ESSAYS

BY THE LATE

MARK PATTISON

SOMETIME RECTOR OF LINCOLN COLLEGE

COLLECTED AND ARRANGED

BY

HENRY NETTLESHIP, M.A.

CORPUS PROFESSOR OF LATIN IN THE UNIVERSITY OF OXFORD

VOL. II

𝔒𝔵𝔣𝔬𝔯𝔡

AT THE CLARENDON PRESS

1889

XII.

CALVIN AT GENEVA.[1]

———◆———

[*Westminster Review,* 1858.]

WHEN Casaubon, on his first visit to Paris, was shown over the great hall of the Sorbonne, he was told by his guide—'This is where the theologians have disputed for five hundred years.' 'Indeed!' was the reply; 'and pray what have they settled?' Something like this is the feeling of every reflective mind on a review of the last three centuries of the history of Europe. We see the most civilized part of mankind, the nations of the West, 'the root and crown of things,' devoting their best energies, and lavishing all their resources, mental and material, upon a doctrinal quarrel. Nor at the end of a three hundred years' experience are we at all wiser. Among our educated classes, at least, far the larger number still think that there exist no questions of more momentous interest for themselves and the world at large than those tenets by which the Protestant Churches are separated from the Church of Rome.

No philosophic mind at this day sympathizes with the scoffers of the last century, or with the 'profane of every age, who have derided the furious contests which the difference of a single diphthong excited between the Homoousians and the Homoiousians[2].' The buffoon wit

---

[1] 1. CALVIN (JEAN), *Lettres recueillies pour la première fois et publiées d'après les Manuscrits originaux.* Par JULES BONNET. Vols. I and II. Lettres Françoises. 8vo. Paris, 1854.

2. GABEREL (J.), *Histoire de l'Église de Genève depuis le commencement de la Réformation jusqu'en* 1815. Vols. I and II. 8vo. Genève, 1855.

[2] Gibbon, chap. XXI.

of *The Tale of a Tub* is not much to our taste. We are now ready to recognize that—whatever may be the case in China or in Lilliput—in Europe nations do not go to war about a diphthong. The great European quarrel of the last three centuries has not been about words and syllables. Foolish, petty, litigious, and blind to their real interests as the peoples are, yet theirs has not, on the whole, been the mere frenzy of two Irish septs, who, after fighting the live-long day, and strewing the ground with the slain, have at nightfall endeavoured in vain to discover the cause of the battle. We are disposed now to think that moral effects are not without adequate causes; that some mighty issue has been trying in the great historical Oyer of the Reformation against the See of Rome; an issue which the Confession of Augsburg does not state, and which is not once alluded to in the Thirty-nine Articles. It is not from any sentimental desire of saving the honour of human nature, but from a better understanding of history, that we derive the belief that great movements originate in the deeps; and that if there is a spring-tide, it is only because some disturbing force is present. We study the religious wars in France and Germany with different eyes from the wits who ridiculed, or the sects who adopt, their party-cries. In what terms to describe the motive force which was developed with such energy in the century of the Reformation, is the problem which all historians of the present day are endeavouring, with more or less success, to solve. But all are agreed that the theological distinctions which were established in the Confessions of that century, and perpetuated in the various religious bodies which then came into being, were only a form or exterior mould into which the heated metal ran, and not the heat itself which fused it. Men do not assign their real motives, not because they will not, but because they cannot. They cannot analyze their own complex feelings with steadiness and impartiality. To do so is the function of the historian. Hence a contemporary cannot write the history of his own times. How trivial and beside the mark read to us the *Defences* of the early Christian Apologists! They are shallow in proportion to the depth of the Christian movement, its radical and subversive spirit; a spirit which those who were swept along with it were possessed by, but knew not what it signified. The only key to a revolutionary epoch is the results which actually establish themselves. Posterity, which witnesses these, may by their aid interpret the quarrel out of which they arose. The issue between Christianity and Paganism in the second century is not expressed in the feeble rhetoric of the Apologists. The issue between Protestantism and Catholicism is not that which is discussed in the scholastic pedantries of Bellarmine.

It is not to be supposed, however, that the formularies of any age are totally irrelevant or immaterial to its sentiments. Its dicta will not exhaust or express, but they will approach, its social necessities. When its language is theological, it is probable that its excitement is, at bottom, religious. The shout of battle may be raised the loudest about some insignificant or harmless quibble, but we may find out from it in which direction the danger was felt to lie. When public opinion is in a sore and irritable state, a very remote allusion will rack all its nerves. In certain feverish moods it is ready to declare any abstract proposition a fundamental matter, and to erect some special definition of justification into an 'articulus stantis aut cadentis ecclesiae.' The mischief lies not in the temporary importance thus forced upon some partial form of truth, but in its perpetuation. The dogma, consecrated by the blood of the martyrs, becomes in lapse of time a tyrant over reason ; and from having been the bulwark of faith, settles into its chief impediment. Systems, and institutions founded on them, thus doom themselves to destruction. A new revolution becomes necessary to displace the charter which the old had inaugurated.

The programme of opinions advertized by any party will fall short of expressing the real tendencies of the party movement, in proportion as the movement is deeply seated and extensively spread. Sympathy is so much more catching than intelligence; and while sentiment cements union, ideas dislocate it. In reducing the aspirations with which the mass was instinct to a scheme of doctrine, partisans split off in all directions. Few can express their own mind; no one can express another's.

Nonne videmus,
Quid sibi quisque velit nescire et quaerere semper?

These considerations offer the true explanation of a fact in the history of the sixteenth century, which has been often observed, and variously accounted for.

There are two results which have accrued to modern Europe, and are unmistakably traceable to the Reformation of the sixteenth century. The first lies in the domain of intelligence, and is known as the Right of Free Inquiry. The second, a consequence of the foregoing, is a fact of politics, and is known as Liberty of Conscience, or Toleration. It is not to the purpose to object that there are many who deny the first, and that the second is carried into effect over a very limited area of Europe, and very imperfectly even there. It must be admitted by all, that this claim of the human understanding to possess and to exercise rights, is made, and that the attempts, successful or not, to enforce the claim, have been the cardinal points of modern history. The principle of Free Intellect has revolutionized Philosophy. The claim of Free Conscience has been, and is at this moment, the substantial dispute between the two classes into which Europe is divided— viz. the unarmed people, and their armed governments. That such a doctrine and such a claim should have flowed from the Reformation may well appear astonishing to

those who read for themselves what the leading Reformers said and did. For it cannot be denied, that
neither in their acts nor their words is there any recognition of such views. The Protestant Churches replaced
Papal infallibility by a not less stern and uncompromising
dogmatism, and claimed, and exercised, the right of
punishing the heretic as unhesitatingly as the Inquisition
itself. This inconsequence on the part of the Protestants
has been the standing indictment of their Catholic opponents, from the time of Erasmus. The leaders of the
Reformation, it is said, first revolted against the authority
of the Church, and the consent of universal Christendom ;
and, when their insurrection was successful, they turned
round on their followers, and required the same unconditional submission of the understanding as had been
exacted by the old Church.

Turning from the abstract controversy to the historical
personages, this illogical spirit of Protestant tyranny is
seen embodied in the person and institutions of CALVIN.
There is a peculiar animosity provoked by the Genevan
Reformer, his doctrines, and his acts, which is shared
by all the world, except the sect which bears his name.
This implacable antipathy is in part due to the severe,
acrimonious, and proud temper of the man. But it is in
no small degree to be ascribed to his successful efforts
in impressing upon the religious movement a character of
despotic control of the understanding, and a spiritual
police of the conscience, far more intrusive and imper-
tinent than that against which it had just rebelled. The
monopoly, too, of Calvin's name and reputation which
some of the narrowest ecclesiastical bodies have secured
for themselves as their founder and patron, has contributed
to cut him off from the sympathies of those whose hopes
and wishes are embarked in the cause of European progress. The hero and prophet of an existing religious
faction has little chance of historical justice.

Historical justice, however, or our decision on the character of the individual Calvin, is a trifling matter. The life and acts of the German reformer have a far higher import. Looked at as biography, his life lends itself very naturally to the conclusions usually accepted. It is useless to tell us, on grounds of abstract historical scepticism, to suspend our judgment. There is no room for doubt. We condemn, by antipathy, as we read. Calvin appears before us as the too successful champion of intolerance; the promoter of what we know as the pre-eminently narrow and exclusive theology; as the man who has done more than any other man to deprive Protestantism of its character as a protest in favour of freedom. We see him overthrowing the liberties of the little State which so generously sheltered him; conspiring to put 'a bridle into its jaws[1];' exiling, or shedding the blood of, its noblest patriots. We shall hate him personally for his bigotry, inhumanity, vindictiveness; above all, as the author of the great crime of the age—the murder of the heroic Servetus. And we shall conclude, on the whole, with the Ultramontane biographer, Audin, that his career was 'funeste à la civilisation, à l'art, aux libertés.'

But when we look off from Geneva upon Europe, when we turn from the person to the course of events, our judgment changes. We then see that the vices of the individual may be the welfare of the community. For on the independence of Geneva hung, at one moment, the very existence of Protestantism. And the independence of Geneva—without an army, without territory, a defence-less city, like a frail boat between two icebergs, France and the Empire—was secured by the spirit evoked by Calvin. That iron will, that inexorable temper and merciless determination which subjugated Geneva, were also the means of concentrating in that narrow corner a moral force which saved the Reformation. On this little

---

[1] Quod eam urbem videret his fraenis indigere.—*Beza, Vit. Calv.*
Westminster Review, 1858.]

fortress, reared on the rugged rock of Predestination, the overwhelming material force of the Empire spent itself in vain. Not only this; Geneva, under Calvin, became the centre of a new strength, which went out into all Europe, to cope not unsuccessfully with the enormous powers of repression which the Inquisition began to put forth. In checking the febrile turbulence which attended the nascent liberty of the Republic, Calvin did so, not in the cause of a mechanical 'order,' but to replace it with a more vigorous sense of personality. Geneva became a seminary of martyrs. Steeled by her Spartan discipline, they went forth to seek danger wherever it could be found, and disseminated through the nations not only the ideas, but the spirit, of the master. Hence the strange paradox, that in the suppression of the liberties of Geneva was sown the seed of liberty in Europe; that, by the demoralizing tenet of fatalism was evoked a moral energy which Christianity had not felt since the era of persecution.

No part of this mighty result was foreseen or schemed by Calvin. Like many other men who have done the greatest things, his purposes were immediate; his energy expended on what was very near at hand. He had greatness thrust upon him. A chance brought him to Geneva. The importunity of another minister, Farel, detained him there. And after he had left it, it was the urgency of others, against his own settled purpose, which recalled him to it. He was a man with a single aim, towards which he bent all the powers of his soul. But this aim was no distant one. It was no conquest on a grand scale which he meditated. The tactic which plans a whole campaign, and out-generals an adversary, was incompatible with the passionate conviction which had absolute possession of his breast. He thought only of Geneva while he was doing the work of the Reformation; and dealt vigorous blows at Amied Perrin, which told upon Europe.

A brief review shall here be attempted of the conditions, moral and political, which gave to one will and one intellect an influence so commanding, and so widely spread.

In the year 1536, Calvin, for whom, as a zealous Reformer, neither Italy nor France was any longer a safe residence, arrived in the city of Geneva. He was on his way to Strasburg, then a free city of the Empire, and Protestant. There he hoped to find a secure refuge for the retired and studious life which it was his sole ambition to lead. So little were his thoughts at this time turned towards active life, or influence of any kind, that he did not even contemplate undertaking the labours of a preacher. He was just at that age—twenty-seven—when, to such intellects as his, not broad and sceptical, but deep and profoundly convinced, knowledge presents itself with allurements irresistible. He had just published the first sketch of his *Institute of Christian Religion*, and his mind was doubtless revolving the larger and more matured dogmatic treatise, as we now have it. 'I was wholly given up to my own interior thoughts and private studies,' he says of himself, looking back on this period of his life. A constitution delicate and irritable, and health already broken by suffering and study, seemed to disqualify him for the stormy career of preacher of the Gospel in those troublous times. Farel, however, the Reformed minister of Geneva, heard that the author of the *Institute* was in the town. He hastened to him; explained to him the urgent need in which Geneva at that moment stood of a well-instructed minister—'the fields white for the harvest'—his own failing strength, and the feebleness of his colleagues. Calvin refused. His health was unequal to the labour, his character too unpliant for negotiation with adversaries. He could serve the Reformed faith far more effectually by his pen, and to that service he meant to devote his life. 'I perceive what it is,' said Farel; 'you are wrapt up in selfish love of leisure and books. May God's curse rest upon these studies, if you now refuse your aid to His Church in her time of need!'

Such was Calvin's call to the ministry at Geneva. The story reads like a scene dramatically dressed up by a modern historian. But we have it on the unquestionable authority of Calvin himself[1], of whom even his enemies will admit, that he knows not how to decorate or disguise a fact. His obstinate will, proof against persuasion, yielded to the terrors of the malediction, and he remained with Farel. He was chosen one of the preachers, and nominated 'Teacher in Theology.' His name occurs in the Register of the Council for September, 1536, with the designation of 'iste Gallus.'

Geneva, which was to become the centre of French Protestantism, was the last of the Subalpine cities to revolt from Rome. In the course of the summer, 1535, the transition to the Reformed faith was effected. Mass ceased to be celebrated on the 10th of August of that year, and the usages of the Helvetian churches gradually received legal establishment in the city. The writers of religious annals, apt to be content with names and forms, regard this exterior change as the critical date in Genevan history. But the real emancipation of the citizens of Geneva had been worked before, and was no less a civil than a religious revolution. The foundation of Genevan reform was not laid by the preaching of Farel, but in the long struggle of the gallant burghers against the encroachments of the Dukes of Savoy. If we wish to understand the elements of moral life which, in 1536, lay ready to the moulding hand of the great Reformer, we must look to another and earlier source than the rise of Lutheranism.

The city and territory of Geneva, like the ecclesiastical principalities of Germany, was, technically, a free town of the Empire; practically, was under the sovereignty of its own Prince-Bishop. The bishop delegated his temporal

[1] Praef. in Comm. in Psalmos.

jurisdiction to a *vidomme* (vice-dominus), who was in the sixteenth century the Duke of Savoy. The dukes garrisoned the castle of the island within the walls, as well as two strong fortresses outside—one on the Rhone, the other on the Arve. But alongside of these seignorial rights the burghers enjoyed large municipal franchises, and governed themselves, not only regulating the police of the town and the markets, but imposing taxes, and electing the syndics, as the chief magistrates were styled. The population, in the earlier part of the sixteenth century, is computed at twelve thousand. The clergy, in an episcopal city, were naturally very strong. Including the thirty-two canons of the cathedral of St. Peter, there were at least three hundred ecclesiastics, regular and secular, officiating in the town.

The consolidation of the territories of the House of Savoy between the Jura and the Alps began seriously to threaten the liberties of Geneva. And when, in 1504, Charles III succeeded to the ducal coronet, a death struggle ensued between the burghers and the vidomme. It lasted twenty years, long enough to call out the spirit of heroic resistance in a good cause—the cause of liberty—to a superior force. For though the Dukes of Savoy could not dispose of any great force, they would have been far more than a match for the little republic, with its insignificant population. But in their distress the *eidguenots* [1], as the party of liberty were called (confederates), had the support of the now free cantons of Switzerland, and especially of their neighbours of Berne and Friburg. The final victory was achieved in 1526, the leaders of the monarchical party, the *mamelukes* (meaning Mahometans), were banished, the vidommate abolished, and its jurisdiction transferred to a board of magistrates. Though the rescue came, at last, from foreign aid, the twenty years' conflict had been a school of patriotic virtue and manly

---

[1] [The form which the German *eidgenossen* assumed in the Genevan *patois*.] *Westminster Review*, 1858.]

sentiment. The impulse and energy of Swiss independence had been communicated to the Genevese. Their
adoption of the Reformed faith was the consequence, not
the cause, of their political emancipation. It is of the first
importance to observe this, in order to appreciate the
nature of Calvin's power. To understand that which he
added, it is indispensable to have a clear conception of
that which he found.

To read the usual ecclesiastical narrative of these
transactions[1], one must believe that, previously to the
arrival of Calvin, the most frightful disorder reigned
unchecked throughout the city. The anarchy is represented as complete, the licence of manners carried to
debauchery. Having thrown off the authority of the
clergy, and the irksome restraints of fasting, penance, and
auricular confession, the people, we are told, gave themselves up to every kind of dissolute excess. The Catholic
historians dwell on this picture because it sullies the
Reformation ; the Protestant biographers of Calvin repeat
it because it exalts the merit of their hero in effecting the
cure. 'The transition,' says Dyer, 'was almost as abrupt
and striking as if a man, after spending all Saturday night
at an opera or masquerade, should, without any preparation, walk into a Friends' meeting on the Sabbath morning.'
Those who believe in miraculous conversion will have
no difficulty in extending their hypothesis to the case of a
whole people, and may affirm that the Genevese were
'converted' by the preaching of 'the Gospel.' But one
might ask the more reasonable among these historians—
those who believe that moral effects must have moral
causes—How came the people of Geneva, then, to submit
themselves to Calvin's discipline, to surrender themselves
of their own free will to this solitary and unarmed invader ?

The truth is that the representations of the anarchical

[1] See in Dyer, *Life of Calvin*, pp. 59–80 ; and in Gaberel, *Hist. de l'Église de
Gen.*, chap. VIII.

and corrupt state of Geneva during the ten years which
intervened between the abolition of the vidommate of the
House of Savoy and the arrival of Calvin (1526-1536), are
greatly overdrawn. We must remember that the details
come to us mainly from ministers or lay-elders, in whose
eyes dancing was a profane amusement, and cards a
device of Satan; who inflicted fine and imprisonment for
the offence of dressing a girl's hair in long ringlets. Their
accusations of vice, profligacy, and dissoluteness must not
be construed literally. To Hooker, who lived under the
despotism of Elizabeth, the 'popular,' or democratic polity
of Geneva seemed of itself rank licence. Nothing that is
brought forward to prove the corruption of morals indicates that Geneva was worse than other towns of its size.
Many of the practices complained of were usages of long
standing, and derived from Catholic times. On the other
hand, it may readily be admitted that in the first hours of
recovered liberty some extravagances of behaviour and
language are likely enough to have occurred. The creed
of childhood is never parted with without some shock to the
character. The police of the streets cannot be so severely
enforced where the life and property of the free citizens
are duly respected, as it may when they are at the disposal
of an absolute prince. Add to this that the religious
persecution just beginning in France was filling Geneva
with refugees. Among the honourable exiles were found
not a few fugitives from justice, persons of ruined character, who sought to pass their crimes under the disguise
of political misfortunes, or worthless monks who had
apostatized in order to fly with a mistress. Nor must we
omit a small but insidious element of discord in the
Catholics who still remained in the city, still cherishing
the silent hope that their country would, before long,
return to the bosom of the Church, and seeing in its
discontents and intestine divisions the hopeful signs of
such a termination.

Westminster Review, 1858.]

Such, in general, was the situation of affairs in Geneva when, in 1536, the young Frenchman, 'iste Gallus,' became one of its ministers. To an aspiring and far-sighted ambition it was just the theatre for a signal personal success. Provided that the Dukes of Savoy were kept at a distance—and this the strength of the Republic of Berne seemed to guarantee—here was just the opening for a purely political career. The scale to be sure was small—a town of 12,000 souls, a territory of a few square miles. But where, at that day, was there any prospect of fame and fortune to the unaided adventurer except through servile dependence on the capricious favour of some king or noble? But Calvin thought neither of fame nor fortune. The narrowness of his views, and the disinterestedness of his soul, alike precluded him from regarding Geneva as a stage for the gratification of personal ambition. This abnegation of self was one great part of his success. Even at periods when his unpopularity was at its height, all parties recognized this disinterestedness, and secretly respected and feared a man who wanted nothing for himself. One idea possessed him, governed, impelled him. For so profound and consecutive a reasoner no man was ever less reflective. He had no self-consciousness. His theory was not a part of his mental furniture, as other men's theories are to them. It was the whole of his intellect. No question had to him two sides. There was but one right reason. All other modes of thought were depravity; not reason at all, but moral perversity. To resist God's Word is blasphemy, to be met not by argument, but by coercion. There must then be authority to compel obedience to God's Word, since all deviation from it is a criminal act, not a corrigible error of judgment. It was no offended self-love that rendered him so violent and implacable towards his adversaries, but impatience at the obstacles they opposed to the establishment of truth which was to him as clear as the day. Authority then, external force, is the one remedy he would employ. Neither art, nor eloquence, nor intrigue, nor soft words, nor gentle influences ; such means never occurred to him.   Here is the absolute truth, the revealed Word of God ; those who will conform themselves to it—well ; those who will not must be compelled into submission.   Nor must individuals only be reduced to subjection ; the civil power in the State must learn to bow to the spiritual authority. This was the astonishing enterprise which a solitary exile, without friends, money, or resources of any kind, undertook, and successfully achieved.   It may be doubted if all history can furnish another instance of such a victory of moral force.

No sooner was Calvin associated with Farel in the ministerial office than the two colleagues applied themselves to frame ecclesiastical ordinances in this spirit.   A doctrinal confession in twenty-one articles which they drew up first, met with some, but not very serious, opposition.   But when they proceeded to call on the Council to put in force some regulations which were already in existence, prohibiting games of chance and dancing, and in other ways curtailing freedom of action, a spirit of resistance began to manifest itself.   Calvin would not yield an inch.   The public registers present us with such entries as this :—

1537. Mai 20. Une épouse étant sortie dimanche dernier avec les cheveux plus abattus qu'il ne se doit faire, ce qui est d'une mauvaise exemple, et contraire à ce qu'on leur évangelise, on fait mettre en prison la maîtresse, les dames qui l'ont menée, et celle qui l'a coiffée.

Another time, a man seized playing cards is exhibited in the pillory with the pack of cards round his neck. Another, who had set on foot a masquerade, is made to ask pardon on his knees before the congregation in St. Peter's Church.   Every citizen was obliged to attend sermon twice on the Sunday under pain of fine, and to be at home by nine in the evening; and tavern-keepers were ordered to see that their customers observed these regulations. Every week produced some new ordinance more meddling and inquisitorial than the previous. The exasperation of the young men daily increased. The more liberal and independent minds began seriously to feel that a new tyranny was being established over them, at a time when they had hoped to begin to enjoy in peace the liberty they had conquered at so much cost. That two strangers, interlopers from France, should thus lord it over those who had hazarded their lives and fortunes to deliver their city from the Duke of Savoy, was not to be borne. Many of these citizens, besides, were not in sympathy with Protestantism at all. They had forsaken Catholicism, it is true. But it was only because, in so doing, they felt that they disposed most effectually of the civil authority of their bishop. Their motives had been political rather than religious, and their devotion was rather to their country than to 'the Gospel.'

A party of opposition was thus gradually formed to resist the encroachments of the pastors, and of the spirit of control which animated them. This party united in itself the two extremes of the population—the best and the worst—the rabble and the most distinguished citizens who had led the van of the movement of emancipation. This party of *Libertins*, as they began to be called, occupied a conservative position. They claimed their right to enjoy in peace the liberties they had fought for against the innovations of the preachers. In November, 1537, there was a scene in the Council. The councillors of the Libertine party went so far as to draw their swords, and reminded the Council that by what they had gained their freedom, by the same they would keep it. 'Le tout,' says Roset, 'sous ce prétexte de maintenir les franchises.'

The more the young men chafed against the bit, and

the high-minded and liberal patriots struggled in the net which was closing on them, the greater was the satisfaction of the mass of respectable middle and lower-class citizens who supported the ministers. They had no difficulty themselves in submitting to any amount of restraints. The narrowest creed imposes no fetters on the understanding of such men. The grosser portions of sensual pleasure satisfy the demands of their taste, without the accessories of social sympathy. It was sweet to them to see the talented, the wealthy, the distinguished, struck down by the levelling hand of Calvin. His maxim was, 'Eminent services to the State, so far from standing in mitigation of moral delinquency, aggravate it. If a citizen has shed his blood for his country, is he to ask in return the liberty to do what he likes?' A moral code levels distinctions in a way no other code can. Birth, and pride, and blood secure an upper class from the petty and mercenary temptations which would bring them within the grasp of criminal law. But let fornication and intrigue be made punishable offences, and whose turn is it then to stand at the bar?

A republic, however, such as Geneva became, is not built on so rotten a foundation as the mere spirit of envy of superiority. This base passion worked here, as elsewhere, doubtless. It worked negatively in balancing the pretensions of the more educated and superior class. But the positive strength of the party lay in the French refugees, and in the religious spirit which they brought with them. This peculiar temperament of religious stoicism, with the stress that it lays on the ethical virtues of temperance, fortitude, and self-control, is, under the name of Puritanism, too well known to English readers to need description. It is not so generally understood that, though it derives to this country directly from Geneva, and is popularly associated with the name of Calvin, it was not the home-growth of Geneva, nor was it originated by the Calvinistic discipline.

This concentrated, severe type of character was brought to Geneva from France, where it had been generated by a reckless and cruel persecution. Virtue, strung to an intensity often almost savage, could scarcely have sprung into existence under the ordinary conditions of society, in which, if there is much sorrow, there is also some enjoyment. The peculiar ethical temper of Calvinism is precisely that of primitive Christianity—of the catacombs and the desert—and was created under the same stimulants.

Formidable from their intensified moral energy, the French emigrants were not inconsiderable in point of number. It was part of Calvin's policy to admit strangers to the freedom of the city unrestrictedly. Towards his later years we find (1558) as many as three hundred incorporated in a single day, of whom two hundred were French, fifty English, twenty-five Italians, and five Spaniards. But even in 1536 they were numerous enough to excite the jealousy of the native patriots. And, organized as a State party by the master-spirit of Calvin, their influence was out of all proportion greater than their numbers. For a period of more than twelve months after Calvin's association into the pastorate, his power was slowly and surely mounting. But, as will always be the case, the encroachments of a party of innovation call into action the spirit of opposition. The friends of liberty had been surprised rather than routed. They had time in their turn to organize, and they were soon in a position to make an effectual stand. Matters were brought to a crisis, as usual, not on the merits of the new discipline, but on a point of ceremony.

The Republic of Berne, in consideration of the services it had rendered to that of Geneva, considered itself entitled from time to time to tender its advice on the internal affairs of its young ally. This interference had hitherto been always well received by the Government to which it was addressed, and had generally been adopted. But, following the example of the civil power, the pastors of Berne ventured to make suggestions, in a tone of admonition, to their brother ministers of Geneva. The Bernese Church used stone fonts for baptism; retained four *fêtes* during the year, viz. Christmas, New-year's Day, the Annunciation, and the Ascension, and employed unleavened bread in the Lord's Supper. All these ceremonial observances Calvin had suppressed, not in the spirit of contradiction, but conducted to the conclusion by the strictest logic from the principles of the Reformation. The Bernese mistook their man if they thought Calvin would be docile to their theological suggestions. It was not that Calvin laid any stress on ceremonies, or shared the fanaticism of his ignorant sect, who thought the Catholic ceremonial pagan and profane. Narrow as was his theology in many respects, he was above such weakness. His remark on the English Prayer-book is well known, from the irritation it caused in the minds of some of the Anglican High Church prelates. 'The Book of Common Prayer had in it,' he said, 'tolerabiles ineptias; some follies, which, however, might be easily allowed to pass.' In this very year (1538), in the preface to a Catechism which he published at Basle, he wrote these words:—'We should rather endeavour a unity of doctrine and spirit among Christians than pettily insist on establishing certain ceremonies. Little will be said of forms on the Day of Judgment.' When, however, summoned to conform to the Bernese usages, he at once refused to compromise the independence of the Church of Geneva by accepting the authority of a neighbour republic, however respected, however intimately allied to his own. The Libertine party instantly saw the opportunity afforded of turning opinion against the pastors. The Libertines had now the majority in the Council, and they espoused the side of the Bernese with affected zeal. They sent for the pastors, Calvin, Farel, and Courault, and ordered them to celebrate the Supper with unleavened wafers at the approaching Easter Communion. The ministers replied that they could not recognize the authority, but were willing to submit to the decision of the collective Helvetic Churches in the synod of Zürich, which was to be held after Easter. The Council was equally firm on its side. It prohibited any celebration on Easter Day except with the wafer. Easter Sunday arrived. The excitement of the people was at its height. Farel preached as usual at St. Gervaise, and Calvin at St. Peter's. Both addressed the people on the same topic—on the Communion—and concluded their sermons with declaring that they would not administer it in the present state of passion and division in which the city was. The next day the Council decreed the banishment of Calvin and Farel. On Tuesday the sentence was adopted in the Council General without discussion, and notice was served upon the two Reformers to leave the city within forty-eight hours. Nor was this a temporary outburst of popular dislike ; for.when the Bernese espoused their cause, and despatched a special embassy to persuade the people of Geneva to receive back their ministers, the proposal was rejected. And in a General Council, held on the 27th of May, the decree of banishment was confirmed almost unanimously.

In this unanimity of voices against him, we seem to see the disappearance of Calvin's authority as abrupt as its rise had been. Entering the city a friendless and penniless exile in August, 1536, he had found himself in the short space of a few months dictating restraints, and enforcing rigorous laws which the established authorities of the place, the Little Council and the Syndics, could not have dreamed of proposing. But he, like all suddenly successful men, strains his power till it breaks; opinion deserts him. Not satisfied with a vast moral influence, he will have despotic control. He disgusts every one, and

the people tear down their own idol.   This is in April,
1538.   Wait but two years more, and we find the syndics
and Council of Geneva 'affectionately recommending'
themselves to their 'good brother and singular friend,
Docteur Calvin,' then in exile at Strasburg, imploring his
return—

Vous pryons tres affectes vous volloyr transporter par devers nous,
et en vostre prestine place et ministere retourne.   Et esperons en
layde de Dieu que ce seray ung grand bien et fruyct a laugmentation
de la se. Evangile.   Voyeant que nostre peuple vous desire.   Et ferons
avec vous de sorte que aurez occasion vous contenter.—*A Geneve,*
22 *Octobre,* 1540.

We cannot be surprised that the historians and biographers flounder helplessly among conjecture and
hypothesis on the causes of these rapid fluctuations. Their
most laboured surmises are little better, possibly are
further from the truth, than the simple philosophy of the
Pastor Bernard—'This is the Lord's doing, and it is
marvellous in our eyes[1]!' or the more learned theory of
Hooker, moralizing in a strain borrowed from the Latin
classics over the levity of popular humour.   In a free
constitution, where the acts of the Government are
determined by the opinion of the majority, such fluctuations of policy indicate the alternate prevalence of nearly-
balanced parties.   When in April, 1538, the party of the
Libertines triumphed over Calvin and the Reformers, a
discerning eye might have seen that the triumph, complete
as it seemed for the moment, was destined to be short-
lived.   The Libertine party in Geneva, as against the
Calvinists, laboured under the same disadvantage as the
Protestant party in Europe at large did against the
Catholics.   They had no rallying principle, only a negative protest against constraint; powerful to overthrow, but
perishing by suicide as soon as they had conquered.   On
the other hand, the Reforming party were strong in the

[1] Bernard to Calvin, Feb. 6, 1541.

possession of that exalted idea of moral duty and purity of life which was beginning to form itself among the French Protestants. Such a party may be extirpated by the sword; but where the free play of opinion is possible, it is no matter of doubt that it will prevail over the partisans of a mere abstract liberty.

On reviewing Calvin's letters written during exile, there can be little doubt that he foresaw his own restoration as certain. He had committed faults during his career as pastor of Geneva, and his imperious and peremptory manner had contributed to his unpopularity. But during his exile he showed a magnanimity truly noble. He maintained a correspondence with his friends and former flock in the city. But it was to urge them to respect their ministers *de facto*; to avoid all occasions of offence, and to submit in matters indifferent. When Sadolet, at the suggestion of the Pope, addressed his conciliatory epistle to the city of Geneva, and there was no one in Geneva competent to make a fitting reply, Calvin undertook it. He would not intrigue for a restoration; he would not speak of it, or propose it. He withdrew to Basle, and occupied himself with other things, with the second edition of *The Institutes*, or the *Commentary on the Romans*. While at Basle he received a 'call' to the French Church at Strasburg. He was employed as deputy to the Diet at Worms, and again at Ratisbon. In all these various duties and employments his merit and services to the Reformed cause became every day more conspicuous. His position with respect to Geneva was altered. It was their turn, if they wanted him, to sue to him. When they did so, by the letter of the 22nd October, 1540, he delayed his consent, and put them off. But it was not in the spirit of a Coriolanus, or to enhance his own value. The hesitation proceeded from his having contracted engagements with his Strasburg congregation, which he did not feel at liberty to break off at once. On the 13th September, 1541, he re-entered Geneva, after an exile of three years and a half.

On the very day of his entry he waited on the Council, and gave in his demand for the establishment of a system of discipline, and a tribunal, or consistory, to enforce it. He was received with every mark of honour and affection, and was presented with a coat of broad-cloth (*drap*), a token of distinction, as private citizens wore serge. A committee was appointed to draw up an ecclesiastical constitution. A very few weeks sufficed for their task of legislation. It was but to draw, in the form of enactments, the principles explained in Calvin's *Institution.*

The *Ordinances Ecclesiastiques de l'Eglise de Genéve*[1] well deserve the careful attention of the historian. We have in them not the mere arrangements of a single Swiss town, but the one form of Church polity which best expresses the spirit of the Reformation. The religious instinct of the Reformed communions, instantly sympathizing with the simplicity with which it went straight to its mark, diffused it over a large part of Europe. Calvin had provided a form of government for all the countries where the civil power had not already set up one. Wherever individual liberty was able to assert itself, the Calvinistic discipline instantly followed. It reformed Scotland, emancipated Holland, attained a brief but brilliant reign in England, and maintained a struggle of sixty years against the royal authority in France.

We must not, however, imagine that any mere form of polity could have power to work this renovation. The Genevan discipline armed the spirit of independence in Europe, but it did not call it forth. At its source, in Geneva itself, the discipline did not create freedom; it organized and affirmed it.

The distinction of Calvin as a Reformer is not to be sought in the doctrine which now bears his name, or in

[1] They are in print. Geneva, 1577.

any doctrinal peculiarity. His great merit lies in his comparative neglect of dogma. He seized the idea of reformation as a real renovation of human character. While the German Reformers were scholastically engaged in remodelling abstract metaphysical statements, Calvin had embraced the lofty idea of the Church of Christ as a society of regenerate men. The moral purification of humanity, as the original idea of Christianity, is the guiding idea of his system. The Communion of Saints is held together by a moral, not by a metaphysical, still less by a sacramental bond. In casting about for the ultimate ground of this spiritual virtue which was the earthly condition of the renewed man, the logical mind of Calvin refused to rest in any intermediate causes. He swept away at once the sacramental machinery of material media of salvation which the middle-age Church had provided in such abundance, and which Luther frowned upon, but did not reject. He was not satisfied to go back only to the historical origin of Christianity, but would found human virtue on the eternal, antemundane will of God. If he left the Atonement, he seemed to deprive it of any original efficacy or inherent virtue by referring it, too, back to an absolute decree, in conformity with which it was arranged.

Hence, too, the religious society is necessarily democratic. For all other inequalities among men sink into nothing in the presence of the levelling decree, which sets apart a select few out of the mass to be recipients of the divine favour. But as our eyes cannot distinguish the elect from the rest of the visible Church, all must, in this world, be treated alike. The citizens of this spiritual republic must govern themselves. Doctors and pastors, indeed, there must be, but they are servants to the community, not lords over it. The function of the doctor is very slightly touched in the *Institution*. It is only to teach, and reduces itself to a pure interpretation of Scripture. That of the pastors is more important, as to them belongs reproof, exhortation, admonition, advice. But in this ministration, they are but the exponents of the word or law of God, and have no power or authority of themselves, or as belonging to any privileged order. As their duty will often place them in collision with their flocks, their rights must be clear and well defined. The civil authority, though distinct from the spiritual, is bound to support it. The magistrate must enforce the penalties imposed by the ecclesiastical tribunal, preserve the exterior form of religion, and suppress by force crimes against public religion, as idolatry and blasphemy.

These general principles of government, as expounded in the *Institution*, were embodied in the arrangements now carried out by Calvin in Geneva. The details are these :—

The five pastors of the city parishes, the pastors of the rural districts, and the teachers of theology (when any), were embodied under the style of 'The Venerable Company.' This board of ministers superintended the theological students, selected the ministers for ordination, subject to the approbation of the flock, and had the ordinary administration of the Church. When a minister's place was vacant, the candidates were first examined in the interpretation of Scripture. The examination was conducted by the Company of Pastors, but in the presence of (lay) delegates deputed by the Council of State. After the examination the councillors withdrew, and the election was made by the Venerable Company, and determined by the majority of voices. Their choice was first submitted to the Council for its approbation, and on the following Sunday announced to the people from the pulpits. The members of the congregation were requested to transmit in writing to the Syndics any objections they had to make against the minister-elect. Eight days were allowed for this purpose. If no objections were brought, the candidate was ordained. This was the pastoral organization.

Westminster Review, 1858.]

More important was the disciplinal organization. This, the working element of the whole system, was not entrusted to the pastors, but to a body called the Consistory. In this board the five pastors of the city parishes were united with twelve elders (*anciens*) elected out of the members of the Councils, by the Councils and the Company united. It was a main point with Calvin, that the lay element in this body should outnumber the ecclesiastical. For the control given to this Consistory over the morals and deportment of the citizens was so searching and domestic, that to be at all tolerable, it was necessary it should be lodged in the hands of the congregation itself; exercised by the people themselves upon themselves. To the Consistory belonged an absolute and irresponsible authority of censure, enforced by the power of excommunication, which the civil arm was obliged to give effect to. From his cradle to his grave, the Genevese citizen was pursued by this inquisitorial eye. Those parts of life which are most private and withdrawn were here exposed to public view, and made an affair of public concernment and welfare. It must suffice to cite a few of these regulations as a specimen of the rest :—

Dress.—Est defendu à tous citoyens . . . . tout usage d'or ou d'argent en porfillures, broderies, passemens, couetilles, filets, ou autres tels enrichissemens d'habits, en quelque sorte et manière que ce soit.

Sont defendues toutes chaînes, bracelets, carquans, fers, boutons, pendans d'or sur habits, cordons d'or ou d'argent, et ceintures d'or, et en general tout usage d'or et de pierrerie, soyent pierres, perles, grenats ou autres, sur habits, en ceintures, colliers ni autrement.

. . . . Est defendu aux hommes de porter de longs cheveux, avec passe fillons, et bagues aux oreilles.

Est defendu aux femmes et filles tout frisure, relevement et entortillement des cheveux, et de porter aucuns grenats ou pierreries, en leur coiffures et cornettes. Toutes façons superflues et excessives de poinct coupé ou autre ouvrage ou pointes excessives, soit en valeur ou grandeur sur les collets et rabats.

Toutes fraises excessives et fraises en poinct coupé, tant aux hommes q'au femmes, et touts rabats doubles excessifs.

Que nulles filles de qualité que elles soyent, n'ayent à porter aucuns anneaux avant qu'estre fiancées, a'l peine de 60 sols, et confiscation des dites bagues.

Entertainments.—Item, que nul faisant nopces, banquets ou festins, n'ait à faire au service d'iceux plus haut d'une venue ou mise de chairs ou de poisson, et de cinq plats au plus, honnestes et raissonables, en ce non comprinses les mesmes entrées, et huict plats de tout dessert et q'au dit dessert y'nait pastisserie, ou piece de four, sinon une tourt seulement, et cela en chacune table de 10 personnes.

Sont defendues aus dites nopces ou banquets toutes sortes de confitures seches, excepté la drogée le tout à ferise de 60 sols.

Est defendu à toutes personnes de provoquer autruy à boire, ni l'accepter, en aucuns festins, ou autres répas.

Wedding presents.—Est defendu aux espoux et espouses de faire aucuns dons et presens a autres qu'a eux, ni mesme aux servants et filles, et que ceux qui se feront mutuellement soyent en toute médiocrité.

Est défendu de donner aus dites fiançailles, nopces, ou baptisailles, des bouquets liés d'or ou canetilles, ou garnis de grénats, perles, et autres pierreries.

Many legislators have enacted sumptuary laws. What is surprising is, not that Calvin should have proposed this code, but that it should have been accepted by, and acceptable to, the people, and should have been acted upon without difficulty. The regulations, some two hundred articles in all, were published, and for some weeks the people had the opportunity of considering them, and talking them over in their family circles. On November 20th, a solemn Council-General was convoked in St. Peter's Church. Each article was read and put to the vote separately. Before they quitted the church, a whole people, between two and three thousand free and independent citizens, had voluntarily engaged to observe the whole circle of moral duties in this rigorous form; to attend divine service regularly, to bring up their children 'in the fear of the Lord,' to renounce not only sensual indulgences, but nearly every form of amusement, to adopt the severest simplicity in their dress, the strictest frugality and order in their abodes.

Nor were these vain promises. The Ordinances were not only accepted, they were carried out in the letter and the spirit. Pastor Gaberel gives us some curious instances. They are extracted from the Registers of the Council, and those of the Consistory, from 1545 to 1557.

A man, who swore by the 'body and blood of Christ,' was condemned to sit in the public square in the stocks, and to be fined.

Another, hearing an ass bray, and saying jestingly, 'Il chante un beau psaume,' was sentenced to temporary banishment from the city.

A man was sentenced to the 'amende honorable,' for saying in church, at the moment of the benediction of the Communion, 'Taisé vos, y est prou prié.'

A young man, presenting his bride with an accompt-book, said, 'Tenez, madame, voici votre meilleur psaume.' Another, a working-man, for saying in a wine-shop, 'S'il y a un Dieu, q'il me paie mon écot;' both had to undergo some penalty. A young girl, in church, singing the words of a song to the tune of the psalm, was ordered to be whipped by her parents.

Drunkenness and debauchery were visited with more severe penalties; adultery, more than once with death. Prostitutes who ventured back to Geneva were mercilessly thrown into the Rhone. Cards were altogether prohibited. Rope-dancers and conjurers were forbidden to exhibit. Usury was restricted, no higher rate of interest being allowed than 6⅔ per cent.

In 1544, the Consistory, laying a complaint before the Council against the Sr. Roseti, that he 'had given the Sr. Morel the lie, and had said that he was as good a man as he was, et est *soupçonné* de paillardise,'—the delinquent, or *suspect*, was sent to prison.

1553. On complaint by the Consistory, that 'last Sunday, at a christening of a child of T——, there had been singing and dancing, which is against God and the ordinances;' ordered, that this be not again allowed.

The romance of *Amadis* having found its way into the book-shops, the Council forbid the reading, and order the copies to be destroyed.

The rigour which the ministers, through the Consistory,

exercised over their flocks, they did not spare each other. On certain days the pastors met for mutual censorship, when they were bound to produce, without reserve, whatever they knew or believed to be faulty in each other's deportment. To take an instance, after Calvin's death :—

A M. Druson, minister of one of the country parishes, is complained of on more than one account. His sermons are not understood; he does not visit his flock. Further, it was alleged that, having engaged himself in marriage to a young person, he broke it off just before the contract was to be signed, on the plea that her portion was insufficient. The scandal was judged heinous: M. Druson was deposed from his functions, and forbidden to approach the Communion.

It would be easy to multiply these instances. The Register of the Consistory is said [1] to contain the record of four hundred and fourteen cases in the two years 1558 and 1559 alone. But it is not the aim of these pages to attract ridicule to the subject of them; or to discuss the labours of the most earnest of men, in that style of ghastly buffoonery which is becoming more and more the tone of the periodical press in this country. The thoughtful reader will read these minutiae neither with scorn nor pity. He will recognize in them, in the first place, the character of fact; a disclosure, in undress, of human character and actions which the lofty philosophic generalities of history have too much the power to control or disguise. In the second place, if we are disposed to think that the historical picture is 'frittered'; that the grand and masculine figure of Calvin is degraded by the miserable details of the petty strife, we shall remember that principles are nothing except in their applications. The story of Genevan reform may instruct us how the insignificant squabbles of a municipal council may be ennobled into one of the most important chapters of the history of civiliza-

[1] Henry, *Calvin's Leben*, II. 217.

tion. The educated man of our day is paralyzed by this fastidious intellectualism, which disdains the littlenesses of ordinary life. Hence, superior mental endowments are retiring more and more from the field of action. In spite of the advances of education, of which we hear so much, society and affairs are more than ever in the hands of the 'practical' man, of the vigorous will, but uninstructed intellect. Refined knowledge is entrenching itself in literature ; but literature is becoming less and less powerful in its action on society, as the element of will becomes more palpably deficient in it.

The movement of the Reformation, as being so largely an intellectual one, incurred the same danger as that which thus threatens our modern civilizing progress. The scientific spirit, which reached its height in the earlier part of the sixteenth century, saw the rise of the Reformation with anything but a favourable eye. Erasmus complains heavily of the damage Luther is doing to letters. Bembo is all astonishment at the piety of Melanchthon. The men of the Renaissance turned with disgust from the men of the Reform. Their taste was offended by the barbarous violence ; their critical impartiality, by the headstrong one-sidedness of the new movement. But more than this. Their culture, by enervating their character, had placed them in antipathy to the moral earnestness of the German Reformers. By touching the deeper sources of moral life, however, Luther was able to do what Erasmus could not have done. The intellectual movement of Humanism was swept into the mightier movement of the Reformation. But the Reformation itself very soon began to betray an interior weakness of the same kind with that which had neutralized the effort of the Humanists. In the earlier days of Luther, while Protestant effort was directed to realize the conditions of human redemption and moral recovery, the movement expanded with an elastic force which carried all before it. The moral revolt against the mechanical salvation by church and sacraments, further strengthened itself by allying, or absorbing, the intellectual revolt against the Church as teacher, which we may designate as the Renaissance. But a moral effort soon gave place to controversy on dogma. From enforcing justification by faith, the Reformers soon began to think the mode of stating the doctrine the all-important point. The intellectual was no longer for the sake of the moral. The Reformation impulse was fast dying out in dispute on symbol and dogma, as little sanctifying in the production of character as the scholastic pedantry of Roman theology. The effort of the Protestant teachers was beginning to be directed to the propagation of theological opinions. The old idea of orthodoxy remained unshaken, only that the particular opinions qualified as orthodox were slightly varied.

The Protestant movement was saved from being sunk in the quicksands of doctrinal dispute, chiefly by the new moral direction given to it in Geneva. The religious instinct of Calvin discerned the crying need of human nature to be a social discipline, rather than a metaphysical correctness. The scheme of polity which he contrived, however mixed with the erroneous notions of his day, enforced at least the two cardinal laws of human society ; viz. self-control as the foundation of virtue ; self-sacrifice as the condition of the common weal. His legislation did not create, but it concentrated and directed, this moral force. We are tempted to laugh at the record of the day by day enforcement of his code. Let us remember the axiom of the schools that, 'All actions are in singulars,' and that only in single instances is the practice of rules possible. Had Calvin, like Plato, left only a paper-sketch of a republic, in glowing language and magnificent imagery, how much more would he have been admired by the world! He did how much more than describe a virtuous society—he created one! Calvin's ideal is, doubtless, vastly inferior to that of Plato, but it is under the disadvantage of having been worked in practice. With what surprising effect it worked, the whole history of Protestant Europe is witness. It was a rude attempt, indeed, but then it was the first which modern times had seen, to combine individual and equal freedom with strict self-imposed law; to found society on the common endeavour after moral perfection. The Christianity of the middle ages had preached the base and demoralizing surrender of the individual; the surrender of his understanding to the Church; of his conscience to the priest; of his will to the prince. Protestantism, as an insurrection against this subjugation, laboured under the same weakness as all other revolutions. It threw off a yoke and got rid of an exterior control, but it was destitute of any basis of interior life. True freedom can only be founded on a strong sense of personality; the conscious possession of a moral force, from which the outward actions flow. Mere emancipation from the tutelage of a church or a government will not convey this basis of self-reliance. The will is not free, merely because it is relieved from outward restraint. But this is all that any revolution does; to destroy impediments to free agency, not to regenerate the forces of action.

The polity of Calvin was a vigorous effort to supply that which the revolutionary movement wanted,—a positive education of the individual soul. Crushed under the weight of a spiritual aristocracy on the one side, and ground down by the huge machine of administrative monarchy on the other, all personal freedom, all moral attributes, had nearly disappeared among the people on whom this superincumbent mass pressed. To raise up the enfeebled will, to stir the individual conscience, to incite the soul not only to reclaim its rights, but to feel its obligations; to substitute free obedience for passive sub-

mission,—this was the lofty aim of the simple, not to say
barbarous, legislation of Calvin.   The inquisitorial rigours
of the Consistory encouraged, instead of humbling, independence.   Government at Geneva was not police,
but education; self-government mutually enforced by
equals on each other.   The power thus generated was
too expansive to be confined to Geneva.   It went forth
into all countries.   From every part of Protestant Europe,
eager hearts flocked hither to catch something of the
inspiration.   The Reformed Communions, which doctrinal
discussion was fast splitting up into ever-multiplying sects,
began to feel in this moral sympathy a new centre of
union.   This, and this alone, enabled the Reformation
to make head against the terrible repressive forces brought
to bear by Spain,—the Inquisition and the Jesuits.   Sparta
against Persia was not such odds as Geneva against Spain.
Calvinism saved Europe.   The rugged and grotesque
discipline of Calvin raised up, from St. Andrews to
Geneva, that little band, not very polished, not very refined, but free men.

> That which we are, we are;
> One equal temper of heroic hearts
> Made weak by time and fate, but strong in will
> To strive, to seek, to find, and not to yield.

Such is the admirable force upon the human conscience
of the simple virtues of sincerity and self-denial.   Where
they are exhibited in a distinct and recognizable form, they
never fail to conquer, and to spread themselves.   Hence-
forward Calvinism tended to take up into itself all the
moral worth existing anywhere in Protestantism.   As the
Humanistic movement had been absorbed into the Protestant, so the first, or Lutheran, reform was gradually
overborne by the Calvinistic, save where State interests
interfered to prevent it.   Such is the law of all great
movements.   The truly great exert a magical influence.
Character is more powerful than intellect.   The lesser

stream empties itself into the greater. Lutheranism was incapable of propagating itself. Calvinism reappeared again and again, with no less vitality than at first. It animated the Cameronians of Cleland, no less than the Independents of Cromwell or the defenders of La Rochelle.

It is necessary to dwell on the services rendered by Calvin to human liberty, for his sins against it were of the deepest dye. These may be brought under two heads :— 1. His political intolerance shows itself in the suppression of the Libertine party in 1555. 2. His theological intolerance, as shown by the cruel execution of Servetus and of Gruet, and his conduct to Bolzec, Castellio, Gentilis, etc.

1. For the overthrow of the *Libertins* in 1555, Calvin will be acquitted by history. The necessities of his position may be held to excuse him. It was a struggle *à outrance* for power in Geneva. Not, on Calvin's part, for selfish power, but for the maintenance of that system which was unmistakably working for the best interests of the city, and which was, besides, acceptable to the majority of the inhabitants.

The Libertine party, which had triumphed in the expulsion of Calvin and Farel in 1538, and had again succumbed to the restoration of the former in 1541, slowly and steadily regained their lost ground. The severity and painfulness of the discipline galled the weak brethren and the 'outsiders.' Though Calvin never lost the steady support of the thorough-going men, a formidable amount of unpopularity gradually accumulated against him. The young men of the *Liberal* party gave the tone. It was eagerly adopted. Calvin was not safe from insult in the street; they hissed him as he passed along. The children were encouraged to make faces at him. They turned his name into Caïn. The opposition succeeded in penetrating into the Council; and at the elections of 1549,

Amied Perrin, the leader of the Liberals, was chosen First Syndic.

Amied Perrin, captain-general of the republic, had married into the family of Favre, one of the leaders in the liberation of Geneva.   Old François Favre, the father-in-law, retained all the fiery spirit of the *Eidgenossen.*   His son-in-law, Amied, equally chivalrous and patriotic, had much less sense and ballast.   A man of fine commanding figure, who dressed with elegance, wore his sword well, and conversed with the skill of a French courtier, but vain-glorious, full of himself, unable to control his loquacious vanity at table, or in the council, he was particularly exposed to the sarcasms of the grave and censorious citizens of the new stamp.   The hatred that grew up between this man and the Reformer was one of those intense, immortal hates which a character like Calvin's is alone capable of provoking and sustaining.   On Calvin's side it was only slightly relieved by the contempt which he felt for the ' Stage Caesar,' as he called Amied.   But in describing his wife Françoise, and his father-in-law Favre, Calvin has withheld none of the colours of religious malignity.   With this family his struggle was long ; it ran through several years, with alternating success.   Perrin was no match for Calvin face to face before the Council. But he was sustained by his party, and by the secret inclinations of the people, who, while they lamented his principles, conceded some latitude of speech and conduct to the gallant soldier.   Once Calvin succeeded in getting him dismissed from his employments, expelled from the Council, and imprisoned.   But he soon recovered his liberty, his office, and the public favour.   More than once, during the struggle, the Liberal party seemed on the point of triumphing, and Calvin was expecting a second exile. Thus, he has been compared [1] to one of those middle-age Popes who, while Europe trembled at their frown, were

---

[1] Lerminier, *Revue d. d. Mondes*, 1842.
Westminster Review, 1858.]

themselves ever on the point of being driven out of their own capital. Sometimes the parties broke out into open violence. But to the credit of the republic it may be observed that wherever Calvin appeared on the scene, a certain degree of respect and forbearance was shown him.

The sort of feeling with which he was regarded may be gathered from one of these incidents. Viret happened to be on a visit in Geneva. A personal enemy of Calvin succeeded in getting into his hands, through Viret's servant, some of Calvin's letters; Viret, who was minister at Lausanne, being one of the persons with whom Calvin maintained a confidential correspondence. In one of these letters Calvin had said, in his usual style, severe things of the Genevese. One passage was—'The people here assume the name of Christ, but they desire to live without him. I have to wage an incessant war with this hypocrisy.' This letter was handed about in the town, where it excited the greatest indignation, and finally was made a charge against Calvin before the Council. He had added in the same letter, 'I expect little of the syndics of this year.' On this the accusation of 'defaming the Government' was founded. Calvin's answer was obvious. 'A confidential letter to a friend was not a published opinion at all. Besides, the expressions referred to events now three years old; and he was ready to uphold their truth.' After Calvin had been heard, and had withdrawn, Farel, who happened to be present, said— 'Troth, sirs, but ye ought to handle more tenderly with a man such as is Calvin, a man who hath not his equal in knowledge or in repute throughout all the churches. His censures be something rough, but ye should not be so delicate. He hath not spared Luther or Melanchthon, and they have borne it meekly. Nor is it meet that magistrates should be thus occupying themselves with the scandal of the taverns.' The Council felt the justice of these remarks, and the matter was let drop.

At length in 1555 the crisis came. The *dénouement* was simple enough, and the victory was complete. The leaders of the Liberal party were either exiled or beheaded, their property confiscated, and to propose their recall was made a capital offence. But what was exactly the nature of the treason in which they were implicated, whether it was political or ecclesiastical, whether it was plot, riot, or armed insurrection, we try in vain to make out from the confused and contradictory statements of the historians and biographers. The defeat of the Libertines is almost as great a historical enigma as the conspiracy of Catiline. It is not that there is a lack of original evidence. But this is so overlaid by the partisan statements of controversial or apologetic biographers, that it will require the careful and tedious process of a thoroughly critical sifting before any notion can be formed of the real character of these transactions. No life has been more written and re-written than that of Calvin[1]. None stands in greater need of a really critical biographer. The letters of Calvin, which have as yet been only very partially published, are in process of collection by M. Bonnet. The 'Société d'Histoire et d'Archéologie' of Geneva, in publishing some of the remains of Bonivard, and the 'Société de l'Histoire Protestante' of France, have done useful service in preparing original material. But what is above all wanted is the publication, in their integrity, of the Registers of the Councils and the Consistory. Without these before him, the writer of history can only be misled by the partial and garbled extracts which are scattered up

---

[1] [The most important contribution to the subject since this Essay was written is Calvin's *Opera Omnia*, published in the *Corpus Reformatorum*, by Baum, Cunitz, and Reuss. In this edition (not yet finished), the Letters are fully collected. Besides this should be mentioned Herminjard, *Correspondance des Réformateurs dans les Pays de la Langue Française* (1866–1878): several *Mémoires* by the younger Galiffe, in the publications of the Genevan *Société d'Histoire et d'Archéologie* : D'Aubigné's *Reformation in Europe in the time of Calvin* : Kampfschulte's *Calvin, seine Kirche und sein Staat in Genf* (1869) ; and Roget, *Histoire du Peuple de Genève depuis la Réformation jusqu'à l'Escalade* (1877).]

Westminster Review, 1858.]

and down the various books which treat of this period of the annals of Geneva. The most complete selection which has as yet been printed comprehends no more than the five years from 1532 to 1536. This, which is annexed to M. Gustave Révilliod's edition of 'Froment,' is only an extract, and omits those extracts which had previously been printed by Baron Grénus; an omission which detracts considerably from the utility, as well as the authenticity, of the volume. M. Révilliod promises a continuation of his labours. It were much to be wished that, in that part which covers the early history of Calvinism, the most faithful reproduction of the original documents should be made the rule of editing.

In the case of the Libertines, the accusation against Calvin is, that the men who had founded the liberties of their country were put to death, exiled, ruined to make way for the establishment of his own authority. This charge is only partially met by M. Gaberel's list of names[1]. He shows by a tabular comparison of the *Eidgenossen* of 1519—1530 with the *Libertins* of 1555, that only five of the latter are included among the former. This is true. But, though the older liberators had been removed by death in the interval, it is undeniable that the Libertines of 1555 were the true political representatives of the patriots of 1530. In many cases they were their sons, nephews, or otherwise related. But what if they were, if they refused to submit to the institutions established by the free choice of the free community? Calvin argued that previous merit only enhanced the guilt of lawlessness. He would not have admitted the plea of Tancred for Rinaldo—

> Ti sovvegna
> Saggio Signor, chi sia Rinaldo, e quale;
> Non del chi regna
> Nel castigo con tutti esser uguale.

[1] Gaberel, I. 303.

Neither, again, must we be misled by the historians
who blacken the moral character of the Libertines, and
adopt, in their ordinary sense, the epithets 'vicious,
dissolute, debauched,' which the Calvinists applied to
their opponents. The Libertines wished to live as other
people live, nothing more. What they opposed was,
judicial cognizance of offences against morals, which were
not also offences against society. The name which the
Calvinists succeeded in imposing on their adversaries
has prejudged their case. The term 'Libertin' was
transferred to the Liberal party in Geneva, the remnant
of the old Liberators, from an Anabaptist sect which had
arisen in the Low Countries. The antinomian doctrines
of Quentin and Cop, the Spiritual Libertines, were never
adopted by the Genevese patriots, who were neither
theologians nor metaphysicians. They were no systematic defenders of sensuality; but claimed, as Michel
Roset reports their own words—'vivre en liberté, et ne
vouloir être contraints au dire des prêcheurs.' They did
not theoretically deny the obligation of morality; but they
thought it too much to be obliged to swear that they
would keep the Ten Commandments.

The historian must never consider himself the apologist
of his characters, or think that his business is to obtain
a verdict. But if the view we have taken of Calvin's
enterprise be at all correct, we see that the success of
that enterprise involved the fall of the Libertines. To
submit or to withdraw from the city was the only
alternative that could be offered them. Neither had
Calvin any choice. Either he must destroy them, or
they would destroy—not himself, but his work, which
he believed to be the work of God. His fight with the
Libertines was not persecution of opinion, or an attempt
to bring dissidents into the Church by force. · The Libertines never alleged that their consciences were violated,
but only that they did not like the constraint. If they

were compelled, it is only as any recalcitrant minority is compelled, in every free State, by the majority. Such a minority can only claim our sympathy for their resistance, either when they suffer for conscience' sake, or for some noble cause. In this case no ground of conscience was or could be alleged. The Libertines had reasons and a good cause, but their opponents had better.

There is, indeed, a seeming paradox in the situation, when the Liberal party appear as the enemies of freedom. But this is not the solitary instance in history of the same phenomenon. It may easily happen that Liberalism may be found on one side and Liberty on the other. For Liberalism is only the irreflective desire to be quit of constraint; the natural instinct of the free man, but nothing more. It is not till that instinct has been deepened into consciousness, till the impulse has been educated into spontaneity, that the liberty of a truly free will begins to be exercised. The roving savage and the citizens of a Republic are both free, but in a different sort. Any anarchy has in it more opportunity for manly virtue, than the strait-waistcoat of 'order' imposed by the political keeper. But true liberty is only realized through self-control, when 'the weight of chance desires' has been felt, and been shaken off by an effort of the will. The modern State, a mere engine of police and property, is wholly incapable of conferring freedom on the individual. It only attains its end by encroaching on the individual. To this policed society the old 'social contract' theory strictly applied, when it represented each as sacrificing some of his own liberty for the benefit of all. Law is conceived as so much surrender of right, and justice as 'the good of others.' 'In pessimâ Republicâ plurimae leges.' But in the pure State, which is founded on virtue, or 'the law of Christ,' restraint is not imposed from without, but issues from within. The state of salvation within which the elect is placed, is the 'kingdom of Heaven,' in which he has no superior but God, and is himself the only aristocrat. Holiness, or strictness of life, becomes his point of honour. The inward 'assurance' of his election elevates the 'saint' above the difficulties of virtue. Morality is to him not a law which he is under the disagreeable necessity of obeying, but the only sphere in which he can exhibit the energies of his spiritual character. The will is the man. 'Il peut tout en étant soi; il ne peut rien sans l'être. De la vérité et l'originalité de l'âme procède la puissance [1].'

2. The political intolerance of Calvin was his strength; and the tyranny of the discipline became the cradle of liberty. It was very different with his intolerance of opinion. We must side with Calvin as against the Libertines. Every philosophic mind will say with Gibbon—'I am more scandalized by the burning of Servetus than by the whole hecatombs of human beings immolated in the *auto da fés* of Spain and Portugal.' But it has been our intention in this paper to consider Calvin in his political action only. His doctrinal and philosophical views form a separate subject. Suffice it to say that though Calvinism was an advance on the earlier Protestantism, in endowing it with the idea of the Church, as the society of the Believers, it did not make a step beyond it in the direction of emancipating Reason. Calvinism conferred on the human will its true freedom of action through restraint. His own powerful will impelled him to modify the ethics of Protestantism. But intensity of will is ever in an inverse ratio to breadth of intelligence. Calvin had a passionate desire to live as a free man under the law of God. He felt no corresponding necessity for intellectual emancipation. His mind had not compassed the idea of truths of reason. He knew only traditional dogma. And, to save the good character of Protestantism, it was desirable that the world should

[1] Sayous, *Études sur les Écrivains Français.*
Westminster Review, 1858].

understand that religious Protestants repudiated all idea of touching the dogma as much as the Catholics themselves. The punishment of Servetus was a stroke of policy. Calvin gained in character with his contemporaries by it. He had justified his faith by his acts, and not left the Church of Rome the sole glory of taking vengeance on the enemies of Christ. All the Protestants approved; Melanchthon emphatically so. Calvin never repented it. Greatly as the Calvinistic Churches have served the cause of political liberty, they have contributed nothing to the progress of knowledge.

XIII.

TENDENCIES OF RELIGIOUS THOUGHT IN ENGLAND, 1688–1750.

[Essays and Reviews, 1860.]

THE thirty years of peace which succeeded the Peace of Utrecht (1714), 'was the most prosperous season that England had ever experienced; and the progression, though slow, being uniform, the reign of George II might not disadvantageously be compared for the real happiness of the community with that more brilliant, but uncertain and oscillatory condition which has ensued. A labourer's wages have never for many ages commanded so large a portion of subsistence as in this part of the eighteenth century[1].'

This is the aspect which that period of history wears to the political philosopher. The historian of moral and religious progress, on the other hand, is under the necessity of depicting the same period as one of decay of religion, licentiousness of morals, public corruption, profaneness of language—a day of 'rebuke and blasphemy.' Even those who look with suspicion on the contemporary complaints from the Jacobite clergy of 'decay of religion' will not hesitate to say that it was an age destitute of depth or earnestness; an age whose poetry was without romance, whose philosophy was without insight, and whose public men were without character: an age of 'light without love,' whose 'very merits were of the earth, earthy.' In this

---

[1] Hallam, *Const. Hist.* II. 464.

Essays and Reviews, 1850.

estimate the followers of Mill and Carlyle will agree with those of Dr. Newman.

The stoical moralists of the second century, who witnessed a similar coincidence of moral degradation and material welfare, had no difficulty in connecting them together as effect with cause. 'Bona rerum secundarum optabilia, adversarum mirabilia[1].' But the famous theory which satisfied the political philosophers of antiquity, viz. that the degeneracy of nations is due to the inroads of luxury, is laughed to scorn by modern economists. It is at any rate a theory which can hardly be adopted by those who pour unmeasured contempt on the eighteenth, by way of contrast with the revival of higher principles by the nineteenth century. It is especially since the High Church movement commenced that the theology of the eighteenth century has become a byword. The genuine Anglican omits that period from the history of the Church altogether. In constructing his *Catena Patrum* he closes his list with Waterland or Brett, and leaps at once to 1833, when the *Tracts for the Times* commenced—as Charles II dated his reign from his father's death. Such a legal fiction may be harmless or useful for purposes of mere form, but the facts of history cannot be disposed of by forgetting them. Both the Church and the world of to-day are what they are as the result of the whole of their antecedents. The history of a party may be written on the theory of periodical occultation; but he who wishes to trace the descent of religious thought, and the practical working of the religious ideas, must follow these through all the phases they have actually assumed. We have not yet learnt, in this country, to write our ecclesiastical history on any better footing than that of praising up the party, in or out of the Church, to which we happen to belong. Still further are we from any attempt to apply the laws of thought, and of the succession of opinion, to the course of

[1] Seneca, *ad Lucil.* 66.

English theology. The recognition of the fact, that the view of the eternal verities of religion which prevails in any given age is in part determined by the view taken in the age which preceded it, is incompatible with the hypothesis generally prevalent among us as to the mode in which we form our notions of religious truth. Upon none of the prevailing theories as to this mode is a deductive history of theology possible. 1. The Catholic theory, which is really that of Roman-Catholics, and professedly that of Anglo-Catholics, withdraws Christianity altogether from human experience and the operation of the ordinary laws of thought. 2. The Protestant theory of free inquiry, which supposes that each mind takes a survey of the evidence, and strikes the balance of probability according to the best of its judgment—this theory defers indeed to the abstract laws of logic, but overlooks the influences of education. If, without hypothesis, we are content to observe facts, we shall find that we cannot decline to study the opinions of any age only because they are not our own opinions. There is a law of continuity in the progress of theology which, whatever we may wish, is never broken off. In tracing the filiation of consecutive systems, we cannot afford to overlook any link in the chain, any age, except one in which religious opinion did not exist. Certainly we, in this our time, if we would understand our own position in the Church, and that of the Church in the age, if we would hold any clue through the maze of religious pretension which surrounds us, cannot neglect those immediate agencies in the production of the present, which had their origin towards the beginning of the eighteenth century.

Of these agencies there are three, the present influence of which cannot escape the most inattentive. 1. The formation and gradual growth of that compromise between Church and State, which is called Toleration, and which,

believed by many to be a principle, is a mere arrangement
between two principles. But such as it is, it is part of our
heritage from the last age, and is the foundation, if foundation it can be called, upon which we still continue to build,
as in the late Act for the admission of Jews to Parliament.
2. The great rekindling of the religious consciousness of
the people which, without the Established Church, became
Methodism, and within its pale has obtained the name of
the *Evangelical* movement. However decayed may be
the Evangelical party as a party, it cannot be denied that
its influence, both on our religious ideas, and on our
Church life, has penetrated far beyond those party limits.
3. The growth and gradual diffusion through all religious
thinking of the supremacy of reason. This, which is
rather a principle, or a mode of thinking, than a doctrine,
may be properly enough called *Rationalism.* This term
is used in this country with so much laxity that it is
impossible to define the sense in which it is generally
intended. It is often taken to mean a system opposed to
revealed religion, and imported into this country from
Germany at the beginning of the present century. A
person, however, who surveys the course of English
theology during the eighteenth century will have no
difficulty in recognizing, that throughout all discussions,
underneath all controversies, and common to all parties,
lies the assumption of the supremacy of reason in matters
of religion. The Kantian philosophy did but bring forward into light, and give scientific form and a recognized
position to, a principle which had long unconsciously
guided all treatment of religious topics both in Germany
and in England. Rationalism was not an anti-Christian
sect outside the Church making war against religion. It
was a habit of thought ruling all minds, under the conditions of which all alike tried to make good the peculiar
opinions they might happen to cherish. The Churchman
differed from the Socinian, and the Socinian from the

Deist, as to the number of articles in his creed; but all alike consented to test their belief by the rational evidence for it. Whether given doctrines or miracles were conformable to reason or not was disputed between the defence and the assault: but that all doctrines were to stand or fall by that criterion was not questioned. The principles and the priority of natural religion formed the common hypothesis on the ground of which the disputants argued whether anything, and what, had been subsequently communicated to man in a supernatural way. The line between those who believed much and those who believed little cannot be sharply drawn. Some of the so-called Deists were, in fact, Socinians; as Toland, who expressly admits all those parts of the New Testament revelation which are, or seem to him, comprehensible by reason[1]. Nor is there any ground for thinking that Toland was insincere in his profession of rational Christianity, as was insinuated by his opponents—e. g. Leland[2]. A more candid adversary, Leibnitz, who knew Toland personally, is 'glad to believe that the design of this author, a man of no common ability, and as I think, a well-disposed person, was to withdraw men from speculative theology to the practice of its precepts[3].' Hardly one here and there, as Hume, professed Rationalism in the extent of Atheism; the great majority of writers were employed in constructing a *via media* between Atheism and Athanasianism, while the most orthodox were diligently 'hewing and chiselling Christianity into an intelligible human system, which they then represented, as thus mutilated, as affording a remarkable evidence of the truth of the Bible[4].' The title of Locke's treatise, *The Reasonableness of Christianity*, may be said to have been the solitary thesis of Christian theology in England for great part of a century.

---

[1] *Christianity not Mysterious.*
[2] *Annotatiunculae subitaneae.*
Essays and Reviews, 1860.]
[3] *View of the Deistical Writers*, vol. I. p. 49.
[4] *Tracts for the Times*, vol. II. No. 73.

If we were to put chronological limits to this system of religious opinion in England, we might, for the sake of a convenient landmark, say that it came in with the Revolution of 1688, and began to decline in vigour with the reaction against the Reform movement about 1830. Locke's *Reasonableness of Christianity* would thus open, and the commencement of the *Tracts for the Times* mark, the fall of Rationalism. Not that chronology can ever be exactly applied to the mutations of opinion. For there were Rationalists before Locke, e. g. Hales of Eton, and other Arminians, nor has the Church of England unanimously adopted the principles of the *Tracts for the Times*. But if we were to follow up Cave's nomenclature, the appellation *Saeculum Rationalisticum* might be affixed to the eighteenth century with greater precision than many of his names apply to the previous centuries. For it was not merely that Rationalism then obtruded itself as a heresy, or obtained a footing of toleration within the Church, but the rationalizing method possessed itself absolutely of the whole field of theology. With some trifling exceptions, the whole of religious literature was drawn into the endeavour to 'prove the truth' of Christianity. The essay and the sermon, the learned treatise and the philosophical disquisition, Addison the polite writer, and Bentley the classical philologian[1], the astronomer Newton[2], no less than the theologians by profession, were all engaged upon the same task. To one book of A. Collins, *A Discourse on the Grounds and Reasons of the Christian Religion* (London, 1724), are counted no less than thirty-five answers[3]. Dogmatic theology had ceased to exist; the exhibition of religious truth for practical purposes was confined to a few obscure writers.

---

[1] Addison, *Evidences of the Christian Religion*, a posthumous publication; Bentley, *Eight Sermons at Boyle's Lecture*, 1692.

[2] *Four Letters, &c.*, Lond. 1756.

[3] [This refers to a list given in the Preface to Collins's later book, *Scheme of Literal Prophecy* (1727).]

Every one who had anything to say on sacred subjects drilled it into an array of argument against a supposed objector. Christianity appeared made for nothing else but to be 'proved'; what use to make of it when it was proved was not much thought about. Reason was at first offered as the basis of faith, but gradually became its substitute. The mind never advanced as far as the stage of belief, for it was unceasingly engaged in reasoning up to it. The only quality in Scripture which was dwelt upon was its 'credibility.' Even the 'Evangelical' school, which had its origin in a reaction against the dominant Rationalism, and began in endeavours to kindle religious feeling, was obliged to succumb at last. It, too, drew out its rational 'scheme of Christianity,' in which the atonement was made the central point of a system, and the death of Christ was accounted for as necessary to satisfy the Divine Justice.

This whole rationalist age must again be subdivided into two periods, the theology of which, though belonging to the common type, has distinct specific characters. These periods are of nearly equal length, and we may conveniently take the middle year of the century, 1750, as our terminus of division. Though both periods were engaged upon the proof of Christianity, the distinction between them is that the first period was chiefly devoted to the internal, the second to the external, attestations. In the first period the main endeavour was to show that there was nothing in the contents of the revelation which was not agreeable to reason. In the second, from 1750 onwards, the controversy was narrowed to what are usually called the 'Evidences,' or the historical proof of the genuineness and authenticity of the Christian records. From this distinction of topic arises an important difference of value between the theological produce of the two periods. A great injustice is done to the eighteenth century, when its whole speculative product is set down under the description of that Old Bailey theology in which, to use Johnson's illustration, the Apostles are being tried once a week for the capital crime of forgery. This evidential school—the school of Paley, and Whately—belongs strictly to the latter half only of the period now under consideration. This school, which treated the exterior evidence, was the natural sequel and supplement of that which had preceded it, which dealt with the intrinsic credibility of the Christian revelation. This historical succession of the schools is the logical order ôf the argument. For when we have first shown that the facts of Christianity are not incredible, the whole burden of proof is shifted to the evidence that the facts did really occur. Neither branch of the argument can claim to be religious instruction at all, but the former does incidentally enter upon the substance of the Gospel. It may be philosophy rather than theology, but it raises in its course some of the most momentous problems which can engage the human mind. On the other hand, a mind which occupies itself with the 'external evidences'. knows nothing of the spiritual intuition, of which it renounces at once the difficulties and the consolations. The supply of evidences in what for the sake of a name may be called the Georgian period (1750–1830), was not occasioned by any demands of controversy. The attacks through the press were nearly at an end; the Deists had ceased to be. The clergy continued to manufacture evidence as an ingenious exercise, a literature which was avowedly professional, a study which might seem theology without being it, which could awaken none of the scepticism then dormant beneath the surface of society. Evidences are not edged tools; they stir no feeling; they were the proper theology of an age whose literature consisted in writing Latin hexameters. The orthodox school no longer dared to scrutinize the contents of revelation. The preceding period had eliminated the religious experience, the

Georgian had lost besides the power of using the speculative reason.

The historical investigation, indeed, of the *Origines* of Christianity, is a study scarcely second in importance to a philosophical arrangement of its doctrines. But for a genuine inquiry of this nature the English writers of the period had neither the taste nor the knowledge. Gibbon alone approached the true difficulties, but met only with opponents 'victory over whom was a sufficient humiliation[1].' No Englishman will refuse to join with Coleridge in 'the admiration' he expresses 'for the head and heart' of Paley, 'the incomparable grace, propriety, and persuasive facility of his writings[2].' But Paley had unfortunately dedicated his powers to a factitious thesis; his demonstration, however perfect, is in unreal matter. The case, as the apologists of that day stated it, is wholly conventional. The breadth of their assumptions is out of all proportion to the narrow dimensions of the point they succeed in proving. Of an honest critical inquiry into the origin and composition of the canonical writings there is but one trace, Herbert Marsh's Lectures at Cambridge; and that was suggested from a foreign source, and died away without exciting imitators. That investigation, introduced by a bishop and professor of divinity, has scarcely yet obtained a footing in the English Church. But it is excluded, not from a conviction of its barrenness, but from a fear that it might prove too fertile in results. This unwholesome state of theological feeling among us is perhaps traceable in part to the falsetto of the evidential method of the last generation. We cannot justify, but we may perhaps make our predecessors bear part of the blame of, that inconsistency, which, while it professes that its religious belief rests on historical evidence, refuses to allow that evidence to be freely examined in open court.

[1] *Autobiography.*   [2] *Aids to Reflection*, p. 401.
Essays and Reviews, 1860.]

It seems, indeed, a singular infelicity that the construction of the historical proof should have been the task
which the course of events allotted to the latter half of the
eighteenth century. The critical knowledge of antiquity
had disappeared from the Universities. The past, discredited by a false conservatism, was regarded with
aversion, and the minds of men directed habitually to the
future, some with fear, others with hope. 'The disrespect
in which history was held by the French *philosophes* is
notorious; one of the soberest of them; D'Alembert, we
believe, was the author of the wish that all record of past
events could be blotted out[1].' The same sentiment was
prevalent, though not in the same degree, in this country[2].
Hume, writing to an Englishman in 1756, speaks of 'your
countrymen' as 'given over to barbarous and absurd
faction.' Of his own history the publisher, Millar, told
him he had only sold forty-five copies in a twelvemonth[3].
Warburton had long before complained of the Chronicles
published by Hearne that 'there is not one that is not a
disgrace to letters; most of them are so to common sense,
and some even to human nature[4].' The oblivion into
which the remains of Christian antiquity had sunk, till
disinterred by the Tractarian movement, is well known.
Having neither the critical tools to work with, nor the
historical materials to work upon, it is no wonder if they
failed in their art. Theology had almost died out when it
received a new impulse and a new direction from Coleridge.
The evidence-makers ceased from their futile labours all
at once, as beneath the spell of some magician. Englishmen heard with as much surprise as if the doctrine was
new, that the Christian faith, the Athanasian Creed, of
which they had come to wish that the Church was well

[1] Mill, *Dissertations*, vol. I. p. 426.
[2] [The historical sense was very feeble, but many important historical books
were being written.]
[3] *My Own Life*, p. 5.   [4] Parr's *Tracts, &c.*, p. 109.

rid, was 'the perfection of human intelligence'; that 'the compatibility of a document with the conclusions of self-evident reason, and with the laws of conscience, is a condition *a priori* of any evidence adequate to the proof of its having been revealed by God,' and that this 'is a principle clearly laid down by Moses and St. Paul'; lastly, that 'there are mysteries in Christianity, but that these mysteries are reason, reason in its highest form of self-affirmation[1].' In this position of Coleridge, the rationalist theology of England, which was in the last stage of decay and dotage, seemed to recover a second youth, and to revert at once to the point from which it had started a century before.

Should the religious historian then acknowledge that the impatient contempt with which 'the last century' is now spoken of, is justifiable with respect to the later period, with its artificial monotone of proof that is no proof, he will by no means allow the same of the earlier period, 1688–1750. The superiority which the theological writing of this period has over that which succeeded it, is to be referred in part to the superiority of the internal, over the external, proof of Christianity, as an object of thought.

Both methods alike, as methods of argumentative proof, place the mind in an unfavourable attitude for the consideration of religious truth. It is like removing ourselves, for the purpose of examining an object, to the furthest point from which the object is visible. Neither the external nor the internal evidences are properly theology at all. Theology is—1st, and primarily, the contemplative, speculative habit, by means of which the mind places itself already in another world than this; a habit begun here, to be raised to perfect vision hereafter. 2ndly, and in an inferior degree, it is ethical and regulative of our conduct as men, in those relations which are temporal and

[1] *Aids to Reflection*, Pref. *Lit. Remains*, III. 293.
Essays and Reviews, 1860.]

transitory. Argumentative proof that such knowledge is possible can never be substituted for the knowledge without detriment to the mental habit. What is true of an individual is true of an age. When an age is found occupied in proving its creed, this is but a token that the age has ceased to have a proper belief in it. Nevertheless, there is a difference in this respect between the sources from which proof may be fetched. Where it is busied in establishing the 'genuineness and authenticity' of the books of Scripture, neglecting its religious lessons, and drawing out instead 'the undesigned coincidences,' Rationalism is seen in its dullest and least spiritual form. When, on the other hand, the contents of the Revelation are being freely examined, and reason, as it is called, but really the philosophy in vogue, is being applied to determine whether the voice be the voice of God or not, the reasoner is indeed approaching his subject from a false point of view, but he is still engaged with the eternal verities. The reason has prescribed itself an impossible task when it has undertaken to prove, instead of evolve them; to argue, instead of appropriate them. But anyhow, it is handling them; and by the contact is raised in some measure to the 'height of that great argument.'

This acknowledgment seems due to the period now referred to. It is, perhaps, rather thinking of its pulpit eloquence than its controversies, that Professor Fraser does not hesitate to call this 'the golden age of English theology[1].' Such language, as applied to our great preachers, was once a matter of course, but would now hardly be used by any Anglican, and has to be sought for in the mouth of members of another communion. The names which once commanded universal homage among us excite, perhaps, only a smile of pity. Literary taste is proverbially inconstant; but theological is still more so, for

[1] *Essays in Philosophy*, p. 205.

here we have no rule or chart to guide us but the taste of our age.   Bossuet, Bourdaloue, and Massillon have survived a dozen political revolutions.   We have no classical theology, though we have not had a political revolution since 1660. For in this subject-matter the most of Englishmen have no other standard of merit than the prejudices of sect. Eminence only marks out a great man for more cordial hatred; every flippant High Church reviewer has learnt to fling at Locke, the father of English Rationalism, and the greatest name among its worthies.   Others are, perhaps, only less disliked because less known; 'qui n'a pas de lecteurs, n'a pas d'adversaires.'   The principal writers in the Deistical Controversy, on either side of it, have expiated the attention they once engrossed by as universal an oblivion.

The Deistical Controversy, the all-absorbing topic of religious writers and preachers during the whole of this first period, has pretty well defined limits.   Stillingfleet, who died Bishop of Worcester, in the last year (1699) of the seventeenth century, marks the transition from the old to the new argument.   In the six folios of Stillingfleet's works may be found the latest echoes of the Romanist Controversy, and the first declaration of war against Locke.   The Deistical Controversy attained its greatest intensity in the twenties (1720–1740), after the subsidence of the Bangorian controversy, which for a time had diverted attention to itself, and it gradually died out towards the middle of the century.   The decay of interest in the topic is sufficiently marked by the fact that the opinions of Hume failed to stimulate curiosity or antagonism.   His *Treatise of Human Nature* (1739) 'fell dead-born from the press,' and the only one of his philosophical writings which was received with favour on its first appearance was one on the new topic—*Political Discourses* (1752).   Of this he says 'it was the only work of mine which was successful on the first publication,

being well received both abroad and at home[1].' Bolingbroke, who died in 1751, was the last of the professed
Deists. When his works were brought out by his
executor, Mallet, in 1754, the interest in them was already
gone; they found the public cold or indisposed. 'It was
a rusty blunderbuss, which he need not have been afraid
to have discharged himself, instead of leaving half-a-crown
to a Scotchman to let it off after his death[2].' To talk Deism
had ceased to be fashionable as soon as it ceased to attract
attention.

The rationalism, which is the common character of all
the writers of this time, is a method rather than a doctrine;
an unconscious assumption rather than a principle from
which they reason. They would, however, all have consented in statements such as the following:

Bishop Gibson, *Second Pastoral Letter,* 1730. 'Those
among us who have laboured of late years to set up reason
against revelation would make it pass for an established
truth, that if you will embrace revelation you must of course
quit your reason, which if it were true, would doubtless be
a strong prejudice against revelation. But so far is this
from being true, that *it is universally acknowledged that
revelation itself is to stand or fall by the test of reason,* or, in
other words, according as reason finds the evidences of its
coming from God to be or not to be sufficient and con-
clusive, and the matter of it to contradict or not contradict
the natural notions which reason gives us of the being
and attributes of God.'

Prideaux (Humphrey, Dean of Norwich), *Letter to the
Deists,* 1708. 'Let what is written in all the books of the
New Testament be tried by that which is the touchstone of
all religions, I mean that religion of nature and reason which
God has written in the hearts of every one of us from the
first creation; and if it varies from it in any one particular,
if it prescribes any one thing which may in the minutest

---

[1] *My Own Life.*   [2] *Boswell,* p. 88.

circumstances thereof be contrary to its righteousness, I will then acknowledge this to be an argument against us, strong enough to overthrow the whole cause, and make all things else that can be said for it totally ineffectual for its support.'

Tillotson (Archbishop of Canterbury), *Sermons*, vol. III. p. 485. 'All our reasonings about revelation are necessarily gathered by our natural notions about religion, and therefore he who sincerely desires to do the will of God is not apt to be imposed on by vain pretences of divine revelation; but if any doctrine be proposed to him which is pretended to come from God, he measures it by those sure and steady notions which he has of the divine nature and perfections; he will consider the nature and tendency of it, or whether it be a doctrine according to godliness, such as is agreeable to the divine nature and perfections, and tends to make us like unto God; if it be not, though an angel should bring it, he would not receive it.'

Rogers (John, D.D.), *Sermons at Boyle's Lecture*, 1727, p. 59. 'Our religion desires no other favour than a sober and dispassionate examination. It submits its grounds and reasons to an unprejudiced trial, and hopes to approve itself to the conviction of any equitable enquirer.'

Butler (Joseph, Bishop of Durham), *Analogy*, &c., pt. II, ch. 1. 'Indeed, if in revelation there be found any passages, the seeming meaning of which is contrary to natural religion, we may most certainly conclude such seeming meaning not to be the real one.' *Ibid.*, ch. 8: 'I have argued upon the principles of the fatalists, which I do not believe; and have omitted a thing of the utmost importance which I do believe: the moral fitness and unfitness of actions, prior to all will whatever, which I apprehend as certainly to determine the divine conduct, as speculative truth and falsehood necessarily determine the divine judgment.'

Essays and Reviews, 1860.]

To the same effect the leading preacher among the
Dissenters, James Foster, *Truth and Excellency of the
Christian Revelation*, 1731. 'The faculty of reason which
God hath implanted in mankind, however it may have
been abused and neglected in times past, will, whenever
they begin to exercise it aright, enable them to judge of
all these things. As by means of this they were capable
of discovering at first the being and perfections of God,
and that he governs the world with absolute wisdom,
equity, and goodness, and what those duties are which
they owe to him and one another, they must be as capable,
if they will divest themselves of prejudice, and reason
impartially, of rectifying any mistakes they may have
fallen into about these important points. It matters
not whether they have hitherto thought right or wrong,
nor indeed whether they have thought at all; let them
but begin to consider seriously and examine carefully
and impartially, and they must be able to find out all
those truths which as reasonable creatures they are
capable of knowing, and which affect their duty and
happiness.'

Finally, Warburton, displaying at once his disdain and
his ignorance of catholic theology, affirms on his own
authority, *Works*, III. p. 620, that 'the image of God in
which man was at first created, lay in the faculty of reason
only.'

But it is needless to multiply quotations. The received
theology of the day taught on this point the doctrine of
Locke, as clearly stated by himself [1]. 'Reason is natural
revelation, whereby the eternal Father of light and
fountain of all knowledge communicates to mankind that
portion of truth which he has laid within the reach
of their natural faculties; revelation is natural reason
enlarged by a new set of discoveries communicated by
God immediately, which reason vouches the truth of, by

[1] *Essay*, Bk. IV. ch. 19, § 4.

the testimony and proofs it gives, that they come from God.   So that he that takes away reason to make way for revelation, puts out the light of both, and does much-what the same as if he would persuade a man to put out his eyes the better to receive the remote light of an invisible star by a telescope.'

According to this assumption, a man's religious belief is a result which issues at the end of an intellectual process.   In arranging the steps of this process, they conceived natural religion to form the first stage of the journey.   That stage theologians of all shades and parties travelled in company.   It was only when they had reached the end of it that the Deists and the Christian apologists parted.   The former found that the light of reason which had guided them so far indicated no road beyond.   The Christian writers declared that the same natural powers enabled them to recognize the truth of revealed religion.   The sufficiency of natural religion thus became the turning point of the dispute.   The natural law of right and duty, argued the Deists, is so absolutely perfect that God could not add anything to it. It is commensurate with all the real relations in which man stands.   To suppose that God has created artificial relations, and laid upon man positive precepts, is to take away the very notion of morality.   The moral law is nothing but the conditions of our actual being, apparent alike to those of the meanest and of the highest capacity. It is inconsistent with this to suppose that God has gone on to enact arbitrary statutes, and to declare them to man in an obscure and uncertain light.   This was the ground taken by the great champion of Deism—Tindal, and expressed in the title of the treatise which he published in 1732, when upwards of seventy, *Christianity as old as the Creation: or, the Gospel a Republication of the Religion of Nature*[1].   This was the point which the Christian

[1] [It was published in different editions in 1710, 1730, and 1732.] *Essays and Reviews*, 1860.]

defenders laboured most, to construct the bridge which should unite the revealed to the natural. They never demur to making the Natural the basis on which the Christian rests; to considering the natural knowledge of God as the starting-point both of the individual mind and of the human race. This assumption is necessary to their scheme, in which revelation is an argument addressed to the reason. Christianity is a *résumé* of the knowledge of God already attained by reason, and a disclosure of further truths. These further truths could not have been thought out by reason; but when divinely communicated, they approve themselves to the same reason which has already put us in possession of so much. The new truths are not of another order of ideas, for 'Christianity is a particular scheme under the general plan of Providence[1],' and the whole scheme is of a piece and uniform. ' If the dispensation be indeed from God, all the parts of it will be seen to be the correspondent members of one entire whole, which orderly disposition of things essential to a religious system will assure us of the true theory of the Christian faith[2].' 'How these relations are made known, whether by reason or revelation, makes no alteration in the case, because the duties arise out of the relations themselves, not out of the manner in which we are informed of them[3].' 'Those very articles of belief and duties of obedience, which were formerly natural with respect to their manner of promulgation, are now in the declaration of them also supernatural[4].' The relations to the Redeemer and the Sanctifier are not artificial, but as real as those to the Maker and Preserver, and the obligations arising out of the one set of relations as natural as those arising out of the other.

The deference paid to natural religion is further seen

[1] *Analogy*, pt. II, ch. 4.
[2] Warburton, *Divine Legation, &c.*, Bk. IX. Introd. *Works*, vol. III. p. 600.
[3] *Analogy*, pt. II. ch. 1.
[4] Ferguson, *Reason in Religion*, 1675, p. 29.

in the attempts to establish *a priori* the *necessity* of a
revelation. To make this out it was requisite to show
that the knowledge with which reason could supply us
was inadequate to be the guide of life, yet reason must
not be too much depressed, inasmuch as it was needed
for the proof of Christianity. On the other hand, the
moral state of the heathen world prior to the preaching
of Christianity, and of Pagan and savage tribes in Africa
and America now, the superstitions of the most civilized
nations of antiquity, the intellectual follies of the wisest
philosophers, are exhibited in great detail. The usual
arguments of scepticism on the conscious weakness of
reason are brought forward, but not pushed very far.
Reason is to be humiliated so far as that supernatural
light shall be seen to be necessary, but it must retain its
competence to judge of the evidence of the supernatural
message. Natural religion is insufficient as a light and
a motive to show us our way, and to make us walk in it ;
it is sufficient as a light and a motive to lead us to revelation, and to induce us to embrace it.   How much of
religious truth was contained in natural knowledge, or
how much was due to supernatural communication, was
very variously estimated. Locke, especially, had warned
against our liability to attribute to reason much of moral
truth that had in fact been derived from revelation. But
the uncertainty of the demarcation between the two is
only additional proof of the identity of the scheme which
they disclose between them. The whole of God's government and dealings with man forms one widespread and
consistent scheme, of which natural reason apprehends
a part, and of which Christianity was the manifestation
of a further part. Consistently herewith they treated
natural religion, not as an historical dispensation, but as
an abstract demonstration. There never was a time when
mankind had realized or established an actual system of
natural religion, but it lies always potentially in his reason.

Essays and Reviews, 1860.]

It held the same place as the social contract in political history. The 'original contract' had never had historical existence, but it was a hypothesis necessary to explain the existing fact of society. No society had, in fact, arisen on that basis, yet it is the theoretical basis on which all society can be shown to rest. So there was no time or country where the religion of nature had been fully known, yet the natural knowledge of God is the only foundation in the human mind on which can be built a rational Christianity. Though not an original condition of any part of mankind, it is an ever-originating condition of every human mind, as soon as it begins to reason on the facts of religion, rendering all the moral phenomena available for the construction of a scientific theory of religion.

In accordance with this view they interpreted the passages in St. Paul which speak of the religion of the heathen; e. g. Rom. ii. 14. Since the time of Augustine[1] the orthodox interpretation had applied this verse, either to the Gentile converts, or to the favoured few among the heathen who had extraordinary divine assistance. The Protestant expositors, to whom the words 'do by nature the things contained in the law' could never bear their literal force, sedulously preserved the Augustinian explanation. Even the Pelagian Jeremy Taylor is obliged to gloss the phrase 'by nature,' thus: 'By fears and secret opinions which the Spirit of God, who is never wanting to men in things necessary, was pleased to put into the hearts of men[2].' The rationalists, however, find the expression 'by nature,' in its literal sense, exactly conformable to their own views[3], and have no difficulty even in supposing the acceptableness of these works, and the salvability of those who do them. Burnet on Art. XVIII., in his usual confused style of eclecticism,

---

[1] *De Spir. et Lit.* § 27.   [2] *Duct. Dubit.* Bk. II. ch. 1, § 3.
[3] John Wilkins (1614–1672), *Of Nat. Rel.* II. c. 9.

suggests both opinions without seeming to see that they are incompatible relics of divergent schools of doctrine.

Consequent with such a theory of religion was their notion of its practical bearings. Christianity was a republication of the moral law—a republication rendered necessary by the helpless state of moral debasement into which the world was come by the practice of vice. The experience of ages had proved that, though our duty might be discoverable by the light of nature, yet virtue was not able to maintain itself in the world without additional sanctions. The disinterestedness of virtue was here a point much debated. The Deists, in general, argued from the notion of morality, that so far as any private regard to my own interest, whether present or future, influences my conduct, so far my actions have no moral worth. From this they drew the inference that the rewards and punishments of Christianity—these additional sanctions—could not be a divine ordinance, inasmuch as they were subversive of morality. The orthodox writers had to maintain the theory of rewards and punishments in such a way as not to be inconsistent with the theory of the disinterestedness of virtue which they had made part of their theology. Even here no precise line can be drawn between the Deistical and the Christian moralists. For we find Shaftesbury placing in a very clear light the mode in which religious sanctions do, in fact, as society is constituted, support and strengthen virtue in the world, though he does not deny that the principle of virtue in the individual may suffer from the selfish passion being appealed to by the hope of reward or the fear of punishment[1]. But with whatever variation in individual disputants, the tone of the discussions is unmistakable. When Collins was asked, 'Why he was careful to make his servants go to Church?' he is said to

[1] *Characteristicks*, vol. II. p. 66. (Inquiry concerning virtue, pt. III. § 3.)
Essays and Reviews, 1860.]

have answered, 'I do it that they may neither rob nor murder me.' This is but an exaggerated form of the practical religion of the age. Tillotson's Sermon [1] ' On the Advantages of Religion to Societies,' is like Collins's reply at fuller length. The Deists and their opponents alike assume that the purpose of the supernatural interference of the Deity in revelation must have been to secure the good behaviour of man in this world; that the future life and our knowledge of it may be a means to this great end; that the next world, if it exist at all, bears that relation to the present. We are chiefly familiar with these views from their having been long the butt of the Evangelical pulpit, a chief topic in which was to decry the mere 'legal' preaching of a preceding age. To abstain from vice, to cultivate virtue, to fill our station in life with propriety, to bear the ills of life with resignation, and to use its pleasures moderately—these things are indeed not little; perhaps no one can name in his circle of friends a man whom he thinks equal to these demands. Yet the experience of the last age has shown us unmistakably that where this is our best ideal of life, whether, with the Deists, we establish the obligation of morality on 'independent' grounds; or, with the orthodox, add the religious sanction—in Mr. Mill's rather startling mode of putting it [2], 'Because God is stronger than we, and able to damn us if we don't'—it argues a sleek and sordid epicurism, in which religion and a good conscience have their place among the means by which life is to be made comfortable. To accuse the divines of this age of a leaning to Arminianism is quite beside the mark. They did not intend to be other than orthodox. They did not take the Arminian side rather than the Calvinistic in the old conflict or concordat between Faith and Works, between Justification and Sanctification. They had dropped the terminology, and with it the mode of thinking, which

[1] *Works*, vol. III. p. 43.   [2] *Dissertations*, vol. II. p. 436.

the terms implied. They had adopted the language and ideas of the moralists. They spoke not of sin, but of vice, and of virtue, not of works. In the old Protestant theology actions had only a certain exterior relation to the justified man; 'gute fromme Werke machen nimmermehr einen guten frommen Mann, sondern ein guter frommer Mann macht gute Werke[1].' Now, our conduct was thought of, not as a product or efflux of our character, but as regulated by our understanding; by a perception of relations, or a calculation of consequences. This intellectual perception of regulative truth is religious Faith. Faith is no longer the devout condition of the entire inner man. Its dynamic nature, and interior working, are not denied, but they are unknown; and religion is made to regulate life from without, through the logical proof of the being and attributes of God, upon which an obligation to obey him can be raised.

The preachers of any period are not to be censured for adapting their style of address and mode of arguing to their hearers. They are as necessarily bound to the preconceived notions, as to the language, of those whom they have to exhort. The pulpit does not mould the forms into which religious thought in any age runs, it simply accommodates itself to those that exist. For this very reason, because they must follow and cannot lead, sermons are the surest index of the prevailing religious feeling of their age. When we are reminded of the powerful influence of the pulpit at the Reformation, in the time of the Long Parliament, or at the Methodist revival, it must also be remembered that these preachers addressed a different class of society from that for which our classical pulpit oratory was written. If it could be said that 'Sherlock, Hare, and Gibson preach in vain[2],' it was because the populace were gone to hear mad Henley on his tub. To charge Tillotson or Foster with not

---

[1] Luther.   [2] Dunciad, III. 204.

moving the masses which Whitefield moved, is to charge them with not having preached to another congregation than that to which they had to preach. Nor did they preach to empty pews, though their carefully-written 'discourses' could never produce effects such as are recorded of Burnet's extempore addresses, when he 'was often interrupted by the deep hum of his audience, and when, after preaching out the hour-glass, he held it up in his hand, the congregation clamorously encouraged him to go on till the sand had run off once more[1].' The dramatic oratory of Whitefield could not have sustained its power over the same auditors; he had a fresh congregation every Sunday. And, in the judgment of one quite disposed to do justice to Whitefield, there is nothing in his printed sermons. Johnson[2], speaking of the comparisons drawn between the preaching in the Church and that of the Methodists to the disadvantage of the former, says, 'I never treated Whitefield's ministry with contempt; I believe he did good. But when familiarity and noise claim the praise due to knowledge, art, and elegance, we must beat down such pretensions.' It is, however, the substance, and not the manner, of the classical sermons of the eighteenth century which is meant, when they are complained of as cold and barren. From this accusation they cannot be vindicated. But let it be rightly understood that it is a charge, not against the preachers, but against the religious ideas of the period. In the pulpit, the speaker has no choice but to take his audience as he finds them. He can but draw them on to the conclusions already involved in their premises. He cannot supply them with a new set of principles, or alter their fixed forms of thought. The ideas out of which the Protestant or the Puritan movement proceeded were generated elsewhere than in the pulpit.

The Rationalist preachers of the eighteenth century

[1] Macaulay, vol. II. p. 177.   [2] Ap. Boswell.

are usually contrasted with the Evangelical pulpit which displaced them. Mr. Neale has compared them disadvantageously with the medieval preachers in respect of Scripture knowledge. He selects a sermon of the eighteenth and one of the twelfth century; the one by the well-known Evangelical preacher John Newton, Rector of St. Mary Woolnoth; the other by Guarric, Abbot of Igniac. 'In Newton's sermon we find nine references to the Gospels, two to the Epistles, nine to the Prophets, one to the Psalms, and none to any other part of Scripture. In the sermon of Guarric we find seven references to the Gospels, one to the Epistles, twenty-two to the Psalms, nine to the Prophets, and eighteen to other parts of Scripture. Thus the total number of quotations made by the Evangelical preacher is twenty-one, by Guarric fifty-seven, and this in sermons of about equal length [1].' Mr. Neale has, perhaps, not been fortunate in his selection of a specimen sermon. For having the curiosity to apply this somewhat childish test to a sermon of James Blair, taken at random out of his four volumes, I found the number of texts quoted thirty-seven. But, passing this by, Mr. Neale misses his inference. He means to show how much more Scripture knowledge was possessed by the preachers of the 'dark ages.' This is very likely, if familiarity with the mere words of the Vulgate version be Scripture knowledge. But it is not proved by the abstinence of the eighteenth century preacher from the use of Biblical phraseology. The fact, so far as it is one, only shows that our divines understood Scripture differently from, some will say better than, the Middle Age ecclesiastics. The latter had, in the mystical theology of the Christian Church, a rich store of religious sentiment, which it was an exercise of their ingenuity to find in the poetical books of the Hebrew canon. Great part of this fanciful allegorizing is lost, apart from the Vulgate translation.

[1] *Medieval Preaching*, Introd. xxvi.

But of this the more learned of them were quite aware, and on their theory of Scripture interpretation, according to which the Church was its guaranteed expositor, the verbal meanings of the Latin version were equally the inspired sense of the sacred record. It was otherwise with the English divine of the eighteenth century. According to the then received view of Scripture, its meaning was not assigned by the Church, but its language was interpreted by criticism—i. e. by reason. The aids of history, the ordinary rules of grammar and logic, were applied to find out what the sacred writers actually said. *That* was the meaning of Scripture, the message supernaturally communicated. Where each text of Scripture has but one sense—that sense in which the writer penned it—it can only be cited in that sense without doing it violence. This was the turn by which Selden so discomfited the Puritan divines, who, like the Catholic mystics, made Scripture words the vehicle of their own feelings. 'Perhaps in your little pocket Bibles with gilt leaves the translation may be thus, but the Greek or Hebrew signifies otherwise[1].' If the preacher in the eighteenth century had allowed himself to make these allusions, the taste of his audience would have rejected them. He would have weakened his argument instead of giving it effect.

No quality of these 'Discourses' strikes us more now than the good sense which pervades them. They are the complete reaction against the Puritan sermon of the seventeenth century. We have nothing far-fetched, fanciful, allegoric. The practice of our duty is recommended to us on the most undeniable grounds of prudence. Barrow had indulged in ambitious periods, and South had been jocular. Neither of these faults can be alleged against the model sermon of the Hanoverian period. No topic is produced which does not compel our assent as soon

[1] Whitelocke, in Johnson's *Life of Selden*, p. 303.

as it is understood, and none is there which is not understood as soon as uttered. It is one man of the world
speaking to another. Collins said of St. Paul, 'that he
had a great respect for him as both a man of sense and
a gentleman[1].' He might have said the same of the best
pulpit divines of his own time. They bear the closest
resemblance to each other, because they all use the
language of fashionable society, and say exactly the
proper thing. 'A person,' says Waterland, 'must have
some knowledge of men, besides that of books, to succeed
well here; and must have a kind of practical sagacity
which nothing but the grace of God joined with recollec-
tion and wise observation can bring, to be able to represent
truths to the life, or to any considerable degree of advantage.' This is from his recommendatory preface prefixed
to the second edition of Blair's Sermons (1732); not the
Presbyterian Dr. Hugh Blair, but James Blair, the founder
and first President of the William and Mary College in
Virginia, whose Sermons on the Beatitudes were among
the most approved models of the day, and recommended
by the bishops to their candidates for orders. Dr. Hugh
Blair's Sermons, which Johnson thought 'excellently
written, both as to doctrine and language[2],' are in a
different taste—that of the latter half of the century, when
solid and sensible reasoning was superseded by polished
periods and flowery rhetoric. 'Polished as marble,' says
Hugh J. Rose, 'but also as lifeless and as cold.' The
sermons which Waterland recommends to young students
of divinity comprise Tillotson, Sharp, Calamy, Sprat,
Blackhall, Hoadly, South, Claggett, and Atterbury. Of
these, 'Sharp's, Calamy's, and Blackhall's are the best
models for an easy, natural, and familiar way of writing.
Sprat is fine, florid and elaborate in his style, artful in his
method, and not so open as the former, but harder to be

[1] [*Biog. Brit.* Art. 'Barrington, John Shute'.]
[2] Ap. Boswell, p. 528.

Essays and Reviews, 1860.]

imitated. Hoadly is very exact and judicious, and both his sense and style just, close, and clear. The others are very sound, clear writers, only Scot[1] is too swelling and pompous, and South is something too full of wit and satire, and does not always observe a decorum in his style.' He advises the student to begin his divinity course with reading sermons, because 'they are the easiest, plainest, and most entertaining of any books of divinity; and might be digested into a better body of divinity than any that is yet extant[2].'

Not only the pulpit, but the whole theological literature of the age, takes the same tone of appeal. Books are no longer addressed by the cloistered academic to a learnedly educated class, they are written by popular divines—'men of leisure,' Butler calls them—for the use of fashionable society. There is an epoch in the history of letters when readers and writers change places; when it ceases to be the reader's business to come to the writer to be instructed, and the writer begins to endeavour to engage the attention of the reader. The same necessity was now laid upon the religious writer. He appeared at the bar of criticism, and must gain the wits and the town. At the debate between the Deists and the Christian apologists the public was umpire. The time was past when Baxter 'talked about another world like one that had been there, and was come as a sort of express from thence to make a report concerning it[3].' As the preacher now no longer spake with the authority of a heavenly mission, but laid the state of the argument before his hearers, so philosophy was no longer a self-centred speculation, an oracle of wisdom. The divine went out into the streets, with his demonstration of the being and attributes of God printed on a broadside; he solicits your

---

[1] [John Scott, D.D. (1638-1694), best known as author of the *Christian Life.*]
[2] *Advice to a Young Student,* 1730.
[3] Calamy, *Life,* I. 220.

assent in 'the new court-jargon.' When Collins visited
Lord Barrington at Tofts, 'as they were all men of letters,
and had a taste for Scripture criticism, it is said to have
been their custom after dinner, to have a Greek Testament laid on the table[1].' These discussions were not
necessarily unprofitable. Lord Bolingbroke 'was seldom
in the company of the Countess of Huntingdon without
discussing some topic beneficial to his eternal interests,
and he always paid the utmost respect and deference to
her ladyship's opinion[2].' Bishop Butler gives his clergy
hints how to conduct themselves when 'sceptical and
profane men bring up the subject (religion) at meetings
of entertainment, and such as are of the freer sort; innocent ones, I mean, otherwise I should not suppose you
would be present at them[3].' Tindal's reconversion from
Romanism is said to have been brought about by the
arguments he heard in the coffee-houses. This anecdote,
given in Curll's catch-penny 'Life,' rests, not on that
bookseller's authority, which is worthless, but on that of
the medical man who attended him in his last illness. It
was the same with the controversy on the Trinity, of
which Waterland says, in 1723, that it was 'spread abroad
among all ranks and degrees of men, and the Athanasian
creed become the subject of common and ordinary conversation[4].' The Universities were invaded by the spirit
of the age, and instead of taking students through a
laborious course of philosophy, natural and moral, turned
out accomplished gentlemen upon 'the classics' and a
scantling of logic. Berkeley's ironical portrait of the
modish philosopher is of date 1732. 'Lysicles smiled,
and said he believed Euphranor had figured to himself
philosophers in square caps and long gowns, but thanks
to these happy times, the reign of pedantry was over.

[1] *Biog. Brit.* Art. ' Barrington.'
[2] *Memoirs of Countess of Hunt.*, I. 180.
[3] *Durham Charge*, 1751.
[4] *Critical Hist. of the Athan. Creed.* Introd.

Essays and Reviews, 1860.]

Our philosophers are of a very different kind from those awkward students who think to come at knowledge by poring on dead languages and old authors, or by sequestering themselves from the cares of the world to meditate in solitude and retirement. They are the best bred men of the age, men who know the world, men of pleasure, men of fashion, and fine gentlemen. EUPH.: I have some small notion of the people you mention, but should never have taken them for philosophers. CRI.: Nor would any one else till of late. The world was long under a mistake about the way to knowledge, thinking it lay through a tedious course of academical education and study. But among the discoveries of the present age, one of the principal is the finding out that such a method doth rather retard and obstruct, than promote knowledge. LYS.: I will undertake, a lad of fourteen, bred in the modern way, shall make a better figure, and be more considered in any drawing-room, or assembly of polite people, than one at four-and-twenty, who hath lain by a long time at school and college. He shall say better things, in a better manner, and be more liked by good judges. EUPH.: Where doth he pick up this improvement? CRI.: Where our grave ancestors would never have looked for it, in a drawing-room, a coffee-house, a chocolate-house, at the tavern, or groom-porter's. In these and the like fashionable places of resort, it is the custom for polite persons to speak freely on all subjects, religious, moral, or political. So that a young gentleman who frequents them is in the way of hearing many instructive lectures, seasoned with wit and raillery, and uttered with spirit. Three or four sentences, from a man of quality, spoken with a good air, make more impression, and convey more knowledge, than a dozen dissertations in a dry academical way. . . . You may now commonly see a young lady, or a *petit maître*, non-plus a divine or an old-fashioned gentleman who hath read many a Greek and Latin author, and spent much time in hard methodical study[1].'

Among a host of mischiefs thus arising, one positive good may be signalized. If there must be debate, there ought to be fair play; and of this, publicity is the best guarantee. To make the public arbiter in an abstract question of metaphysics is doubtless absurd; yet it is at least a safeguard against extravagance and metaphysical lunacy. The verdict of public opinion on such topics is worthless, but it checks the inevitable tendency of closet speculation to become visionary. There is but one sort of scepticism that is genuine, and deadly in proportion as it is real; that, namely, which is forced upon the mind by its experience of the hollowness of mankind; for 'men may be read, as well as books, too much.' That other logical scepticism which is hatched by over-thinking can be cured by an easy remedy; ceasing to think.

The objections urged against revelation in the course of the Deistical controversy were no chimeras of a sickly brain, but solid charges; the points brought into public discussion were the points at which the revealed system itself impinges on human reason. No time can lessen whatever force there may be in the objection against a miracle; it is felt as strongly in one century as another. The debate was not frivolous; the objections were worth answering, because they were not pitched metaphysically high. To a platonizing divine they look trivial; picked up in the street. So Origen naturally thought 'that a faith which could be shaken by such objections as those of Celsus was not worth much[2].' Just such were the objections of the Deists; such as come spontaneously into the thoughts of practical men, who never think systematically, but who are not to be imposed upon by fancies. Persons sneer at the 'shallow Deism' of the last century; and it is customary to reply that the an-

<hr />

[1] *Alciphron*, Dial. I. § 11.   [2] *Cont Cels.*, Pref. § 4.
Essays and Reviews, 1860.]

tagonist orthodoxy was at least as shallow. The truth is, the 'shallowness' imputed belongs to the mental sphere into which the debate was for the time transported. The philosophy of the age was not above its mission. 'Philosophy,' thought Thomas Reid, in 1764, 'has no other root but the principles of common sense; it grows out of them, it draws its nourishment from them; severed from this root, its honours wither, its sap is dried up, it dies and rots[1].' We, in the present generation, have seen the great speculative movement in Germany die out from this very cause, because it became divorced from the facts on which it speculated. Shut up in the Universities, it turned inwards on itself, and preyed on its own vitals. It has only been neglected by the world, because it first neglected the great facts in which the world has, and feels, an interest.

If ever there was a time when abstract speculation was brought down from inaccessible heights and compelled to be intelligible, it was the period from the Revolution to the middle of the last century. Closet speculation had been discredited; the cobwebs of scholasticism were exploded; the age of feverish doubt and egotistical retrospection had not arrived. In that age the English higher education acquired its practical aim; an aim in which the development of the understanding and the acquisition of knowledge are considered secondary objects to the formation of a sound secular judgment, of the 'scholar and the gentleman' of the old race of schoolmasters. Burke, contrasting his own times with the preceding age, 'considered our forefathers as deeper thinkers than ourselves, because they set a higher value on good sense than on knowledge in various sciences, and their good sense was derived very often from as much study and more knowledge, though of another sort[2].'

---

[1] *Inquiry*, &c., Intr. § 4.   [2] *Recollections by Samuel Rogers*, p. 81.

When a dispute is joined, e. g. on the origin and composition of the Gospels, it is, from the nature of the case,
confined to an inner circle of Biblical scholars. The
mass of the public must wait outside, and receive the
result on their authority. The religious public were
very reluctant to resign the verse 1 John v. 7, but they
did so at last on the just ground that after a philological
controversy conducted with open doors, it had been
decided to be spurious. No serious man would consider
a popular assembly a proper court to decide on the
doctrine of transubstantiation, or on the Hegelian definition of God, though either is easily capable of being
held up to the ridicule of the half educated from the
platform or the pulpit. It is otherwise with the greater
part of the points raised in the Deistical controversy.
It is not the speculative reason of the few, but the
natural conscience of the many, that questions the ex-
tirpation of the Canaanites, or the eternity of hell-torments.
These are points of divinity which are at once fundamental and popular. Butler, though not approving 'of
entering into an argumentative defence of religion in
common conversation,' recommends his clergy to do so
from the pulpit on the ground that, 'such as are capable
of seeing the force of objections, are also capable of
seeing the force of the answers which are given to
them[1].' If the philosophic intellect be dissatisfied with
the answers which the divines of that day gave to the
difficulties started, let it show how, on the rationalist
hypothesis, these difficulties are removable for the mass
of those who feel them. The transcendental reason
provides an answer which possibly satisfies itself; but
to the common reason the answer is more perplexing
than the difficulty it would clear.

M. Villemain has remarked in Pascal 'that foresight

---

[1] *Durham Charge.*

which revealed to him so many objections unknown to his generation, and which inspired him with the idea of fortifying and intrenching positions which were not threatened.' The objections which Pascal is engaged with are not only not those of his age, they are not such as could ever become general in any age. They are those of the higher reason, and the replies are from the same inspiration. Pascal's view of human depravity seems to the ordinary man but the despair and delirium of the self-tormenting ascetic. The cynical view of our fallen nature, however, is at least a possible view. It is well that it should be explored, and it will always have its prophets, Calvin or Rochefoucault. But to ordinary men an argument in favour of revelation, founded on such an assumption, will seem to be in contradiction to his daily experience. Pascal's *Pensées* stand alone; a work of individual genius, not belonging to any age. The celebrity which the *Analogy* of Bishop Butler has gained is due to the opposite reason. It is no paradox to say that the merit of the *Analogy* lies in its want of originality. It came (1736) towards the end of the Deistical period. It is the result of twenty years' study—the very twenty years during which the Deistical notions formed the atmosphere which educated people breathed. The objections it meets are not new and unseasoned objections, but such as had worn well, and had borne the rub of controversy, because they were genuine. And it will be equally hard to find in the *Analogy* any topic in reply, which had not been suggested in the pamphlets and sermons of the preceding half century. Like Aristotle's physical and political treatises, it is a *résumé* of the discussions of more than one generation. Its admirable arrangement only is all its own. Its closely packed and carefully fitted order speaks of many years' contrivance. Its substance are the thoughts of a whole age, not barely compiled, but each reconsidered and digested. Every brick in the building has been rung before it has been relaid, and replaced in its true relation to the complex and various whole. In more than one passage we see that the construction of this fabric of evidence, which 'consists in a long series of things, one preparatory to and confirming another from the beginning of the world to the present time[1],' was what occupied Butler's attention. 'Compass of thought, even amongst persons of the lowest rank[2],' is that form of the reflective faculty to which he is fond of looking both for good and evil. He never will forget that 'justice must be done to every part of a subject when we are considering it[3].' Harmony, and law, and order, he will suppose even where he does not find them. The tendency of his reason was that which Bacon indicates; 'the spirit of a man being of an equal and uniform substance doth usually suppose and feign in nature a greater equality and uniformity than is in truth[4].' This is, probably, the true explanation of the 'obscurity' which persons sometimes complain of in Butler's style. The reason or matter he is producing is palpable and plain enough. But he is so solicitous to find its due place in the then stage of the argument, so scrupulous to give it its exact weight and no more, so careful in arranging its situation relatively to the other members of the proof, that a reader who does not bear in mind that 'the effect of the whole' is what the architect is preparing, is apt to become embarrassed, and to think that obscurity which is really logical precision. The generality of men are better qualified for understanding particulars one by one, than for taking a comprehensive view of the whole. The philosophical breadth which we miss in Butler's mode of conceiving is compensated for by this judicial breadth in his mode of arguing, which gives its place to each consideration, but regards

[1]. *Durham Charge.*   [3] *Sermon IV.*
[2] *Pref. to Sermons.*   [4] *Advancement of Learning.*
Essays and Reviews, 1860.]

rather the cumulative force of the whole. Many writers before Butler had insisted on this character of the Christian evidences. Dr. Jenkin, Margaret Professor at Cambridge, whose *Reasonableness and Certainty of the Christian Religion* (1721) was the 'Paley' of divinity students then, says, 'there is an excellency in every part of our religion separately considered, but the strength and vigour of each part is in the relation it has to the rest, and the several parts must be taken altogether, if we would have a true knowledge, and make a just estimate of the whole[1].' But Butler does not merely take the hint from others. It is so entirely the guiding rule of his hand and pen that it would appear to have been forced upon him by some peculiar experience of his own. It was in society, and not in his study, that he had learned the weight of the Deistical arguments. At the Queen's philosophical parties, where these topics were canvassed with earnestness and freedom, he must have often felt the impotence of reply in detail, and seen, as he says, 'how impossible it must be, in a cursory conversation, to unite all this into one argument, and represent it as it ought[2].' Hence his own labour to work up his materials into a connected framework, a methodized encyclopaedia of all the extant topics.

Not that he did not pay attention to the parts. Butler's eminence over his contemporary apologists is seen in nothing more than in that superior sagacity which rejects the use of any plea that is not entitled to consideration singly. In the other evidential books of the time we find a miscellaneous crowd of suggestions of very various value; never fanciful, but often trivial; undeniable, but weak as proof of the point they are brought to prove. Butler seems as if he had sifted these books, and retained all that was solid in them. If he built with brick, and not

---

[1] *Reasonableness*, &c., Pt. II. Pref. 1721.
[2] *Durham Charge.*

with marble, it was because he was not thinking of reputation, but of utility, and an immediate purpose. Mackintosh wished Butler had had the elegance and ornament of Berkeley. They would have been sadly out of place. 'There was not a spark of the littleness of literary ambition about him. There was a certain natural-ness in Butler's mind, which took him straight to the questions on which men differed around him. Generally it is safer to prove what no one denies, and easier to explain difficulties which no one has ever felt. A quiet reputation is best obtained in the literary *quaestiunculae* of important subjects. But a simple and straightforward man studies great topics because he feels a want of the knowledge which they contain. He goes straight to the real doubts and fundamental discrepancies, to those on which it is easy to excite odium, and difficult to give satisfaction; he leaves to others the amusing skirmishing and superficial literature accessory to such studies. Thus there is nothing light in Butler, all is grave, serious, and essential; nothing else would be characteristic of him[1].' Though he has rifled their books he makes no display of reading. In the *Analogy* he never names the author he is answering. In the *Sermons* he quotes, directly, only Hobbes, Shaftesbury, Wollaston, Rochefoucault, and Fénelon. From his writings we should infer that his reading was not promiscuous, even had he not him-self given us to understand how much opportunity he had of seeing the idleness and waste of time occasioned by light reading[2].

This popular appeal to the common reason of men, which is one characteristic of the rationalist period, was a first effort of English theology to find a new basis for doctrine which should replace those foundations which had failed it. The Reformation had destroyed the authority of the Church upon which Revelation had so

---

[1] Bagehot, *Estimates*, &c., p. 189.   [2] *Sermons*, Pref.
Essays and Reviews, 1860.]

long rested. The attempt of the Laudian divines to substitute the voice of the national Church for that of the Church universal had met with only very partial and temporary success. When the Revolution of 1688 introduced the freedom of the press and a general toleration, even that artificial authority which, by ignoring non-conformity, had produced an appearance of unity, and erected a conventional standard of truth and falsehood, fell to the ground. The old and venerated authority had been broken by the Reformation. The new authority of the Anglican establishment had existed in theory only, and never in fact, and the Revolution had crushed the theory, which was now confined to a small band of non-jurors. In reaction against Anglican 'authority,' the Puritan movement had tended to rest faith and doctrine upon the inward light within each man's breast. This tendency of the new Puritanism, which we may call Independency, was a development of the old, purely scriptural, Puritanism of Presbyterianism. But it was its natural and necessary development. It was a consequence of the controversy with the establishment. For both the Church and Dissent agreed in acknowledging Scripture as their foundation, and the controversy turned on the interpreter of Scripture. Nor was the doctrine of the inner light, which individualized the basis of faith, confined to the Nonconformists. It was shared by a section of the Church, of whom Cudworth is the type, to whom 'Scripture faith is not a mere believing of historical things, and upon artificial arguments or testimonies only, but a certain higher and diviner power in the soul that peculiarly correspondeth with the Deity[1].' The inner light, or witness of the Spirit in the soul of the individual believer, had, in its turn, fallen into discredit through the extravagances to which it had given birth. It was disowned alike by Churchmen and Non-

[1] *Intellectual System,* Pref.

conformists, who agree in speaking with contemptuous
pity of the 'sectaries of the last age.' The reaction
against individual religion led to this first attempt to
base revealed truth on reason. And for the purpose for
which reason was now wanted, the higher, or philosophic,
reason was far less fitted than that universal understanding in which all men can claim a share. The 'inner
light,' which had made each man the dictator of his own
creed, had exploded in ecclesiastical anarchy. The appeal
from the frantic discord of the enthusiasts to reason must
needs be, not to an arbitrary or particular reason in each
man, but to a *common* sense, a natural discernment, a
reason of universal obligation. As it was to be universally
binding, it must be generally recognizable. It must be
something not confined to the select few, a gift of the
self-styled elect, but a faculty belonging to all men of
sound mind and average capacity. Truth must be accessible to 'the bulk of mankind.' It was a time when
the only refuge from a hopeless maze, or wild chaos,
seemed to be the rational consent of the sensible and
unprejudiced. 'Have the bulk of mankind,' writes Locke,
'no other guide but accident and blind chance to conduct
them to their happiness or misery? Are the current
opinions and licensed guides of every country sufficient
evidence and security to every man to venture his great
concernments on? Or, can those be the certain and
infallible oracles and standards of truth which teach one
thing in Christendom, and another in Turkey? Or shall
a poor countryman be eternally happy for having the
chance to be born in Italy? Or a day labourer be
unavoidably lost because he had the ill-luck to be born
in England? How ready some men may be to say some
of these things, I will not here examine; but this I am
sure, that men must allow one or other of these to be
true, or else grant that God has furnished men with
faculties sufficient to direct them in the way they should

take, if they will but seriously employ them that way, when their ordinary vocations allow them the leisure [1].'

Such an attempt to secure a foundation in a new consensus will obviously forfeit depth to gain in comprehensiveness. This phase of rationalism—'Rationalismus vulgaris'—resigns the transcendental, that it may gain adherents. It wants, not the elect, but all men. It cannot afford to embarrass itself with the attempt to prove what all may not be required to receive. Accordingly there can be no mysteries in Christianity. The word μυστήριον, as Archbishop Whately points out [2], always means in the New Testament not that which is incomprehensible, but that which was once a secret, though now it is revealed it is no longer so. Whately, who elsewhere [3] speaks so contemptuously of the 'cast-off clothes' of the Deists, is here but adopting the argument of Toland in his *Christianity not Mysterious* [4]. There needs no special 'preparation of heart' to receive the Gospel, the evidences of religion are sufficient to convince every unprejudiced inquirer. Unbelievers are blameworthy, as deaf to an argument which is so plain that they cannot but understand it, and so convincing that they cannot but be aware of its force. Under such self-imposed conditions religious proof seems to divest itself of all that is divine, and out of an excess of accommodation to the recipient faculty to cease to be a transforming thought. Rationalism can object to the old sacramental system that it degrades a spiritual influence into a physical effect. But rationalism itself, in order to make the proof of revelation universal, is obliged to resolve religion into the moral government of God by rewards and punishments, and especially the latter. It is this anthropomorphic conception of God as the 'Governor of the universe,' which is presented to us in

---

[1] *Essay*, Book IV. ch. 19, § 3.
[2] *Essays*, 2nd ser., 5th ed., p. 288.
[3] Paley's *Evidences*, new ed.
[4] Cf. Balguy, *Discourses*, p. 237.

the theology of the Hanoverian divines, a theology which excludes on principle not only all that is poetical in life, but all that is sublime in religious speculation. 'To degrade religion to the position of a mere purveyor of motive to morality is not more dishonourable to the ethics which must ask, than to the religion which will render such assistance[1].' It is this character that makes the reading even of the *Analogy* so depressing to the soul; as Tholuck[2] says of it, 'we weary of a long journey on foot, especially through deep sand.' Human nature is not only humbled, but crushed. It is a common charge against the eighteenth century divines that they exalt man too much, by insisting on the dignity of human nature, and its native capacities for virtue. This was the charge urged against the orthodox by the evangelical pulpit. But only very superficial and incompetent critics of doctrine can suppose that man is exalted by being thrown upon his moral faculties. The history of doctrine teaches a very different lesson. Those periods when morals have been represented as the proper study of man, and his only business, have been periods of spiritual abasement and poverty. The denial of scientific theology, the keeping in the background the transcendental objects of faith, and the restriction of our faculties to the regulation of our conduct, seem indeed to be placing man in the foreground of the picture, to make human nature the centre round which all things revolve. But this seeming effect is produced not by exalting the visible, but by materializing the invisible. 'If there be a sphere of knowledge level to our capacities and of the utmost importance to us, we ought surely to apply ourselves with all diligence to this our proper business, and esteem everything else nothing, nothing as to us, in comparison of it. . . . Our province is virtue and religion, life and

[1] A. J. Vaughan, *Essays*, vol. I. p. 61.
[2] *Vermischte Schriften*, I. 193.

manners; the science of improving the temper and making the heart better. This is the field assigned to us to cultivate; how much it has lain neglected is indeed astonishing. . . . He who should find out one rule to assist us in this work would deserve infinitely better of mankind than all the improvers of other knowledge put together[1].' This is the theology of Butler and his contemporaries; a utilitarian theology, like the Baconian philosophy, contemning all employment of mental power which does not bring in fruit. 'Intellectui non plumae, sed plumbum addendum et pondera[2],' might be its device.

In the *Analogy* it is the same. His term of comparison, the 'constitution and course of *nature*,' is not what we should understand by that term; not what science can disclose to us of the laws of the *cosmos*, but a narrow observation of what men do in ordinary life. We see what he means by the 'constitution of things,' by his saying[1] that 'the writings of Solomon are very much taken up with reflections upon human nature and human life; to which he hath added, in Ecclesiastes, reflections upon the constitution of things.' In Part I. ch. 3 of the *Analogy*, he compares the *moral* government of God with the *natural*—the distinction is perhaps from Balguy[3]— that is to say, one part of natural religion with another; for the distinction vanishes, except upon a very conventional sense of the term 'moral.' Altogether we miss in these divines not only distinct philosophical conceptions, but a scientific use of terms. Dr. Whewell considers that Butler shunned 'the appearance of technical terms for the elements of our moral constitution on which he speculated,' and thinks that he 'was driven to indirect modes of expression[4].' The truth is that Butler uses the language of his day upon the topics on which he

---

[1] Sermon XV.   [2] Bacon, *Nov. Or.*, I. 104.   [3] *Divine Rectitude*, p. 39.
[4] *Moral Philosophy in England*, p. 109.

writes. The technical terms, and strict logical forms, which had been adhered to by the writers, small as well as great, of the seventeenth century, had been disused as pedantic; banished first from literature, and then from education. They did not appear in style, because they did not form part of the mental habit of the writers. Butler does not, as Dr. Whewell supposes, think in one form, and write in another, out of condescension to his readers. He thinks in the same language in which he and those around him speak. Mr. Hort's remark, that 'Butler's writings are stoic to the core in the true and ancient sense of the word [1],' must be extended to their style. The English style of philosophical writing in the Hanoverian period is to the English of the seventeenth century, as the Greek of Epictetus, Antoninus, or Plutarch is to that of Aristotle. And for the same reason. The English stoics and their Greek predecessors were practical men who moralized in a practical way on the facts of common life, and in the language of common life. Neither the rhetorical Schools of the Empire, nor the Universities of England, any longer taught the correct use of metaphysical language. To imitate classical Latin was become the chief aim of the University man in his public exercises, and precision of language became under that discipline very speedily a lost art.

Upon the whole, the writings of that period are serviceable to us chiefly, as showing what can, and what cannot, be effected by common-sense thinking in theology. It is of little consequence to inquire, whether or not the objections of the Deists and the Socinians were removed by the answers brought to meet them. Perhaps, on the whole, we might be borne out in saying that the defence is at least as good as the attack; and so, that even on the ground of common reason, the Christian evidences may

[1] *Cambridge Essays,* 1856, p. 337.
Essays and Reviews, 1860.]

be arranged in such a way as to balance the common-sense improbability of the supernatural—that 'there are three chances to one for revelation, and only two against it[1].' Had not circumstances given a new direction to religious interests, the Deistical controversy might have gone on indefinitely, and the amoebean strain of objection and reply, 'et cantare pares et respondere parati'—have been prolonged to this day without any other result. But that result forces on the mind the suggestion that either religious faith has no existence, or that it must be to be reached by some other road than that of the 'trial of the witnesses.' It is a reductio ad absurdum of common-sense philosophy, of home-baked theology, when we find that the result of the whole is that 'it is safer to believe in a God, lest, if there should happen to be one, he might send us to hell for denying his existence[2].' If a religion be wanted which shall debase instead of ele-vating, this should be its creed. If the religious history of the eighteenth century proves anything it is this:— That good sense, the best good sense, when it sets to work with the materials of human nature and Scripture to construct a religion, will find its way to an ethical code, irreproachable in its contents, and based on a just estimate and wise observation of the facts of life, ratified by Divine sanctions in the shape of hope and fear, of future rewards and penalties of obedience and dis-obedience. This the eighteenth century did and did well. It has enforced the truths of natural morality with a solidity of argument and variety of proof which they have not received since the Stoical epoch, if then. But there its ability ended. When it came to the supernatural part of Christianity its embarrassment began. It was forced to keep it as much in the background as possible, or to bolster it up by lame and inadequate reasonings. The philosophy of common sense had done its own work; it

[1] *Tracts for the Times*, No. 85.   [2] Maurice, *Essays*, p. 236.

attempted more only to show, by its failure, that some higher organon was needed for the establishment of supernatural truth.   The career of the evidential school, its success and failure,—its success in vindicating the ethical part of Christianity and the regulative aspect of revealed truth, its failure in establishing the supernatural and speculative part—have enriched the history of doctrine with a complete refutation of that method as an instrument of theological investigation.

This judgment, however, must not be left unbalanced by a consideration on the other side.   It will hardly be supposed that the drift of what has been said is that common sense is out of place in religion, or in any other matter.   The defect of the eighteenth-century theology was not in having too much good sense, but in having nothing besides.   In the present day, when a godless orthodoxy threatens, as in the fifteenth century, to extinguish religious thought altogether, and nothing is allowed in the Church of England but the formulae of past thinkings, which have long lost all sense of any kind, it may seem out of season to be bringing forward a misapplication of common sense in a bygone age.   There are times and circumstances when religious ideas will be greatly benefited by being submitted to the rough and ready tests by which busy men try what comes in their way; by being made to stand their trial, and be freely canvassed, *coram populo.*   As poetry is not for the critics, so religion is not for the theologians.   When it is stiffened into phrases, and these phrases are declared to be objects of reverence but not of intelligence, it is on the way to become a useless encumbrance, the rubbish of the past, blocking the road.   Theology then retires into the position it occupies in the Church of Rome at present, an un-meaning frostwork of dogma, out of all relation to the actual history of man.   In that system, theological virtue is an artificial life quite distinct from the moral virtues

Essays and Reviews, 1860.]

of real life. 'Parmi nous,' says Rémusat, 'un homme
religieux est trop souvent un homme qui se croit entouré
d'ennemis, qui voit avec défiance ou scandale les événe-
ments et les institutions du siècle, qui se désole d'être né
dans les jours maudits, et qui a besoin d'un grand fond de
bonté innée pour empêcher ses pieuses aversions de
devenir de mortelles haines.' This system is equally fatal
to popular morality and to religious theory. It locks up
virtue in the cloister, and theology in the library. It
originates caste sanctity, and a traditional philosophy.
The ideal of holiness striven after may once have been
lofty, the philosophy now petrified into tradition may
once have been a vital faith ; but now that they are
withdrawn from public life, they have ceased to be social
influences. On the other hand, the eighteenth century exhibits human attainment levelled to the lowest secular
model of prudence and honesty, but still, such as it was,
proposed to all men as their rule of life. Practical life
as it was, was the theme of the pulpit, the press, and
the drawing-room. Its theory of life was not lofty, but
it was true as far as it went. It did not substitute a
factitious phraseology, the pass-words of the modern
pulpit, for the simple facts of life, but called things by
their right names. 'Nullum numen habes si sit pru-
dentia' was its motto, not denying the 'numen,' but
bringing him very close to the individual person, as his
'moral governor.' The prevailing philosophy was not
a profound metaphysic, but it was a soundly based arrangement of the facts of society ; it was not a scheme
of the sciences, but a manual for every-day use. Nothing
of the wild spirit of universal negation which was spread
over the Continent fifty years later belonged to the solid
rationalism of this period. The human understanding
wished to be satisfied, and did not care to believe that
of which it could not see the substantial ground. The
reason was coming slowly to see that it had duties which

it could not devolve upon others; that a man must think
for himself, protect his own rights, and administer his own
affairs.   The reason was never less extravagant than in
this its first essay of its strength.   Its demands were
modest, it was easily satisfied; far too easily, we must
think, when we look at some of the reasonings which
passed as valid.

The habits of controversy in which they lived deceived
the belligerents themselves.   The controversial form of
their theology, which has been fatal to its credit since,
was no less detrimental to its soundness at the time.
They could not discern the line between what they did,
and what they could not, prove.   The polemical temper
deforms the books they have written.   Literature was
indeed partially refined from the coarser scurrilities with
which the Caroline divines, a century before, had assailed
their Romanist opponents.   But there is still an air of
vulgarity about the polite writing of the age, which the
divines adopt along with its style.   The cassocked divine
assumes the airs of the 'roaring blade,' and ruffles it on
the Mall with a horsewhip under his arm.   Warburton's
stock argument is a threat to cudgel any one who disputes
his opinion.   All that can be said is that this was a habit
of treating your opponent which pervaded society.   At a
much later period Porson complains, 'In these ticklish
times . . . talk of religion it is odds but you have infidel,
blasphemer, atheist, or schismatic, thundered in your
ears; touch upon politics, you will be in luck if you are
only charged with a tendency to treason.   Nor is the
innocence of your intention any safeguard.   It is not the
publication that shows the character of the author, but
the character of the author that shows the tendency of
the publication[1].'   A licence of party vituperation in the
House of Commons existed, from the time of the opposition to Walpole onwards, which has long been banished

[1] Luard's ' Porson,' *Cambridge Essays*, 1857.
Essays and Reviews, 1860.]

by more humane manners. 'The men who took a fore-most part seemed to be intent on disparaging each other, and proving that neither possessed any qualification of wisdom, knowledge, or public virtue. . . . Epithets of reproach were lavished personally on Lord North, which were applicable only to the vilest and most contemptible of mankind [1].'

Were this blustering language a blemish of style and nothing more, it would taint their books with vulgarity as literature, but it would not vitiate their matter. But the fault reaches deeper than skin-deep. It is a most serious drawback on the good sense of the age that it wanted justice in its estimate of persons. They were no more capable of judging their friends than their foes. In Pope's satire there is no medium; our enemies combine all the odious vices, however incongruous; our friends have 'every virtue under heaven.' We hear sometimes of Pope's peculiar 'malignity.' But he was only doing what every one around him was doing, only with a greatly superior literary skill. Their savage invective against each other is not a morally worse feature than the style of fulsome compliment in which friends address each other. The private correspondence of intimate friends betrays an unwholesome insincerity, which con-trasts strangely with their general manliness of character. The burly intellect of Warburton displays an appetite for flattery as insatiable as that of Miss Seward and her coterie.

This habit of exaggerating both good and evil the divines share with the other writers of the time. But theological literature, as a written debate, had a form of malignant imputation peculiar to itself. This is one arising out of the rationalistic fiction which both parties assumed, viz. that their respective beliefs were deter-mined by an impartial inquiry into the evidence. The orthodox writers considered this evidence so clear and

[1] Massey, *Hist. of England*, II. 218.

certain for their own conclusions, that they could account for its not seeming so to others only by the supposition of some moral obliquity which darkened the understanding in such cases.   Hence the obnoxious assumption of the divines that the Deists were men of corrupt morals, and the retort of the infidel writers, that the clergy were hired advocates.   Moral imputation, which is justly banished from legal argument, seems to find a proper place in theological.   Those Christian Deists who, like Toland or Collins, approached most nearly in their belief to Revelation, were treated, not better, but worse, by the orthodox champion; their larger admissions being imputed to disingenuousness or calculated reserve.   This stamp of advocacy, which was impressed on English theology at the Reformation—its first work of consideration was an 'Apology'—it has not to this day shaken off.   Our theologians, with rare exceptions, do not penetrate below the surface of their subject, but are engaged in defending or vindicating it.   The current phrases of 'the bulwarks of our faith,' 'dangerous to Christianity,' are but instances of the habitual position in which we assume ourselves to stand.   Even more philosophic minds cannot get rid of the idea that theology is polemical.   Theological study is still the study of topics of defence.   Even Professor Fraser can exhort us 'that by the study of these topics we might not merely disarm the enemies of religion of what in other times has been, and will continue to be, a favourite weapon of assault, but we might even convert that weapon into an instrument of use in the Christian service[1].'   'Modern science,' as it is called, is recommended to the young divine, because in it he may find means of 'confuting infidelity.'

A little consideration will show that the grounds on which advocacy before a legal tribunal rests make it inappropriate in theological reasoning.   It is not pre-

[1] *Essays in Philosophy,* p. 4.

Essays and Reviews, 1860.]

tended that municipal law is coextensive with universal law, and therefore incapable of admitting right on both sides. It is allowed that the natural right may be, at times, on one side, and the legal title on the other; not to mention the extreme case where 'communis error facit jus.' The advocate is not there to supply all the materials out of which the judge is to form his decision, but only one side of the case. He is the mere representative of his client's interests, and has not to discuss the abstract merits of the juridical point which may be involved. He does not undertake to show that the law is conformable to natural right, but to establish the condition of his client relatively to the law. But the rational defender of the faith has no place in his system for the variable, or the indifferent, or the non-natural. He proceeds on the supposition that the whole system of the Church is the one and exclusively true expression of reason upon the subject on which it legislates. He claims for the whole of received knowledge what the jurist claims for international law, that it is a universal science. He lays before us, on the one hand, the traditional canon or symbol of doctrine. On the other hand, he teaches that the free use of reason upon the facts of nature and Scripture is the real mode by which this traditional symbol is arrived at. To show, then, that the candid pursuit of truth leads every impartial intellect to the Anglican conclusion was the task which, on their theory of religious proof, their theology had to undertake. The process, accordingly, should have been analogous to that of the jurist or legislator with regard to the internal evidence, and to that of the judge with regard to the external evidence. If theological argument forgets the judge and assumes the advocate, or betrays the least bias to one side, the conclusion is valueless, the principle of free inquiry has been violated. Roman Catholic theologians consistently enough teach that 'apologetics,' as

usually conducted by way of reply to special objections
urged, make no part of theology, but that a true apologetic
must be founded (1) on a discovery of the general principle
from which the attack proceeds, and (2) on the exhibition,
per contra, of that general ground-thought of which the
single Christian truths are developments[1].

With rare exceptions the theology of the Hanoverian
period is of the most violent partisan character. It seats
itself, by its theory, in the judicial chair, but it is only to
comport itself there like Judge Jeffrey. One of the
favourite books of the time was Sherlock's *Trial of the
Witnesses.* First published in 1729, it speedily went
through fourteen editions. It concludes in this way :—

'*Judge.*—"What say you? Are the Apostles guilty of
giving false evidence in the case of the resurrection of
Jesus, or not guilty?"

'*Foreman.*—"Not guilty."

'*Judge.*—"Very well; and now, gentlemen, I resign my
commission, and am your humble servant." The company
then rose up, and were beginning to pay their compliments to the Judge and the counsel, but were interrupted
by a gentleman, who went up to the Judge and offered
him a fee. "What is this?" says the Judge. "A fee, sir,"
said the gentleman. "A fee to a judge is a bribe," said
the Judge. "True, sir," said the gentleman; "but you
have resigned your commission, and will not be the first
judge who has come from the bench to the bar without
any diminution of honour. Now, Lazarus's case is to
come on next, and this fee is to retain you on his side."'
One might say that the apologists of that day had in like
manner left the bench for the bar, and taken a brief for
the Apostles. They are impatient at the smallest demur,
and deny loudly that there is any weight in anything
advanced by their opponents. In the way they override
the most serious difficulties, they show anything but the

[1] Hagemann, *Die Aufgabe der Catholischen Apologetik.*
Essays and Reviews, 1860.]

temper which is supposed to qualify for the weighing of evidence. The astonishing want of candour in their reasoning, their blindness to real difficulty, the ill-concealed predetermination to find a particular verdict, the rise of their style in passion in the same proportion as their argument fails in strength, constitute a class of writers more calculated than any other to damage their own cause with young ingenuous minds, bred in the school of Locke to believe that 'to love truth for truth's sake is the principal part of human perfection in this world, and the seed-plot of all other virtues[1].' Spalding has described the moral shock his faith received on hearing an eminent clergyman in confidential conversation with another, who had cited some powerful argument against revelation, say, 'That's truly awkward; let us consider a little how we get out of that;' *wie wir uns salviren*[2]. A truthful mind is a much rarer possession than is commonly supposed, for 'it is as easy to close the eyes of the mind as those of the body[3].' And in this rarity there is a natural limit to the injury which uncandid vindications of revelation can cause. To whatever causes is to be attributed the decline of Deism, from 1750 onwards, the books polemically written against it cannot reckon among them. When Casaubon first visited Paris, and was being shown over the Sorbonne, his guide said, 'This is the hall in which the doctors have *disputed* for 300 years.' 'Ay! and what have they settled?' was his remark.

Some exceptions, doubtless, there are to the inconclusiveness of this debate. Here again the eminent instance is the *Analogy*. Butler, it is true, comes forward not as an investigator, but as a pleader. But when we pass from his inferior brethren to this great master of the art, we find ourselves in the hands of one who knows the

---

[1] Locke, act. 73. *Letter to Collins.*   [2] *Selbstbiographie*, p. 128.
[3] Butler, Sermon X.

laws of evidence, and carefully keeps his statements within them. Butler does not, like his fellow apologists, disguise the fact that the evidence is no stronger than it is. 'If it be a *poor* thing,' to argue in this way, 'the epithet *poor* may be applied, I fear, as properly to great part, or the whole, of human life, as it is to the things mentioned[1].' Archbishop Whately, defining the temper .of the rational theologian, says:—'A good man will, indeed, wish to find the evidence of the Christian religion satisfactory; but a wise man will not, for that reason, think it satisfactory, but will weigh the evidence the more carefully on account of the importance of the question[2].' This character Butler's argument exemplifies. We can feel, as we read, how his judgment must have been offended in his contemporaries by the disproportion between the positiveness of their assertion and the feebleness of their argument. Nor should we expect that Butler satisfied them. They thought him 'a little too little vigorous,' and 'wished he would have spoke more earnestly[3].' Men who believed that they were in possession of a 'demonstration' of Christianity were not likely to be satisfied with one who saw so strongly 'the doubtfulness in which things were involved' that he could not comprehend 'men's being impatient out of action or vehement in it[4].' Warburton, who has a proof which 'is very little short of mathematical certainty, and to which nothing but a mere physical possibility of the contrary can be opposed[5],' was the man for the age, which did not care to stand higgling with Butler over the degrees of probability. What could the world do with a man who 'designed the search after truth as the business of my life[6],' and who was so little prepared to dogmatize about the future world that he rather felt that 'there is no

[1] *Analogy*, Part II. ch. 8.
[2] *Essays*, 2nd series, p. 24.
[3] Byrom's *Journal*, March, 1737.
[4] *Unpublished Remains, &c.*
[5] *Divine Leg.*, b. I. § 1.
[6] *Correspondence with Dr. Clarke.*
Essays and Reviews, 1860.]

account to be given in the way of reason of men's so
strong attachments to the present world[1].' Butler's
doubtfulness, however, it should be remarked, is not the
unsteadiness of the sceptical, but the wariness of the
judicial mind; a mind determined for itself by its own
instincts, but careful to confine its statements to others
within the evidence produced in court. The *Analogy*
does not depict an inward struggle in his own mind,
but as 'he told a friend, his way of writing it had been to
endeavour to answer as he went along, every possible
objection that might occur to any one against any position
of his in his book[2].' He does not doubt himself, but he
sees, what others do not see, the difficulty of proving
religion to others. There is a saying of Pitt circulating
to the effect that the *Analog* is 'a dangerous book; it
raises more doubts than it solves.' All that is true in this
is, that to a mind which has never nourished objections
to revelation a book of evidences may be the means of
first suggesting them. But in 1736 the objections were
everywhere current, and the answers to them were mostly
of that truly 'dangerous' sort in which assertion runs
ahead of proof. The merit of Butler lies not in the
'irrefragable proof,' which Southey's epitaph attributes
to his construction, but in his showing the nature of the
proof, and daring to admit that it was less than certain;
to own that 'a man may be fully convinced of the truth of a
matter and upon the strongest reasons, and yet not be able
to answer all the difficulties which may be raised upon it[3].'

Another, perhaps the only other, book of this polemical
tribe which can be said to have been completely successful
as an answer, is one most unlike the *Analogy* in all its
nobler features. This is Bentley's *Remarks upon a late
Discourse of Freethinking, by Phileleutherus Lipsiensis, 1713*.
Coarse, arrogant, and abusive, with all Bentley's worst

[1] Sermon VII. [2] Bartlett's *Life of Butler*, p. 50.
[3] *Durham Charge*, 1; 51.

faults of style and temper, this masterly critique is decisive. Not, of course, of the Deistical controversy, on which the critic avoids entering. The *Discourse of Free-thinking* was a small tract published in 1713 by Anthony Collins. Collins was a gentleman of independent fortune, whose high personal character and general respectability seemed to give a weight to his words, which assuredly they do not carry of themselves. By 'free-thinking,' he means liberty of thought—the right of bringing all received opinions whatsoever to the touch-stone of reason. Among the grounds or authorities by which he supports this natural right, Collins unluckily had recourse to history, and largely, of course, to the precedent of the Greek philosophers. Collins, who had been bred at Eton and King's, was probably no worse a scholar than his contemporary Kingsmen, and the range of his reading was that of a man who had made the classics the companions of his maturer years. But that scholarship which can supply a quotation from Lucan, or flavour the style with an occasional allusion to Tully or Seneca, is quite incompetent to apply Greek or Roman precedent properly to a modern case. Addison, the pride of Oxford, had done no better. In his *Essays on the Evidences of Christianity*, Addison 'assigns as grounds for his religious belief, stories as absurd as the Cock-lane ghost, and forgeries as rank as Ireland's *Vortigern*, puts faith in the lie about the thundering legion, is convinced that Tiberius moved the Senate to admit Jesus among the gods, and pronounces the letter of Agbarus, King of Edessa, to be a record of great authority[1].' But the public was quite satisfied with Addison's citations, in which a public, which had given the victory to Boyle in the *Phalaris* controversy, could hardly suspect anything wrong. Collins was not to escape so easily. The Freethinker flounders hopelessly

[1] Macaulay, *Essays.*

among the authorities he has invoked. Like the necro-
mancer's apprentice, he is worried by the fiends he has
summoned but cannot lay, and Bentley, on whose nod
they wait, is there like another Cornelius Agrippa
hounding them on and enjoying the sport. Collins's
mistakes, mistranslations, misconceptions, and distortions
are so monstrous, that it is difficult for us now, forgetful
how low classical learning had sunk, to believe that they
are mistakes, and not wilful errors. It is rare sport to
Bentley, this rat-hunting in an old rick, and he lays about
him in high glee, braining an authority at every blow.
When he left off abruptly, in the middle of a 'Third Part,'
it was not because he was satiated with slaughter, but to
substitute a new excitement, no less congenial to his
temper—a quarrel with the University about his fees. A
grace, voted 1715, tendering him the public thanks of the
University, and 'praying him in the name of the University
to finish what remains of so useful a work,' could not
induce him to resume his pen. The *Remarks of Phileleutherus Lipsiensis*, unfinished though they are, and
trifling as was the book which gave occasion to them,
are perhaps the best of all Bentley's performances. They
have all the merits of the *Phalaris* dissertation, with the
advantage of a far nobler subject. They show how
Bentley's exact appreciation of the value of terms could,
when he chose to apply it to that purpose, serve him as
a key to the philosophical ideas of past times, no less
than to those of poetical metaphor. The tone of the
pamphlet is most offensive, 'not only not insipid, but
exceedingly bad-tasted.' We can only say the taste is
that of his age, while the knowledge is all his own. It
was fair to show that his antagonist undertook 'to interpret the Prophets and Solomon without Hebrew;
Plutarch and Zosimus (Collins spells it Zozimus) without
Greek; and Cicero and Lucan without Latin [1].' But the

---

[1] *Remarks*, Part I. No. 3.

dirt endeavoured to be thrown on Collins will cleave to the hand that throws it. It may be worth mention that this tract of Bentley contains the original of Sydney Smith's celebrated defence of the 'prizes' in the 'Church.' The passage is a favourable specimen of the moral level of a polemic who was accusing his opponent of holding 'opinions the most abject and base that human nature is capable of[1].'

'He can never conceive or wish a priesthood either quieter for him, or cheaper, than that of the present Church of England. Of your quietness himself is a convincing proof, who has writ this outrageous book, and has met with no punishment nor prosecution. And for the cheapness, that appeared lately in one of your parliaments, when the accounts exhibited showed that 5000 of your clergy, the greater part of your whole number, had, at a middle rate one with another, not fifty pounds a year. A poor emolument for so long, so laborious, so expensive an education, as must qualify them for holy orders. While I resided at Oxford, and saw such a conflux of youth to their annual admissions, I have often studied and admired why their parents would, under such mean encouragements, design their sons for the Church; and those the most towardly and capable, and select geniuses among their children, who must needs have emerged in a secular life. I congratulated, indeed, the felicity of your establishment, which attracted the choice youth of your nation for such very low pay; but my wonder was at the parents, who generally have interest, maintenance and wealth, the first thing in their view, till at last one of your state-lotteries ceased my astonishment. For as in that, a few glittering prizes, 1,000, 5,000, 10,000 pounds among an infinity of blanks, drew troops of adventurers, who if the whole fund had been equally ticketted, would never have come in; so a

[1] Letter prefixed to *Remarks.*

Essays and Reviews, 1860.]

few shining dignities in your Church, prebends, deaneries, bishopricks, are the pious fraud that induces and decoys the parents to risk their child's fortune in it. Everyone hopes his own will get some prize in the Church, and never reflects on the thousands of blanks in poor country livings. And if a foreigner may tell you his mind, from what he sees at home, 'tis this part of your establishment that makes your clergy excel ours [i. e. in Germany, from which *Phileleutherus Lipsiensis* is supposed to write]. Do but once level all your preferments, and you'll soon be as level in your learning. For, instead of the flower of the English youth, you'll have only the refuse sent to your academies, and those, too, cramped and crippled in their studies, for want of aim and emulation. So that, if your Freethinkers had any politics, instead of suppressing your whole order, they should make you all alike; or if that cannot be done, make your preferments a very lottery in the whole similitude. Let your Church dignities be pure chance prizes, without regard to abilities, or morals, or letters[1].'

It has been mentioned that Bentley does not attempt to reply to the argument of the *Discourse on Freethinking*. His tactic is to ignore it, and to assume that it is only meant as a covert attack on Christianity; that Collins is an Atheist fighting under the disguise of a Deist. Some excuse, perhaps, may be made for a man nourished on pedagogic Latin, and accustomed to launch furious sarcasm at any opponent who betrayed a brutal ignorance of the difference between 'ac' and 'et.' But Collins was not a sharper, and would have disdained practices to which Bentley stooped for the sake of a professorship. When Bentley, in the pride of academic dignity, could thus browbeat a person of Collins's consideration, it was not to be expected that the inferior fry of Deistical writers,—Toland, a writer for the press; Tindal, a fellow of

---

[1] *Remarks, &c*, Part II. § 40.

H 2

a college; or Chubb, a journeyman glover—should meet
with fairer treatment from their opponents. The only exception to this is the case of Shaftesbury, to whom, as
well after his death as in his lifetime, his privileges as
a peer seem to have secured immunity from hangman's
usage. He is simply 'a late noble author.' Nor was
this respect inspired by the Earl's profession of Christianity. He does, indeed, make this profession with the
utmost unreserve. He asserts his 'steady orthodoxy,'
and 'entire submission to the truly Christian and Catholic
doctrines of our holy Church, as by law established,' and
that he holds 'the mysteries of our religion even in the
minutest particulars[1].' But this outward profession
would only have brought down upon any other writer
an aggravated charge of cowardly malice and concealment of Atheism. If Shaftesbury was spared on account
of his rank, the orthodox writers were not altogether
wrong in fastening upon this disingenuousness as a moral
characteristic of their antagonists. The excuse for this
want of manliness in men who please themselves with
insinuating unpopular opinions which they dare not advocate openly, is that an injustice is perpetrated by
those who have public feeling on their side. 'They
make,' says Mr. Tayler, 'the honest expression of opinion
penal, and then condemn men for disingenuousness.
They invite to free discussion, but determine beforehand
that only one conclusion can be sound and moral. They
fill the arena of public debate with every instrument of
torture and annoyance for the feeling heart, the sensitive
imagination, and the scrupulous intellect, and then are
angry that men do not rush headlong into the martyrdom
that has been prepared for them[2].'

In days when the pillory was the punishment for
common libel, it cannot be thought much that heresy
and infidelity should be punished by public opprobrium.

[1] *Characteristicks*, Vol. III. p. 315.   [2] *Religious Life of England*, p. 282.
Essays and Reviews, 1860.]

And public abhorrence was the most that a writer against revelation had now to fear. Mandeville's *Fable of the Bees*, indeed, was presented as a nuisance by the grand jury of Middlesex, in 1723, as were Bolingbroke's collected *Works*, in 1752, and Toland's *Christianity not Mysterious*, in 1699. We find, too, that Toland had to fly from Dublin, and Collins to go out of the way to Holland, for fear of further consequences. But nothing ever came of these presentments. The only [1] prosecution for religious libel was that of Woolston, 2 George II, in which the defendant, who was not of sound mind, provoked and even compelled the law officers of the crown to proceed against him, though they were very reluctant to do so. When thus compelled to declare the law, on this occasion, the Lord Chief Justice (Raymond) 'would not allow it to be doubted that to write against Christianity in general was punishable at common law.' Yet both then and since, judges and prosecutors have shown themselves shy of insisting upon the naked offence of 'impugning the truth of Christianity.' That it is an offence at common law, independent of 9 & 10 William III, no lawyer will deny. But an instinctive sense of the incompatibility of this legal doctrine with the fundamental tenet of Protestant rationalism has always served to keep it in the background. 'The judges seem to have played fast and loose in this matter, in such sort as might enable the future judge to quote the tolerant or the intolerant side of their doctrine as might prove convenient; and while seemingly disavowing all interference with fair discussion, they still kept a wary hold of the precedents of Hale and Raymond, and of the great arcanum of "part

---

[1] [The statement is a little too sweeping. In 1703, in Dublin, Thomas Emlyn was sentenced to a year's imprisonment, and a fine of £1000, for Arianism. In 1721 Joseph Hall was convicted and sentenced to the pillory, a fine of £200, and three months' imprisonment, for a blasphemous pamphlet; the pillory, however, was remitted, and the fine reduced to £50. Peter Annet, in 1763, was sentenced to a year's hard labour for blasphemous libel.]

and parcel;" semianimesque micant digiti, ferrumque
retractant[1].'

Whatever excuse the Deistical writers might have for
their insidious manner of writing, it is more to the present
purpose to observe that we may draw from it the conclusion that public opinion was throughout on the side
of the defenders of Christianity. It might seem almost
superfluous to say this, were it not that complaints meet
us on every side, which seem to imply the very contrary;
that in the words of Mr. Gregory, 'the doctrine of our
Church is exploded, and our holy religion become only
a name which is everywhere spoken against[2].' Thirty
years later Butler writes, that 'it is come to be taken for
granted that Christianity is not so much as a subject of
inquiry; but that it is now, at length, discovered to be
fictitious. Accordingly they treat it as if in the present
age this were an agreed point among all people of discernment, and nothing remained but to set it up as a
principal subject of mirth and ridicule, as it were by way
of reprisals for its having so long interrupted the pleasures
of the world[3].' However a loose kind of Deism might
be the tone of fashionable circles, it is clear that distinct
disbelief of Christianity was by no means the general
state of the public mind. The leaders of the Low-church
and Whig party were quite aware of this. Notwithstanding the universal complaints of the High-church
party of the prevalence of infidelity, it is obvious that
this mode of thinking was confined to a very small
section of society. The *Independent Whig* (May 4, 1720),
in the middle of its blustering and endeavours to terrify
the clergy with their unpopularity, is obliged to admit
that 'the High-church Popish clergy will laugh in their
sleeves at this advice, and think there is folly enough

[1] *Considerations on the Law of Libel.* By John Scarch, 1833. See also James
Paterson, *Liberty of the Press, Speech, and Public Worship* (Macmillan, 1880).
[2] *Pref. to Beveridge's Private Thoughts*, 1709.
[3] *Advertisement to Analogy*, 1736.
  Essays and Reviews, 1860.]

yet left among the laity to support their authority; and will laugh themselves, and rejoice over the ignorance of the Universities, the stupidity of the drunken squires, the panic of the tender sex, and the never-to-be-shaken constancy of the multitude.' A still better evidence is the confidence and success with which the writers on the side of Revelation appealed to the popular passions, and cowed their Deistical opponents into the use of that indirect and disingenuous procedure with which they then taunted them. The clerical sphere was much more a sphere by itself than it has since become. Notwithstanding the large toleration really practised, strict professional etiquette was still observed in the Church and in the Universities. The horizontal hat, the starched band, and the cassock, were still worn in public, and certain proprieties of outward manner were expected from 'the cloth.' The violation of these proprieties was punished by the forfeiture of the offender's prospects of preferment, a point on which the most extreme sensitiveness existed. In the Balguy and Waterland set an officious spirit of delation seems to have flourished. The general habit of publicly canvassing religious topics was very favourable to this espionage; as, at the Reformation, the Catholics gathered their best calumnies against Luther from his unreserved 'table-talk.' It was not difficult to draw the unhappy Middleton into 'unguarded expressions[1]'; and something which had fallen from Rundle in his younger days was used against him so successfully that even the Talbot interest was able to procure him only an Irish bishoprick. Lord Chesterfield, seeing[2] what advantage the High-church party derived from this tactic, endeavoured to turn it against them. He gives a circum-

---

[1] Van Mildert, *Life of Waterland*, p. 162.

[2] [Too much seems here to be attributed to a mere repetition of a bit of scandal, which was, moreover, never published by Chesterfield, but only left among his papers.]

stantial account of a conversation with Pope, which would tend to prove that Atterbury was, nearly all his life, a sceptic. The thing was not true, as Mr. Carruthers has shown[1]; and true or false, the weapon in Chesterfield's hands was pointless.

Though the general feeling of the country was sufficiently decided to oblige all who wished to write against Christianity to do so under a mask, this was not the case with attacks upon the clergy. Since the days of the Lollards there had never been a time when the established ministers of religion were held in so much contempt as in the Hanoverian period, or when satire upon Churchmen was so congenial to general feeling. This too was the more extraordinary, as there was no feeling against the Church Establishment, nor was non-conformity as a theory ever less in favour. The contempt was for the persons, manners, and character of the ecclesiastics. When Macaulay brought out his portrait of the clergyman of the Revolution period, his critics endeavoured to show that that portrait was not true to life. They seem to have brought out the fact that it was pretty fairly true to literature. The difficult point is to estimate how far the satirical and popular literature of any age may be taken as representative of life. Satire to be popular must exaggerate, but it must be ex-aggeration of known and recognized facts. Mr. Churchill Babington[2] sets aside two of Macaulay's authorities, Oldham and T. Wood, because Oldham was an Atheist and Wood a Deist. Admitting that an Atheist and a Deist can be under no obligation to truth, yet a satirist, who intends to be read, is under the most inevitable engagement to the probable. Satire does not create the sentiment to which it appeals. A portrait of the country parson *temp*. George the Second which should

[1] *Life of Pope*, 2nd ed. p. 213.
[2] *Character of the Clergy, &c., considered*, p. 48.

Essays and Reviews, 1860.]

be drawn verbatim from the pamphlets of the day, would be no more historical than is that portrait of the begging friar of the sixteenth century which our historians repeat after Erasmus and the *Epistolae Obscurorum Virorum.* History may be extracted from them, but these caricatures are not themselves history.

One inference which we may safely draw is that public feeling encouraged such representations. It is a symptom of the religious temper of the times, that the same public which compelled the Deist to wear the mask of 'solemn sneer' in his assaults upon Christian doctrine, required no such disguise or reserve when the ministers of the Church were spoken of. Nor does the evidence consist in a few stray extracts from here and there a Deist or a cynic, it is the tone of all the popular writers of that time. The unedifying lives of the clergy are a standard theme of sarcasm, and continue to be so till a late period in the century, when a gradual change may be observed in the language of literature. This antipathy to the clergy visible in the Hanoverian period, admits of comparison with that vein which colours the popular songs of the Wickliffite era. In the fifteenth century, the satire is not indiscriminate. It is against the monks and friars, the bishops and cardinals, as distinct from the 'poure persoun of a toun.' Its point against the organized hypocrisy of the Papal Churchmen is given it by the picture of the ideal minister of 'Christe's Gospel' which always accompanies the burlesque. In the eighteenth century the license of satire goes much beyond this. In the early part of the century we find clerical satire observing to some extent a similar discrimination. The Tory parson is libelled always with an ostentatious reserve of commendation for the more enlightened and liberal Hanoverian, the staunch maintainer of the Protestant succession. This is the tone of the *Independent Whig*, one of the numerous weekly sheets called into being in imitation of the *Tatler*[1]. It was started in 1720, taking for its exclusive theme the clergy, whom it was its avowed object to abuse. A paper came out every Wednesday. It was not a newspaper, and does not deal in libel or personalities, hardly ever mentioning a name, very rarely quoting a fact, but dilating in general terms upon clerical ignorance and bigotry. This dull and worthless trash not only had a considerable circulation at the time, but was reprinted, and passed through several editions in a collected form. The Bishops talked of prohibiting it, but, on second thoughts, acted more wisely in taking no notice of it. The only part of the kingdom into which it could not find entrance was the Isle of Man, where the saintly Wilson combined with apostolic virtues much of the old episcopal claims over the consciences of his flock. The *Independent Whig*, though manifestly written by a man of no religion, yet finds it necessary to keep up the appearance of encouraging the 'better sort' of clergy, and affecting to despise only the political priests, the meddling chaplain, the preferment-hunter, the toper, who is notable at bowls, and dexterous at whisk.

As we advance towards the middle of the century, and the French influence begins to mingle with pure English Deism, the spirit of contempt spreads till it involves all priests of all religions. The language now is, ' The established clergy in every country are generally the greatest enemies to all kinds of reformation, as they are generally the most narrow-minded and most worthless set of men in every country. Fortunately for the present times, the wings of clerical power and influence are pretty

---

[1] [By Thomas Gordon, also translator of Tacitus, in co-operation with Trenchard. It carried on the Whig opposition to the Church, previously shown in the Sacheverel and Bangorian controversies. It represents Hoadly as against Atterbury, but does not imply a general estimate of the clergy from an extra-political standpoint. It is really an imitation of Swift's *Examiner*, Defoe's *Review*, &c., not of the *Tatler*, which was outside politics.]

Essays and Reviews, 1860.]

close trimmed, so that I do not think their opposition to the proposed reformations could be of any great consequence, more of the people being inclined to despise them, than to follow them blindly[1].' It was no longer for their vices that the clergy were reviled, for the philosopher now had come to understand that 'their virtues were more dangerous' to society. Strictness of life did but increase the dislike with which the clergyman was regarded; his morality was but double-dyed hypocrisy; religious language from his mouth was methodistical cant. Nor did the orthodox attempt to struggle with this sentiment. They yielded to it, and adopted for their maxim of conduct, 'surtout point de zèle.' Their sermons and pamphlets were now directed against 'Enthusiasm,' which became the bugbear of that time. Every clergyman who wished to retain any influence over the minds of his parishioners, was anxious to vindicate himself from all suspicion of enthusiasm. When he had set himself right in this respect, he endeavoured to do the same good office for the Apostles. But if he were not an 'enthusiast,' he was an 'impostor.' For every clergyman of the Church had against him an antecedent presumption as a 'priest.' It was now well understood, by all enlightened men, that the whole sacerdotal brood were but a set of impostors, who lived by deceiving the people, and who had invented religion for their own benefit. Natural religion needed no 'priests' to uphold it; it was obvious to every understanding, and could maintain itself in the world without any confraternity sworn to the secret.

Again came a change. As the Methodist movement gradually leavened the mass beneath, zeal came again into credit. The old Wickliffite, or Puritan, distinction

---

[1] Burgh, *Political Disquisitions*, 1774. [The French influence can hardly be perceived till after the middle of the century. Voltaire, in his sceptical writings, and Rousseau, introduced this influence, itself partly affected by English Deism.]

is revived between the 'Gospel preachers' and the 'dumb dogs.' The antipathy to priests was no longer promiscuous. Popular indignation was reserved for the fox-hunter and the pluralist; the Hophni-and-Phinehas generation; the men, who are described as 'careless of dispensing the bread of life to their flocks, preaching a carnal and soul-benumbing morality, and trafficking in the souls of men by receiving money for discharging the pastoral office in parishes where they did not so much as look on the faces of the people more than once a year.' In the well-known satire of Cowper, it is no longer irreligious mocking at sacred things under pretence of a virtuous indignation. It becomes again what it was before the Reformation—an earnest feeling, a religious sentiment, the moral sense of man; Huss or Savonarola appealing to the written morality of the Gospel against the practical immorality consecrated by the Church.

Something too of the old anti-hierarchical feeling accompanies this revival of the influence of the inferior clergy; a faint reflection of the bitter hatred which the Lollard had borne to Pope and Cardinal, or the Puritan to 'Prelacy.' The utility of the episcopal and capitular dignities continued to be questioned long after the evangelical parish pastor had re-established himself in the affections of his flock, and 1832 saw the cathedrals go down amid the general approbation of all classes. In the earlier half of the century the reverse was the case. The boorish country parson was the man whose order was despised then, and his utility questioned. The Freethinkers themselves could not deny that the bench and the stalls were graced by some whose wit, reputation, and learning would have made them considerable in any profession. The higher clergy had with them the town and the court, the country clergy sided with the squires. The mass of the clergy were not in sympathy, either politically or intellectually, with their ecclesiastical su-

Essays and Reviews, 1860.]

periors. The Tory fox-hunter in the *Freeholder* (No. 22) thinks 'the neighbouring shire very happy for having scarce a Presbyterian in it except the Bishop;' while Hickes 'thanks God that the main body of the clergy are in their hearts Jacobites.' The bishops of George the Second deserved the respect they met with. At no period in the history of our Church has the ecclesiastical patronage of the crown been better directed than while it was secretly dispensed by Queen Caroline. For a brief period, liberality and cultivation of mind were passports to promotion in the Church. Nor were politics a hindrance; the queen earnestly pressed an English see upon Bishop Wilson. The corruption which began with the Duke of Newcastle (1746) gradually deepened in the subsequent reign, as political orthodoxy and connexion were made the tests, and the borough-holders divided the dignities of the Church among their adherents.

Of an age so solid and practical it was not to be expected that its theologians and metaphysicians would mount into the more remote spheres of abstraction. Their line of argument was, as has been seen, regulated by the necessity they laid themselves under of appealing to sound sense and common reason. But not only was their treatment of their topic popular, the motive of their writings was an immediate practical necessity. Bishops and deans might be made for merit, but it was not mere literary merit, classical scholarship, or University distinction. The Deistical controversy did not originate, like some other controversies which have made much noise in their time, in speculative fancy, in the leisure of the cloister, or the college. It had a living practical interest in its complication with the questions of the day. The endeavour of the moralists and divines of the period to rationalize religion was in fact an effort to preserve the practical principles of moral and religious conduct for society. It was not an academical disputation, or a

contest of wits for superiority, but a life and death
struggle of religious and moral feeling to maintain itself.
What they felt they had to contend against was moral
depravity, and not theological error; they wrote less in
the interest of truth than in that of virtue. A general relaxation of manners, in all classes of society, is universally
affirmed to be characteristic of that time; and theology
and philosophy applied themselves to combat this. A
striking instance of this is Bishop Berkeley, the only metaphysical writer of the time, besides Locke and Hume, who
has maintained a very high name in philosophical history.
He forms a solitary—it might seem a singular—exception
to what has been said of the prosaic and unmetaphysical
character of this moralizing age. The two peculiar
metaphysical notions which are connected with Berkeley's
name, and which, though he did not originate, he propounded with a novelty and distinctness equal to
originality, have always ranked as being on the extreme
verge of rational speculation, if not actually within the
region of unfruitful paradox and metaphysical romance.
These two memorable speculations, as propounded by
Berkeley in the *Alciphron,* come before us not as a
Utopian dream, or an ingenious play of reason, but inter-
woven in a polemic against the prevailing unbelief. They
are made to bend to a most practical purpose, and are
Berkeley's contributions to the Deistical controversy.
The character of the man, too, was more in harmony
with the plain utilitarian spirit of his time than with his
own refining intellect. He was not a closet-thinker, like
his master Malebranche, but a man of the world and of
society, inquisitive and well informed in many branches
of practical science. Practical schemes, social and
philanthropic, occupied his mind more than abstract
thinking. In pushing the received metaphysical creed
to its paradoxical consequences, as much as in prescribing
'tar-water,' he was thinking only of an immediate 'benefit

to mankind.' He seems to have thought nothing of his argument until he had brought it to bear on the practical questions of the day.

Were the 'corruption of manners' merely the complaint of one party or set of writers, a cry of factious Puritanism, or of men who were at war with society, like the Non-juring clergy, or of a few isolated individuals of superior piety, like William Law, it would be easily explicable. The 'world' at all times, and in all countries, can be described with truth as 'lying in wickedness,' and the rebuke of the preacher of righteousness is equally needed in every age. There cannot be a darker picture than that drawn by the Fathers of the third century of the morals of the Christians in their time[1]. The rigorous moralist, heathen or Christian, can always paint in sharp contrast the vices and the belief of mankind. But, after making every allowance for the exaggeration of religious rhetoric, and the querulousness of defeated parties, there seems to remain *some* real evidence for ascribing to that age a more than usual moral licence and contempt of external restraints. It is the concurrent testimony of men of all parties, it is the general strain of the most sensible and worldly divines, prosperous men who lived with this very world they censure, men whose code of morals was not large, nor their standard exacting. To attempt the inquiry what specific evils were meant by the general expressions 'decay of religion,' and 'corruption of maners,' —the stereotype phrases of the time—is not within the limits of this paper. No historian, as far as I am aware, has attempted this examination; all have been content to render, without valuation, the charges as they find them. I shall content myself with producing here one statement of contemporary opinion on this point; for which purpose I select a layman, David Hartley[2].

---

[1] See passages in Jewel's *Apology*.
[2] *Observations on Man*, Vol. II, p. 441.

There are six things which seem more especially to threaten ruin and dissolution to the present States of Christendom.

1st. The great growth of atheism and infidelity, particularly amongst the governing parts of these States.

2nd. The open and abandoned lewdness to which great numbers of both sexes, especially in the high ranks of life, have given themselves up.

3rd. The sordid and avowed self-interest, which is almost the sole motive of action in those who are concerned in the administration of public affairs.

4th. The licentiousness and contempt of every kind of authority, divine or human, which is so notorious in inferiors of all ranks.

5th. The great worldly-mindedness of the clergy, and their gross neglect in the discharge of their proper functions.

6th. The carelessness and infatuation of parents and magistrates with respect to the education of youth, and the consequent early corruption of the rising generation.

All these things have evident mutual connexions and influences; and as they all seem likely to increase from time to time, so it can scarce be doubted by a considerate man, whether he be a religious one or no, but that they will, sooner or latter, bring on a total dissolution of all the forms of government that subsist at present in the Christian countries of Europe.

Though there is entire unanimity as to the fact of the prevailing corruption, there is the greatest diversity of opinion as to its cause. Each party is found in turn attributing it to the neglect or disbelief of the abstract propositions in which its own particular creed is expressed. The Nonjurors and High-Churchmen attribute it to the Toleration Act and the latitudinarianism allowed in high places. One of the very popular pamphlets of the year 1721 was a fast-sermon preached before the Lord Mayor by Edmund Massey, in which he enumerates the evils of the time, and affirms that they 'are justly chargeable upon the corrupt explication of those words of our Saviour, My kingdom is not of this world'—i. e., upon Hoadly's celebrated sermon. The latitudinarian clergy divide the blame between the Freethinkers and the Nonjurors. The Freethinkers point to the hypocrisy of the Clergy, who, they say, lost all credit with the people by having preached 'passive obedience' up to 1688, and then suddenly finding out that it was not a scriptural truth. The Nonconformists lay it to the enforcement of conformity and unscriptural terms of communion; while the Catholics rejoice to see in it the Protestant Reformation at last bearing its natural fruit. Warburton characteristically attributes it to the bestowal of 'preferment' by the Walpole administration[1]. The power of preferment was not under-estimated then. George II maintained to the last that the growth of Methodism .was entirely owing to ministers not having listened to his advice, and 'made Whitefield a bishop.' Lastly, that every one may have his say, a professor of moral philosophy in our day is found attributing the same facts to the prevalence of 'that low view of morality which rests its rules upon consequences merely.'

'The reverence which,' says Dr. Whewell, 'handed down by the tradition of ages of moral and religious teaching, had hitherto protected the accustomed forms of moral good, was gradually removed. Vice, and crime, and sin, ceased to be words that terrified the popular speculator. Virtue, and goodness, and purity were no longer things which he looked up to with mute respect. He ventured to lay a sacrilegious hand even upon these hallowed shapes. He saw that when this had been dared by audacious theorists, those objects, so long venerated, seemed to have no power of punishing the bold intruder. There was a scene like that which occurred when the barbarians broke into the Eternal City. At first, in spite of themselves, they were awed by the divine aspect of the ancient magistrates; but when once their leader had smitten one of these venerable figures with impunity,

---

[1] Dedication to Lord Mansfield, *Works*, II. 268.

the coarse and violent mob rushed onwards, and exultingly mingled all in one common destruction [1].'

The actual sequence of cause and effect seems, if it be not presumptuous to say so, to be as nearly as possible inverted in this eloquent statement. The licentiousness of talk and manners was not produced by the moral doctrines promulgated: but the doctrine of moral consequences was had recourse to by the divines and moralists as the most likely remedy of the prevailing licentiousness. It was an attempt, well-meant but not successful, to arrest the wanton proceedings of 'the coarse and violent mob.' Good men saw with alarm, almost with despair, that what they said in the obsolete language of religious teaching was not listened to, and tried to address the age in plain and unmistakable terms. The new theory of consequences was not introduced by 'men of leisure' to supplant and overthrow a nobler and purer view of religion and morality, it was a plain fact of religion stated in plain language, in the hope of deterring the wicked from his wickedness. It was the address of the Old Testament prophet, 'Why will ye die, O house of Israel?' That there is a God and moral Governor, and that obedience to His commands is necessary to secure our interests in this world and the next—if any form of rational belief can control the actions of a rational being, it is surely this. On the rationalist hypothesis, the morality of consequences ought to produce the most salutary effects on the general behaviour of mankind. This obligation of obedience, the appeal to our desire of our own welfare, was the substance of the practical teaching of the age. It was stated with great cogency of reasoning, and enforced with every variety of illustration. Put its proof at the lowest, let it be granted that they did not succeed in removing all the objections of the Deistical writers, it must, at least, be allowed that they

[1] *Moral Philosophy in England*, p. 79.
Essays and Reviews, 1860.]

showed, to the satisfaction of all prudent and thinking men, that it was *safer* to believe Christianity true than not. The obligation to practice in point of prudence was as perfect as though the proof had been demonstrative. And what was the surprising result? That the more they demonstrated the less people believed. As the proof of morality was elaborated and strengthened, the more it was disregarded, the more ungodliness and profaneness flourished and grew. This is certainly not what we should antecedently expect. If, as Dr. Whewell assumes, and the whole *doctrinaire* school with him, the speculative belief of an age determines its moral character, that should be the purest epoch where the morality of consequences is placed in the strongest light—when it is most convincingly set before men that their present and future welfare depends on how they act: that 'all we enjoy, and great part of what we suffer, is placed in our own hands.'

Experience, however, the testimony of history, displays to us a result the very reverse. The experiment of the eighteenth century may surely be considered as a decisive one on this point. The failure of a prudential system of ethics as a restraining force upon society was perceived, or felt in the way of reaction, by the Evangelical and Methodist generation of teachers who succeeded the Hanoverian divines. So far their perception was just. They went on to infer that, because the circulation of one system of belief had been inefficacious, they should try the effect of inculcating a set of truths as widely remote from the former as possible. Because legal preaching, as they phrased it, had failed, they would essay Gospel preaching. The preaching of justification by works had not the power to check wickedness, therefore justification by faith, the doctrine of the Reformation, was the only saving truth. This is not meant as a complete account of the origin of the Evangelical school.

It is only one point of view—that point which connects the school with the general line of thought this paper has been pursuing. Their doctrine of conversion by supernatural influence must on no account be forgotten. Yet it appears that they thought, that the channel of this supernatural influence was, in some way or other, preaching:—preaching, too, not as rhetoric, but as the annunciation of a specific doctrine—the Gospel. They certainly insisted 'on the heart' being touched, and that the Spirit only had the power savingly to affect the heart; but they acted as though this were done by an appeal to the reason, and scornfully rejected the idea of religious education.

It should also be remarked that even the divines of the Hanoverian school were not wholly blind to some flaw in their theory, and to the practical inefficacy of their doctrine. Not that they underrated the force of their demonstrations. As has been already said, the greater part of them over-estimated their convincingness; but they could not but see that they did not, in fact, convince. When this was forced upon their observation, when they perceived that an *a priori* demonstration of religion might be placed before a man, and that he did not see its force, then, inconsequent with their own theory, they had recourse to the notion of moral culpability. If a person refused to admit the evidence for revelation, it was because he did not examine it with a dispassionate mind. His understanding was biassed by his wishes; some illicit passion he was resolved on gratifying, but which prudence, forsooth, would not have allowed him to gratify so long as he continued to believe in a future judgment. The wish that there *were* no God suggested the thought that there *was* not. Speculative unbelief is thus asserted to be a consequence of a bad heart: it is the ground upon which we endeavour to prove to ourselves and others that the indulgence of our passions is consistent

with a rational prudence. As levelled against an individual
opponent, this is a poor controversial shift. Many of the
Deists were men of worth and probity; of none of them
is anything known which would make them worse men
than the average of their class in life. Mr. Chichester[1]
says, 'Tindal was infamous for vice in general'; but I
have not been able to trace his authority for the assertion.
As an imputation, not against individual unbelievers, but
against the competency of reason in general, it may be
true, but is quite inconsistent with the general hypothesis
of the school of reasoners who brought it. If reason be
liable to an influence which warps it, then there is required
some force which shall keep this influence under, and
reason alone is no longer the all-sufficient judge of truth.
In this way we should be forced back to the old orthodox
doctrine of the chronic impotence of reason, superinduced
upon it by the Fall; a doctrine which the reigning orthodoxy had tacitly renounced.

In the Catholic theory the feebleness of Reason is met
half-way and made good by the authority of the Church.
When the Protestants threw off this authority, they did
not assign to Reason what they took from the Church,
but to Scripture. Calvin did not shrink from saying
that Scripture 'shone sufficiently by its own light.' As
long as this could be kept to, the Protestant theory of
belief was whole and sound. At least it was as sound as
the Catholic. In both, Reason, aided by spiritual illumi-
nation, performs the subordinate function of recognizing
the supreme authority of the Church, and of the Bible,
respectively. Time, learned controversy, and abatement
of zeal drove the Protestants generally from the hardy
but irrational assertion of Calvin. Every foot of ground
that Scripture lost was gained by one or other of the
three substitutes: Church-authority, the Spirit, or Reason.
Church-authority was essayed by the Laudian divines,

---

[1] *Deism compared with Christianity*, 1821, vol. II p. 220.

but was soon found untenable, for on that footing it was
found impossible to justify the Reformation and the breach
with Rome. The Spirit then came into favour along
with Independency. But it was still more quickly discovered that on such a basis only discord and disunion
could be reared. There remained to be tried Common
Reason, carefully distinguished from recondite learning,
and not based on metaphysical assumptions. To apply
this instrument to the contents of Revelation was the
occupation of the early half of the eighteenth century:
with what success has been seen. In the latter part of
the century the same Common Reason was applied to
the external evidences. But here the method fails in a
first requisite—universality; for even the shallowest array
of historical proof requires some book-learning to apprehend. Further than this, the Lardner and Paley school
could not complete their proof satisfactorily, inasmuch
as the materials for the investigation of the first and
second centuries of the Christian era were not at hand.

Such appears to be the past history of the Theory of
Belief in the Church of England. Whoever would take
the religious literature of the present day as a whole, and
endeavour to make out clearly on what basis Revelation
is supposed by it to rest, whether on Authority, on the
Inward Light, on Reason, on self-evidencing Scripture,
or on the combination of the four, or some of them,
and in what proportions, would probably find that he
had undertaken a perplexing but not altogether profitless
inquiry.

Essays and Reviews, 1860.]

XIV.

LIFE OF BISHOP WARBURTON [1].

———•———

(*National Review*, 1863.)

ABOUT fifteen years after Warburton's death, that
which his friends wished to be known of his
life was given to the world by his confidential disciple
and admirer, Hurd, Bishop of Worcester. The same
editor and literary executor left ready for press a volume
of Warburton's correspondence with himself, which
appeared immediately after Hurd's death in 1808. Warburton, who always expressed himself without fear or
favour, softening or disguise, about friend or foe, has
in these letters left a piece of self-portraiture. The
correspondence is the corrective of the Life, and reveals
Warburton and the Warburtonians in a thousand characteristic traits which Hurd's decorum had varnished over.

To these two primary sources, coupled with Warburton's
own works, which fill thirteen volumes 8vo, Mr. Selby
Watson has added a diligent search through the ephemeral
literature of the period,—periodicals, pamphlets, sermons,
and charges [2]. He does not seem to have enjoyed the use
of any new materials hitherto unprinted. Warburton's
own letters are understood to have been almost all
destroyed by his widow. One cannot help asking,
Where are those which were not destroyed? Where

---

[1] *The Life of William Warburton, D.D., Lord Bishop of Gloucester from* 1760
to 1779 ; *with Remarks on his Works.* By the Rev. JOHN SELBY WATSON, M.A.,
M.R.S.L. Longmans, 1863.

[2] [There is also a great deal of information about Warburton in Nichols's
Literary Anecdotes, which Mr. Watson seems to have fully used.]

are the letters of Warburton's correspondents? Where
are the papers from which Mr. Kilvert printed a 'Selection' in 1841? and where are the collections which
Mr. James Crossley has been many years making?
No *subsidia* from these sources are to be found in
the present biography. But as this volume is already
650 pages thick, most readers will think they have too
much, rather than too little. And, for a complete estimate
of Warburton and his doings, we have enough. There
may be many letters yet recoverable. But it is impossible
that anything can be now brought to light which could
modify perceptibly the well-defined image of the man
which may be traced from the materials already in our
hands. All that is required for this task, beyond some
skill in delineating character, is to place the man in
his right relation to the social life and ideas of the time.
The biographer must know his way about among religious
parties in the latter half of George II's reign,—perhaps
the least-known portion of the history of the English
Church. Warburton belonged to none of these, and came
athwart all of them at one period or another of his bellicose
career. It is on such invisible attractions and repulsions
that the main interest of a career of antagonism such as
Warburton's lies. His life was a succession of battles,—
battles of the pen. All Warburton's books, like those of
St. Augustine, are written against some adversary. But
instead of handling the great public themes of Divinity,
natural and revealed, Warburton is always defending some
peculiar notion of his own, to which no one attached
any importance, himself as little as any. The zest lay
in the fighting, of which, while he was young, he never
could get enough. The most famous of Warburton's
battles,—and the most serious; indeed the Waterloo of his
critical empire,—was that with Lowth. In this celebrated
encounter, in which the whole reading public, from the
king downwards, participated with the liveliest interest,

the points of sacred antiquity debated are mostly of no moment. Or where they are of moment, as, e. g. the date of the Book of Job, the disputants lack the requisite knowledge for throwing even the feeblest ray of light upon them. But though we can learn nothing respecting the Pentateuch and Job, we may glean much to instruct us in the inner history of the Church of England during a period in which that history is very little known to the present generation. What is wanted here, is not so much fresh materials, as the hand to reduce to order and system those which are already extant. The life of Warburton, which was passed wholly on the highways, and open to public inspection, is peculiarly calculated as a mirror of the clerical life of the eighteenth century, or at least of the literary section of it, and contrasts in this respect with the noiseless and inexpressive existence of men like Secker and Porteus.

Though Warburton inherited an ancient name, he was born (1698) to humble, or rather no fortunes. Bred to the law, his passion for literature—though Hurd pretends an early seriousness of temper—led him into the Church at the age of twenty-five. At the age of thirty he obtained from a private patron, Sir Robert Sutton, a living of some value. At this parsonage, Brant-Broughton, near Newark, he fixed himself with his mother and sisters, and spent the eighteen best years of his life in unintermitted study. An athletic frame and a vigorous constitution, seconded by abstemious habits, enabled him to support, at least without immediate injury, this severe tax on the brain. Nature, however, exacted the penalty—a penalty which may be deferred, but is never remitted—at the end of life. Though he lived to old age, his memory became impaired, and some time before death he sank into a general torpor of the faculties. One of his sisters, Mrs. Frances Warburton, told Hurd that, even at this early period, they became apprehensive for his health, and 'would some-

times invite themselves to take coffee in his library
after dinner, and contrive to make their stay with him
as long as possible; but that, when they retired, they
always found that he returned again to his books, and
continued at them till the demands of sleep obliged
him to retire[1].' His absorption in his books is illustrated by a story told of his going to dine at Lord
Tyrconnel's, at Bilton Hall, where a fire was raging
at a house which Warburton had to pass on the road
from Brant-Broughton. When he arrived at Bilton he
had nothing to tell; though he had ridden close by the
house, he had not noticed the fire. The company began
to hope the report was not true. But it was soon
confirmed by the arrival of another guest, who said
he had noticed Mr. Warburton ride by without turning his
head, apparently absorbed in some subject of meditation.

With these habits seconding the native energy of his
mind, his knowledge of books became immense. Johnson
told the king that 'he had not read much, compared
with Warburton[2],'—a modest admission, yet strictly true,
even understood of bare quantity. But Johnson was
not thinking of volumes by number. He knew that
Warburton's reading ranged over whole classes of books
into which he himself had barely dipped. Johnson's own
stock of learning had been acquired, he once told Boswell,
by eighteen, and that he had added little to it at any
subsequent period. And Warburton said of himself that
'he was a great reader of history, but a greater still of
romances; for that nothing came amiss to a man who
consulted his appetite more than his digestion.' An
indication, perhaps, that Bentley's sarcasm had come to his
ears. The great critic, on being shown the first volume of
the *Divine Legation*, about three years before his death,
had remarked, 'This man has a monstrous appetite,
but very bad digestion.' 'A change in the object of

[1] *Life*, p. 34.
National Review, 1863.]   [2] [See Hill's *Boswell*, II. 36.]

his pursuit,' says Whitaker[1], 'was his only relaxation. He could pass and repass from fathers and philosophers to *Don Quixote* in the original, with perfect ease and pleasure.' Of his method of reading, nothing is reported by any one who knew him during his period of acquisition. Cradock, in a conversation with Mrs. Warburton, observed that Hurd had expressed his wonder how the Bishop had acquired all the anecdotes in which he so much abounded. 'I could readily have informed him,' replied Mrs. Warburton. 'When we passed our winters in London, he would often, after his long and severe studies, send out for a whole basketful of books from the circulating libraries, and at times I have gone into his study and found him laughing, though alone.' And he writes to Doddridge that 'his melancholy habit impelled him to seek refuge from the uneasiness of thought in wild and desultory reading.' He was well acquainted with the history of the Civil War, and told Hurd that 'there was scarcely a memoir or a pamphlet published between 1640 and 1660 which he had not read.' These are all the testimonies we can find on the subject. Beyond this we are left to the evidence his writings themselves afford of the compass and depth of his acquaintance with books.

However great Warburton's receptive capacity, his instinct to communicate thought was quite as vigorous. All this reading could not go on without a corresponding effort to write. The first direction was given to his pen, as to most men's before they have found their own vein, by the taste of those with whom he lived. Warburton had found his way, in his occasional visits to London, into a coffee-house set of fourth-rate literati,— Concanen, Dennis, James Moore, Hesiod Cooke, and Broome. The best man of the set was Theobald. When Theobald brought out his *Shakespeare* in 1733, he said

[1] [Article on Warburton in the *Quarterly Review*, vol. VII.]

that he owed Warburton 'no small part of his best criticisms,'—an acknowledgment which went rather beyond than within the mark.   After another emendatory attempt, of which Velleius Paterculus was the unfortunate object, Warburton forsook a track into which he had only been drawn by imitation for one proper to his own bent. He certainly did not relinquish verbal criticism because he thought he had failed in it, notwithstanding a friendly hint from Bishop Hare, intended to suggest that conclusion to him.   To the last he believed in himself as a restorer of Shakespeare.   Even Johnson's edition in 1765 could not open his eyes.   He was very far from adopting the good-natured suggestion of the Preface that 'he (Warburton) cannot now be very solicitous what is thought of notes which he ought never to have considered as a part of his serious employments, and which, I suppose, he no longer numbers among his happy effusions.'   But, though perfectly satisfied of his own 'happy sagacity to restore an author's text[1]' his mind was formed with a more ambitious grasp, and impelled him to marshal ideas.

In 1736 he struck into the vein which made him famous. The *Alliance of Church and State*, brought out in that year, is widely different by its title and argument from the *Divine Legation*, which followed it in 1738.   But the mould in which the thought of both works is cast is one and the same, viz. the politician's view of religion.

The immediate effect of these publications in riveting upon themselves the attention of all the reading public is only to be accounted for by their union of two qualities : they occupied themselves with the thought with which every body was occupied, and they treated it with more force and weight than any body.   The originality of Warburton's manner would not have told as it did, had it

---

[1] *Letters to Hurd*, p. 367.

not been laid out upon a topic which was anxiously
engaging the minds of practical men. His work fell at a
time when the interest of the speculative part of the
Deistical controversy had well-nigh exhausted itself. On
the question, Does Christianity contain any supernatural
elements ? that generation had said on both sides nearly
all it could say. The interest had merged in a new
and more practical phase of inquiry, viz. What remedy
could be found for the growing licentiousness of manners,
and relaxation of the bonds of civil society ? The title
and professed thesis of the *Divine Legation* hide from us
this bearing upon contemporary feeling. It was this
secret bearing which recommended an otherwise barren
paradox to general attention. When this engrossing
subject was treated with singular force, and with a learned
apparatus which had not been seen in theological
controversy since Stillingfleet, the author became at once,
in that frivolous world of pamphleteers, the mark for
adulation and for envy. From the associate of Concanen
and Theobald, he became the friend and adviser of Pope,
the correspondent of Charles Yorke, received open favour
from Hare, and timid encouragement from Sherlock.
To the Bishop of Chichester (Hare) he owed a recom-
mendation to the queen. Her majesty chanced one day,
in the autumn of 1737, to ask the bishop if he could
recommend her a person of learning and ability to be
about her, to read and converse. Hare immediately
named Warburton. The promised opening was closed by
the queen's death in November,—an event disastrous not
only to Warburton's rising fortunes, but to the whole
Church of England.

His preferment was retarded by this event, but not
ultimately forfeited. The intrinsic merit and ingenuity
of the *Divine Legation* must ultimately have won it
attention ; but an immediate and exaggerated *éclat* was
conferred upon it by the cloud of insect assailants who

immediately fastened upon it. The liberal section of
the clergy, represented by Hare, commended, but with an
evident coldness. The moderate orthodox, represented
by the feeble Sherlock, timidly gave in their adhesion,
rather as if they feared to alienate so much power than as
heartily appropriating it. But the high-church party,
standing aloof in sullen opposition, felt at once, by an
instinct far surer than intelligence, that the new candidate
in the field of theology, however carefully he might have
avoided committing himself against them, yet was not
of them. They fell upon him immediately, to bury and to
stifle, with the usual arms of the party—denunciation,
not argument. From the pulpit of St. Mary's, Oxford, they
called for 'the secular arm' to cut off the heretic. They
misrepresented, twisted meanings, drew inferences, and
gave a momentary interest to their malignant trash by
promiscuous revilings. Warburton complains that 'propositions were invented, conversations betrayed, and
forged letters written.' A hireling writer, whom the party,
though not trusting him, occasionally used, inserted, if he
did not write, in a paper, *The Weekly Miscellany*, edited by
him, one of the worst of these attacks[1]. In it the 'clergy
who are sincere friends to Christianity' are put on their
guard against this new pretended advocate of revelation,
who is really a subtle enemy. The author of the *Divine
Legation*, it is insinuated, denies the divinity of Christ,
the merits of his death, the obligation and effects of the
sacraments, and the doctrine of grace; and he 'under-
values the evidence arising from miracles.' The letter,
signed a 'Country Clergyman,' winds up with a naïve
disclosure of the writer's purpose in a hint that Mr.
Warburton 'should be hindered from any further advancement in the church.' Of the imputations on Warburton's
orthodoxy no proof was attempted, because none could

[1] [The *Weekly Miscellany* (1733–1741) was edited by William Webster. See
Nichols's *Lit. Anecd.*, II. 36, V. 160–175.]

National Review, 1863.]

be found. But as his friends, Sherlock included, thought he ought to take some notice of this assault, Warburton made the best defence he could. To the repeated cautions of Sherlock and Hare we must ascribe it that this 'Vindication' is in a higher tone, and almost pure from that intemperate invective against assailants in which Warburton afterwards allowed himself. But that which did him most credit in it was the way in which he treated Conyers Middleton. In the *Divine Legation* he had spoken of Middleton, who was his personal friend, as a 'formidable adversary to the Freethinkers.' To have mentioned Middleton's name without proscribing it was enough to give a handle to cavil. Warburton's allusion was immediately transformed by the 'Country Clergyman' into his being 'a warmer advocate for Dr. Middleton, who denies the divine inspiration of the Scriptures, than for the Scriptures themselves.' In his 'Vindication' Warburton extricates himself without sacrificing his friend with a tact for which he deserved the commendation of the Bishop of Chichester, who told him that the bishops thought this part, which was the only difficult part, extremely well done. 'It cannot but please every candid reader to see you do justice to yourself, and yet not do it at his (Middleton's) expense.' It is to be regretted that Warburton had not always such prudent friends as Hare and Sherlock to advise him. He had probably escaped one of the worst blots upon his reputation,—the unmannerly violence towards opponents, which was the tone of his later controversy.

Meanwhile he pursued a better method of shaking off adversaries than writing against them; that of continuing at his own labour. The second volume of the *Divine Legation*, containing books 4, 5, and 6, came out in 1741. It had the fate of continuations,—of not being thought equal to the first part. But in this instance with justice. It wants the elasticity and point of the earlier books, being

at once less strong and more violent. It almost seems as
if the author was angry with himself at being so little able
to prove the thesis he had undertaken to prove, and making so little way with so much effort. But he had no reason
to be dissatisfied with its reception by the world. Any
decay of interest in the argument was made up for by
personalities. He had now erected the notes to the *Divine
Legation* into 'the ordinary place of his literary execu-
tions, where offenders by the dozen were whipped at the
cart's tail,' to use Lowth's comparison. The stir among
the pamphleteers was far greater than on the occasion of
the first volume. Then, Warburton contradicted as a
man who has to make his way by pulling down those
above him; now, he called criminals before him as already
seated on the judge's bench. He no longer reasoned;
he sentenced. It was not now necessary to show that
Warburton's opinion was right; the man who disputed
it was, to begin with, a 'scoundrel.' Though here, to be
sure, he is too apt to forget his own maxim that 'the
proving a man a scoundrel is putting him in the way to
thrive[1],' and Charles Yorke's suggestion that the opponents were 'like the spectres whom Æneas encountered,
whom you cannot hurt with any weapons.' And, in fact,
the more heads Warburton cut off, the more the foe
multiplied upon his hands. The fight waxed hotter, and
promised to last. A row in the theological world did
not die out so speedily in those days, when the steam-
press was not yet invented. Warburton had taken the
place of Hoadly. In 1746, five years after the appearance of the second volume of the *Divine Legation*, Hurd
writes to Devey: 'The attention of the learned world at
present turns entirely almost on the author of the *Divine
Legation*, who is mowing down his adversaries with as
great zeal and success as ever old Bentley did before
him.' By this time he had become literary executor to

[1] *Letter to Doddridge.*

Pope, and entered upon the inheritance of Pope's feuds in addition to his own.

Mr. Selby Watson devotes some chapters to the 'Answerers'—'Answerer' is a proper term in Warburtonian history, meaning those who wrote pamphlets against the *Divine Legation*. The writers themselves were of very various capacity and position. One character is common to all, that is, the insignificance of the points they choose to dispute, and their total want of the critical knowledge necessary for settling even those points. The two parties oppose opinion to opinion; and because Warburton vociferates most loudly in defence of his, it carries the day. It is observable that the attempts to make out Warburton unorthodox gradually die away. This kind of imputation is the first weapon at which a clerical assailant grasps, and the most deadly. Warburton had succeeded in parrying it, and there was no other he had to fear. It was settled that he was orthodox, and he was therefore in a condition to hurl it back upon his assailants. He had not always magnanimity enough to abstain from doing so.

The violence of the attacks on him had no blighting effect upon his reputation. During the ten years, 1740–1750, his credit was steadily rising, his circle of connexion extending, his fortunes improving. A man who rouses opponents is not seldom found to be capable of attaching friends in the same proportion. All Warburton's friendships were formed late, and as the result of literature. They had nothing about them of early association and comradeship. His introduction into the Pope circle was perhaps the most influential event in his life. This he obtained by writing expressly for it. In his struggling days, through his relations with Theobald, he had been accustomed to sneer at Pope. A very little insight into the life of the town taught him that, with a view to his own interest in literature, it would be better to propitiate

Twickenham.   He took the opportunity of Crousaz's
critique on the *Essay on Man* to draw up an elaborate
defence of the moral doctrine enforced in it.   In these
papers, which appeared in the *Works of the Learned* for
1739, Warburton forced his own meaning on the poet,
with his usual paradox and force.   'If you did not find
him a philosopher, you have made him one,' Middleton
told him ; and Pope, who was not very sure what moral
doctrine he had intended to teach, was delighted to discover of himself that he was *not* a fatalist.   He addressed a letter of thanks to the author, who was till
then an entire stranger to him.   The friendship thus
begun proved of more worth than literary friendships
usually are, being cemented by the bond of mutual
interest.   Pope wanted a commentator and a champion
against the crowd of enemies his provocative spirit had
called up against himself.   Warburton wanted an introduction to the great and powerful.   When Pope died
(1744) he left Warburton his literary executor—a legacy
which was worth to him at least £4000, a considerable
sum to a poor man.   Pope had introduced him to Allen.
This led to his marrying Allen's favourite niece, to whom
Allen left by his will the bulk of his property,—a very
large fortune ; and before his death he obtained for his
son-in-law, first the deanery, and afterwards the bishopric,
of Gloucester.   All this grew from a few flimsy pages
in the *Works of the Learned*, which happened to please
Pope.

Pope had made a great point of introducing Warburton
to Bolingbroke, and had calculated upon the certainty
of 'their being pleased to meet each other.'   After many
delays a meeting was at last effected.   The three dined
together at Lord Mansfield's, a short time before Pope's
death.   Bolingbroke made a remark about the moral attributes of the Deity which did not please Warburton.
He replied with some asperity, and a debate ensued,

National Review, 1863.]

which ended in making each thoroughly detestable to the other; a very common result of such prearranged friendships! They had been forced into contact without any natural attraction: the result was a deadly animosity. Before his death, Bolingbroke scattered over his pages sarcasm by the handful against the *Divine Legation* and its author; and a whole volume of Warburton's works is devoted to tirade against Bolingbroke and Bolingbroke's philosophy.

Of the friends made by literature, the best man was Jortin, and the most intimate, Hurd. The acquaintance with Jortin was not longer-lived than literary friendships usually are; but the fault of its disruption was wholly Warburton's, and in none of his many enmities did he show to greater disadvantage. To Bishop Newton, who has left in his Memoirs a parallel between Jortin and Warburton, and to the public in common with Bishop Newton, both appeared 'men of great parts, both men of uncommon learning, both able critics, both copious writers;' he adds, indeed, that Jortin 'was *perhaps* the better Greek and Latin scholar.' 'Better' implies comparison. The fact was that Jortin was a scholar in every sense of the word; Warburton in none: and in the matter of the disagreement between them, Jortin shows as much above Warburton in magnanimity as he is in learning. The two were exactly of an age, having been born in the same year, 1698. But the modesty, not to say reserve, of Jortin, together with what Parr calls his 'unfettered opinions,' kept him longer in the background, and he was in a condition to be patronized by Warburton. Warburton employed him as an occasional substitute in Lincoln's Inn Chapel, and dropt an encouraging word for him in some preface to a second edition: 'The world might soon expect to be gratified with the learned Mr. Jortin's Dissertations, composed, like his life, not in the spirit of controversy, but of truth and candour.' A neat compliment, but in the present case not more than strictly true. These very Dissertations, when they came out in 1755, contained a confession of dissent from the Warburtonian hypothesis on Virgil's descent into hell. That it was indicated with the writer's habitual modesty and gentleness made no difference. Hurd was commissioned to fall upon Jortin with the sword of vengeance. This he did in a 'Seventh Dissertation addressed to the Author of the Six,' a long and rambling piece of irony, which, however, the contemporary world called 'Attic.' In spite of the 'Attic irony,' the public who interested themselves in all these 'quarrels of authors' sided with Jortin. They translated out of the Attic irony the following rules in plain English[1], for the proper guidance of writers in their demeanour towards the sovereign of letters ;

1. You must not write on the same subject that he does. 2. You must not write against him. 3. You must not glance at his arguments without naming him. 4. You must not oppose his principles. 7. Where you design him a compliment, you must express it in form, with all the circumstance of panegyrical approbation. 8. You must call his suggestions 'discoveries,' not 'conjectures.'

Though the public condemned Hurd, Warburton was delighted that Jortin's 'mean, low, and ungrateful conduct' towards him had been properly chastised. Those who espoused Jortin's side were 'dirty fellows indeed,' and the compliment to Jortin was erased from the next edition of *Julian.* For all this, Jortin's revenge—neat and quiet, after his manner—was but to correct a childish mistake as to the meaning of the word *princeps,* which Warburton had committed. It was done without naming Warburton, though the application to him was made by a line from Terence, with which the correction wound up. Warburton had pretended to 'prove' that *primus* meant *chief,* and

---

[1] [Watson, p. 440, quotes this from a pamphlet of 1757, entitled *Remarks on Dr. Warburton's account of the Sentiments of the early Jews concerning the Soul.*]

National Review, 1863.]

had collected passages in which it has that signification.
'He has omitted one,' says Jortin, 'which would "suit
him better" than any: "Est genus hominum qui esse
primos se omnium rerum volunt, Nec sunt[1]."' This
little reproof was buried out of sight in a note to Jortin's
Life of Erasmus. But though whispered to the reeds, it
struck Warburton in his most vulnerable part,—his conceit of classical knowledge. Before his equanimity could
be restored, Hurd was obliged to 'prove' that *princeps*,
in the passage of Cicero [2], actually meant what Warburton
had made it mean. This he did to Warburton's entire
satisfaction; but, as Mr. Watson remarks, Hurd knew
Latin enough to refrain from going before the public
with these proofs, and was satisfied at having appeased
his patron's wrath by a private exposure of 'the poor
man's criticism.' Warburton sent Jortin, in an indirect
way, a letter reproaching him, in return for his criticism,
with the fact that, 'from the first moment of my acquaintance with him to the last that he would allow me
to call him friend, I had the vanity to be always recommending him to those of the first quality whom I knew.'
Jortin replied as follows:

LONDON, *October 3d*, 1758.

REV. SIR,—I had the favour of yours, which gave me a mixture of
pain and pleasure,—of pain for ever having been at variance with you;
of pleasure from some prospect of seeing an end of it, unless I deceive
myself.

You complain; I could complain too; but to what purpose
would that serve? To irritate, perhaps; but that is not my present
design.

You say that you never was concerned in the attacks made upon
me. I ought to believe you; and I do believe you. But before you
informed me of it, I thought otherwise; and so did many a person
besides me.

That you recommended me to persons who had it in their power

---

[1] Terent. *Eun.* II. 2, 17. [248 in Umpfenbach.]
[2] *De Legg.* II. 6, 14

to do me service, I doubt not. Vouchers are needless. Your own word suffices with me, and I thank you for it.

As to the passage in Cicero, which I ought in civility to have mentioned to you ; if I did not mention it, my memory deceives me egregiously. Surely, unless I am utterly mistaken, I did tell you of it, and you replied, that Bishop Hare had once said the same thing to you.

[Your correction of my translation of *apud inferos*] I would take occasion, unless you forbid it, to mention in the next volume, with respect and with thanks. 'Sit simultatis depositae et nunquam resumendae pignus et monumentum !' . . . .

I am, sir, your most humble servant,

J. JORTIN.'

When we find that this generous proffer of the right hand of reconciliation was not accepted, we are ready to welcome Parr's ebullient sentences in the preface to *Tracts by Warburton and a Warburtonian :*

'While they (Leland and Jortin) were living, no balm was poured into their wounded spirits by the hand that pierced them ; and if their characters after death remain unimpaired by the rude shocks of controversy and the secret crimes of slander, their triumph is to be ascribed to their own strength, and to the conscious weakness of their antagonist, rather than to his love of justice, or his love of peace.'

In the quarrel with Jortin, the public feeling was on Jortin's side. But the sense of the public was not manifested with any thing like the strength and unanimity which was shown on the next occasion,—his controversy with Lowth,—his most desperate battle, and his last. Though Lowth had on the main issue far the best of it, yet both the combatants were severely maimed in the fight —Warburton by his enemy's spear, Lowth by his own impetuosity. As it gave a blow to Warburton's dictatorship which it never recovered, we shall give the narrative at more length.

In the year 1753 the Clarendon Press at Oxford brought
out, in a splendid quarto with all the honours of typo-
graphy, the series of Lectures which Lowth had delivered
during his ten years' occupancy of the chair of poetry in
that University. It was not the externals only of the
volume of which the University was proud. It was no
less remarkable for its matter. It was the first sign of the
awakening of Oxford from that torpor under which two
generations had now lain, under the besotting influence of
Jacobite and high-church politics. The Lectures *De
Sacra Poesi Hebraeorum* seemed to combine the polish of
a past generation, long gone, with the learning of a new
period to come. The lore of Michaelis was here dressed
out in Latin as classical as, and more vigorous than, that
of Addison. Kocher has indeed shown[1] that Lowth's
Hebrew skill was not equal to his pretensions ; and Parr
has pointed out that the professor was capable of writing
poterit after *ut.* Still the effect of the Lectures was
great. The Jacobite University had at last produced a
work which might vie in solidity with anything that proceeded from Hanoverian Göttingen, and with the finished
style of which Göttingen had nothing to compare. The
'classic elegance of Lowth' became a standard phrase,
and continued to be so till into the present century ; and
German Hebraists occupied themselves in refuting the
temerity of his numerous emendations of the Hebrew text.
In England, the monopoly of learned theology had been
for nearly twenty years in the author of the *Divine Legation*—an outsider. The tyrant of clerical literature was
not only sprung from the *plebs*, but had seized the Acro-
polis of letters over the heads of the true aristocrats of Eton
and Westminster, of King's and Christ Church. Many
murmurs had been heard from time to time from various
parts of the usurper's realm, but they had only drawn
down his vengeance upon the heads of the disaffected.

[1] Laurence, *On Translations of the Bible*, 1820.

The malcontents had been 'hung, as they do vermin in a warren, and left to posterity, to stink and blacken in the wind[1],' as a warning to the rest. The new rebel was sprung from the very core of orthodoxy, the inner guild of traditional discipline. Robert Lowth was the son and grandson of clergymen; his father was the well-known commentator, and Prebendary of Winchester. The son was a Wykehamist, a member of that close and jealous corporation—a university within the University—which was supposed in former times to exaggerate at once the faults and the excellences of the academical training. He chose to reside on his fellowship at New College, and at thirty years of age he stood forward as the most rising academic of his day. In 1741 he was placed, by the unanimous voice of the Masters of Arts, in the chair of poetry, the only possible competitor, Townson, declining to try the strength of Magdalen and Christ Church against the Wykehamist interest. The qualifications for the poetry professorship at that day were scholastic skill of Latin versification. In this art Lowth confessedly excelled his contemporaries. But in choosing the subject of his *Praelectiones* he resolved not merely to be satisfied with exhibiting the graces of his Latin style, but to instruct his auditory, inviting them into an entirely new field of criticism. 'Why,' he asked 'should we be ever repeating our eulogies of Homer and Pindar, while Moses, David, and Isaiah, poets not inferior to them, are passed by in silence?' Lowth's audience, though no judges of Hebrew, were connoisseurs in Latin ; and these Lectures, interspersed with frequent passages of tasteful Latin translation, were delivered to thronging crowds, such as professorial lecture-rooms had long ceased to hold. In the ten years (1741–1751) of Lowth's tenure of the chair, he could boast that[2] the study of Hebrew, which had been almost extinct, 'nimium diu neglectam et paene obsoletam,'

---

[1] *Warburton to Birch.*   [2] *Praelect.* 32.

had been rekindled by his exertions. In 1755 Warburton
and Lowth met on the same stage of the ladder of Church
preferment, each of them obtaining in that year a stall at
Durham.   But Warburton was fifty-seven, Lowth only
forty-five ; regular breeding had been equivalent to just
twelve years' start in the race. From this time Warburton
began to regard Lowth as his rival for the mitre. A
suppressed jealousy, embittered by the inequality of age,
made him quick to suppose meanings never meant.
Though Lowth's Lectures had appeared in the spring of
1753, it was only in the summer of 1756, the year after the
double Durham promotion, that Warburton took it into
his head to be offended with some of the criticisms in that
volume, and to look upon them as aimed against himself.
He accordingly desired two common friends, Dr. Chapman [1] and Mr. Spence,—for so, we have little doubt, ought
to be filled up the blanks in the published Correspondence,—to call upon Lowth at Winchester, and demand
satisfaction for this constructive treason. Lowth replied
to this summons by addressing a letter to the autocrat
himself. What must have been Warburton's surprise and
rage when, instead of the apologetic submission to which
he had been accustomed, he was met with the easy
courtesy of an equal, aware of his strength, and yet dis-
guising it under a thin veil of polished indifference. Had
the offender come in on his knees, with the cord round his
neck, the surrender had been graciously accepted. Had
he flown to arms, the conqueror would have dealt with
him according to precedent. The attitude which Lowth
assumed, firm without defiance, foiled Warburton. Warburton's complaint had been, that his opinion on the age
of ' Job' was controverted in the Lectures. Lowth replies
by an intimation, that he intended to pursue his critical
inquiries in any direction that might be convenient to

---

[1] [This is doubtful, as Chapman does not appear to have been a friend of
Warburton's.]

himself, without thinking it necessary to obtain leave from the author of the *Divine Legation*. As to the opinion on the age of ' Job,' as Warburton was only one of many who had held the same opinion, there was no reason why he should take the refutation all to himself. And that, in fact, however surprising it might seem, in writing the criticism in question he neither had the *Divine Legation* by him, nor was thinking of it.

The correspondence extended to several letters. Warburton saw enough of his man to see that he was one whom it would be advisable to have as a friend rather than an enemy. He determined upon a bold stroke. At the end of his fourth letter, dating from Grosvenor Square, he adds a postscript :

' I am here in waiting. I mention it to you from a selfish view. Regis (i. e. King's chaplain) of this month is dying. What should hinder your stepping into his place ?'

In the subsequent letters the tone of irritation relaxes, and from 'obedient humble servant' the correspondents leave off 'your most faithful and affectionate,' etc. So the affair rested for a time. But Warburton's tactic had not the success expected from it. Neither threats nor favours could subdue Lowth's independence of spirit. In 1763 he brought out a second edition of the *Praelectiones*, in which he not only did not modify the objectionable opinion on Job, but strengthened its point by additions which seemed unmistakably to aim at the views patronized in the *Divine Legation*. Castigation for this insolence could not be withheld without direct abdication. The next edition of the *Divine Legation*, 1765, accordingly pilloried the offender in an Appendix specially devoted to him. All temporizing was discarded, and Lowth was finally settled with his 'business being done' in a 'few strictures.' This prompt execution, however, so far from crushing the foe, only put him on his mettle. Though the dictator had in the interim become Bishop of Gloucester, Lowth was not daunted. Nay,

Warburton's promotion did but point his pen to give
words to the long-pent-up spleen with which Oxford had
regarded the gradual progress of the intruder from the
attorney's office to the bench. The manifesto appeared at
the close of the long vacation of 1765 in a 'Letter to the
Right Rev. Author of the *D. L.*,'—a pamphlet of one
hundred pages, printed at 'the Clarendon Printing-house.'
In polished dexterity of argument, tinged, and not more
than tinged, with the raillery of one who knows exactly
what is due both to himself and his antagonist, this short
piece has perhaps never been surpassed in literary
warfare. At that period of paper ruffianism, when the
courtesies of legitimate warfare were unpractised and
unknown, such moderate language, combined with such
superiority of demeanour, was wholly new. Even the
mere English composition of the 'Letter' was an event
which opened a new era in writing, and made the public
wonder that it could ever have admired the lame sentences
and clumsy English of Warburton and his followers. 'It
would be difficult to find in the English language of equal
variety and length four such compositions as Burke's
Speech to the Electors of Bristol, Johnson's Preface to
Shakespeare, Parr's Dedication, and Lowth's Letter to
Warburton[1].' Nor was it in composition only that the
author of the English Grammar had the advantage over
his antagonist. In his knowledge of the learned languages, Lowth, though a child by the side of Bentley,
was beyond his contemporaries. Learning enough to
qualify him as a critic of ancient writings he had not;
he had enough to expose the clumsy blunders of the
Divine Legation. In the correspondence of 1756 Lowth
appears to give Warburton credit for all the knowledge
which the dictator's tone arrogated to him. The closer
scrutiny of Warburton's writings to which the second
provocation led him, must have revealed to his astonish-

[1] *Diary of a Lover of Literature.*

ment that the demonstrator of the divine legation of Moses could not read the writings of Moses except in a translation,—must have awakened his suspicions that Greek was not altogether familiar to one who had talked so largely of Pythagoras and Plato and the Tὸ ῎Εν; and one or two gross mistakes in the Bishop's Latin, which Lowth pauses upon, might have led him to the further conclusion at which we have ourselves arrived, had not the incredible nature of that conclusion apparently closed Lowth's eyes to the inevitable inference from such mistranslations as those of which the bishop is guilty when he has to render Lowth's Latin where he was left without an English version to guide him.

This pamphlet contains the inimitable retort which will adhere to Warburton as long as his name continues to be mentioned among men,—'one of those lucky hits,' says Whitaker, 'which are given to the most witty and dextrous of mankind but once in a life.' The bishop had said, 'The learned professor has been hardily brought up in the keen atmosphere of *wholesome severities,* and early taught to distinguish between *de facto* and *de jure*[1].' To understand the bitterness of this taunt, we must recur to Lowth's peculiar position before the world in 1765. The University of Oxford was committed by all the traditions of seventy years to the principles of High-church and Jacobitism. Convicted of scarcely disguised disaffection to the reigning dynasty, it had been treated by successive ministries with neglect and contempt. Lowth stood forward as the foremost man and representative of this disgraced and semi-outlaw society. To fasten upon him the stigma of being the champion of disloyalty and persecuting principles, the presumed atmosphere in which Lowth had been brought up, would have been a fatal bar to his prospects in the Church. Nothing, therefore, could be more malignant than Warburton's hints, while at the

[1] *Div. Leg., Works,* vol. VI. p. 150.

same time nothing could be more unjust; for though the
public and the government were not yet aware of it, a
great change had been working in the opinions and
feelings of the University. The old High-church and
High-Tory party, of which Dr. King was the representative, had been slowly losing in numbers and influence,
and a new generation forming in a mould less alien from
the general feeling and opinion of England. To this
party, which comprehended the younger and better minds
in the University, the doctrines of the old Tory, his Stuart
attachments, and his passion for 'wholesome severities'
against Nonconformists, were already distasteful; and it
was of this party that Lowth was the representative.
Stung at once by the unfairness of the taunt and by its
damning nature, Lowth threw all his force into his reply
to it. He distinctly and emphatically repudiates, as he
could with truth, the insinuation of intolerance and persecuting tenets. 'I have never omitted any opportunity
that fairly offered itself of bearing my testimony against
these very principles, and of expressing my abhorrence of
them both in public and in private.' And then he turns
upon the bishop:

Pray, my lord, what is it to the purpose where I have been
brought up? You charge me with principles of intolerance and
disaffection to the present royal family and government. You infer
these principles, it seems, from the place of my education. Is this
a necessary consequence? Is it even a fair conclusion? May not
one have had the good sense or the good fortune to have avoided,
or to have gotten the better of the ordinary prejudices of education?
Why, then, should you think that I must still necessarily labour
under the bad influence of an atmosphere which I happened to breathe
in my youth?

To have made a proper use of the advantages of a good education,
is a just praise; but to have overcome the disadvantages of a bad one,
is a much greater. Had I not your lordship's example to justify me,
I should think it a piece of extreme impertinence to inquire where
you were bred. It is commonly said your lordship's education was

of that particular kind concerning which it is a remark of that great judge of men and manners, Lord Clarendon, that it particularly disposes them to be proud, insolent, and pragmatical. 'Colonel Harrison was the son of a butcher, and had been bred up in the place of a clerk, under a lawyer of good account in those parts ; which kind of education introduces men into the language and practice of business ; and if it be not resisted by the great ingenuity of the person, inclines young men to more pride than any other kind of breeding, and disposes them to be pragmatical and insolent.'   Now, my lord, as you have in your whole behaviour, and in all your writings, remarkably distinguished yourself by your humility, lenity, meekness, forbearance, candour, humanity, civility, decency, good manners, good temper, moderation with regard to the opinions of others, and a modest diffidence of your own, this unpromising circumstance of your education is so far from being a disgrace to you, that it highly redounds to your praise.

For myself, on the contrary, it is well if I can acquit myself of the burden of being responsible for the great advantages which I enjoyed.   For, my lord, I was educated in the University of Oxford ; I enjoyed all the advantages, both public and private, which that famous seat of learning so largely affords.   I spent many happy years in that illustrious society, in a well-regulated course of useful discipline and studies, and in the agreeable and improving commerce of gentlemen and scholars ; in a society where emulation without envy, ambition without jealousy, contention without animosity, incited industry and awakened genius ; where a liberal pursuit of knowledge, and a generous freedom of thought, was raised, encouraged, and put forward by example, by commendation, and by authority.   I breathed the same atmosphere that the Hookers, the Chillingworths, and the Lockes had breathed before. . . . . And do you reproach me with my education in this place, and this most respectable body, which I shall always esteem my greatest advantage and my highest honour ?

We must remark, by the way, the very significant fact which this controversy brings before us, that in 1765 the favourite alumnus of the Tory University finds it necessary to his self-preservation to declare himself an adherent of Locke, and to purge himself from the ruinous suspicion of having been poisoned by the persecuting principles of

Locke's opponents—'wholesome severities' had been the cant phrase of the Tory party in the controversy on toleration in 1688.

Lowth's victory was complete. Warburton had the discretion to attempt no answer. 'Whatsoever might be the merits of an insignificant controversy,' says Gibbon[1], 'Lowth's victory was clearly established by the silent confession of Warburton and his slaves.' It was, too, as public a triumph as the most ambitious man could have desired. Never had the public taken a keener interest in any literary dispute. Lowth's 'Letter' went through four editions in eighteen months. It had indeed this good fortune, that it appeared precisely in the interval between the proceedings against Wilkes and the Stamp Act, and the public attention was not preoccupied by greater matters. The town hailed, with the Monthly Reviewers, the fall of 'the haughty and overbearing Colossus,' and the 'ample vengeance that had been taken upon the imperious aggressor.' The newspapers teemed with squibs, parodies, and *jeux d'esprit.* Even the king participated in the interest generally felt. George III, in that celebrated interview in the Queen's Library, called for Johnson's opinion of the controversy, which 'his Majesty seemed to have read[2].'

But Lowth had committed one error of judgment, of so grave a nature as not only to mar his triumph, but even in some measure to compromise his character as a man of the world. At the end of his pamphlet he gave an 'Appendix containing a former literary correspondence.' These were the letters that had passed between himself and Warburton in 1756; thus publishing Warburton's letters without asking his permission. Lowth's general behaviour throughout his life was that of a gentleman. We are therefore compelled to think that on this occasion he was guilty only of an inadvertence. But it was an inadvertence

---

[1] *Memoirs of My Life.*   [2] Boswell, 1767.

which gave the enemy the only point of advantage he obtained in the affair. Warburton could say, with justice, 'Is not this universally esteemed dishonourable conduct, to publish a man's letters without his knowledge and consent?' Mr. Watson says Warburton 'affected to complain.' But it is evident that public opinion justified the complaint, and that Lowth himself immediately became aware of the false step he had taken. He became angry, as a man so often does, at his own blunder. He vented his rage in some very intemperate letters to the bishop, who, as Johnson represented the affair, drew him on to expose himself, and then asked his leave to publish the correspondence, which he knew Lowth could not refuse after what he had done. After such a rencontre, and between men of such ripe age, it might have been thought the foes never could have met again. But they did do so; and the reconciliation is one among the many evidences we can cite of the goodness of heart and placability of temper which lurked beneath Warburton's coarse and rude exterior.

Lowth's victory had been won by the weapon of refined irony and sarcasm, against which the Warburtonian cudgel was a very poor defence. If any of Warburton's contemporaries could have handled this weapon against him, it might have been expected that Bolingbroke would have been the man. Between Bolingbroke and Warburton, ever since their meeting at Murray's table, there had been deadly hatred, 'Ira fuit capitalis, ut ultima divideret mors.' But Bolingbroke chose to use the stick instead of the rapier; and instead of setting down, as he alone could, *de haut en bas*, the insolent adventurer, has merely scattered over his pages the epithets of vulgar abuse,—'scribbler,' 'stupid fellow,' etc.,—in which Warburton himself dealt.

It is on record that he was set down in company by Quin on more than one occasion. One of these is related, perhaps improved, by Horace Walpole. Warburton was haranguing in behalf of prerogative. Quin said, 'Pray, my lord, spare me; you are not acquainted with my principles; I am a republican; and perhaps I even think that the execution of Charles I may be justified.' 'Ay,' said Warburton, 'by what law?' Quin replied, 'By all the laws that he had left them.' The bishop would have got off upon judgments, and bade the player remember that all the regicides came to violent ends. 'That, if I am not mistaken, was also the case of the twelve Apostles,' was Quin's reply. Walpole comments on this: 'There was great wit *ad hominem* in the latter reply; but I think the former equal to anything I ever heard.'

The other, though not so good as a story, was, no doubt, made very effective by Quin's acting. When Quin was staying at Prior Park, Warburton always made a point of addressing him in a way to make him feel that he was an actor. One evening he begged Quin, whom he should never see on the stage, to oblige the company with a specimen of his great powers. Quin replied, that plays were then almost out of his head, but that he would declaim a passage out of *Venice Preserved.* He stood up and gave the passage which contains the words:

> Honest men
> Are the soft easy cushions on which knaves
> Repose and fatten.

As he pronounced the words 'honest men' and 'knaves,' he took care that the application to Allen and Warburton should not be lost on the assembled company.

Warburton's friends were certainly not so numerous as his enemies. The first place is of course due to Hurd, whose name is as inseparably united with that of Warburton as Boswell with Johnson. Hurd was a man who, having many qualities that obtain respect, and none that attach regard, has been more hardly treated by the biographers than he deserved to be. That he provoked a peculiar animosity among his contemporaries may well be understood. For if men ill brooked the domineering arrogance of Warburton, they were little likely to tolerate the irritable superciliousness of Warburton's toady.

The 'terse, neat, little, thin man,' as one of his college contemporaries describes him, was sadly deficient in the warmth and geniality which the impetuous and choleric Warburton possessed in excess. This contrast of character promoted the intimacy which sprang up between the two. Of the origin of their acquaintance we have Hurd's own account:

For the first years of residence at the University, when I was labouring through the usual courses of logic, mathematics, and philosophy, I heard little of your name and writings; and the little I did hear was not likely to encourage a young man that was under direction to inquire farther. In the mean time I grew up into the use of a little common-sense; my commerce with the people of the place was enlarged. . . . . When I became B.A., I was led by a spirit of perverseness to see what there was in these decried volumes that had given such offence. I wished, perhaps out of pure spite, to find the invectives I had heard unfounded.

I took the *Divine Legation* with me down into the country, where I was going to spend the summer of 1741 with my friends. I read there the three volumes at my leisure, and with an impression I shall never forget. I returned to college the winter following, not so properly your convert, as all over spleen and prejudice against your defamers. From that time I am to date my friendship with you.

He means, that he had formed a friendship for Warburton from reading his books, before making his acquaintance. Towards the commencement of their personal intimacy Hurd made the first advance in print by a compliment in his Commentary on Horace, sending Warburton, at the same time, a copy of the book. But the rosewater of dedications in those days so usually turned to vinegar, that a peculiar adaptation of the pair to each other was necessary to cement a union so firm and lasting as that which ensued between them. The equivalents in this combina-

tion of dissimilar characters have been touched by the
master-hand of a critic, whose genius was buried beneath
genealogical parchments and the minutiae of parochial
history—Thomas Dunham Whitaker.

It is not always true, in fact, that unequal friendships (we mean
those of unequal minds) are quite as frail as they are represented.
Great men, especially in the decline of life, often grow indolent con-
versers; they love to dictate rather than dispute; they decline the
irritating and laborious collision of equal intellects; and an humble
friend, just able to understand, and very willing to applaud, is a
more acceptable companion than an equal, who dares to contradict,
and who may chance to confute. If Warburton were a tyrant, he
was a magnanimous tyrant, and, the point of unconditional submission once secured, a warm and generous friend. Over the mind of
Pope himself, in his declining years, the friend and commentator
enjoyed an ascendant unperceived, it may be, by the bard himself.
In his intercourse with Murray and Yorke, his ferocity was blunted,
not by timid assent, but by the impenetrable and unassailable
polish of high breeding. Under the predominant and overbearing
influence of a superior mind, Hurd, in addition to an affection as
warm as his constitution was capable of, is understood to have
been uniformly supple and obsequious. In all the extravagance of
his wildest hypotheses, assailed by the contradiction of scholars and
the laughter of wits, Warburton had one kindred bosom on which he
could repose, one understanding which never questioned the legitimacy of his reasonings, or failed to perceive the validity of his
conclusions.

Nothing can be added, it appears to us, to the delicate
precision of this classical passage, to which Parr's laboured
comparison of Hurd and Warburton is as inferior in truth
as it is in expression. Parr entitled his pamphlet *Tracts
by Warburton and a Warburtonian.* By 'a Warburtonian'
is meant Hurd. For though 'the Warburtonian School'
is a phrase of common occurrence in the writings of the
end of the 18th century, Hurd is really the only man
to whom the designation properly applies. We may
perhaps include Brown[1] and Towne. Towne was arch-

---

[1] [John Brown (1715-1756) of the 'Estimate.']

deacon of Stowe, and a man of considerable reading. He had studied Warburton's writings with such attention, that Warburton was wont to say that Towne understood them better than himself.   He wrote a good deal, but so badly that Warburton, who revised for him, used to complain that 'he had more trouble in reforming the style and method of them than it would have cost him to write the whole fresh in his own manner.'

Dr. Brown was at one time an obsequious attendant on Warburton.   Dr. Monsey once dined at Garrick's in company with them both.   After dinner, Garrick checked Monsey, who was running on in what Garrick thought too free a style.   'Oh,' said Brown, 'you may be sure Dr. Monsey will restrain his humour before Dr. Warburton, as he is afraid of him.'   Monsey retorted, 'I am afraid neither of Warburton nor of his jackpudding!' Afterwards Brown fell off from his allegiance.   Two years before his melancholy end, he observed that he was sorry for having far overpainted Warburton[1].   'I cannot bring myself,' said he, 'to give up the freedom of my mind to Warburton, and therefore we do not agree.   Dr. Hurd will never quarrel with him.'

Warburton's reputation by his writings, his controversies, his connexions, and the confessed ascendancy of his talents and temper, was already higher than that of any other clergyman in the Church of the same standing. Yet the author of the *Divine Legation*, of the *Alliance*, and of *Julian*, still remained in a country parish; and, but for his marriage with Allen's niece, he might have died rector of Brant-Broughton.   Pope had shown much anxiety to bring him 'in the way of some proud and powerful persons,' and had actually made some application for him through Lord Granville, but without effect.   But Pope died in 1744, and even had he lived, the Pelhams required other influence than such as Pope could exert.

---

[1] [Watson, p. 586, from Davies's Garrick, I. 42.]

Dedications were all in vain. Edwards twitted him with this in the *Canons of Criticism.* 'The first edition of the *Alliance* was presented to all the bishops; when nothing came of that, the second was addressed to both the Universities; and when nothing came of that, the third was dedicated to a noble earl; and nothing has yet come of that.' His marriage, however, in 1745, which gave him a new position, a wealthy home, and a political connexion, entirely altered his prospects. From this moment the career of his preferment was uninterrupted and rapid. In 1746 he became preacher of Lincoln's Inn, through Murray, the solicitor-general. In 1753, prebendary of Gloucester, from Lord Hardwicke; in 1754, king's chaplain; in 1755, prebendary of Durham, through Murray, now attorney-general; in 1757, dean of Bristol, from Pitt, whom Allen had just brought in for Bath; and finally, in 1759, he was advanced to the bishopric of Gloucester.

These are the plain facts, which biographical decorum still persists in rendering into 'William Warburton, whose talents and learning raised him from a humble station to the highest honours of his profession,' etc.

Hurd had seen a letter of Pitt (Earl of Chatham), in which he said that 'nothing of a private nature, since he had been in office, had given him so much pleasure as his bringing Dr. Warburton upon the bench.' Warburton himself regarded these honours with a manly indifference, which is one of the best traits in his character. It was impossible for him to be insensible to the attractions of preferment, more especially at a period when, more than at most times, so much of a clergyman's thoughts was absorbed by them. If his mind had not turned in that direction of itself, it must have been drawn into it by the constant hints of friends and correspondents. His own letters are tinged with expectancy; but it is kept under by a real superiority of nature, and by an intellect occupied with other thoughts. Occasionally only a hint is dropped in public, as where he tells Lord Chesterfield, in the dedication of a new edition of the *Alliance*, that 'of all the strange connexions which the revolutions of time bring about, the rarest and most accidental is that between merit and reward.' He was well aware of what those around him were about, and his pride kept him from falling into ways of petty intrigue, which he saw through and despised. He writes to Mr. Jane:

> The general body of the clergy have been, and, I am afraid, always will be, very intent upon pushing their temporal fortunes,—a fact so apparent to government, both civil and ecclesiastical, that they have found it necessary to provide rewards and honours for such advances in learning and piety as may best enable the clergy to serve and advance the interests of the Church of Christ. . . . I endeavoured to show, that if these rewards and honours be so mis-employed, that instead of giving them to learning and merit, they were diverted upon such as can only promote the interests and flatter the passions of the great, young men, upon entrance into life, seeing how matters were carried, would be tempted rather to cultivate the sordid arts of intrigue and adulation, than the liberal endowments of learning and piety.

It would be difficult to find a more naked avowal of the dependence of the supply of 'learning and piety' upon the demand created by endowments. He who thought thus of others shared largely, it cannot be doubted, in their motives. All that can be said is, that while inferior men were entirely dominated by such sordid views, Warburton's larger nature could never be so absorbed. We must remember, too, that before promotion came within his reach he was already in comfortable, if not affluent, circumstances. Allen left Mrs. Warburton £5000, and the reversion, on Mrs. Allen's death, of £3000 a year. Warburton too had made a considerable sum by his writings,—e. g. for his edition of *Shakespeare* he had £560 from Tonson. And besides his own books, he had the copyright of Pope's works. So that altogether, when

Paul Knapton the publisher failed in 1755, Warburton was the largest creditor.

We cannot therefore wonder, when at the age of fifty-five his first preferment came to him, that he viewed it with indifference. He had been reluctant to take the preachership at Lincoln's Inn seven years before, though the society had done him the unprecedented honour of making him the offer of it. The trouble of writing the sermons, the five or six months' attendance in town, and the additional house-rent, were not compensated, to his mind, by the distinction. When the stall at Gloucester came in 1753, Dr. Birch gave him instruction as to the mode of taking possession, observing that 'it was so long since he had had any preferment, that he must have forgotten all the formalities.' 'There was another thing,' said Warburton, 'he did not dream of; that it is so long since I had occasion to inquire about the formalities, that I am become very indifferent about the things themselves.' His health too was becoming such as to detract from all enjoyment. Soon after his appointment to the bishopric we find him complaining of his 'usual dizziness,' in a way that implies it to be no new visitant. He made attempts to complete the *Divine Legation*, writing portions of the ninth book, Hurd says, 'by snatches, and with difficulty,' and unable to make any real progress with it. The ninth book remains a fragment, and has scarce any trace of the merits of the early books. It has, besides, inconsistencies of expression and lapses of memory, sad indications of failing faculty, such, e. g., as speaking of St. Paul as author of the Epistle to the Hebrews[1], whereas in 1741 he had been careful, through a long argument, to observe the distinction[2]. Mr. Watson says he is 'generally supposed' to have held the non-Pauline origin of the epistle. We do not know on what authority

[1] *Works*, VI. p. 309.
[2] *Works*, V. p. 430 seq.

this is supposed; and against his opinion in 1741 we may set his opinion in 1738, when he cites the Hebrews as St. Paul's. The inconsistency is only curious as show-ing the inconstant nature of his ideas, which only became fixed when they were opposed. Had any disputant chal-lenged either the one or the other of these 'opinions' on the authorship of Hebrews, we can imagine the fury with which it would have been defended, and the 'folly and knavery' which would have been imputed to the alternative view.

In his sixty-ninth year we find him complaining of rheumatism in the shoulder, of a disorder of the gall-bladder, with symptoms of gravel, for which he was desired to drink the Selzer-waters, then just come into fashion. The pains he at first thought rheumatic, he afterwards suspected to be 'St. Anthony's fire.' More rapid than the strides of physical were those of mental decay. It showed itself as disinclination before it became incapacity. Very early in his work he required the stimulus of compulsion to rouse his mind to effort. In 1741 he had recourse to the expedient of setting the press prematurely to work, that he might be forced to supply it with copy. That part of the *Divine Legation* (viz. books IV, V, VI) written under this artificial pressure betrays its origin in its manifest inferiority in vigour to the fresh and spontaneous offspring of his earliest thoughts. In 1766 he had lost the power of exciting himself to effort by any device, and shrank, disheartened and disgusted, from the task of completing his great work. Looking back in 1770 upon some of his writings, he says, 'The retrospect is accompanied with a mortifying conviction that the time is past when I was able to write with that force. Expect to find in my future writings the marks of intellectual decay.' 'You talk,' says he again to Hurd, 'of your golden age of study long past. For myself, I can only say I have the same appetite for knowledge and learned converse I ever had, though not the same appetite for writing and printing. It is time to begin to live for myself; I have lived for others longer than they deserved of me.' Hurd, who wrote much more freely to Mrs. Warburton than to his patron, marked the rapid decline, and in 1771 took occasion to assure Mrs. Warburton that 'the bishop would now write no more.' She communicated this to her husband, who heard it with composure. He replied to Hurd that he had received the news 'with an approving smile. I was charmed with the tenderness of friendship, which conveyed in so inoffensive a manner that fatal secret which Gil Blas was incapable of doing as he ought to the Archbishop of Granada.' The seasons began to tell more on him. He had always considered the months of February and March to be his sterile season. In 1769 he writes (aet. 71):

I think you have heard me say that my delicious season is the autumn, the season which gives most life and vigour to my mental faculties. The light mists, or, as Milton calls them, the steams, that rise from the fields in one of these mornings give the same relief to the view that the blue of the plum gives to the appetite. But I now enjoy little of this pleasure compared to what I formerly had in an autumn morning, when I used, with a book in my hand, to traverse the delightful lanes and hedgerows round about the town of Newark, the unthinking place of my nativity. Besides, my rheumatism now keeps me within in a morning, till the sun has exhaled the blue of the plum.

'Old age,' he truly says, 'is a losing game.' Yet, with his robust frame and strictly temperate habits,—not only temperate, but abstinent, in eating and drinking, is Bishop Newton's testimony,—we should have hardly expected to find this failing from age before seventy. He speaks of himself as a 'slender supper-man,' and as 'being obliged to old age, like Cato, for having diminished his care for eating and drinking, while it increased his desire for conversation.' But excess in food is not the only excess that revenges itself on the constitution. He had discounted life in those nights of prolonged study at Brant-Broughton. A voracious appetite for reading had been indulged without restraint, for a time with impunity. But the hour was come when it had to be paid for; and, like Swift, Scott, and Southey at the same age and from the same cause, Warburton outlived himself. The death of his only son, of consumption, in 1775, gave the final blow. It put an end to his labours and amusements.

Not, says Hurd, that his memory and faculties, though very much impaired, were ever wholly disabled. I saw him so late as October 1778, when I went into his diocese to confirm for him. On our first meeting, before his family, he expressed his concern that I should take that journey, and put myself to so much trouble on his account. . . . The evening before I left, he desired the family to withdraw, and then entered into a confidential discourse with me on some private affairs with as much pertinence as he could have done in any former part of his life. Such was the power he had over his mind when roused to exert himself by some interesting occasion. But this was an effort which could not be sustained. In less than half an hour the family returned, and he relapsed into his usual forgetfulness and inattention (*Life*, p. 93).

The melancholy scene was closed 7th June, 1779, in the eighty-first year of his age and the nineteenth of his episcopate. Just before his death a momentary rally of his faculties took place. He asked his attendant in a quiet, rational tone, 'Is my son really dead or not?' The servant hesitated, and the bishop repeated the question. The attendant then answered, 'As your lordship presses the question, I must say, he is dead.' 'I thought so,' said Warburton, and soon after expired. He had been forgotten by the world long before his decease; and when he actually passed to the tomb, it was without more notice than a few lines in the *Gentleman's Magazine.* His works were not collected till 1788, and the impression then limited to 250 copies, the public having shown, as Parr insinuated, 'some inauspicious symptoms of indifference about Warburton's writings.' The fame, however, of the *Divine Legation* underwent a revival in the course of time; and besides taking an octavo edition of the Works in 1811, the public called for several reprints of the principal treatise.

In the performance of his episcopal duties Warburton has been censured as remiss. And Whitaker has expressed this opinion strongly. But we must not judge a bishop of the eighteenth century by what is expected of one at this day. Yet when Hurd acknowledges that though 'he performed the ordinary duties of his office with regularity; further than this he could not prevail with himself to go,'—we cannot deny that there must have been some foundation for such a conclusion. Habits of study, so fixed that they cannot be thrown aside, no doubt interfere with pastoral vigilance; and Warburton himself, we are told, confessed that they did so in his case. Yet we cannot wish that theological learning should be excluded from the bench, and bishops become the tail of the paper-kite of opinion. And there were other causes, physical and moral, which made him an inactive bishop over and above that now assigned. Of these, the chief must undoubtedly be sought in failing vigour. For though the symptoms of decline did not manifest themselves as grave till 1764, yet the influence must have begun to make itself felt as an impediment to exertion some time before. It is his '*usual* dizziness for which he is going to be bled.'

It was perhaps as well that he was thus disabled for diocesan activity; for his peremptory despotic temper unfitted him for dealing with men. Regarding the Church, as he did, exclusively as an institution of government, his manner with his clergy was that of an officer to the common soldier. He knew not the arts of persuasion; and if he was resisted, he could only either sulk or cajole. This is the way he writes to a clergyman of his diocese.

The Rev. John Andrews was suspected of Methodism, but had also written an insignificant pamphlet against the *Divine Legation.*

> MR. ANDREWS,—I have received several complaints of you. Those which concern your own curacy are on account of your frequent absence, and for not giving your parish service both morning and afternoon on a Sunday. Unless I have satisfaction on these two particulars, I shall revoke your license. I shall insist on your constant residence, not so much from the good you are likely to do there, as to prevent the mischief you may do by rambling about in other places.—Your bishop, and, though your fanatic conduct has almost made me ashamed to own it, your patron,   W. GLOUCESTER.

He tells Hurd that the effect of some directions he had issued will 'depend upon the clergy's observing my direction; an attention to me which I do not expect.' He was indeed little likely to obtain more attention than he could enforce at the law's point. Mr. Watson gives some passages from his Charges, which truly are not composed to the prim decorum of our day. But here again it must be remembered that bishops formerly addressed their clergy as a king did his parliament,—in much more familiar and easy tones than are now thought suitable. Bating some eccentric and truly Warburtonian metaphors, the passages produced do not strike us as remarkably differing from the pulpit style of the day. After all, he must occasionally have been carried by his impetuosity in preaching beyond the limits even then prescribed. Mr. Cradock has reported of one sermon preached at St. Lawrence's on behalf of the London Hospital, that a few passages in it were ludicrous; and that when he proceeded to describe some monks who had robbed their own begging-boxes, he excited 'more than a smile' among his audience. Cradock told Hurd afterwards he was not sorry he had not been there; 'for I know you would not absolutely have approved.' 'Approved, sir!' replied Hurd; 'I should have agonised.'

National Review, 1863.]

But his great defect as a minister of religion was his want of religious earnestness. We shall have occasion a little further on to notice this in its influence on his theological writings. We only refer to it now, because the secular and official tone which appears in all their ministerial relations is ultimately traceable to that want of personal religion common to Warburton with a large part of his contemporaries.

The slow approaches of mental infirmity will also account for his disappointing expectation in the House of Lords; if indeed any other explanation is wanting than that which Curran gave of Flood's failure in the British Parliament,—that an oak of the forest cannot be transplanted at fifty. Hurd says he had heard of a 'certain minister' who dreaded Warburton's promotion, and thought he would turn out 'a second Atterbury.' But, as Warburton himself told the Duke of Cumberland, 'haranguing is a trade, like other trades, which the bishops generally come to this bench too old to learn.' His only reported appearance was in 1763, on the occasion when Lord Sandwich brought Wilkes's *Essay on Woman* before the House. The business was altogether an unlucky one, being mismanaged by the prosecutors of Wilkes from first to last. But though we may justly disregard the opinion of Horace Walpole and the men about town, that Warburton 'made himself ridiculous' in it[1], yet he had the bad taste to occupy the House with himself and his labours in 'defence of revelation,' and to sound his own praises in the style of his later prefaces. This, too, apropos of a ruined profligate like Wilkes! Nothing that could have been hit upon could have served that demagogue's purposes better than Lord Sandwich's attack, and Warburton's defence of himself.

Of Warburton's manner in society the notices preserved are extremely meagre. The little that is recorded goes to

[1] *Letters,* I. 312.

bear out Hurd's representation, according to which the
overbearing tone of his books was not carried into company, or only showed itself as a disposition 'to take a
somewhat larger share of the conversation than very exact
breeding is thought to allow.'   Malone has preserved an
anecdote of his meeting with Burke.   Burke sat next
Warburton at dinner without knowing who he was, and at
last observed, 'I think it is impossible I can mistake, you
must be Dr. Warburton.' Johnson and Warburton appear
to have met but twice.   Johnson's own account of one
of these meetings was: 'At first he looked surlily at
me; but after we had been jostled into conversation, he
took me to a window, asked me some questions; and
before we parted was so well pleased with me, that he
patted me.'   Johnson always remembered with gratitude
that he had been praised by Warburton at a time (1745)
when, as Macaulay says, to be praised by Warburton was
no light thing.   And he did not know the contemptuous
and brutal language in which Warburton had written of
him to Hurd only two years after the 'praise.' 'Of this
Johnson, you and I, I believe, think much alike.   His
remarks have in them as much folly as malignity.' Dr.
Kippis, who had seen Warburton once, found him 'instructive and entertaining.' And one more conversant in the
society of the best men of the day, Charles Yorke, who had
met him frequently, describes the fluency and correctness
of his conversation as 'beyond most men,' though marred
by his turn for paradox.

To his own family and connexions, where he doubtless
received all the deference he exacted, he was attached and
generous.   He watched over, and provided for, the family
of a sister, who were 'the more endeared to him by their
sole dependence on him.' And he reckoned it a lucky
year in which he married a niece to a reputable grocer at
York, and got a commission in the artillery for a nephew.
The commentator on Pope, who thought that 'every

woman is at heart a rake,' may have shared in the degrading estimate of the sex common to the generation of Walpole and Chesterfield. And he spoke in theory of woman as a being 'in whose capricious and variable fancy discordant and monstrous ideas are, by the force of the passions, whimsically daubed on at random.' But in practice, married at the age of forty-seven, he lived happily with Mrs. Warburton for thirty-four years. This notwithstanding an irritable temper, which made the arrival of a visitor, to pour oil on the bishop's vinegar, occasionally not an unwelcome domestic incident. 'Your gentleness wins,' he said to Hurd, 'where my roughness revolts.' Mrs. Warburton is described to us as 'elegant in her person, possessed of an excellent understanding, great politeness, and an engaging *naïveté* in conversation.' After thirty-four years' experience of married life, she entered the state a second time within two years after Warburton's death. She died in 1796.

Of the durability of his affection in friendship a touching instance is recorded by (we believe) Mr. Markland. One day in his last years, the character of Pope was being freely censured in his presence, the party not supposing the bishop capable of attending to what was passing. He suddenly woke up, and exclaimed, 'Who talks against Pope? He was the best of friends, and best of men,' and then relapsed into his former insensibility[1]. Yet his friendship with Pope had been built on the quicksand of literary flattery; a treacherous foundation, which had given way in the cases of Middleton, Richardson, and Jortin. His placability was equal to his irritability. He patted Johnson, as we have seen, after his preface to *Shakespeare.* He was reconciled to Lowth after receiving his most signal overthrow at his hands. It is told[2] that for some years he had not been on speaking terms with Tucker, dean of Gloucester. On a Good Friday they met

---

[1] *British Critic,* April, 1841. [2] Barker's *Parriana,* I. 345.

at the holy table, when the bishop was administering. On giving the cup to the dean, he stooped down and said, with tremulous emotion, ' Let this cup be the cup of reconciliation between us.'

We have already related some of Warburton's more signal enmities. They are samples only of a whole career. Nay, the man himself is in this but the representative man of his age. Theological literature was a Babel of loud vociferation, coarse contradiction, and mean imputation. The prize in this *mêlée* was to the noisiest lungs and the foulest tongue. The Warburtonians must not bear the blame alone; nor was the disease of detraction confined to divines[1]. The progress of refinement cannot tame the passions, but has curbed the directness with which they then vented themselves in words. Even now malignant imputation, banished from higher literature, still lingers in clerical controversy. But, after every deduction made, we still find there rests upon the Warburtonian school an extraordinary opprobrium on the score of dirt-throwing. Warburton's superiority and his generous temper ought to have exempted him from this weakness of inferior writers. Instead of that he is the worst offender. He rejoices in ' chastising'—*saevo laetus negotio*. He considers it on principle ' suitable to his clerical function to hunt down, as good King Edgar did his wolves, that pestilent herd of libertine scribblers with which the island is overrun.' Only half a generation later, Johnson, quite as irritable, and almost as much libelled by critics as Warburton, set the noble example of taking no notice of attacks. ' A hundred bad writers,' says Macaulay, ' misrepresented him and reviled him ; but not one of the hundred could boast of having been thought by him worthy of a retort.' It may be said that the mutual abuse in which Warburton and his contemporaries indulge in print is bad taste, and

[1] [See *Tendencies of Religious Thought*, etc. p. 88.]

nothing more. It is, in fact, of a piece with the lavish compliments which friends and correspondents unblush- ingly offer each other,—compliments which, on the slightest offence, they were ready to exchange for savage invective; and the one had as little meaning as the other. That their rounded and fulsome compliments and their contumelious insults are gross faults in taste, is true. But they are surely something more. The manners of the ruffian here betray the morals of the savage. This prevailing license of censure is only another side of that want of depth of character which marks every product of that frivolous and superficial age. Their manners, their politics, their literature, their theology, all bear the same stamp. Never was there an age in which there was less zeal and more vehemence, less faith and more demon- stration of 'revelation.' Knowledge and the power of weighing evidence had vanished for a time, and a talkative opinionativeness overspread the world of books. Such writers could not respect each other. Conscious of the want of solid worth, they endeavoured to supply its place by forming coteries for mutual laudation, and for setting down their enemies. Such a coterie was Pope's, and the *Dunciad* the public vehicle of its resentments and its favouritism. It was a great stroke of policy on Warbur- ton's part by which he became legatee and proprietor of this private pillory, though he afterwards erected an independent and original scaffold of his own in the notes to the *Divine Legation.* The Warburtonians—i. e. Warbur- ton and Hurd—kept each other in countenance by the same device. The more the tide of opposition ran against them, the more cloying became the mutual eulogies, the more sweeping the denunciations of every body else. We can trace the gradual strengthening of this delusion in the correspondence between the two, till they have arrived at the conviction at last that all the worth, sense, and talent in England is concentrated in themselves.

Hurd says he gives the Letters 'to this wretched world, to shame it into a better opinion of that excellent man, by showing the regard he had to real merit.' If we except Balguy and Towne, we shall find no other single name mentioned in these letters except coupled with an expression of contempt. Hurd's favourite word is 'coxcomb.' 'Toup is certainly well skilled in the Greek tongue, but with all this he is a piece of a coxcomb.' He writes against Leland 'out of pure indignation, as a coxcomb.' Priestley is 'a wretched coxcomb.' Bishop Shipley is 'a very coxcomb'; and Dr. Chapman 'an insolent coxcomb.' Of Dr. Richard Farmer he knows nothing; but he is 'an author,' and 'the prince of coxcombs is the scribbling coxcomb.' He may well ask in naïve astonishment, 'How is it there are so many coxcombs,—indeed, so many, one hardly meets with anything else?' Warburton, who unites in his own person 'the virtues of Aristotle and Longinus,' finds more variety in the characters by which this wretched world is peopled. Johnson is 'this Johnson,' of whom Warburton and Hurd 'think much alike.' Jortin is 'as vain as he is dirty.' Dean Tucker has 'a flow of transcendent nonsense.' Priestley is a 'wretched fellow'; and Voltaire 'a scoundrel.' Young is the 'finest writer of nonsense of this or any age;' Rutherforth 'the meanest pedant of the age.' Spence is 'an extreme poor creature.' Smollett is 'a vagabond Scot, who writes nonsense ten thousand strong.' Taylor has 'less understanding than the dunce Webster.' Jackson is 'a wretch who has spent his days in one unvaried course of begging, railing, and stealing.' Romaine 'has amazingly played the scoundrel.' The court is an 'earthly pandemonium'; and the church, 'like Noah's ark, full of unclean beasts and vermin.' These are not citations from angry philippics hurled against assailants under provocation; it is their settled and habitual mode of thinking and speaking of their contemporaries. One, at least, of the correspondents was so well satisfied of the justice of these opinions, that he printed them for publication, after the interval of thirty years, to show the world the regard the pair had 'to real merit.' And Warburton himself boasted to the House of Lords of his zeal in 'defence of revelation,' 'services' to which he attributed all the abuse that had been heaped upon him. Though Horace Walpole found this appeal ridiculous, yet it could not have been made without the expectation of sympathy. In his own age the violence of Warburton passed for zeal on behalf of religion. The generation which thought Butler 'too little vigorous' did not think Warburton's bluster out of place. A few cultivated men even then, like Charles Yorke, may have disapproved. Charles Yorke was the only friend who could address Warburton in terms other than those of submissive adulation. His station, talents, tact, and power of serving Warburton retained for him a superior influence over a temper to which all others gave way. He ventured to hint to Warburton that 'the unguarded sallies of a generous mind' might be sometimes 'too warm,' and were 'scarce forgiven' him[1]. This is the solitary protest against vindicating religion by foul language which proceeded from a contemporary.

Their contemptuous violence towards others argues a defect of moral breadth in themselves. It is, further, an indication of want of intellectual breadth. The greatest minds, fully possessed by great objects, are never controversial. In contrasting himself with Lessing, Goethe drew two contrasted types of men. 'Lessing's polemical instincts make him at home in the region of contradictions; he is great in distinctions. I am different; I never dealt in contradictions; I have given utterance only to results.' If this contrast be true of life, it holds good equally of religious life. By an intellect which is habitually filled

[1] Sept. 30, 1746.

M 2

with the wisdom which is from heaven in all its length and breadth, 'objections' against religion are perceived at once to proceed from imperfect apprehension. Such an intellect cannot rage against those who give words to such objections. It sees that the objectors do but intimate the partial character of their own knowledge. Warburton, like his contemporaries, approached religion from the outside. They never got beyond the scaffolding. They added demonstration to demonstration, till the thing to be proved grew more and more obscure behind the forest of arguments. Warburton was essentially one of these demonstrators. He had no real grasp of the essence of religion, or he would have understood that it did not possess that character of certainty which he attributed to his own reasonings. What Mr. Gladstone has said of his *Alliance* is equally applicable to all his writings:

The greatest intellectual defect of [the *Alliance*, &c.] appears to be the absolute and rigid form of its propositions in indeterminate subject-matter. The writer argues for his particular scheme of the support of an establishment with full toleration of dissent, and the maintenance of an exclusive test, as though it were the single and mathematically necessary result of all general arguments from the nature of the State and the Church; whereas his is, in fact, only *one* mode of constructing the social equation; adapted perhaps to one particular stage of the progression of religious freedom, but not distinguished by any inherent properties of truth from other modes, which may be equally suitable to the preceding or the following stages [1].

Warburton offers nothing to his readers that is short of moral certainty. His pages are full of the language of proof. It is evident; it necessarily follows. The *Divine Legation* is laid out on a syllogism, with a major and a minor premiss, separately established, and then the conclusion drawn. That all this logical array should fail to carry conviction on the instant, seemed to him a thing incredible. Those who withstood it must be men

---

[1] *Gladstone on Church and State*, I. p. 20.

National Review, 1863.]

of perverse minds, and must be 'chastised' into submission. Nor does he only offer his readers certainties. He sees nothing but certainties all around him; he is thoroughly convinced himself. There is no laborious groping after truth amid doubts and perplexities, to arrive, after all, at a qualified and provisional judgment. He catches from the first at some view of the case, and proceeds to make all the evidence support that view.

He has himself said of Bayle, that he 'struck into the province of paradox as an exercise for the unwearied vigour of his mind.' What he said of Bayle was applied to himself by Charles Yorke; and the application has been repeated since by all the critics who have ever sat in judgment upon Warburton. That the desire of originality influenced what he wrote is undeniable. He says arrogantly, 'It is not my manner to say what others have said before me.' And that the love of contradiction was strong in him, we have already seen abundantly. But the paradoxical taint which pervades all that Warburton has written has its cause in an intellectual foible still more vicious than the spirit of contradiction, or the ambition of originality. His so-called paradox is really a capriciousness of opinion. It is a want of judgment in the subject on which he writes. He is under the imperious necessity of adopting an opinion on every subject, without the power of forming one. His mind plunges into the bewildering chaos of fact and opinion, like the Irishman into the fight, with a 'God grant I may take the right side!' To take his side is at the beginning, and not at the end of his intellectual process. To follow the evidence up to its edge, and not beyond it, to suspend the judgment, to balance probabilities, to wait upon the slow discoveries of time and experience,—these are not Warburton's arts. He must start at once with a proposition, and then ransack libraries for material out of which to forge the proof of it. It is an injustice to Bayle to compare his paradoxes with

those of Warburton. Bayle is not seldom right. Where
Bayle runs counter to the prevailing opinion of his time,
he does so because he saw further; and posterity has
vindicated the correctness of his view by coming round to
it. Warburton, where he differs from the received opinion,
is always wrong. His paradoxes will never make a convert.
The more copious his citation, the more dexterous his
ingenuity, the more irrefragable his logic, the more
vehement his determination to make us think so, the
more the reason revolts from the demonstration. The
intellectual character exemplified by Warburton is common
enough in life. But it only attracts wonder when it is
coupled with powers and industry like Warburton's, and
dedicated to some literary theme of widely-extended
interest. In reviewing the *Divine Legation*, we cannot
help being forcibly reminded of the *Homeric Studies* of
Mr. Gladstone. The differences between the two men
are many and radical; the intellectual character of the two
works is the same. A comprehensive general reading; an
heroic industry in marshalling the particulars of the proof;
a dialectical force of arm which would twist a bar of iron
to its purposes; and all brought to bear to prove a
perverse and preposterous proposition. The mischief
done by such powerful efforts of human reason is not in
the diffusion of erroneous opinion on the subjects of which
they treat, but in setting brilliant examples of a false
method. A visionary projector carries his own refutation
with him; but when a first-rate calculator devotes his
powers to squaring the circle, there is so much method
in his madness, that his example is sure to be influential
on similarly constituted minds.

In Warburton's famous work the paradox so commonly
imputed is to be found, we conceive, not in the main
positions proposed to be proved, but in the connexion
or inference attempted to be established between the
positions; in the absolute statement of those positions

without any qualification; and lastly, in the supposition
that this connexion or inference could be shown by proof
of demonstrative cogency. Bishop Bull had remarked[1]
that in reference to the doctrine of a future state, the Old
Testament must be separated into an earlier and a later
part; and that while the Law contained no promise of
eternal life, in the Prophetic books a distinct and direct
promise could hardly be said to be found ('clarum ac
disertum promissum vix ac ne vix quidem reperias').
This guarded statement probably meets, as nearly as
possible, the exact requirements of the language of the
Jewish canon.   But it is a point of critical judgment, to be
founded on a consideration of all the passages, not admitting of being either proved or disproved.   The constant
opinion of all moderate and impartial persons has been,
as Mr. Lancaster[2] puts it, that 'this doctrine was both
recognized and countenanced, but not explicitly and
directly taught, in the Pentateuch.'   In Warburton's
hands this opinion becomes the affirmation that future
rewards and punishments were not taught in the Mosaic
dispensation at all, and that the Israelites, from the time
of Moses to the time of the Captivity, had not the doctrine
of a future state.   This he declares that he shows by the
clearest and most incontestable arguments.   Then he
proceeds to draw the inference, that a people who could
have been placed under such a system must have had an
immediate providential superintendence to replace a doctrine
which is found to be the very bond and cement of human
society.   Finally, the propositions here involved, and the
inference from one to the other, are put forward, not with
the modest diffidence of an inquirer, but with the arrogant
swagger of a demonstration, and an insulting challenge to
all the world to yield an immediate assent.   Gibbon,
speaking of one of his later productions, says: 'The
secret intentions of Julian are revealed by the late Bishop

---

[1] *Harmon. Apost.* II. 10. 8.   [2] *Harmony of Law and Gospel*, p. 409.

of Gloucester, the learned and dogmatic Warburton, who, with the authority of a theologian, prescribes the motives and conduct of the Supreme Being.'

We cannot help thinking that in the epithet 'learned' in this quotation lurks a Gibbonian sneer. No one knew better than the historian, that to have read many books and remembered their contents, is 'learning' only in a very popular acceptation of the word. But in no other sense was Warburton entitled to be called a 'learned' man. His temper was too arrogant to 'learn,' too impatient to inquire. He went the *a priori* road, and, having formed a very decided opinion, searched books to find arguments with which to support it. For some employments, for metaphysical speculation, for arbitrating between predestination and free-will, for framing an ideal polity, or for any theorizing where the facts are few and obvious, such an intellect is well fitted. But it was Warburton's ill fortune that his own bent no less than that of his age determined his pen to social and historical topics. The crying evils of society, both in France and England, were forcing the minds of men upon the consideration of their causes and their remedies. Political institutions appeared to them the most influential of these causes. The great work of Montesquieu, the *Esprit des Lois,* is the epochal book of this phase of speculation, which was only closed by the revolution of '88. To the same mode of thought must be referred Warburton's speculations, however deficient in those qualities of judgment, profound observation of human character, and attentive induction of fact, which made the *Esprit des Lois* overlive the epoch which produced it. The idea of a future state of reward and punishment employed as a restraining force over human passion and appetite in aid of civil sanctions, this view of religion, which belongs entirely to his age, Warburton took up, and the greater part of what he wrote turns on it. To detect the presence or absence of this idea through past times, and the amount of its influence at various periods, is by no means an uninteresting inquiry. But it is an inquiry which demands not only the most extensive survey of ancient literature, but a delicate appreciation of modes of thought, and an exact knowledge of the ancient languages. Of 'learning' in this sense Warburton was hopelessly destitute. That he was not a philologian of the calibre of Bentley, every one is prepared to admit. That he was not as a classical scholar equal to many of his own generation—Jortin or Markland, Lowth or Parr—may perhaps surprise no one to hear. But the truth goes far beyond even this. Warburton was wholly without any tincture of what we understand by scholarship. Of the Greek language he had scarcely any knowledge. Latin he knew very badly. He was not competent to decide upon the sense of any difficult passage in a classical author, and was wholly at the mercy of translators and commentators. Yet so impudently did he assume the privileges of a scholar, and so cleverly did he disguise his amazing ignorance, that he succeeded in imposing his opinion on the world, as one that was at least entitled to a refutation. Even his professed biographers have not sounded the depths of his deficiencies. All that Dr. Whitaker says is, 'In the mind of Warburton the foundation of classical literature had been well laid, yet not so as to pursue the science of ancient criticism with an exactness equal to the extent in which he grasped it.' And the present biographer only speaks of his 'imperfect acquaintance with Greek,' and 'unskilfulness in the niceties of Latin'; phrases far too lenient for the imposture in this respect actually practised by Warburton. The secret was divined by more than one of his contemporaries, though even by them hardly in its full extent. If we compare the correspondence with Lowth in 1756 with Lowth's letter of Sept. 1765, we see that in the interim Lowth's eyes had been opened to the fact he had not suspected,—that one who undertook in such dogmatic tone to settle the age of the book of Job, had not, and could not, read it, and that the demonstrator of Moses' legation never read the Hebrew Pentateuch! This discovery may have led him to surmise that similar dogmatism in the use of Greek and Latin concealed similar ignorance. He accordingly concludes his letter with the threat that he would take in hand the *Divine Legation*, as he had demolished the Appendix. As this threat was never executed, we have no means of knowing how far Lowth was in the secret. Upton, referring to Warburton having cited Homer in this fashion, δ' ἐνδυνε χιτῶνα καλόν, remarked that as νῦν and καί begin sentences, so might δέ for aught Warburton knew to the contrary. The Rev. Henry Taylor detected him, in citing the *Phoenissae*, copying Brumoy's French (very French) version. Dr. John Taylor had denounced him in Cambridge combination-rooms as 'no scholar.' The story bears marks of having been improved, but is perhaps not untrue in the main point. It is, that Warburton sent a friend to ask Taylor, if he had really used the words? And that Taylor replied, 'He did not remember ever having said that Warburton was no scholar, but he had certainly always thought so.' Jortin's gentle admonition in his correction of Warburton's translation of 'princeps' has been already mentioned.

Forearmed with these hints, we approach Warburton's writings with the distrust they are calculated to create. Recollecting the case of Gibbon, and considering that want of the language of the Greeks does not absolutely exclude a critic from *all* use of the wisdom of the Greeks, we could not say beforehand that Warburton might not have ascertained correctly some of the forms of Greek life and opinion, and reasoned soundly upon them. A cautious man, conscious of labouring under one heavy disqualification for the task he had undertaken, might have done this. But Warburton was not conscious of the limited range of his acquirements in Greek and Latin, and was the reverse of cautious. He thought he could refute Bentley; he had 'a very poor opinion of both Markland and Taylor's critical abilities [1]'; and he confidently undertook to emend the text, not only of Shakespeare, but of Cicero and Velleius Paterculus. The emendations of Paterculus which he sent to the *Bibliothèque Britannique* in 1736 were specimens of an edition which he contemplated. Of the loss that letters have sustained by the non-execution of this scheme, one example may enable the reader to judge. Speaking of Cumae and Neapolis, two Greek settlements in Italy, the text of Velleius had 'Utriusque urbis semper eximia in Romanos fides. Sed aliis diligentior ritus patrii mansit custodia. Cumanos Osca mutavit vicinia.' 'Aliis' in this passage is certainly not above suspicion, and Ruhnken printed 'illis;' a neat conjecture, which has been received with the favour it deserved. Warburton's note is: 'I read, *sed Neapolis diligentior ritus patrii mansit custodia*; which makes it a pertinent observation, and worthy the notice of an exact historian. And it is not difficult to conceive *Neapolis* being corrupted to *aliis* by a stupid copier.' We cannot help Mr. Selby Watson in his grave perplexity, whether 'he means *Neapolis* for *Neapolitanis*, or for the genitive case of *Neapolis*.' But the critic who could turn Shakespeare's 'past the *infinite* of thought' [2] into 'past the *definite* of thought'; who could explain 'prayers from preserved souls' [3] as a metaphor taken from fruit *preserved* in sugar, will scarcely be thought to have more skill in his own language than in Latin. We could fill a page with his verbal mistakes; show him restricting ἀθάνατος to the immortality of gods; explaining δεισιδαιμονία as the fear of demons or inferior gods; and misconstruing his own citations so frequently, that at last we cannot avoid thinking that he does not apprehend the meaning of

[1] *Letter to Birch.*   [2] *Much Ado,* II. 3.   [3] *Measure for Measure,* II. 2.

Vergil's 'sub luce maligna[1],' or understand 'testari' in its sense of 'to cite[2]'; though we should be disposed to give any one else the benefit of the doubt, which the reader, who chooses to turn to the references, will see exists in these two cases.

Such verbal mistakes might be but slight deformities on the surface of a grand and noble work. To make much of them would then be only worthy of those 'little grammarians,' for whom Warburton so habitually expressed his contempt, including therein, as Jortin slyly suggested[3], a contempt for grammar. But the truth is, they are not flaws in the fabric; they are of its texture. When he is writing of 'the ancients,'—Warburton always speaks of 'the ancients' or 'pagan antiquity' in the lump, and this when he is investigating the history of opinion,—his notions are one mass of misconception from beginning to end; a misconception in which his misunderstanding of single passages is but a subordinate element. His reasoning is such, that anything whatever might be proved in the same way of argumentation, as Mosheim told him, while at the same time doing ample homage to his talents[4], in a compliment which Warburton himself transcribed into his own pages. Of all the tasks which have exercised the ingenuity of scholars, that of reproducing the religious and philosophical opinion of the Greek schools from the fragmentary and contradictory accounts which remain to us, is the most delicate and precarious. Warburton is hampered by no doubts; he rushes in where Wolf or Heyne fears to tread, and 'presumes to enter the very penetralia of antiquity[5].' Entering these dark recesses under the conduct of our self-confident guide, we are

---

[1] *Works*, IV. 416.   [2] *Works*, III. 203.   [3] *Life*, p. 446.

[4] Ego quidem mediocris ingenii homo, et tanto viro quantus est Warburtonus longe inferior, omnes Theologos nihil eorum quae publice tradunt credere, et callide hominum mentibus impietatis venenum afflare velle convincam, si mihi eadem eos via invadendi potestas concedatur, qua Philosophos vir doctissimus aggressus est.

[5] *Works*, III. 215.

surprised to find how plainly and clearly all objects are visible there; the 'double doctrine' and Τὸ Ἕν are everywhere round us; Aristotle is cleared up by 'his best interpreter, Bossu[1]'; 'Lucian of all the ancients best understood the intrigues and intricacies of ancient philosophy' (III. 105); and Socrates 'was in morals a dogmatist, as appears largely by Xenophon and the less fabulous parts of Plato' (III. 52). If there is any 'obscurity in Plato's writings, it is caused by the double doctrine, and by the joint profession of two such contrary philosophies as the Pythagorean and the Socratic' (III. 87). But it need not give us much concern if there be; for 'all the Greek philosophers are shown for knaves in practice and fools in theory' (III. 201); unless perhaps it be Socrates, who 'being perpetually ironical, take him in the reverse, and he is in his right senses' (XI. 161); or Zeno, who seems to have been only a fool, for 'the man had forgot sure that he was writing laws for a community, while he thus impertinently philosophizes to the Stoical sage' (III. 102, so in 1st ed.). Socrates might have been witty as well as ironical, had Simmias anticipated the suggestion of the *Divine Legation,* that to his cock he should add a bull (III. 357). That of all philosophic tenets the Pantheistical are 'the most absurd' (III. 209), we might have scored down as one of Warburton's random shots, but that Bayle appears to have said the same before him. And that Homer's invocation to the Muses 'is an intimation that he took his account from authentic records, and not from uncertain tradition' (IV. 434), is an opinion which, whatever else it may be, must at least be orthodox, since it is sanctioned by the authority of Mr. Gladstone and of the University of Oxford.

Notwithstanding the preposterous nature of his argument, the coarse vulgarity of his style, the supercilious dogmatism of his manner, most dictatorial when he is

---

[1] *Works,* II. 80.

most wrong, there is still some quality latent in Warburton's writings which will make them 'ever be read
with delight, even by those who are indifferent to their
subject.' Perhaps we ought to restrict this to the first
three books of the *Divine Legation*; for neither the later
books of that work, nor anything else that he has written,
appear to us to stand on the same level with that effort.
This quality is intellectual vigour; a quality so rare in
literature, and above all in theological literature, that its
exhibition, even in its most undisciplined state, always
commands respect. 'His rants are amazing, and so are
his parts,' said Horace Walpole of Lord Chatham; and
the rant and fustian of his speeches were forgiven the
orator, in consideration of the moral vigour of the man.
The causes which concur to break down vigour in a
writer are so many, that before the thought comes to the
birth it has mostly lost all the raciness of the soil from
which it springs. Of these causes, classical education and a
nice and conscientious sense of truth are among the more
powerful. He who can set at nought the traditions of
taste, and take up an opinion irrespective of the facts, can
employ the whole unimpeded energies of his mind in
giving momentum to the view he happens to have
espoused. 'The manners of a gentleman,' says Whitaker,
'the formalities of argument, and the niceties of composition, would have been unwillingly accepted in exchange
for that glorious extravagance, which dazzles while it is
unable to convince, and that haughty defiance of form and
decorum, which, in its rudest transgressions against
charity and manners, never failed to combine the powers
of a giant with the temper of a ruffian.'

It would be unjust to quit Warburton without drawing
attention to one or two instances in which his vigour was
not employed in the maintenance of paradox. At a time
when copyright was generally regarded as a legal monopoly, he argued the natural right of an author in the

produce of his mind[1]. He had the courage to denounce
the slave-trade in indignant terms from the pulpit (X. 57).
A poor-law he declares to be a 'beneficent but ill-judged
policy' (X. 253). He had formed from his own observation
a just estimate of the effect of mathematics on the mental
faculties (VIII. 14). He dismisses the sophism, which has
imposed on many besides Akenside, that 'ridicule is a
test of truth' (I. 181). Dr. Whewell has bestowed approbation on his discriminating the power of reason as
sufficient to *perceive* truth when proposed to it, but not to
discover it[2]. And Dugald Stewart[3] has noticed that Malebranche's extraordinary merit has been recognized by few
English writers except Warburton, 'who even where he
thinks the most unsoundly, has always the rare merit of
thinking for himself.' Of his solid good sense we cannot
give a better instance than his remarks on the Lauder
forgery. He writes to Jortin:

> Lauder has offered much amusement to the public, and they are
> obliged to him. What the public wants or subsists on is news. Milton
> was their reigning favourite; yet they took it well of a man they never
> heard of before to tell them the news of Milton's being a thief and a
> plagiary. Had he been proved a ——, it had pleased them better.
> When this was no longer news, they were equally delighted with an-
> other [Dr. Douglas], as much a stranger to them, who entertained them
> with another piece of news,—that Lauder was an impostor. Had he
> proved him to be a Jesuit in disguise, nothing had equalled the satis-
> faction (*Life*, p. 368).

The vigour of his thought does not concentrate itself in
telling paragraphs. It is a rude—we had almost said
brute—force penetrating the whole. And his English
style is so slipslop, that it would be difficult to find in all
the thirteen volumes of his works half a dozen passages
which might be taken as fair specimens of his peculiar
powers. We will conclude our notice with one of the best
of these:

[1] *Works*, XII. 406.   [2] *Moral Philosophy*, p. 145.
[3] *Dissert.* p. 161.

Those who are upon the records of history for having failed [in their projects] were either mere enthusiasts, who knew not how to push their projects when they had disposed the people to support them; or else mere politicians, who could never advance their wise schemes so far as to engage a fanatic populace to support them; or lastly, which most deserves our observation, such as had the two qualities in conjunction, but in a reverted order.

Of each of these defects we have domestic examples in the three great companions of the last successful imposture; I mean Fleetwood, Lambert, and Vane. Cromwell had prepared the way for their succession to his power as thoroughly as Mahomet had done for that of Abubeker, Omar, and Othman. Yet these various wants rendered all his preparations fruitless. Fleetwood was a fervent enthusiast without parts or capacity; Lambert, a cool contriver without fanaticism; and Sir Harry Vane, who had great parts and as great enthusiasm, yet had them and used them in so preposterous an order as to do him no kind of service. He began a sober plotter. But when come in view of the goal, he started out the wildest and most extravagant of fanatics. He ended where his master began; so that we need not wonder his fortune proved so different. But this was a course as rare as it was retrograde. The affections naturally keep another order. The most successful impostors have set out in all the blaze of fanaticism, and completed their schemes amid the cool depth and stillness of politics. Though this be common to them all, yet I don't know any who exemplifies it so strongly as the famous Ignatius Loyola. This illustrious personage —who confirms the observation of one who came after him, and almost equalled him in his trade, 'that a man never rises so high as when he does not know whither he is going'—began his ecstasies in the mire, and completed his schemes with the direction of Councils that, even in his own lifetime, were ready to give the law to Christendom. The same spirit built up old and new Rome. When the city had not six miles of dominion beyond its walls, it indulged the dream of universal monarchy. When the jurisdiction of the bishops of Rome extended not beyond a small diocese, they entertained the celestial vision of a popedom. And it was this spirit which, in defiance and to the destruction of civil policy and religion, made the fortune of both.

National Review, 1863.]

XV.

THE CALAS TRAGEDY[1].

(*Westminster Review*, 1858.)

IT happens, from time to time, that the world is called upon to alter or reverse one of its settled judgments on some character or event of the past time. Some new evidence turns up, or the old facts are more carefully and critically inquired into, and the result is that the traditional view of the case has to be modified or corrected. This is the legitimate advance of knowledge. This is the way in which history can take its place among the progressive studies; and to make such a discovery is one of the most prized rewards of its critical study.

A very different complexion belongs to those fluctuations of the popular taste which dispose it at one time to admire, and soon again to hate, the same objects. This mutability of opinion,—the 'turba Remi' burning the gods which once it worshipped—does not operate upon the living hero or statesman only, it is extended far back into history. The shifting of opinion is a process, like the other, incessantly at work, and inevitable in its operations as the law of elevation and depression in terrestrial physics. But it is not a legitimate process. It is not one worked out by the science of criticism. It is no part of the solid victory of the human understanding.

[1] *Jean Calas, et sa Famille, Étude Historique d'après les Documents Originaux, suivie des Dépêches du Comte Saint-Florentin, Ministre Secrétaire d'État, etc.* Par ATHANASE COQUEREL Fils, Pasteur Suffragant de l'Église Réformée de Paris. Paris: Joel Cherbuliez. 1858.

It is rather the play of human passion, and the confession of human infirmity.

A very remarkable instance of this instability of historical belief is brought before us by a *brochure* of a young writer, who bears the honoured name of Athanase Coquerel. It offers a complete narrative, far the most complete that has ever been published, of the case of Jean Calas, a Protestant, who was executed at Toulouse, in 1762, on the charge of having murdered his eldest son, but who was afterwards discovered to have been innocent. The publication has been called forth by perceiving a fashion growing up, first in Catholic circles and religious periodicals, and extending gradually from them to society at large, of believing Calas guilty. This 'view,' which is thus spreading itself to the sun, has no foundation on any new documents or facts that have only now been brought to light. It is a mere sign of the great general reaction of opinion in France—one of the straws which show which way the wind is setting. More than two years ago Emile Montégut said *(Revue des Deux Mondes)*—

'What do you think of the Calas business—what of that of the Chevalier Labarre? Are you for or against the revocation of the Edict of Nantes?' Such is the conversation, full of present meaning, which one hears in the salons of Paris—Paris of the nineteenth century.

This disposition is not mere levity and fickleness, the caprice of the mob which turns upon its own idol—'odit damnatos'—it is a part of that general Catholic revival which has been working for some years, and which, like a fog, is spreading over the face of opinion, and giving its own views and altered proportions to all objects, past, present, and future. This change of opinion about an event which happened nearly one hundred years back, proceeds not from the growth of knowledge on the topic on which the opinion is formed, but from the accretion of ignorance. The facts and proof once known are convincing. But the innocence of the unhappy victim is, for reasons which will be seen in the following pages, a truth extremely unpleasant to the Catholics. If they can only get inquiry stifled and criticism gagged, then they may safely maintain their thesis. This application of force, however, to drown the truth of history, is one for which opinion in France is not yet ripe, though it is rapidly advancing in that direction. M. Coquerel has taken advantage of that remnant of freedom which is still left to the French writer to publish a clear and succinct narrative of the transaction. We have thought it worth while to give our readers a very succinct *résumé* of this narrative. Not only is this *cause célèbre* of the highest interest in itself, but its connexion with existing passions and prejudices curiously illustrates the temper and tendencies of French thought at the present moment.

Toulouse, the theatre of the tragedy, obtained its popular appellation of *La Sainte* from possessing in the crypt of one of its churches the skeletons of seven out of the twelve apostles. This extraordinary accumulation of riches justified the inscription over the vault in which they were contained :—

Non est in toto sanctior orbe locus.

The sanctity of the locality was not without its influence upon the character of the population. From the year 1203, when the 'genius loci' inspired Saint Dominic with the idea of the order to which mankind owes the Inquisition, down even to the murder of General Ramel by the Catholic Royalists in 1815, the history of the Holy City offers a series of fanatical outbursts and ferocious cruelties, which can only be paralleled in ancient Egypt or in modern Turkey. To ascribe these deeds of blood and frenzy to the influence of the Catholic superstition would be an error. But it is too true that the priests and

N 2

ministers of the religion, instead of checking, have
fomented the savage passions of the multitude; instead
of disavowing, have adopted their feats of murder, have
publicly justified them, and endeavoured to make the
Church responsible for them.

One of these achievements of the religious mob of
Toulouse was enacted in the sixteenth century.   In 1562,
a Huguenot procession was accompanying a corpse to
burial, when it was set upon, under some pretext or
other, by the rabble.   The street row grew into a general
fight.   The Reformed population of Toulouse, though a
considerable body, was vastly outnumbered by the
Orthodox, and was obliged to entrench itself in the
Hôtel de Ville, and stand a siege.   The besiegers sent
the Governor of Narbonne to offer terms.   The Protestants accepted them.   They were to march out of their
defences, leaving their arms and munitions, and to retire
unmolested whither they thought fit.   On Whitsunday,
May 17th, the Protestants began their retreat.   Though
they had chosen the hour of vespers designedly to avoid
all risk of commotion in the streets, the Catholics obtained
intelligence of the movement, rushed out of the churches,
seized arms, and massacred upwards of three thousand
unarmed men, women, and children.

But this was the work of an ignorant and fanatical
populace, brutalized by feudal oppression, kindled into
momentary rage by the armed resistance of their enemies.
It was a time of civil war, in fact a war in which both
parties were equally in the wrong, Huguenots as well
as Catholics; and the excesses of the victorious faction
were lamented by all good men, even of their own party.

Nothing of the sort.   The Church adopted the double
crime of perjury and murder.   The Parlement of Toulouse
instituted an annual *fête* to commemorate the massacre of
the 17th of May.   The Pope (Pius IV) hastened to issue
a bull, in which he authorized the religious ceremony

and attached indulgences and benedictions to it. Two centuries afterwards, 1762, the *fête* of ' The Deliverance' had its centenary. It was celebrated with extraordinary fervour and magnificence. Clement XIII renewed the bull of Pius IV with ampler privileges. Such is the aspect of the Church towards crime, when it is committed in its own interest.

The event of which we are about to narrate the chief incidents fell in the year 1761. There lived at Toulouse a certain Jean Calas. He kept a respectable draper's shop in one of the principal streets of the city—Grande Rue des Filetiers, No. 16. He had been forty years established in business; his age was sixty-three, his character simple, his dealings honest, his habits industrious, and his unassuming virtues those which were hereditary in the families of the Protestant *bourgeois*. The piety of the Protestants of that age had lost its harshness, without abating its grave sincerity. Calas was known among his neighbours as uniting steadiness to his inherited religious principles with entire tolerance towards his Catholic fellow-citizens; a tolerance which was very far from being reciprocal, and which was rare in provincial towns in those days, and, indeed, is far from being universal in these. He was, in consequence, generally respected, and among his co-religionists enjoyed, like Isaac Walton, a consideration far above his worldly rank. Limited as were his means, we find him admitted to the society and friendship of the *petite noblesse* of Languedoc, and even connected with some of them by marriage.

His family consisted of his wife, who was eighteen years younger than himself, and who appears, by her conduct during her examination, to have been a woman of strong sense and superior character, six children, and one maid-servant. Of the children four were sons, Marc-Antoine, Jean-Pierre, Louis, Jean-Louis-Donat, and two daughters, Anne-Rose and Anne.

The eldest son, Marc-Antoine, with whom we are
principally concerned, was, in the year 1761, twenty-eight
years old. He had been a law-student at the University,
and taken his Bachelor's degree. He had what is
described as a taste for letters, which seems rather to
have been a taste for a sauntering, easy life, and a decided
distaste for the shop. But no one could, in France, be
admitted to the bar without a certificate of Catholicity,
signed by the curé of the parish. These tyrannical
regulations, by which the professions and many of the
trades were closed to the Protestants, were somewhat
alleviated in practice by the good-nature of many curés,
who used to sign these certificates without inquiry, as
matters of course. In the present case, however, the
curé had refused to give the voucher without an attestation
signed by a priest, to certify that Marc-Antoine had
confessed to him. This disappointment had soured the
temper and broken the spirits of the youth. He became
moody, silent, irritated against the present, and without
prospects for the future. He took no part in the amusements which the household shared together, and sate
by, not joining in any conversation which might be going
on, but appearing occupied with some thoughts of his
own. He read a good deal, and was often heard to
comment on the excuses for suicide urged by Plutarch
and Montaigne.

The maid, Jeanne Viguier, was a zealous Catholic, but
had lived twenty-three years in the family, and brought
up the children, to whom she was much attached. Her
zeal for their spiritual interests had induced her to attempt
their conversion. She had succeeded with one member
of the family only—the only one without character or
good sense—the third son, Louis. These endeavours,
however, were but additional evidence of her zealous
devotion to the family, to whom she adhered through
their terrible trials with a steady fidelity which was rare,

even in those days, and in the southern provinces, which retained more of the old-fashioned manners than the north.

Such was the *personnel* of the family at the time when the quiet course of their existence was broken by a catastrophe so sudden and undeserved, at the same time so blighting and irretrievable, as to excite the compassion and sympathy of all succeeding ages in the highest degree of which our nature is capable.

The following account of the facts is contained in a letter written by Madame Calas herself, for the information of a friend of the family. Its natural and simple language, and the suppressed anguish of spirit which it reveals, make it more touching than the most highly-coloured narrative could be.

I herewith send you an exact and true statement of our unhappy business, as it happened.

On the 13th of October, an evil day for us, M. G. La Vaisse arrived at Toulouse, from Bordeaux, on a visit to his parents. He found they had left town for their country box, and he endeavoured in vain to hire a horse to take him out. Between four and five in the afternoon he came to our house. My husband said to him, that as he was not leaving the city, it would give us great pleasure if he would sup with us. He readily consented, and came up stairs to see me. After the first compliments were past between us, he said, ' I am coming to supper with you ; your husband has asked me.' I expressed my satisfaction, and left him for a few minutes, to give some orders in consequence. When I went down stairs, I found my eldest son alone in the shop, seated, in a very absent mood apparently. I requested him to purchase some Roquefort cheese for supper. This was his ordinary province, as he knew more about cheese than any of the others. I then ascended again to the room where I had left M. La Vaisse, who soon took his leave.

He returned at supper-time (seven o'clock), and we all took our places. The conversation during the meal turned on indifferent matters—the antiquities at the Hôtel de Ville, etc. After supper, which did not last very long, my unhappy boy (Marc-Antoine, the eldest son) rose from table, as usual, and went towards the kitchen.

The servant asked him, 'Are you cold, Monsieur l'aîné?' 'Not at all,' he replied, 'I am burning hot.' We remained seated at table a very short time longer, and then passed into an adjoining room, and continued the conversation. My younger son fell asleep, and about three-quarters after nine, or towards ten o'clock, M. La Vaisse took his leave. We wakened up Pierre, who went down stairs with a light in his hand, to show M. La Vaisse out.

A moment after we heard their cries of alarm, and my husband ran down to see what was the matter, I remaining, all trembling, in the passage at the head of the stairs, not daring to go down, and not knowing what it could mean.

At last, as no one returned, I ventured down, and at the foot of the stairs encountered M. La Vaisse, and asked him hurriedly what it was. He only replied by urging me to go up stairs again; and he went up with me, but left me immediately. I did not know what to do, so I called to Jeannette, and sent her down to see what had happened. As she did not return, I went down again myself; and what was my horror when I saw, great God! my dear son stretched upon the ground! I did not suppose he was dead, so I ran for a bottle of *Reine de Hongrie*, supposing that he was taken suddenly faint, and did everything I could think of to revive him, not being able to persuade myself that it was his dead body which I had before me.

Meanwhile the surgeon had come in, without my seeing that he was there, till I found him telling me that my pains were of no use, for that he was dead. I persisted in asserting that it could not be so, and implored him to use all his efforts to save him. He did so, to appease me, but in vain. All this time my husband was leaning against a desk, in a state of desperation. My heart was torn in two between the sad sight of my son stretched dead before me, and the fear of losing my husband, who abandoned himself to sorrow, and would listen to no consolation. They made us go upstairs; and in that state we were when the officers of justice came and arrested us.

This is, word for word, what happened. May the Almighty, who knows our innocence, punish me eternally if I have exaggerated or diminished one iota, or have not told the pure truth. I am ready to seal this truth with my blood.

Your very humble and very obedient servant,

ANNE ROSE CABIBEL CALAS.

Westminster Review, 1858.]

The mother confines her statement to what she herself saw. From the depositions of other witnesses taken at the time, we can fill up what is wanting to complete the story of the events in the Rue des Filetiers.

When La Vaisse returned to supper at seven o'clock, Pierre Calas, who had been out along with him, shut and barred the outer door of the house towards the street. This circumstance, which was afterwards construed as premeditation of crime, explains itself by the ordinary practice of the shops, where the front door was invariably fastened while the family were at meals.

After retiring from the supper-table the party spent about two hours in chatting in the adjoining parlour, Madame Calas working at her embroidery the while. When they came to wake Pierre, on La Vaisse's departure, the young man tried to deny that he had been asleep. They rallied him playfully on it, and the adieux were mirthful and gay; the last time that gaiety visited that household. Death was already within the walls.

When La Vaisse, accompanied by Pierre, reached the bottom of the stairs, he noticed that the door leading from the passage into the shop was open, which, it seems, was unusual, and raised a momentary suspicion that some person had got into the shop who had no business there. Pierre went in to look. The first object that met his eye was the body of his brother suspended by the neck against the inner door by which the outer shop *(boutique)* communicated with an inner store-room *(magasin)*. Across the two leaves of this folding-door, as it stood open, the unhappy suicide had placed a long billet of wood, and suspended himself by a cord and running knot. Pierre took hold of his brother's hand, on which the body began to swing, and the two then called out for help. Jean, the father, came down instantly, and seeing what had happened, seized the corpse in his arms. The round billet of wood, thus relieved of its burden, rolled off the top of the doors, and fell to the ground. He deposited the body on the floor, and slipped the knot, crying out to Pierre, 'Run for Camoire.' Camoire was a surgeon who lived in the neighbourhood. Pierre and La Vaisse both rushed out, and returned with a young man, a pupil or apprentice of the surgeon.

As soon as Jean Calas came to understand what had happened, his first thought was for the honour of his dead son and the family. 'Let no one know,' he cried, 'that he has died by his own hand.' La Vaisse was easily enjoined to secrecy on this point. This deception may have given an unfavourable colour to the case, but it was extremely natural, if not excusable, when we recollect the hideous barbarity of the French law of suicide.

Such were the occurrences within the house. Misery enough for the afflicted family. But this was but the beginning of sorrow. Outside the house, in the street, a considerable assemblage of the curious had gathered. Misfortune must never expect sympathy or commiseration from a crowd. They began, as usual, to indulge in liberal commentary on the enigmatical proceedings within the house. The usual uncharitableness of such remarks was, in this instance, inflamed by the ardent hatred of French Catholics against a Protestant. The ingenuity and malice of an individual could not have deliberately invented a fiction more plausible or more destructive to its object than that which grew up spontaneously from the passions and imagination of this street-mob. It only needed to be suggested, and these Catholics were sure, that the Protestant parents had murdered their son. But with what motive? why, of course it was to prevent him from turning Catholic. It is the business of justice to crush such scandal, and to sift facts without regard to what may be the popular cry. 'Vanae voces populi non sunt audiendae,' is a maxim of the Roman law. In this instance the magistrate caught eagerly at the suggestion, and thenceforth all the efforts of law were bent towards getting up a plausible proof of a suggestion which had this chance origin.

The public of Toulouse, as well as the administration of justice, both civil and criminal, 'haute et basse,' was in the hands of a municipal council, locally elected. These eight councillors, or aldermen, formed a court, styled 'the Consistory,' each member of which was called a 'Capitoul,' (i. e. member of the chapter, *capitulum*). Out of the total number of eight Capitouls, the majority were changed, or re-elected annually. But two or three of the body were usually persons who had purchased their place, according to the custom which prevailed in France before the Revolution. These held their post for life. This of course gave these 'titular Capitouls,' so they were styled, a very great ascendancy over their annual colleagues. One of these titulars at the present juncture was David de Beaudrigue. This man was not a villain, though he has been made to play that part in some of the tragedies founded on this history. He was one of those self-important officials, to whose well-meaning zeal so much of the evil which takes effect in the world is owing. As a police-officer he was in his place. The impetuous restlessness of his temperament, even in this capacity, made him perpetually over-step the line of usefulness. Such a man is always dangerous except when kept under the strict control of a superior. But as a magistrate, with supreme control over the persons and property of others, there exists no form of character more pregnant of mischief to society. He is ready to become the instrument, and always a most energetic instrument, of the reigning prejudice or passion. In the present case, the Catholic fanaticism of Toulouse was the storm that swept him away. He came into it with all the violence of his character, and displayed, in hunting the Calas to the death, as much blind passion and ferocious determination as if, instead of judge, he had been a party having a private injury to revenge.

David had been roused from his first sleep by the commotion which began to spread through the city.   He hurried to the spot with the watch, ordering at the same time a physician and two surgeons to be fetched.   His first measure was to arrest Pierre Calas, who had re-mained downstairs with the body while the parents had withdrawn above.   He then, without any of the formalities which the law required, or any examination of the premises, ordered off the body of Marc-Antoine to the Hôtel de Ville, and proceeded to arrest Monsieur and Madame Calas, the maid Jeanne, La Vaisse, and a friend of the family named Cazeing, who had come to the house on hearing the terrible news.   The parents of the defunct, absorbed in grief, supposed that they were being con-ducted to the Hôtel de Ville to depose to the circum-stances of the suicide.   Pierre was about leaving a candle burning in the passage, that they might find a light on their return.   David, with a sarcastic leer at his simplicity, bade him put it out.   'They would not get home again so soon.'

It is obvious how this precipitate arrest, and the neglect of an examination of the spot, were calculated to prejudice the case of the Calas family.   It is possible that a proper scrutiny at the time would have established at once the fact of self-murder.   Some essentials of the evidence were irretrievably lost.   Such was the hurry of the proceedings, that David did not even stay to ascertain the name of Cazeing, but described him in the procès-verbal, as 'unè espèce d'abbé.'   This 'sort of clergyman' was a manu-facturer of stuffs, and, as an employer of several hundred hands, perfectly well known in Toulouse.   One of David's colleagues arrived while he was making out this procès, and seeing the trembling eagerness of the zealot, ventured to suggest a little more patience and caution.   'Je prends tout sur moi,' was the reply; 'c'est ici la cause de la religion.'

We shall not follow step by step the subsequent hearings of the five accused, for such they now were, before the Consistory. The procedure of a French court of justice before the Revolution seems to have been arranged, not with a view of eliciting truth, but with that of securing condemnation. In the procès-Calas, even this iniquitous system would have failed of its purpose. It required all the address and management of David to get up a case sufficiently plausible to obtain a sentence against his victims. The prisoners were kept in close confinement, not allowed to communicate with their friends outside, and consequently unable to instruct counsel for their defence. The daughters Calas, and Louis, employed an advocate. But not only had he no access to his clients, he could not approach the tribunal. For there was no public trial. The accused were interrogated separately and secretly by the judges. They could produce no witnesses for the defence, nor state anything except in answer to a question of the court. The advocate's part was reduced to that of presenting 'memoirs,' which it was at the judge's option to treat with neglect. But in this case David had taken care that not even a 'requête' should reach the bench. At the beginning of the process, the attorney employed by the Demoiselles Calas had filed a bill in the court which was calculated, but apparently not judiciously calculated, to stay the proceedings. So irritated was David at this attempt to arrest his course, that he employed all his credit to get the attorney, Duroux, cashiered. He did actually succeed in getting him sentenced to a public apology, and three months' suspension. After this it became impossible for the friends of Calas to find an attorney to act for them. Even the bailiffs declined the hazardous office of serving the memorials which their advocate drew up.

Notwithstanding all these arrangements, the affair did not progress rapidly. More than thirty witnesses had been examined, yet no evidence had been obtained which permitted the Calas to be sentenced. It was found necessary to have recourse to the 'monitory.' This was a resource of the civil tribunals in cases where witnesses were backward. The Attorney-General drew up a list of 'presumed facts' of which the Court was in need of evidence, which list was addressed to the ecclesiastical authority, and by it dispersed to the various parishes, to be read from the pulpits by the curés. The monitory so published informed all those who *knew by hearsay or otherwise* any of the circumstances stated in the requisition, that if they did not appear to disclose what they knew before either the magistrate, *or the curé of their parish*, they rendered themselves liable to excommunication. One of the rules for drawing up this terrible document in point of form required that it should always summon witnesses on both sides—for the defence as well as the prosecution. The provision was necessary, because the tribunals in those days adhered rigorously to the maxim of the Roman law, that no witness can be heard who offers himself. ('Testis se offerens repellitur a testimonio.') As the accused themselves were not allowed to call witnesses, none could appear for the defence at all, were the monitory so worded as to cite them for the prosecution only. In the present case the Attorney-General, with flagrant illegality, drew up his requisition in this partial form.

Meanwhile the passions of the populace were further appealed to by the aid of religion. It was determined to give Marc-Antoine a public funeral. The Attorney-General, by collusion with the Capitouls, demanded, in the King's name, an order for interment on the ground that 'une foule de motifs le rendent nécessaire.' As proper means had been taken to guard against decomposition, there were no other motives that could reasonably be alleged. David, and one of his colleagues, took an opportunity when the rest of the consistory were absent, and they found themselves alone with two of their assessors of whom they were sure, to make an order to that effect. They then engaged the curé of the parish of St. Étienne to undertake the ceremonies. Accordingly the body of a Protestant and a suicide was buried with all the honours of the Catholic Church, attended by all the clergy in Toulouse. It shows the temper of the people, that one of the lay confraternities, called the 'White Penitents,' attended the procession in their colours, on the pretext that the 'martyred' Marc-Antoine had entertained the idea of joining their society. After this one reads with satisfaction, in the *Moniteur* of April 8, 1792, in the decree suppressing the confraternities throughout France, that the part played by the ' Pénitents Blancs' in the affair of Calas is recited as one of the motives of the suppression.

By these means a mass of evidence was slowly gathered which enabled the Capitouls to proceed to judgment. Not that any new facts, either direct or circumstantial, belonging to the tragedy of October 13th had been collected. The depositions are a mass of suspicions and hearsays, proving only the general animosity with which the Protestants were habitually regarded by their neighbours, and pointing constructively to the conclusion that the heretics thought any crime, even assassination, permissible to prevent the conversion of one of their body to the Catholic faith. From this premiss the inference was, that on the 13th October, 1762, Jean Calas, aided and abetted by his wife, his son Pierre, his servant Jeanne Viguier, and the young La Vaisse, had murdered his eldest son, Marc-Antoine. There was no evidence whatever for the murder, but the particular fact was thought to be sufficiently proved, because the general doctrine of the Protestants had been presumptively established. The accused were not proved guilty, but they had been rigorously excluded from offering any evidence of their innocence. It was not to be endured that heretics should be allowed to say that one who had received from the Church the honours of a martyr had been a suicide. Nor, indeed, in the excited state of popular feeling, could any witness have dared, even if the citation had been so framed as to have admitted it, to depose in favour of the accused. There were, indeed, two persons who could and would have come forward to affirm on oath the innocence of Calas and his wife. These two persons were La Vaisse, and the maid Jeanne Viguier. The prosecutors were, indeed, much embarrassed by having arrested these two persons, and by having included them in the charge. Jeanne Viguier was a devout Catholic, who had been the means of converting one of her young masters, Louis Calas, and was supposed to have been urgent with Marc-Antoine to follow his brother's example. The absurdity of the supposition that she had aided in murdering Marc-Antoine, to prevent his conversion, was glaring, and the obvious mode of removing it would have been to have silently released her. But had she been released, she would have immediately appeared in quality of witness to prove that she had never quitted the Calas, father and mother, for an instant, from supper-time to the discovery of the body, and it would have been impossible to bring them in guilty.

As to the state of opinion in Toulouse, it was now the fixed belief of the whole city that one of the articles of the Protestant creed required all Protestants to put to death any member of their body who became a convert to the Church Catholic ; that their own parents were bound to denounce them, nay to aid, if required, in their execution. It was further affirmed by those who pretended to know, that on the morning of the 13th, an assembly of Protestants had been held in a house which they named, at which the assassination of Marc-Antoine had been resolved in solemn conclave. One of the depositions bearing on this charge may be selected as illustrative, not only of the evidence in this case, but of the sort of evidence admissible under the system of secret interrogatory practised in the French Courts before the Revolution:—

Pierre Lagréye, master-tailor, 61st witness, declares, that he *had it from* one Bonnemaison, that he, the said Bonnemaison *had heard say,* that a labourer of Caraman, on hearing of the affair of Calas, *had said,* that there was nothing strange in it, for that five or six persons had been made away with at Caraman in the same fashion.

Evidence enough of this sort had been got, and public opinion in Toulouse was not only ready, but impatient, for a severe sentence. Accordingly, on November 18th, the Capitouls met, and proceeded to what was called a preliminary sentence, which condemned Jean and Madame Calas, with their son Pierre to the rack *(question ordinaire et extraordinarie),* and La Vaisse and Viguier to be 'presented.' This presentation consisted in attaching the persons to the instrument of torture, and making every preparation for proceeding, and in that position interrogating them.

The sentence was immediately read to the victims. They appealed from the sentence of the Consistory to the higher court, the Parlement. Their appeal was met by a counter appeal on the part of the Attorney-General, an appeal *a minimâ,* i. e. on the ground that the sentence on the last two criminals was too light.

The Parlement of Toulouse ranked as the second Supreme Court of justice in the kingdom. The Chambre de Tournelle, so called because the counsellors sate in it in rotation, was a Board, or Judicial Committee of Magistrates for the hearing of criminal appeals. It con-

sisted apparently of fifteen members, though only thirteen
sat and voted on this appeal. None of these magistrates
bear names of historic note, though many of them were
men of high consideration in Languedoc. Under such
a system, however, where offices were purchased, and the
magistracy vied with each other in truckling for ministerial
favours, the highest names give no security for justice
or even for common integrity. Those who know anything
of the history of the provincial Parlements will be prepared to find that the magistracy of Toulouse did but
swim with the stream, and fall in with all the prepossess-
sions and passions of the *bourgeoisie.*

It will be unnecessary to go over again the pleadings
before the Chamber, as the depositions which had already
been taken in the court below were put in in the higher
court, and nothing material was added. The accused
had here, however, the advantage of counsel. They could
not have had an abler advocate than M. Sudre. Combining a thorough knowledge of the civil law with a
classical taste, the pleadings which he drew up for the
defence are in the best style of the French bar, and
far superior in their chastened reserve to the exaggerated
and tumid protocols which were put forth at a later period
of the affair, when it had begun to attract the attention
of Europe. They do not appear to have produced any
effect upon the magistrates. One member of the Chamber
only, M. de La Salle, was, at an early period of the trial,
convinced of the innocence of the unhappy Calas, and
was courageous enough to brave public opinion in the
endeavour to save them. He was easily put aside by
his colleagues, not by argument, but by simple sarcasm,
'Ah, Monsieur, vous êtes tout Calas!' What courage
it required to bear even this useless testimony to
truth may be conceived from the fact that M. Sudre,
for his generosity in undertaking the defence of the
helpless, lost all his practice at the bar, no one daring to

employ a barrister who had so seriously compromised himself.

After ten 'grandes séances' the court proceeded to deliver judgment. M. de La Salle, from highly conscientious motives, abstained from voting, as having already taken a part out of court. Of the thirteen judges who voted, only seven voted for the extreme sentence of the law. This would have saved the prisoner, as the law required an absolute majority of the chamber. Upon this the senior magistrate present, out of complaisance to the court, transferred his vote, and the required majority was obtained.

The sentence condemned Jean Calas—

1. To the rack (la question ordinaire et extraordinaire) to draw from him a confession of his crime, and a betrayal of his accomplices.

2. That in his shirt, head and feet bare, he should be drawn from prison to the cathedral, and there on his knees, at the principal entrance, with a candle of wax two pounds weight in his hands, he should demand pardon for his crime of God, the king, and the laws.

3. That he should then be replaced in the cart, and taken to the Place Saint-Georges, where he should be stretched on a wheel, and have his arms, legs, thighs, and ribs broken by the executioner.

4. That he should then be laid upon his back, with his face toward heaven, to live as long as it should please God to give him life in pain and repentance for his crime and misdeeds, and to serve as an example of terror to other malefactors.

This sentence was pronounced March 9, 1762, and executed the following day.

The horrible details of the torture, ordinary and extraordinary, by rack and by water, are given at length in the official procès-verbal. Human nature shrinks before the repetition of them. Suffice it to say that the spirit of the heroic victim triumphed over his mortal agonies, and that the butchers, assisted by the exhortations of two Jacobin friars, only extorted a consistent and unwavering declaration of innocence.   In the hideous interrogatory between the patient and his judges we have no difficulty in recognizing an error on the one side endeavouring in vain to find any grounds on which to establish itself: on the other, the integrity of innocence reproducing itself in every form, and under the most terrible test to which human nature can be subjected.   When brought out on the scaffold for the final scene of brutality, a single cry escaped his lips at the first blow out of the eleven, each one of which broke a bone.   He endured the rest without a murmur.   When stretched out in the manner prescribed by the sentence, notwithstanding the double torture and the breaking of his limbs, life was still so tenacious in the man of sixty-four, that he lingered in his agony for two hours.   At the expiration of this time the executioner had orders to put a period to his sufferings.   At this moment David, who had presided at the torture, and had been watching the subsequent proceedings, unable any longer to control his rage and disappointment at not having extracted a confession, rushed towards him on the scaffold, 'Wretch, you have but a moment more to live! Confess the truth!'   Calas, unable to speak, but retaining his faculties perfectly, made a sign in the negative with his head, and the executioner put the cord round his neck.

It is some consolation to outraged humanity to record the end of David.   As light was gradually thrown upon this horrible perversion of justice, David found himself become the object of universal detestation.   In 1765 he was turned out of the Capitolate.   The horrors of his situation deranged his mind.   He thought he saw gibbets and executioners on every side of him.   He was taken home to his native place for the benefit of the air.   He threw himself out of window once, but without fatal consequences.   Though carefully watched, he managed to evade his keepers a second time, and killed himself by throwing himself from a window, crying out the name of Calas!

In relating the fate of the wretched Capitoul, we have anticipated. We return to the year 1762.

It had been thought advisable to take the case of Jean Calas first, separate from the others, as it was expected the torture would wring from him such a confession as would furnish a better ground of proceeding to their condemnation, than as yet existed. The heroism of the father saved his family. The day after the execution, the Procureur-Général [1], 'ce Procureur de Beelzebuth,' Voltaire called him in the Sirven affair in 1770, moved the court to proceed to sentence the rest of the prisoners. He demanded that Madame Calas, her son, and La Vaisse should be hanged, and Jeanne Viguier confined for life in the prison of the asylum, after having been present at the execution of her accomplices. On the 18th March the court pronounced its decision. This was—against Pierre Calas, banishment: against the other three, a verdict of acquittal. It is evident from this sentence that the judges had already begun to feel a suspicion of their error. For if Pierre had been guilty as an accessary to the murder of his brother, he should not have been let off with banishment. And if he was not accessary, for what crime was the penalty of banishment inflicted? And as he and the other three were not accessary to the murder, we are to suppose that a man of sixty-four had, unassisted, strangled a vigorous young man of twenty-eight, without his even being able to make sufficient resistance to alarm the rest of the household. This second sentence is the severest censure on the first.

Such was the tragedy enacted in Toulouse. Let us turn to the effect produced as it came to be known beyond the walls.

[1] The *Procureur-Général* was the head of the bar attached to a supreme court. The *Procureur-du-Roi* held the same position at the bar attached to any inferior court.

On the Protestants of France it produced the utmost
degree of consternation. The odious horrors of the torture
and execution of an innocent man, and the blind violence
with which his destruction at all hazards had been pushed
on, struck the imagination with awe.   But more than even
this were they alarmed by finding the whole of the Reformed churches publicly charged in an official document,
authenticated by the Church, with holding the doctrine
that it was the duty of parents to assassinate their children
if they showed a disposition to become Catholics.   They
thought themselves obliged to obtain a solemn disavowal
of the tenet, signed by the 'Venerable Company of the
Pastors, &c., of the Church at Geneva.'   And they further
engaged the most accredited name among the French
Reformed, the illustrious Paul Rabaut, Pastor of the
Desert, to put forth a 'Memorial' in their defence.   This
defence, entitled 'La Calomnie Confondue,' is, in the
opinion of M. Coquerel, not the production of Paul Rabaut
himself.   He was led to this conclusion by the style of the
pamphlet, which is spirited, defiant, and tinged with the
declamatory rhetoric of the man of letters of that age.
Such was not the attitude of the Reformed religion in
France in the eighteenth century. The French Protestants
were terrified at the pluck of their own apologist, and
hastened to let him know that they found his pamphlet
'too severe.' Too severe on the murderers of Calas! To
what can a few generations of unresisted and hopeless
oppression bring a feeble and persecuted class or sect of
men! We may not taunt these unhappy 'sheep in the
desert' with pusillanimity.   But it is too true that the
vigour and life of the Huguenot body had quitted their
country at the time of the revocation of the Edict of Nantes.
Those who stayed behind had to drain to the dregs the
bitter cup of insult and humiliation.   They voluntarily
accepted their lot, and their submission produced its
natural effects on their character. We are reminded of

the description given of them in the indignant appeals of
Saurin to these Nicodemites, as he calls them, who, by
remaining at home, had sacrificed their conscience to their
interests. Saurin reproaches them with betraying their
God and their brethren. It would be more true to say
that they were unfaithful to themselves. They had, like
all defeated parties, lost the consciousness of being in the
right, and seemed to cling to their creed rather from a
stupid tenacity than from conviction. They justified their
oppressors, and really thought it 'treason' to complain.
We must ascribe to this entire subjugation to the opinion
of the majority the fact, that many Protestants in France
at first expressed their full belief in the guilt of Calas.

All that the voice from the Desert dared to call in
question was the ascription to the Protestant body of the
doctrine of assassination. Even for this moderate resistance the memorial of Paul Rabaut was ordered by the
Parlement of Toulouse to be burnt in the public square,
and informations were directed to be taken against all
'concerned in composing, writing, printing, or distributing
the said libel.' The sentence on Jean Calas, a sentence
passed with every solemnity by the second court of
justice in the kingdom, no Protestant would have ventured
to dispute the legality of, whatever suspicion he might
have nursed in private. But even had the Protestants
possessed the will, they had not the power to obtain a
hearing. It required a mind unsubjugated by the reigning
fanaticism, and a voice which could make itself heard,
in order to bring the murderers of Calas to the bar of
public opinion.

About the end of March, 1762, a merchant of Marseilles,
on his way home from Toulouse, stopped at Geneva, paid
a visit to Voltaire, and gave him an account of the dreadful
scene which he had just witnessed. He affirmed most
emphatically that Calas was innocent. Over and above
the indignation inspired by the perversion of justice, there

was that in the character of the business which in an
especial manner addressed itself to Voltaire's interests.
The most sincere and disinterested of his feelings was his
burning indignation against crimes committed in the name
of religion.   In the Toulouse tragedy he had brought
home to him one of the most atrocious of such crimes on
record.   And this, on either alternative.   Was Calas
guilty?   Then would be betrayed a dark and murderous
fanaticism lurking among the crushed relics of French
Calvinism.   Was he innocent?   Then Catholic bigotry
had committed in the sight of day an atrocious wickedness,
which it concerned the honour of the French nation to
atone for as publicly and fully as lay in its power.   With
his accustomed energy he set about obtaining all the
information he could gather; he spared neither time nor
labour, nor any of his accustomed artifice, to elicit, to
surprise, the truth; writing in every direction, checking
one correspondent by another.   If he found one of his
informants zealous in the cause of the Calas, Voltaire
assumed the tone of one who believed their guilt, and
challenged proof of the contrary.   It was not long, however, before he saw his own way.   The task of putting
the evidence in a shape to convince others was much more
serious.   For one species of proof which had most influenced himself could not be represented on paper.
This was his experiments, for so we may call them, on
the two sons.   Donat Calas, the youngest, was then
fifteen; he had been apprenticed to a tradesman at Nimes.
After the arrest and imprisonment of his family, he was
recommended to fly the country, as the only way of escap-
ing being involved in the catastrophe; he took refuge at
Geneva; here Voltaire found him, carried him home to
'Les Délices,' and kept him with him.   By this means he
gained a knowledge not only of the young man's own
disposition, but of the character of the family, and the
interior economy of their household.   Had Voltaire found

in Donat the traces of savage fanaticism and sectarian hatred, it would at least have given possibility to the crime. He recognized, on the contrary, in the family with whose habits he thus made acquaintance, a gentleness of manners, a respectful tolerance towards the Catholic religion, which is most remote from such sacrifices to Moloch as were alleged. In July, Pierre Calas, having escaped from a Dominican convent at Toulouse into which he had been entrapped, made his appearance at Geneva. Voltaire, not content with examining him, placed persons in secret espionage near him for four months. His whole conduct and language, writes Voltaire, at the conclusion of this long trial, 'sont de l'innocence la plus pure, et de la douleur la plus vraie.' The innocence of Calas is not doubtful. Had it been otherwise, the result of Voltaire's experiment upon the sons would have been of the greatest weight in favour of the father. It may be true that it suited Voltaire's purposes to attack the Parlement rather than the Protestants. But it was essential to him, if he did engage in a struggle with the Parlement, to be sure that he had right on his side before beginning. Had he had a bad case, he must have been ignominiously defeated. As it was, with right and justice on his side, success was doubtful.

As soon as he was decided to act, it was necessary to engage the co-operation of the widow Calas. Broken-hearted by a calamity which was irreparable by any human aid, she had retired with Jeanne Viguier into the country, in the neighbourhood of Montauban. Her only desire now was to drag out in privacy the sorrowful remainder of a life whose sunshine had been so cruelly extinguished. When she found herself expected to re-appear in the world, to undertake the journey to Paris, and the harass and shame of a personal canvass, she at first shrank from the effort demanded. Indeed it was a hazardous as well as a difficult enterprise. She had but just escaped, herself

and one of her sons, from participating in her husband's
tortures and death. They might be thought fortunate in
having got off so easily. Was she now to confront
authority, to levy war against the Parlement of Toulouse,
or even against the Capitouls? The same credit and
influence which had been used to procure the unjust
verdict would be exerted with tenfold force to sustain it.

Voltaire better understood the risk run in the attempt
than Madame Calas herself. He knew that now the whole
strength of the Church would be engaged to uphold the
unjust judgment, and with the more pertinacity because
they knew it to have been unjust, and its exposure would
therefore involve signal disgrace. But with his farsighted
and clear understanding, he had calculated his resources,
and saw that it could be done. The closest caution, however, was necessary. Had it been known that Madame
Calas was in motion, the Attorney-General would have
had little difficulty in obtaining a *lettre de cachet*, and
shutting her up in some prison or convent. She went to
Paris alone. Her means were now too narrow—for their
fortune had been wrecked by the imprisonment, and even
their shop pillaged by the mob—for her to afford an
attendant, and the faithful Jeanne was left at home. M.
La Vaisse, who acted in concert with her, also appeared in
Paris under an assumed name. Voltaire from a distance
watched over her proceedings, smoothed her path, and
acted as her protector with that thoughtful delicacy in
which he was unsurpassed. Thanks to his indefatigable
exertions, the lonely woman soon found herself surrounded
by friends, and offers of assistance. But this brought with
it new troubles. Her inexperience of the capital was so
great, that every friend thought himself bound to become
adviser also. The multitude of counsellors became itself
an embarrassment. Voltaire's time was now occupied in
setting aside the impracticable proposals of mistaken well-
wishers, and repairing the blunders of officious but ignorant

zeal. His activity was incessant, and only equalled by his steadiness. The fertility of his invention, his inexhaustible fund of expedients to meet every difficulty, were never more conspicuous than in this cause, into which he threw himself with all his soul.

The difficulties were appalling. First, there was the pervading official difficulty of getting anything done, which is multiplied tenfold when it is a question of getting undone that which has been done. Not public offices only, and professions, but society, swarms with persons who are always convinced that an official sentence is always a just sentence. Such a one was the Duc de Villars, whom Voltaire had endeavoured to enlist in the cause. He had so far complied as to make an application to the Secretary of State, that the grounds of the sentence (*motifs de l'arrêt*) might be produced :—

This is as much as I considered myself justified in saying to M. de Saint-Florentin. I could not venture to assert that the sentence was an unjust sentence, as I have no reason for thinking it so. The papers which you have forwarded to me, and which I hereby acknowledge, have not altered my opinion. I wish I may be wrong in believing that fanaticism can prompt to any crime. But I cannot suppose that thirteen judges would unanimously condemn a man to the most terrible of punishments without a certain assurance of his guilt.

These sentiments, which breathe the refinement and cold good sense of the 'highest circles,' were by no means confined to those circles. They were above all things adapted to damp Voltaire, who, however he might outrage decency at times, was always alive to the proprieties. An anecdote is told by M. Gaberel (*Voltaire et les Génevois*) of a German Baron who happened in passing by Geneva to call at Ferney, in the very height of the business. Having just emerged from his patriarchal Schloss, the Baron was in baronial ignorance of the news of the day. Voltaire, who could think of nothing else, immediately inquired, ' Monsieur, que pensez-vous du pauvre Calas, qui a été roué ?'

' Il a été roué! Ah! il faut que ce soit un grand coquin!'

Voltaire's indignation may be guessed, and the visitor was summarily ejected from Ferney, much to his astonishment. His blunder was explained to him at Geneva. He, on his part, had supposed Calas to be some brigand to whom the Lord of Ferney had been administering seignorial justice.

The coldness of official persons was not the only obstacle to be grappled with. The Calas had a secret opponent in the most powerful personage in the realm, the Secretary of State, the Comte de Saint-Florentin. His opposition was all the more formidable that it was veiled under the cautious and stately reserve of diplomatic forms. What may have been the minister's policy it is impossible to guess. But we. now know, from the secret despatches, what was not penetrated by Voltaire himself, that throughout the affair the Secretary of State was the active and interested patron of the enemies of Calas.

Another danger to be guarded against was the susceptibility of the Catholics. Had the appeal of the Calas for justice been put in its true light, it might easily have been represented on the other side as a conspiracy of the Calvinists, and so not only the Church, but the whole Catholic party, have been roused to resist it. In drawing up the memorials for the appellants, Voltaire had the difficult task of pleading for a Protestant, and before Catholic France, such as Louis XIV had left it. His own account of the nicety of touch this required is found in one of the letters, published for the first time in 1856 (*Lettres Inédites*) :—

My dear Tronchin,—I send you the memorial as I have worded it for our Catholics at home; you see that, like the apostle, I make myself all things to all men. A Protestant, speaking as here in his own name, could not, I thought, conceal his creed, but must speak of it with modesty, to disarm, if possible, the French prejudice against Calvinism. Consider that there are plenty of folks quite ready to say, 'What signifies it if they have beaten a Calvinist to death ! The state has one enemy the less !' Depend upon it, many a good simple ecclesiastic thinks this. We must stop their mouths by a modest exposition of the reasonable side of Protestantism, so stated that the Catholic convert-mongers shall continue to cherish hopes of success.

Many other obstacles of a technical nature, such as the difficulty of obtaining a copy of the original proceedings at Toulouse, arose ; the expense, which was enormous, Voltaire paid out of his own pocket, or by a subscription among his friends ; but finally they were all surmounted by his address and ardour. On the 7th of March, three days short of a year since the death of Jean Calas, Voltaire had the gratification of seeing the first step towards reparation made. The Conseil d'État, on the motion of M. Mariette, made an order for the review of the case of Jean Calas. It had now attracted general attention, not only at the bar, and in legal and official circles, but in the court. The Conseil du Roi was held at Versailles ; and we have the following account from an eye-witness, in a letter dated the following day, March 8th :—

Madame Calas's affair was decided yesterday in the Council. I accompanied her to Versailles, as did several other gentlemen her friends. She met with a most favourable reception from the ministers. She was not obliged to wait anywhere. As soon as ever she presented herself, the doors flew wide open. Every one seemed bent on offering her all the sympathy in their power. The Chancellor said to her, 'Your business, Madam, engages all our thoughts. We desire that you should receive here all the consolation for your troubles which we can give.' She proceeded to the gallery, with her daughters, to see the king pass to council. Several of the great lords addressed her— the Duc d'A., the Comte de Noailles, &c. They undertook that the king should notice her, and placed her on purpose. But owing to a strange accident their design was frustrated. For just as the king came to the place, one of his suite stumbled and fell, and drew all eyes upon him.

This first *arrêt* of the Council, ordering a review, was only the first stage. It took twelve months more to carry the case through all the necessary steps. The 4th of June, the Council having reviewed the case, quashed the judgment of the Parlement of Toulouse (*arrêt de cassation*), and ordered a new trial.

The indignation at Toulouse, when the news reached that city, was extreme. It was indeed an extreme and rare stretch of royal power to reverse the judgment of a Supreme Court of justice. The lawyers at Toulouse maintained that it could not be done. However, they were obliged to content themselves with muttering this constitutional doctrine, and with making an extortionate charge for certified copies of the proceedings. One religious consolation the archbishop (Arthur Richard Dillon) indulgently added. To reward their Catholic zeal, and console them under their cruel humiliation, he permitted each of the counsellors of the Parlement to have mass said at home on Sundays. In the enjoyment of these Christian comforts they had nothing to regret, as they said, in the business, but not having had the whole five broken on the wheel instead of one only.

The Conseil du Roi, or Privy Council, having annulled the sentence as a court of appeal, sent the case for a new trial before a court composed of the ' Maîtres des Requêtes de l'Hôtel au Souverain.' This appears to have been a sort of Palace Court, for the trial of causes arising within the precincts of the palace or royal residence. Its cognizance seems to have been extended, on this and rare occasions, to such cases as the king in council pleased to reserve for his own hearing. This second trial was of the greatest consequence for clearing the memory and establishing the innocence of Jean Calas. Had the

Westminster Review, 1858.]

proceedings ended in annulling the Toulouse judgment, it would have been certainly pretended that the reversal was unfounded. Now the whole evidence was gone into afresh, and the Calas were enabled to produce evidence for the defence, which the iniquitous procedure of the provincial tribunal had not admitted. The examination of the evidence occupied six sittings of about four hours each, the last excepted, which was more than eight. The final sentence, in which the forty judges unanimously concurred, was given on the ninth of March, 1765—the very day three years on which the original sentence had been passed on Jean Calas. This piece of French puerility might better have been spared. 'This theatrical trick,' says Grimm[1], 'in so solemn a business, makes one shudder, as if one was among children playing with knives and axes.' Some of the advisers of Madame Calas, elated with success, urged her to proceed to sue the Parlement of Toulouse for damages. This was judiciously prevented. She received a sum in compensation out of the public purse. It sounds considerable, but it was all exhausted in the costly legal proceedings which had now spread over three years, besides the sums which had been laid out by Voltaire. To the subscription which Voltaire opened foreign countries contributed. The Empress of Russia was said to have given 3000 livres. The English subscription-list contained nearly one hundred and fifty names, headed by those of the Queen and the Archbishop of Canterbury. Long before all the creditors were paid off, these succours were exhausted; and it remained for the National Convention in '92—thirty years after the event—to make this final reparation. On the 23rd Pluviose, the citoyen Bézard made a set harangue before the Convention, reciting the whole story, and bringing forward some facts which had not been produced on the trial, with which he had been furnished by the surviving members of

---

[1] *Corresp. Lit.*, 25 Mars.

the family. This is the last public notice of the Calas tragedy.

One reflection is forced upon us by reviewing the share which law had in this drama. The arm by which Voltaire fought out his success was public opinion. The power by which the Catholic magistrates of Toulouse had worked was also a public opinion, viz. that of the Catholic population of Languedoc. Voltaire was able to upset their judgment by bringing to bear on the tribunals a wider and more comprehensive publicity. The opinion of Europe corrected the narrow bigotry of a remote province. The tribunals play a subordinate part throughout. Law appears as the creature and instrument of the public voice, which controls and directs its findings. Instead of waiting to let the case be sifted in court, confident that justice will be done, the public out of doors dictate what view the bench shall take. The public must assume the office of Dicast, and labour through the evidence, or there is no security that justice will be done. Let us suppose that instead of a sceptical and tolerant age, with a Voltaire to direct opinion, these events had occurred in a reactionary and servile period, when orthodoxy and the infallibility of government were the reigning doctrines, what possible chance would there have been of the reversal of Jean Calas's sentence? The same bigotry which had perverted justice at Toulouse would have sanctioned the perversion at Paris. The rational and instructed minority would have raised their voice, but it would have been heard only in an unavailing and despised protest. There has probably been no age of the history of France in which such a sentence as this passed by the Parlement of Toulouse was impossible. There is hardly any period of that history, besides the one in question, when such a conspicuous act of justice to a Protestant as the reversal of Calas's sentence, was possible.

Westminster Review, 1858.]

Thus it happened that a matter of fact, no more doubtful than any of the most certain facts in history, became a party question. The memory of Calas had been vindicated by Voltaire and the Encyclopedists. That was quite enough for the Catholics. A good Catholic must know no more in order to form his opinion. It is the characteristic of Catholicism that it supersedes reason, and prejudges all matters by the application of fixed principles. And this habit of mind a Catholic carries with him from religion and philosophy into history and matters of fact. His question is not, 'Is there evidence that this man did this thing?' but, 'which view does the Church take?' The mental habit thus engendered is fatal to truth and integrity. M. Coquerel flatters himself, in his closing words, that he has set the matter at rest for ever. The writers on both sides, he says, had followed the same method. They had repeated, out of the histories, the same arguments, the partisans dwelling on those which seemed to tell for the accused,—the adversaries on those which made against them. But no one before himself had undertaken to go through in detail the written depositions and the pleadings of the advocates. M. Coquerel ought to know his countrymen better than to think that even demonstrative evidence will procure from Catholic opinion justice for a Protestant. Reasonable and well-informed men of course will see the truth. But the mass of Catholics are carefully protected from reason and information. We have little doubt that as long as the Catholic religion shall last, their little manuals of falsified history will continue to repeat that Jean Calas murdered his son because he had become a convert to the Catholic faith.

XVI.

PRESENT STATE OF THEOLOGY IN GERMANY[1].

(*Westminster Review*, 1857.)

IN the early sessions of the Council of Constance, the votes of the assembled prelates and divines were taken by nations. The injustice of this arrangement was complained of by the Pope, on the plea that it reduced the learned Italian and French prelates to a level with the English and Germans.

Since the fifteenth century, Theology has emigrated. Extinct in Italy, and all but so in France, it is now in Germany alone that the vital questions of Religion are discussed with the full and free application of all the resources of learning and criticism which our age has at its command. It is not that better books are produced in Germany than elsewhere : it is, that theological inquiry and research are alive there as they are not elsewhere. The colliding elements of which religious sentiment is made up are there circulating with a healthy activity through the intelligence of the educated classes ; and the

---

[1] 1. *Zur Geschichte der neuesten Theologie.* Von KARL SCHWARZ, ausserordentlichem Professor der Theologie zu Halle. 3° Auflage. Leipzig. 1856.

2. *Internal History of German Protestantism since the Middle of the last Century.* By C. F. A. KAHNIS, Professor of Theology in the University of Leipzig. Translated from the German by Theod. Meyer, Hebrew Tutor in the New College, Edinburgh. Edinburgh : (Clark). 1856.

3. *Die Kirchengeschichte des 18en und 19en Jahrhunderts aus dem Standpunkte des evangelischen Protestantismus.* Von Dr. K. R. HAGENBACH. 3° verbesserte Auflage. Leipzig. 1856.

result is that balance of system which is as necessary to sound mental, as to bodily, organization.

We may distinguish two kinds of vital action of the religious sensibility. One which spreads itself through the masses. This rouses to action, originates crusades and religious wars, animates martyrs. Its organ is the pulpit, or the pamphlet; its issues are tried in councils and synods. The other is confined to the educated, perhaps we should say the reading, classes. Its organ is the book, or the Professor's chair. It is speculative, and concerns itself with thought and words, not with acts. It is the religious sentiment manifesting itself through the intelligence, in criticism and reflection, moulding and applying, assimilating and reproducing portions of the religious material which time has accumulated. The product of this process is Theology.

It is of this latter process and its result that the following pages speak. Our object is not to give detailed abstracts of books or systems, but to indicate the broad features of the sections into which theological opinion is at present divided, and to enable an unprejudiced reader to judge how far the religious literature of Germany fulfils the conditions of a healthy theology.

For in this country, it is hardly necessary to say, a very unfavourable opinion of the state of theology in Germany is widely prevalent. We welcome eagerly their historical and critical labours ; the scholars in our universities are content, though with an occasional outburst of impatience, to sit at the feet of German professors in Greek, and in general Philology. But German Theology has been long under a ban. Not to speak of the wholly uninformed, who depend entirely on the reports of others, even educated men participate largely in this undefined prejudice. Undefined it is, but peremptory. And though it is impossible to reduce the contradictory epithets, in which the prejudice expresses itself, to any common term, we may extract from

them at least two separate ideas which seem to be generally shared in.   First, theological speculation in Germany
is wild and lawless, a chaos of reckless criticism and baseless systems which, 'like momentary monsters, rise and
fall,' bearing no relation to religion, and not worthy of a
plain, sensible man's attention.   Secondly, it is not merely
foolish, but impious; not merely superfluous in religion,
but irreligious and antichristian.

To these two may perhaps be reduced the notions
prevalent among intelligent men in this country about
German Theology.   Other, but accidental, impediments
there are which deter them from approaching the subject.
In addition to the natural difficulty of the German language
—a difficulty prodigiously enhanced by the elaborate
sinuosity of the period which German writers now choose
to adopt—there is a discrepancy between their mode of
thinking and ours.   'It has often been remarked with
regret,' says a recent writer[1], 'that while the learned in the
exacter sciences abroad and in England have the most
perfect sympathy with each other,—while the physician or
the mathematician in London is completely at home in the
writings of the physician or the mathematician in Berlin
and Paris, there is a sensible, though invisible, barrier,
which separates the jurists, the moral philosophers, the
politicians, and the historians of the Continent, from those
who follow the same pursuits in England.'   This divergence—a divergence not of opinion, but in our mode of
thinking—is even more manifested in our Theology, than
in the moral and political sciences.   It is therefore an
element of difference which must be discounted in a comparison of conclusions.   As common to many provinces of
thought, the influences of nationality must not be credited
to one.   The national medium of thought must not be
confused with the results of thought.   We make allowance for this variation of form, in our study of ancient

[1] Dr. [lately Sir Henry] Maine, *On Roman Law and Legal Education.*
Westminster Review, 1857.]

literatures, but it is no less indispensable to do so in the case of living and contemporary nations. Yet we do not do it. We are apt to regard language as the only obstacle to complete intercourse with the intellectual produce of a foreign European nation, and to expect that when we have surmounted this barrier, we are to find ourselves at once naturalized. The abundance of translations tends to foster this expectation. We read a translation from the German as we would an original English book. We expect that, because the language difficulty is smoothed for us, we are to meet with no other impediment to apprehension than such as the subject itself may present. When we find that this is not the case, when we still encounter an element which eludes our grasp, and feel ourselves inhaling an atmosphere in which we do not freely breathe, we summarily condemn our book, form and matter, contents and treatment, together. No one does this with an old philosophy. No one expects from an English translation of the Vedas, or of Aristotle's Metaphysics, to find Hindoo or Greek philosophy lying patent before him. The whole of the interpretation is to come, after translation is ended. When we have penetrated the language, there remain many integuments through which we have to make our way to the thought. The intricacies of this process may be greater for an ancient, than for any modern, literature. But they exist in all. No one, certainly, is under any obligation to undertake this labour for the Theology of Germany. But no one has any right to pronounce it 'unintelligible' till he has taken the proper means to understand it.

Other hasty and imperfect notions are also current on the subject. It is believed by some that German criticism is the product of professorial rivalry. Dr. Pusey, e. g. can count on an audience to whom he can say that these theories originate in the pleasure of pulling to pieces 'what has been received for thousands of years;'

Such has been the course which the mind of the German professors has taken, and in part is taking.   One cannot read speculations on Holy Scripture, in which it is dissected into fragments on some arbitrary theory of the professor's, without marvelling at the self-confidence with which conflicting opinions are proposed, and at the same time feeling that the interest which the different theories have in the author's eyes is their supposed ingenuity.   The aim is to achieve something that has not been achieved before.—*Evidence, &c., on the State of the University of Oxford*, p. 24.

That there have been reckless assertions and unqualified critics,—that the revolutionary spirit has at times disturbed the calm temper of historical inquiry,—that the ardour of novelty has carried the discoverer beyond the bounds of sobriety,—all this is certain.   But to think that so pervasive, deep-principled, and epochal a development of thought as has been evolved in Germany during the last hundred years can have had for its sole or its chief cause one of the most puerile and ostentatious of human passions, is a belief which could only satisfy minds of the most superficial order.   This philosophy of 'What great events from trifling causes spring,' is a poor key to history.   Voltaire's *Dictionary*, once thought ' philosophical,' explained the Reformation from a jealousy of the Augustinian monks against the Dominican friars. 'Ce petit intérêt de moines dans un coin de la Saxe produisit plus de cent ans de discordes, de fureurs, et d'infortunes chez trente nations.'   We now believe, on the contrary, that 'tout se tient dans l'ordre des idées,' and that in intellectual, as in social, changes, the state of belief in any age is determined by the conditions of that which preceded.   On this principle only is a history of Theology either possible or instructive.

And the time is now come when German Theology can be historically described.   The noise and confusion of the battle are over.   The dust and smoke are rolled away, and the contending forces may now be seen in position, in orderly and intelligible arrangement.   The critical Theo-

logy has become conscious of its own mission. From a
blind instinct of aimless inquiry, from the eager ebullition
of youthful curiosity which would question everything, it
has matured into a habit of careful research, governed by
a conscientious spirit, and armed with all the resources of
knowledge, direct and collateral. If, indeed, its early
enthusiasm has abated, this is inevitable. All fertile
periods of speculative agitation, such as that which
Germany has just gone through, are only possible because
they are stimulated by hopes too sanguine to be realized.
After a time the human mind is brought-to, in its most
adventurous flights, by the bounds which it cannot pass.
It recognizes, when 'roused by the shock which drives it
back, the wall of adamant which bounds inquiry.' It
lowers its pretensions, but at the same time consolidates
its efforts. In this stage is German theological endeavour.
Never was speculation less wild or capricious. Its every
movement has to be made under the surveillance of the
most vigilant criticism. Its own intense consciousness of
the laws of logical method checks it at every turn. The
enormous wealth of applicable learning which it has
accumulated hampers its operations. It can no longer be
ingenious or inventive, but is under the imperative necessity of being just. It may smile at the crude conjectures
of its young rationalist days, but it must be with a mixture
of regret for the freedom and elasticity with which it then
sallied forth for the conquest of the world.

The critical Theology, then, having attained the
maturity of its growth, perhaps already in the decline of
its strength, but certainly not yet numbered with the
things which belong to the past, is a proper subject for
the historian : and it has not been neglected. Already
histories abound; and the nineteenth century is in a fair
way of being as thoroughly discussed as the sixteenth.
Besides fragments contributed to some of the many
religious periodicals from nearly every theologian of

repute in Germany, there are complete histories of recent Theology by Kahnis, and Gieseler. For the earlier part of the period, that is from the beginnings of Rationalism down to Strauss, Professor Hagenbach's *Lectures on the Church History of the Eighteenth and Nineteenth Centuries* (Leipzig, 1856) offer an excellent introductory sketch. Popularly written, without being superficial, the book is what too many German books are not, readable. For the later and contemporary portion of the period, since the Straussian crisis, the brilliant sketch of Dr. Schwarz leaves nothing to be desired.

It will, of course, be understood that such reviews as the two now mentioned, can but initiate a student into a vast and varied material. To follow out the whole movement of the critical Theology, and of so much of the philosophical revival as is connected with Theology, is a study by itself. It is, too, a study well deserving the time and pains it requires on the part of the student of history. For it must not be supposed that German Theology is some obscure national product, the concern exclusively of the country which has given it birth. It is no insulated phenomenon. Though generated in Germany, it belongs to Christendom. It is the theological movement of the age. It is only because there is fuller intellectual life in Germany than elsewhere,—only because it so happens that, at present, European speculation is transacted by Germans, as our financial affairs are by Jews, that German characteristics are impressed on the substance of the Christian science. The capital of learning is in the hands of Germans, and theirs has been the enterprise which has directed it into theological channels. The stream may be strongly coloured by the peculiarities of the locality through which its course at present lies ; but it is the old stream of Christian tradition still, whose source is in the Galilean Lake. If we have not been drawn into it, or contributed to it, it is not because we have found a better channel for thought, but because we have dispensed with thought on such subjects altogether. So far as there has been speculative movement in any other of the constituents of the European commonwealth of nations, so far they have participated in the German impulse.

For this is the historical law of the progress of the human Mind. In each wave of its advance, in each epoch-making conquest, some one nation has taken the lead, and done the work, while all have shared in the profits. *Sic vos non vobis* is the condition of all industry, intellectual, as well as material. In quite modern times it would seem as if the burden and labour of human progress were pretty evenly shared between the three nations of Europe who have any liberty of action at all. The French have had hitherto the working out of the political problem. To the share of the English has fallen the social and industrial difficulty. Speculative Germany has claimed for her own the problems of thought, the abstract matters of Philosophy and Theology. To each of these separate tasks is attached its own burden, its own peculiar danger. We each do our work at our own risks and perils. It is a venture in which each, if he loses, wrecks only his own fortunes; what each gains is equally gained by all. The political experimentalist, France, undertakes hers, subject to the most terrible casualties,—to violent revolution,— to the sudden transference of power from one extremity of the body politic to the other. The English industrial development is big with the threatening evils of pauperism, fraud, and bankruptcy, of which none can yet foresee the issues. It cannot, therefore, be expected that the work of the intellect should not be subject to its own dangers,— to the destruction of faith,—to the too absolute rupture with the past,—to exhaustion and paralysis from over-exertion, and other diseases incident to vigorous life.

Nor is it only in the most recent times that Germany has been called to this office. There have been, in all,

three epochs at which Christian doctrine has acquired a
new development.   Each of these epochs of development
was determined by a previous excitement of the speculative faculty.

1. The Greek Theology, or the Christological controversies of the fourth and fifth centuries: determined by
the speculative excitement which arose out of the collision
of Greek with Oriental ideas, and to which may be given
the name of the Gnostical Movement.

2. The Latin Theology of the twelfth and thirteenth
centuries : determined by the speculative movement commonly called the Scholastic Philosophy.

3. The Vernacular Theology, or the Reformation
Controversies : determined by the intellectual excitement
known as the Renaissance.

In this last conflict and evolution of Christian doctrine
Germany had, undeniably, the chief, if not the whole
labour.   It is true that the most elaborate of all the
renderings of the Protestant views, Calvin's *Institutes,*
was the work of a Frenchman.   But the inspiration, if not
the substance, of Calvin's scheme of thought came from
the German controversies.

The source of the inspiration, however, was very soon
closed.   How far the Reformation doctrinal development
had exhausted itself from within,—how far it was checked
from without, by the interference of power, is not now for
discussion.   Suffice it that for two centuries or more
theology in Europe was dormant, except so far as the
Quinquarticular controversies at the beginning of the
seventeenth century may be considered an exception.
Future historians of Christianity will have to describe
as—

The *fourth* Epoch of its doctrinal development, that
which commenced in Germany towards the latter part of
the eighteenth century, a movement which is now, at the
middle of the nineteenth, approaching its consummation.

Westminster Review, 1857.]

This movement contains two directions, a speculative and a critical. In its speculative effort, it was determined by the new philosophy which we may designate by the name of Kant. In its critical effort it was inspired by the Philological activity which preceded, and which has outlived the Philosophical properly so called.

These epoch-making movements in the history of Christian doctrine are distinguished from the other portions of its course by being productive. In the long periods which intervene between these Epochs, theology is not lost. Religious ideas always subsist. Books are written. Doctrines are taught, expounded, proved, argued. But though the ideas are there, they do not fecundate. Nothing is developed from them. The mind does not go on to new applications of the old principles. Theology becomes an abstract matter,—gets more and more an affair of books, and less and less applicable to the course of the world. These intervening periods thus become periods of orthodoxy, and merge in the stagnation of Christian thought. The epochs are moments of revival and reform. They are characterized by earnestness, energy, and intensity of thought. The religious consciousness is awakened, and the ideas of religion become again matter of human interest. The inexhaustible applicability of Christian truth strikes the new generation with wonder. Men are engrossed with the rediscovered principles, and absorbed in measuring and comparing, in applying and adapting them to those masses of other knowledge which had been accumulating on their hands during the last long period of abeyance.

Thus, movement is the characteristic of the epoch of religious revival. It follows, that one indispensable condition of such revival is freedom for thought. The natural action of the popular mind must not be interfered with by any controlling force from without. It is here precisely as in morals or politics: free agency is the condition under

which the individual must work out his own happiness.
Political freedom is essential to constitutional development.
That this is the true order of things is now recognized by
foreign theorists on the English Constitution.   It has
been the creation of our freedom.   Our liberty is not
guaranteed by the constitutional forms.   Rightly does a
recent eloquent writer place the freedom of discussion at
the head of his dissection of English politics :—

'Sachons reconnaître en premier lieu,' says Count Montalembert,
' le fait qui est à la fois la condition essentielle de la vie nationale, et la
source des erreurs les plus habituelles aux juges étrangers.   Tout y
[in England] est discuté, critiqué, débattu sans réserve.   Tout s'y
fait au grand jour et au milieu du bruit.   Rien n'échappe à cette loi
universelle.   Religion, politique, guerre, législation, administration, il
faut que tout passe et repasse chaque jour par ce crible redoubt-
able. . . . Telle est d'ailleurs, partout et toujours, la condition de la
vie, de la vraie vie, de la vie virile, la seule dont il vaille la peine de
vivre ! Ce qui fait la force des individus fait aussi la force des nations ;
l'habitude du danger, la perpétuité de l'effort, la liberté du mouve-
ment.   Qui jamais a rêvé la vie avec un garde-vue sur les yeux, avec
du coton dans les oreilles, avec la main d'un maître pour béquille ?
Quand vous me montrez un homme dans cet accoutrement, je plains
et je respecte les infirmités inséparables de la vieillesse, mais je n'y
reconnais pas les conditions de la vie [1].'

These words, descriptive of the freedom and vigour of
political life, are not inapplicable to the Church.   Christian
Theology has been elaborated by controversy.   Out of
the war and collision of opinion, out of an atmosphere of
conflict, each age has had to draw the spiritual truth on
which it has lived.   The indispensable condition of this
process is freedom of opinion.   The natural balance
and consistency of the human mind with itself will
keep it just, only if no alien influence be intruded into its
deliberations.   Under that condition, the formation of doctrine is promoted, and its truth guaranteed, by the fervour,
intensity, and variety of speculative effort, by the con-

[1] *De l'Avenir Politique de l'Angleterre*, p. 23.

flict of mind with mind, by the correction which opposing systems mutually supply each to the other. In the words of V. Cousin—' La victoire absolue, c'est la mort en philosophie; un système rival est nécessaire au meilleur système, et la critique est la vie de la science[1].' Not that contention and strife can be ever other than evil; they are among the evils of imperfect intelligence. In the beatific vision there is no shadow of doubt; the perfect reason does not employ logic. But neither perfect understanding nor perfect virtue is attainable by man in his present state. The Church militant is no more in possession of absolute truth than it is of absolute sanctity. ' Speculative difficulties are of the very same nature as external temptations[2].' We cannot, in this life, place ourselves without the sphere of either.

But the recent German movement is not only a vital movement in the heart of Christian Theology; it is, further, a movement in a direct line from the Reformation. It is the historical consequent of the great Revolution of the sixteenth century. So little is it the arbitrary creation of hallucinating professors, that it were nearer the truth to say it was necessitated by the regular progress of European thought.

The Reformation of the sixteenth century comprised within itself two directions—a revulsion or reaction of popular sentiment, and a development of formal doctrine. The first of these, or the popular commotion, played so important a part in that movement as to have thrown the latter comparatively into the shade. The dogmatic position of the Reformation was undoubtedly its weak side. The ecclesiastical abuses in the Western Church were patent and acknowledged. They were tacitly acknowledged even by the Church itself, inasmuch as the most flagrant of them were gradually corrected and removed. But against the doctrines of the Reformation the Church

---

[1] *Abelard*, p. 179.   [2] Butler, *Analogy.*

of Rome has always been able to make a successful resistance. This is because the Reformation dogmatic rests on an hypothesis which Catholic Theology does not admit—viz. the exclusive sufficiency of Scripture. The Roman theologian smiles to see the self-complacence with which the Protestant divine first assumes as his basis Scripture, interpreted by Reason, as his rule of faith, and then proceeds to make Scripture yield up, as its contents, precisely the confessions of the sixteenth century, and no more. The formal position of the Reformation is often stated as the insurrection of the human reason against the yoke of authority. The movement may have tended in this direction. but it was not this consciously or avowedly. Its formal and avowed basis was an appeal from the Church to the Bible. The Reformers rejected the traditions and beliefs of the Institution in favour of the Document. The force and success of their appeal lay in its presenting itself as an appeal from the human to the divine ; from the Church, now discovered to be a society of men, to a book, thought to be the book of God. Even had they meant reason, it would have been of small avail to say so ; for that would have been to appeal from the human to the human, and would have been but a weak engine against the stronghold of Babylon. They could only have triumphed by being able to produce an admitted infallible on their own side against a fallible on the other. For, while the Romanists admitted the authority of Scripture, the Protestants did not admit the authority of the Church. The claims of Reason, then, were not argued; the question lay, for the sixteenth century, between rival authorities ; and in that form it has been transmitted by tradition, and thoroughly ingrafted into the popular religious sentiment of our own day. But a very slight consideration of the history of the Reformation is sufficient to show that the hypothesis of The Book owed its victory over the rival hypothesis of transmission by an incorporated society, to causes extraneous to any superior probability intrinsic in the hypothesis itself. At any rate, it was inevitable that, when that hypothesis had done its work in controversy as against papal authority and ecclesiastical tradition, it should, in quieter times, be itself subjected to examination. What determined the Reformation was, as has been said, the intellectual revival of the Renaissance. A mass of knowledge was gradually accumulated, and a momentum acquired by speculative curiosity, which became inconsistent with the inert religious ideas that had been kept sedulously isolated from the humanist movement. The human mind at last turned round on its religious system, and found that it had come to bear with its whole weight on the prop of Church authority. Protestantism transferred so much of the superstructure as it retained to the foundation of Scripture. Instead of building on the Church, it built on the 'pure Word of God.' Having done so much, it stopped. The Reformation impulse was exhausted for a time. Theology came to a stand-still. The same process which had prepared the way for the Reformation was gradually going on. Knowledge was accumulating outside : critical inquiry was gathering force. Theological science all the while intrenched itself more and more jealously within the narrow limits of the sixteenth century. Again the human mind turned round upon its inherited religious system, and found that it rested with its whole weight upon a book. It was inevitable that the claims of the book should be submitted to tests. It is imperative that, on a matter so all-important to it, the understanding of Christians should be satisfied that the book is what it is alleged to be,—that it *can* be the sole and exclusive source of our religious hopes and beliefs. Criticism, so far from being imperious and arbitrary, is become the duty to which Theology is summoned. Should it be found that the basis to which Christian doctrine was shifted by the Reformers was an insufficient one, wé have precisely the same right, we are under the same obligations, to transfer it to what appears to the best of our knowledge to be a sounder position, as the Reformers were when they substituted Scripture for the Church. While the Protestant Churches generally have evaded this plain duty, and betaken themselves to anathemas, intrenching themselves behind the 'authority' of the Reformers in the very spirit in which the Reformation was resisted, the inquiry has been honestly and courageously undertaken in Germany, and something, at least, has been done in the last fifty years towards a solution of its difficulties.

It is easy to say that little has been really done—that there is little to show for so much agitation—that the number of questions unsettled is large compared to that which has been settled. We shall not think so when we are sufficiently aware of the complexities and delicacies of the subject. The principles of celestial mechanics are not at all doubtful; yet what long periods of inquiry and debate, what hot opposition had to be encountered, before they could be installed in the place of the traditional hypothesis! The true character of the early history of the Roman republic is but slowly establishing itself in the understanding of educated men. Yet how small the amount of human interest involved in upholding the traditions of Livy! Were the theological question, indeed, a mere question of fact—e.g. a question of the authorship or genuineness of this or that particular book, it would be soon decided. But the relation of the Canonical Books and of the opinions of the first Christians to the opinions of Christians in our own day—this is, in its very nature, a question not admitting of being ruled in the absolute and definitive way which the objection requires. Probability is the essence of historical criticism; nor can that criticism divest its reasonings of their probable character, because the records to which it is applied are religious records.

Westminster Review, 1857.]

So far as divine facts have been suffered to be incorporated into the world's history,—so far as they have become events,—so far they must needs be described, recorded, interpreted, and arranged by the same means as any other events. The transcendent importance and spiritual bearing of the events resides in the nature of the events themselves. The human soul, with its eternal destinies, is lodged in a material body. There are no other means than the universal laws of chemistry and physiology by which we may ascertain the conditions under which that body subsists. There is no short cut, no royal road, whether by way of pope or of council, of fathers or reformers, by which we can grasp so much of the Christian revelation as is matter of fact and record.

We may conveniently classify the existing Theology of Germany into three tendencies, or schools : — 1. The Historico-critical. 2. The Orthodox. 3. The Mediation-Theology, which lies between, and desires to reconcile, Nos. 1 and 2.

1. The first place is due, on many grounds, to the Critical school. Criticism was the problem bequeathed to succeeding times by the Reformation, which had set off the Apostolic age and the Canonical Books, against the middle-age development of Christianity. This the sixteenth century had done with success. But it had made an appeal to history, and had therefore invited a scrutiny of the historical antecedents which itself was unable to apply. And if the Reformation had challenged criticism, it was precisely in this direction that modern discovery had been advancing. Already, in the commencement of the seventeenth century, Joseph Scaliger had turned the stream of historical research into ecclesiastical channels, and had swept away much of the pseudepigraphical literature which had been accepted as genuine equally by the Protestants and Catholics of the sixteenth. The deistical

movement, too, of the eighteenth century, which denied any value to the Christian records on *a priori* and inappropriate grounds, forced upon Theology the task of determining the true character of its own historical monuments.

The Historico-critical process, then, claims attention first as the legitimate continuation of the Protestant movement in Theology.   At the present time, it not only holds the first place, but seems to be in exclusive occupation of the field of Theology.   The speculative movement, which in Schleiermacher advanced with such lofty aims and brilliant promise, is for the present suspended.   It cannot indeed be said that it has borne no fruit, or left no influence behind it, but as an instrument of inquiry, it shares in the general depreciation of philosophy.   We have not therefore thought it necessary, in our classification of existing schools, to reserve a place for the Philosophical process.   All that there is of speculative effort is now subsidiary to the historical inquiry, which cautiously and sparingly employs it in its service.

In this subordination of the speculative to the critical method, lies the great distinction of the Historical, or, as it is familiarly called, the Tübingen school.   Hitherto, philological criticism had been an instrument of speculative theology.   That is to say, the theologian determined his doctrines by some other method, and then had recourse to criticism to fortify a foregone conclusion, or to annoy an opponent in his position.   Interpretation had become, in the most barefaced way, the art of finding in the Bible that which each had determined to believe.   The old satire—

> Hic liber est in quo quaerit sua dogmata quisque,
> Invenit et pariter dogmata quisque sua,

not only applied strictly to the herd of commentators, but more original minds did not escape this vicious circle. This circle, be it observed, is not to be confounded with that vague accusation which is often urged against the Protestant claims of private judgment. Romanist and Anglican controversialists have found no more fertile topic than this of 'prejudice': that education necessarily biasses the mind; that principles of judgment are, in fact, opinions; and that, before we come with matured powers to exercise this so-called 'private judgment' on Scripture, impartiality between competing interpretations is no longer possible to us. This line of argument, an arrow out of the quiver of the sceptics, has been often urged with great force on the side of Authoritative religion, and replied to on the other. Distinct from this question of the qualification of human reason, with all its interest, is that peculiar inconsequence by which the Reformation Theology was embarrassed in its appeal to Scripture. It takes its stand upon a book which it pronounces the sole authentic depositary of the Divine Will. The contents of this book can only be arrived at in the way in which the contents of any book are—by understanding its language. Its language is ancient. The adequate knowledge of a dead language is Scholarship. The proper application of grammatical and historical knowledge to the elucidation of a book requires a very high class of scholarship, or Philology. Philology is eminently the Protestant science. Every advance or improvement in philology was an improvement of the Protestant organum, a strengthening of the Protestant arm. All the great philologers were Protestants. But as the art of interpretation was improved, it was found that a knowledge of authorship, ay, and of constituent ideas, was essential to complete interpretation. Now to do this in the case of Scripture was incompatible, or it was feared might become incompatible, not only with the creeds with which the reformed Churches had over and above burdened themselves, but with the original assumption of Scripture altogether. Protestantism was therefore in this dilemma. It must either give up Scripture, or put

Q 2

a veto on its interpretation.   If the principle of ' Scripture
the only source' was to be maintained, it could only be
maintained by applying the recognized laws of interpretation.   To veto interpretation was to reduce Scripture to
silence.

Critical and exegetical effort had thus, ever since the
Reformation, been confined by an unnatural barrier.
Its free action had been prohibited, and consequently
all its results falsified. A principle derived from speculation had controlled and vitiated Scripture interpretation.
The eminent merit of the Tübingen school is, to have
freed Scripture interpretation from this false position.   It
no longer, by a speculative assumption, makes Scripture
interpretation impossible.   It distinguishes carefully what
is speculative from what is historical in religion.   It
conceives of Christianity as a series of connected events,
having a history, the earliest preserved records of which
are the canonical books.   It does not deny the perennial
source of religious consciousness in the human breast, but
it selects for the special field of its own labours the
historical manifestations.   It makes no pretensions to
fetter speculation, but makes it its humbler object to
ascertain what has occurred, what has been thought and
felt.   It does not enter the lists for or against this or that
doctrine, but analyzes it, tracing its growth and formation.
Ecclesiastical history had been hitherto only a vehicle for
party passion.   Scripture was degraded into a repertory
of texts out of which doctrines were to be supported.
Critical and historical conclusions had been applied by
one side to pull down, by the other to maintain, the
orthodox system, but there was no belief in criticism and
history as scientific methods.   The Tübingen divines did
not invent historical criticism, nor were they the first to
employ it upon dogma.   But they have been the first to
assert its paramount claims, as the method of interpretation,
exclusive of any other hypothesis.   Bacon did not invent

induction, but he was the first to assert it as the supreme and only method of procedure in Physics. Even in the beginnings of philology in the sixteenth century, it had been said by Joseph Scaliger, 'Non aliunde dissidia in religione pendent, quam ab ignoratione grammaticae.' The importance of this pregnant sentence has been slowly making itself felt. The claim of philology as the only key to history has been gradually established. After being successfully applied to every branch of history, its latest conquest was the history of philosophy. The only unconquered territory then left was the history of theological opinion and religious sentiment. This we now see, for the first time, fairly and fully undertaken by men qualified for the task. They have relieved Scripture criticism from the incapacity under which it laboured, from the opprobrium of dishonesty which had attached to it. It is not too much to say that more has been done for the elucidation of the first three centuries during the last twenty years, than in the two hundred years which preceded. This signal success, in a subject seemingly so well worn, must be ascribed chiefly to the distinct and consistent application of their principle of inquiry. It cannot be overlooked, however, that it has been greatly promoted by the genius and unrivalled acquirements of one man, the celebrated head of the critical school—Dr. Baur.

F. Ch. Baur—the initials are necessary to distinguish him from a critic of a very different stamp, Bruno Bauer —is not only the chief of the Tübingen school, but is unquestionably the first of living theologians. His exterior, by which one is involuntarily reminded of Gibbon— heavy, sleepy, and somewhat coarse, gives indication of the intellectual power locked up within. This exhibits itself in his books and lectures, in the rare union of opposite qualifications—viz. the most extensive reading, with the most elastic vigour of original speculation. He has Mosheim's colossal capacity for details, with Schleier-

macher's inventive genius. A deficiency in either of
these points would have equally destroyed his means
of remoulding the subject as he has done. With the
exception of a few, and those certainly interesting, recent
discoveries, all the facts of early Christian history had
been long in the hands of theologians—had been turned
over and over—commented and illustrated on a thousand
sides. On the other hand, the speculative and *a priori*
method had fairly exhausted itself in the various Hegelian
schools. 'Mere theory' had shown its impotence in
Strauss's *Leben Jesu*, in which it professed to dissipate
all fact and reality, to disperse history into air. Forsaking
the illusory path of speculation, Baur undertook to submit
all the remains, genuine and spurious, of early Christianity
to a new examination, on the same rigidly critical method
which had been applied to the remains of classical antiquity. A bare enumeration of his labours may convey
some idea of their compass and drift. No description can
do justice to the fund of learning and vigour of thought
which they contain.

Baur first came forward as a writer in 1824, with his
Symbolik und Mythologie, in which he still stands on
Schleiermacher. In 1831 he published, in the pages of a
theological journal, the *Tübinger Zeitschrift*, two essays, on
The Derivation of Ebionitism from Essenism, and *The Party
of Christ (Christuspartei) in the Corinthian Church*. The
latter of these essays contains already the germ of that view
which he has since much expanded—viz. the view of the
development of Christianity through the antagonism of Petrinism and Paulinism continued within the Church up to the
middle of the second century. In 1833 he first descended
to the times of the Reformation, and stood forward as an
expounder of the principle of Protestantism against Möhler.
After this, there followed in rapid succession a series
of striking monographs :—*The Manichaean System* (1831),
The Christian Gnosis (1835), *On the so-called Pastoral*

Epistles (1835), *On the Design and Occasion of the Epistle to
the Romans* (1836), *The Origin of the Episcopate* (1838);
these were smaller essays preluding to works of greater
extent and compass. These were, *The Christian Doctrine
of the Atonement* (1838), *Tertullian's Doctrine of the Eu-
charist* (*Tübinger Zeitschrift* (1839), *The Christian Doctrine
of the Trinity and Incarnation of God* (1841–43),
The Apostle Paul (1845), *On the Canonical Gospels*
(1847), and lastly, *The Christian Church of the First
Three Centuries* (1853). There are, besides these, many
dissertations scattered through the volumes of the *Theologische Jahrbücher,*—a journal established chiefly by
himself in 1842. In one of the most recent, he has returned
again to the topic which had engaged him in 1833—the distinctive principle of Protestantism, examining the claims
which Lutheranism, Calvinism, and Melanchthonism respectively make to be the orthodox representative of the
Reformation[1].

The characteristic of Baur's method has been already
indicated. The animation and force of his reasoning is
derived from the directness and distinctness of his purpose.
The vigour and inspiration, which many theorists have
drawn from theological passion, is supplied to him from
his confidence in his scientific method. Every fact with
him tells, and is referred to its place. He is no historical
painter, to bring forward events because they make a good
picture. He values nothing but what is significant, and
to him every phrase of an ancient writer is significant.
With the same fine tact with which Niebuhr follows the
trail of a national migration, Baur tracks a dogma. Not
an inflexion, however minute, escapes him; not a complication, however perplexed, that he does not unravel. The
traverses and passes of dialectic, the flights and vagaries of

---

[1] *Theolog. Jahrbücher*, Bd. XIV, Jahrgang 1855. [Baur's method, and his
general results, are expounded in two works, *Epochs in the Treatment of
Ecclesiastical History* (1852), and *Christianity and the Christian Church in the
First Three Centuries* (1853).]

mysticism, the solid and the frivolous, the heights and depths through which the doctrine in its passage down the stream of time has ranged, are all marshalled in their due relation to the general development of the thought.

Out of Baur's strength comes his weakness. The law of the development of thought had become in his hands the master-key of the history of doctrine. The idea, so fertile and seductive, led, not unnaturally, to exaggeration. The Hegelian *a priori* construction was over-driven in its application to Christian history. This speculative genesis of dogma explained so much, that it was too hastily concluded it could explain all. It is quite true that the dogmatic process takes place through successive generations, according to the laws of dialectic. It is further true that this sequence is the thread that must be taken up to follow through the mazes of history. But it should not be overlooked that other influences come in from without, modifying and marring the symmetry of the logical dependence. The impulses to the construction of creeds are not exclusively intellectual conviction. Baur cannot be acquitted of somewhat of scholasticism,—of fixing the attention too exclusively on Christian thought, and neglecting the developments of Christian life and morals. These last he deduces from the doctrine, but he does not allow for their reaction on the doctrine. Other influences, no less momentous, especially the bias received at various epochs by Christian thought from secular power, are too apt to be overlooked. The new solution may justly take its place as the principal determining cause, but it is not the solitary condition, of all the phases of Christian doctrine[1].

The danger of the Historico-Critical school then appears

---

[1] [Dr. Fairbairn, to whom the editors are indebted for several valuable additions and corrections in this Essay, gives the following account of the most important of Baur's writings published since 1857. 'In 1859 appeared his *Apology for the Tübingen School*, and in the same year the second volume of his general Church History, *The Christian Church from the fourth to the sixth Century*. After his death in 1860, his son, Professor F. F. Baur, and his son-in-law, Professor E. Zeller, published the remaining volumes of the History: *The Middle Ages* (1861), *The*

Westminster Review, 1857.]

to be one of one-sidedness, in relying too exclusively on the laws and categories of thought, as the order of historical sequence. If the historical method is to preserve the ascendency it now exercises,—if it is to extend its empire over ecclesiastical annals with the entire right with which it has established itself in the other departments, it must above all things be true to its own principle. The attention which the historico-critical method has drawn on itself has indeed been caused by Baur's brilliant applications of it in detail. But its strength consists in itself. It claims to be the absolute method in history. Errors may be made in its application, as errors may be committed in an inductive process, but the claims of induction as the method in physics are not invalidated by such errors. The danger is not from any mistakes in detail, but from the method not remaining true to its principle. It professes to establish a safe and firm ground outside of the prepossessions of sect or the traditions of the religious parties. It would rescue Christian history from the reproach of being a common stock of material out of which rival creeds select facts for their own justification. Orthodox and heretic alike have used the history of the Church in the light of their own peculiar system of doctrine. Baur has reversed the process, and shown that the doctrine is to be accounted for by the general laws applicable to the whole history. We must not take in our hands any particular scheme of doctrine, and go back requiring to find this in each age of Christian teaching in all its integrity, imposing, e. g. the Athanasian formularies on Origen and Irenaeus. We must not do this, not because such scheme of doctrine is false, which is not the question, but because what we have before us is history, and historical fact cannot be truly dealt with in this arbitrary way. Theology is a science

Reformation to the end of the Eighteenth Century (1863), and *The Nineteenth Century* (1862). To these were added, in 1861, his lectures *On New Testament Theology*, and in 1865–1867 those on *The History of Dogmatic*, in three volumes.]

apart, having its own principles, its own method, its own truths. But these truths of theology are not to be imposed as laws of history. Historical criticism ascertains as far as it can, events, and the general laws which have determined their succession. We must not obtrude into this inquiry the more important, it may be, but alien, conclusions of a distinct order of ideas. The whole power of the critical method lies in its being employed in its purity. Hence its judicial supremacy, it claims to decide without appeal on what is. It has brought the realm of thought within its jurisdiction, which before only extended to occurrences, simply by disclaiming the power to decide for past ages, what they ought to have thought, and limiting itself to the question what they did actually think. It is, in short, a positive science, repudiating theory. It must be said that Baur has not always been sufficiently on his guard against the insidious inroads of theory. In particular, he has allowed his capital discovery, that the historical books of the New Testament were composed with a doctrinal tendency, to glide into the position of an established law, while it is, as yet, only a highly probable hypothesis. Again, the antithesis of Petrinism and Paulinism, which is more than a hypothesis, and must be considered a fact, has yet swelled out of all proportions, extended itself both in time and degree, and has shown a disposition to efface, rather than to bring into light, the other characteristics of the period.

In these instances, and in others which might be quoted, it should be observed that Baur's error consists in the exaggeration of a true principle, not in the employment of a false. Such a source of error, therefore, does not threaten the vitality of the system. It is rather an evidence of luxuriant growth, than a symptom of decay. And it is sure to be soon corrected; it is even now in process of correction, by the retreat of friends from the untenable positions, and the operation of controversy without.

Westminster Review, 1857.]

From this last source of correction less has come than ought to have done. For though the Tübingen views have called forth abundance of hostile writings, the greater part of these productions are entirely worthless in a critical point of view. They do not fairly produce the theory of orthodoxy, or allow it to measure itself against the new historical theory. The mass of these writers are evidently not in possession of the grounds of their own system. The more reasonable and learned antagonists again, such as Dorner and Baumgarten, notwithstanding their apparently determined attitude, do in reality make such concessions, and adopt so much of the critical view, that neither do they bring the pure theory of orthodoxy to bear with its whole weight on the controversy. The most useful of these antagonists is Bleek. He comes, however, from the school of Schleiermacher, not from the camp of orthodoxy. In Bleek's *Beiträge zur Evangelienkritik* (1846), the Tübingen critics are met on their own ground. By purely critical arguments Bleek establishes the Apostle John in the authorship of the fourth Gospel. He has collected with great care all the internal marks of genuineness. He has subjected the external testimonies also to an independent examination. He lays due stress on Tatian's *Diatessaron*, on the early appearance of the Gospel in the school of Valentinus. How, he asks, could this Gospel, if it did not really emanate from John, but first made its appearance about the middle of the second century, so immediately obtain universal reception? How is it that it was adopted unquestioned by opposite parties—by the Judaic Churches as well as by the Valentinians—by those who followed the Asiatic Easter as well as by the orthodox adherents of the Roman computation? To suppose such a universal recognition of a recent and spurious compilation, by all the conflicting parties in the very heat of their conflict, is to suppose nothing short of a miracle.

Some service is thus rendered to criticism by the professed antagonists of the Critical school,—if antagonists they can be called who only combat particular conclusions on the common ground of inquiry. Of greater value are the corrections and modifications that come from within. In these must be included not only the concessions and retractations of the Tübingen critics themselves, but also the revision of some of their ground by independent critics, such as Hilgenfeld. A critic like Hilgenfeld is the very man who ought to come after one like Baur. Without the temerity of the spirit of invasion, without risking hypothesis, without something of the hardihood of paradox, the New World could not have been conquered and taken possession of in the name of criticism. To consolidate the conquest, industry and sober good sense alone are wanted. These are eminently Hilgenfeld's characteristics. He has retired from some of the hasty positions which Baur had taken up; but he retires not in the spirit of one who makes concessions to hostile attacks, but of one who, on a more accurate survey of the ground, finds the positions untenable. He has not betrayed the principle of criticism, but has rather recalled the critics within it when they were in danger of being seduced into speculation. For example: the hypothesis of doctrinal purpose, which in Baur's hands threatened to swallow up every other consideration in accounting for the origin of the historical books, is now reduced to its proper place. It is one, but only one, element. The material which the evangelist, or Church historian, found at his disposal, was a main guide in the composition of his work. Besides Hilgenfeld, K. R. Köstlin, who is a pupil of Baur's, has, in his *Origin and Composition of the Synoptical Gospels* (1853), followed in the same path of cautious revision. Though the moderation of the younger generation of critics is no abandonment of principle, but is only a more exact and rigid compliance with the laws of historical criticism, it may be questioned if their sober procedure has not lost something of its animating spirit. We may perhaps apply to them what has been well said of the Scottish common-sense metaphysicians, as compared with their more unsafe and speculative forerunners. These sensible reasoners, says M. Saisset[1], possessed 'une discrétion spéculative, un esprit de réserve et de défiance, qui n'est pas le doute, mais qui pourrait bien être la stérilité.'

II. We have placed the Historical school first, not for the number of its adherents, but for the decided character of its pretensions. It is the only scientific Theology at present extant. But it is anything but popular, and commands no considerable section of theological opinion. Looking at the number and weight of respectable names, the party which makes the best show in Theology at present is what we must call the Middle Party. To this class belong all the theological writers of any eminence, except the few who, on either extreme, constitute the schools of Orthodoxy or of Criticism. It is indeed not a school or party: it is made up of men of all schools, character, tendencies, and antecedents, who, on the dissolution of the speculative schools, found themselves left, as it were, *in medio*—in a position which they did not choose, but which circumstances had prepared for them. Nothing else leaves on the spectator a more discouraging picture of the utter rout and discomfiture of German intellectual effort than the inspection of this wide region, in which is comprehended nearly every name of theological character in Germany. These *campi patentes* are anything but the abode of faith, of high aspiration, or Science confident in its grasp. They are rather like a battle-field strewed with the shivered wreck of some great combat. The pale heroes are seen sadly amusing

[1] *Revue des deux Mondes,* 1853.

themselves with the ghosts of dead controversies. Among
these melancholy *débris* of a former world we are not
to expect anything like common views, or united effort.
What common character it has, however, is expressed
by the name applied to this section of theologians.
The term 'Mediation-Theology' (Vermittelungs-Theologie)
was first applied to the attempts made in the school
of Schleiermacher, to approximate the old rationalism
to the positive doctrine and ordinances of the Church.
The followers of Schleiermacher (*d.* 1834) endeavoured
this reconciliation on the side of faith and feeling.   At the
same time, Hegel (*d.* 1831) had promised to bring out
orthodox Christianity as one with absolute philosophic
truth.   When this illusion was dispelled on the side
of Hegelianism in the disruption of the Hegelian schools,
it was still cherished as a fond lingering hope among the
followers of Schleiermacher.   This phasis of Mediation-
Theology belongs so entirely to the past, that it ought
hardly to find a place here, where we are discriminating
existing schools.   It must find a place, however, because
its respected representative still lives to propound his
views by the pen and from the pulpit, however little
attention they may now command.   Books, pamphlets,
Ullmann is one
of those amiable, gentle natures, whose activity and
earnestness seem totally unconscious of the neglect and
apathy they have to encounter.   Books, pamphlets,
prefaces, articles in periodicals, sermons,—in all these
the unwearied author repeats the phrases of a long-since
discredited system with all the zeal of a propagandist
who can count his proselytes by the thousand.   Ullmann's
most popular book is his *Reformers before the Reformation.*   This was first published in 1841.   There is
an English translation in Clark's *Foreign Theological
Library,* in 2 vols., 8vo., Edinburgh, 1855.   It is a series
of biographies of some of the more remarkable among the
German divines who preluded to the Reformation in

the sixteenth century—John of Goch, John of Wesel, Cornelius Grapheus, the Brethren of the Common Lot, etc. As biographies they are indistinct and insipid; but the book has recommended itself to general readers by a tone of pious sentiment, a general tint through which, as in Neander's histories, all the characters are seen to look pretty much alike. The key-note of the author's theology at that time was an adaptation of the Theology of the Reformation to the wants of the age. He says in his preface, 'The only course of safety I see, is for every man who can to cleave with conviction to the principles of the Reformers; and firm in the faith, and free in science, to build upon that ground conformably to the wants of the age.' This vague longing for a reconcilement between the Theology of the Reformation and the 'wants of the age,' without any fixed idea how the reconcilement is to be effected, is characteristic of the mind of the Moderates at that period. But it is in his *Essence of Christianity*[1] that we find the average profession of the followers of Schleiermacher, or the 'German Theology' as it called itself. Ullmann's *Essence of Christianity* is a repertory of Schleiermacher phrases, emptied of all their significance. The difficulties with which Schleiermacher really grappled are here smoothed over with sounding words, which but ill disguise the absence of any distinct theology. 'Christianity is not a doctrine, as the Supernaturalists have said; nor a law of morality, as the Kantians; nor redemption, as Schleiermacher would have it; but *Life.*' And the changes are rung on 'Life-power,' and 'Life-principle,' till the doctrine of Schleiermacher disappears, evaporated in its own expression. This indeed was the inevitable fate which awaited the speculative rhetoric of Schleiermacher.

[1] [*Das Wesen des Christenthums*, 1° Auflage, 1845; 4° Auflage, 1854. English Translation. Chapman, 1846.]

Within the brilliant nimbus that surrounded that great name were lodged no distinctive features. Schleiermacher was an impulse, not a doctrine. It is true that his influence has been much more abiding in theology than that of Hegel ; but it has been an influence of personality, not of science. He inspired and stimulated ; but he implanted no idea calculated to fructify. Hence the attempts to develope and continue Schleiermacher have led to nothing. The phrases with which the mighty master conjured became empty sounds in the mouth of the imitators.

Ullmann, then, with his mild and conciliatory generalities, is rather a *souvenir* of the past, than a representative of any tendencies of the present. We place him on the threshold of the Mediation-Theology, because the same character of indecision more or less pervades the whole school. In advancing, however, to its modern representatives, we seem to have before us something more solid and substantial. The Mediation-Theology has its scientific writers. At least Dorner, Liebner, Lange, appear scientific writers by the side of the washy and discursive rhetoric of Ullmann. In these theologians the influence of the spirit of Schleiermacher is still strong, but it is tempered by the logical forms of the Hegelian school. Nor do they aim only at the forms of a systematic theology. There is an honest and well-intended effort to conceive and expound the religious ideas. There is positive thought in this school. Its object is not simply to maintain a position, to argue in favour of received formulae ; it seeks to understand and to represent. It is not satisfied to proclaim a doctrine : it would realize the substance of which the doctrine speaks ; nor does it shrink from attempting for itself the highest mysteries of Christianity. It is true, it is to some extent cowed before the pretensions of traditional orthodoxy. It receives much of the *credenda* of tradition, but with interpretations

and interpolations of its own. The crowning example
of its pretensions to originality is its exposition of the
union of natures in Christ. They complain of the
unproductiveness of Theology as ascribable to the timidity
of theologians. These, they say, have got into the habit
of restricting themselves to secondary and derivative
matters, where emptiness and impotence are easily
concealed, and avoiding all handling of what is fundamental, all reconsideration of primary dogmas[1]. The
Mediation-Theology itself does not shrink from engaging
the Christological problem. It proposes to fill in, in
harmony with the style of the whole building, two of
the gaps which the Lutheran Theology had, even while
amplifying and developing this doctrine, allowed to remain
in it. In order to state these additions, it is necessary to
employ the technical language of Theology, strange to
English ears, since scientific Divinity has ceased to be a
study thought worth requiring, even from the professional
ministers of religion.

1. In the unique person of the God-man, Christ, are
united the two natures, the divine and the human, each in
their completeness and perfection. Each nature therefore
retains, in the new combination, all the properties and
attributes necessary to such independent perfection.
These attributes are related to the nature to which
they belong as its inherent properties *(idiomata)*. But as
the personality is *one*, these properties of the one nature
become, in a secondary sense, the attributes *(modi)* of the
other. Thus, to the human nature of Christ belong, in the
first degree, the attributes of humanity; in the second
degree, the attributes of deity. Thus much all the Catholic
Confessions had asserted. This predication of the properties of the divine nature as accidents of the human, was
known as 'glorification' *(genus majestaticum)*. But it is

---

[1] [See Liebner, *Ueber den Begriff der Dogmatik. Jahrb. für Deut. Theol.* vol. 1,
pp. 198 ff.]

obvious that, in order to make the interchange of attributes complete, it must be reciprocal *(communicatio idiomatum)*. But the Catholic Theology had shrunk from carrying through its own hypothesis, and predicating the attributes of the divine as accidents of the human nature. This is now to be effected by conceiving the Divine Word in becoming man to have imposed a limitation on itself. Retaining all the attributes of deity in their fulness, Christ's divine nature is conditioned in space and time by the attributes of humanity.

2. Another essay of the same character is Dorner's attempt to define the personality of Christ in its relation to the human species. Departing from the historical representations of Schleiermacher, Dorner[1] and Lange have returned to the scholastic ideal Christ. Christ is the typical man, a generic individual. He does not represent, but contain, the personality of the whole human race *(allpersönlichkeit)*. Adam and his descendants are singly only so many dispersed members, portions, of humanity, the whole of which, in its essence, is summed up in the person of Christ.

It is not the place here to enter on any discussion of these doctrines in themselves. They are only cited as instancing the activity of the Mediation-Theology, and indicating the basis of its operations. They evidence vitality of thought, and activity of speculation in this school, in contrast with the stagnant apathy of the Romanist and Anglican Churches, where Divinity consists in repeating by rote obsolete formularies without any attempt to conceive their objects as existing realities. But they disclose at the same time the hollowness and unreality of the basis on which this ingenious fabric is reared. The Mediation-Theology declines the application of modern metaphysic to religion. It keeps at a distance attempts,

[1] *Entwickelungs-Geschichte der Lehre von der Person Christi.* 1º Auflage, 1848. 2º Auflage, 1853. [English Translation in Clark's Foreign Theological Library (1861–1863.)]

Westminster Review, 1857.]

like those of Schleiermacher, to construe religious ideas in terms of modern thought. It will not rebuild from the foundation. But it will build. And it endeavours to work with the metaphysic of the Greek schools. That the Christian Church of the fourth and fifth centuries should have constructed a scientific theology, by employing its own metaphysical conceptions upon the eternal realities— nothing more natural, nothing more inevitable. It is impossible to resuscitate, for theological purposes only, a metaphysical terminology which has ceased to be employed for all other purposes of thought and expression. We have the alternative of not speculating on religion at all. This is the alternative adopted by Orthodoxy. Its penalty is, that the religious ideas disappear from the mental vision, and their place is supplied by words. If we do speculate, we must think in our own language, in conformity with the same forms of thought as we employ in thinking on all other subjects. To speculate is nothing more than to construe consistently with the rest of my conceptions. We can no more think out religious problems in the metaphysics of a past age, than in a dead language. The imitative Christology of the Mediation theologians is like the imitative Gothic churches rising all around us. They are copies after originals—they are no longer expressions in stone of the faith and sentiment of the builders.

Nor has the activity of the moderate theologians been confined to the doctrines of the Incarnation. They have resolutely attempted the still more difficult problems of the origin of things, and the relation of God to the world. Here they are on more original ground even than in the last instance. Cosmological doctrine had been entirely neglected in the Reformation Theology. So far as it had been touched by the Catholic doctors, it had been chiefly apologetically, and in answer to the speculations of the Arabian metaphysicians. Since then it had been

almost entirely abandoned to the philosophers. But as
Theology revived, it was soon felt, not that it might, but
that it must, grapple with this subject. This necessity
comes upon it not only from within, but from without.
From within—the doctrine of Creation is the essential
substructure of the moral truths of Government and
Providence. From without—the growth of physical knowledge drew on, in the train of its extended mastery over
Matter, speculations extra-physical on the origin of the
existing combinations of Matter. Thus, from an isolated
point in the controversy with the Deists, Causation and
Creation have grown into questions of the first magnitude.
From a mere ontological disputation, they are felt to
involve the basis of the whole structure of natural knowledge which the last two centuries have been rearing.
This, much more than the Christological, is the urgent
problem of our age. Historical and Speculative Theology
are similarly embarrassed by a pressure from without.
As the growth of criticism, as independent Science, has
made necessary a reconsideration of the position assigned
to the canonical books in an uncritical age, so the vast
development of Physical Science forces on a reconsideration of the crude conceptions of the relation of God to the
world, which had satisfied men in the infancy of Physics.

This arduous duty the Mediation-Theology has not
shrunk from. Several attempts have been made at a
theory of Creation. The attempt is all that the historian
can chronicle; for there is yet nothing but failure; nor can
anything else be expected as long as the attempt is made
in the spirit of *a priori* speculation. Entirely of this
Hegelian character is the most celebrated among the
recent expositions, that by Rothe. It may, perhaps, be
thought that injustice is done to this original and independent thinker (now Professor of Theology at Heidelberg),
by classing him with the Mediation-theologians. Rothe is
the leading mind in philosophical Theology, as Baur

is in historical. Not only the clearness and energy of his intellect, but the wide sweep of his systematic development of his science, place him on an eminence above the respectable level of the theologians of the Middle school. He is too clear-sighted to be satisfied with the half-truths and adaptations of the popular method. He is too stern a lover of truth to offer to compromise with Orthodoxy in order to secure its countenance. His deduction from his premises is rigid : if you go one step with him, you will have to go the whole road. He seems to lie under a necessity of consecutive thought, and is no patcher-up of many-coloured theories, or promulgator of views. He is ready to follow out the idea, lead where it will. In so following it up, he requires that speculation shall hold itself free from all homage to any alien authority, from all considerations of consequences. It is to own no control but the laws of logic, the intrinsic consistency of thought. This independence is, with Rothe, not a matter of personal, but of doctrinal, importance. He distinguishes speculative Theology from Philosophy, by saying that Philosophy has to develope the pure self-consciousness, while Theology does the same for the God-consciousness, or the idea of God in the human consciousness. The matter, or object, of thought is distinct in each case, but the method is the same. Theology is as strictly dialectical as Philosophy. It is entirely independent of confessional orthodoxy, and scorns synodal determination by majorities. It is not influenced by opinion, but claims to correct and control ecclesiastical opinion. The pretence of churchmen to decide doctrine is as preposterous an invasion of theological science, as their professing to lay down the laws of motion would be of mechanical science.

Notwithstanding this clear enunciation of the sphere and claims of speculative Theology, or, as he calls it, Theosophy, Rothe can be ranked only among the Moderate

theologians. It is true that he is free from their fundamental error, which consists in making Theology a
compromise between opposite views, and so ultimately
dependent on opinion. Rothe does not profess reconcilement as a system. But however absolute his own
point of view, he cannot escape from the necessity of
building it up with the ruins of older speculation. The
soil of Theology is no longer virgin. Rothe comes after
Schleiermacher and Hegel ; and though a follower of
neither, he cannot go to work irrespectively of them.
Some one has expressed the wish that the Bible could be
buried for a hundred years, and then dug up, that men
might begin afresh with its interpretation. Something like
this is necessary for genially moulding doctrine. After the
delicate texture of thought has been torn to shreds by
controversy, it is impossible to weave it at once into
a homogeneous web. Time must elapse, and the topic
must be faded out of memory, before it can become again
a living and profitable substance for organic thought.
Like an atmosphere that has been breathed, it must
be re-oxygenized before it can be healthily inhaled
again.

That he falls in the autumn instead of the spring of
speculation, is Rothe's fortune, not his fault. But, in other
respects, notwithstanding the peremptory self-assertion
of his logic, he is not the man to found a school. He
is wanting in the personal qualities. He obtains recognition as an eminent teacher ; he does not attach followers.
He is often compared to Schleiermacher, whom he
resembles in some qualities : in the union of an energetic
dialectic with the inward life, the deep religious sensitiveness. But he wants that which gave to the same
faculties in Schleiermacher, the victorious force that
carried all before them—greatness. Rothe's personality is
feeble. A small man—sharp, clear, acute, intense, but not
great,—he cannot impose himself upon his fellows.

Rothe's peculiar views can only be stated by those who have habitually followed his lectures; for his great work, his *Theologische Ethik* (1845), was published twelve years ago. Though it has long been out of print, he declines to republish it[1]; and it is known that he is now (1857) dissatisfied with the way in which much was there presented. His leading views, however, have doubtless not undergone much change. The basis of his *Ethik* is the identity of the moral and the religious. The *Ethik* is not a treatise on morals, as its title might seem to indicate, but includes besides the whole of speculative Theology. The moral relations, or the conditions of a Personality—of an Agent, are the central existence in the world. Into the moral is absorbed, on the one side, the material—on the other, the spiritual. As to the material, the lower steps and spheres of Creation are indifferent, till they have evolved out of themselves that unity of self-consciousness and self-activity—a human personality. In a 'Person' matter is ultimately, through the creative power of God, raised above itself—it has evolved its own antithesis. When this personality has been thus evoked, the further problem is, that it becomes the determining principle of everything that is in contact with it. Man must appropriate to himself, subordinate to his uses, material Nature—that is, all the forces in action, whether within, or without, him. This is the moral problem;—a continuation of the process of creation, entrusted to the agency of the creature itself. But this process of adaptation is a gradual one—no less gradual than all the previous steps of creation. The first Adam is the incomplete man; and sin is the inevitable passage to the higher stage of being. The completed human personality is only won through a long course of toil and suffering, and finally culminates in the second Adam.

---

[1] [A second edition began to appear in 1867, the year of Rothe's death. Volumes III–IV were issued in 1870, and Vol. V in 1871, under the editorship of Holtzmann.]

The redeeming action of the Deity is thus a strict and steady continuation of his creative action.   There is nothing arbitrary in the moral development of the race. The spiritual is no intrusive element.   There is no breach of the continuity of law.   The Church, or religious society, finds its completest realization in the State, or moral society.

This is a very meagre notice of a system so articulate and so deeply laid as that of Rothe.   It may perhaps serve to indicate the direction of his thought.   It is an attempt to deduce a consistent scheme from the starting-point of moral personality.   It would deliver religious theory from the arbitrariness involved in the common conceptions. It replaces the purely formal freedom of divine and human will, by a rational, essentially determined series.   In grandeur of design and vastness of compass, the scheme of Rothe raises its head far above any of the extempore theories of the Moderate school.   But it shares in their weakness.   Seemingly intent on its own work, it is unconsciously labouring to comprehend as much of existing opinion as it can.   With all its appearance of vigorous logic, it has a side-eye for the received dogmatic forms. Conscious of not having the right to compel assent, it would insinuate itself.   It is but a transformed orthodoxy. The principle on which Rothe professes to stand—viz. the reduction of the ideas of spirit, grace, etc., into moral relations, is the annihilation of orthodoxy.   But he is not steady to his principle : he is attracted out of his true orbit by the mass of Christological doctrine, to the superior attractions of which the moral explanation is obliged to yield.

III. We come lastly to the Theology of Orthodoxy, or the endeavours at a revival of the Confessions of the sixteenth century.

In a history of the Church, the recent movement of the

orthodox party, its rise and progress, would form an important chapter. It would be difficult to exaggerate the state of feebleness and decay in which this party was sunk at the beginning, and for the first twenty years, of this century. All the learning, all the piety, all the zeal of the age, was gone into other channels. Unsupported by popularity among the masses, or favour at court, Old-Lutheranism was maintained solely by the obstinacy and bigotry of the least enlightened of the rural clergy. And as their numbers were never recruited, the prospect before them seemed to be the same lingering unpitied death in which the Nonjuring schism in this country was extinguished. But just before the fatal moment, the dying man showed signs of new life, the dry stump put forth new shoots. So full of surprises is history! Out of the very weakness of the party came the new strength. The decaying vitality of the principle of confessionalism it was which encouraged the Prussian Government to its attempt to unite (1821–1830) the Lutheran and Reformed into one State Church. The time seemed to be come when the schism which dogma had produced might be closed, since dogma was now unimportant. The bond of nationality might be substituted for that of symbolism. The union was accomplished. The strong hand of Government overbore all external resistance. But it awakened at the same time, within, the spirit of tenacity and exclusiveness. Men were found in that dead age—let their names be mentioned with the honour due—Scheibel, Guericke, Heubner,—who preferred their principles to their preferment, and refused submission to the civil power in a matter where conscience was involved. They suffered, but their resistance awoke the old spirit of Lutheranism. A few short years elapse, and lo! in the Union itself, an exclusive Lutheranism is the fashionable profession. Thirty years ago it led to martyrdom; it is now the only road to preferment. Nay, the reaction no longer rests at Luther and the sixteenth century. It goes back invoking 'church principles,' derived from a time far anterior to the origin of Protestantism.

The Prussian Union was only the turning-point of the reaction. Its cause lay much deeper, and belongs to the history of Europe. Though culminating in Prussia, this 'churchmanship' is no mere Berlin ware. The wave of the orthodox reaction has been perceptible, in one form or another, over a great part of the surface of Europe. It only belongs to our present subject so far as it has produced or coloured theological opinion.

We hear on all sides, and from all parties, of the rapidly hastening return of Germany to 'the Faith.' It is not so much a revival of zeal, as a correction of theological opinion, which is believed to be in progress. Wearied of endless debate, the German mind is preparing, we are told, to seek repose in the principles of the Reformation. It has exhausted itself in unsatisfying speculation, and quits in disgust the chase of philosophical shadows, for the solid and unchanging doctrines of 'the Church.' This current of opinion is attested as well by the alarm and discouragement of the friends of free thought, as by the triumphant self-congratulations of the party now in the ascendant. The phenomena of the day undoubtedly justify in some measure the exultation of the one party, and the consternation of the other. But when we come to look more closely into these appearances, we easily see that they are a disguise, and not a manifestation. They cover indeed a reality solid enough, but it is anything but a revival of the ideas or doctrines of the Protestant Reformation.

The movement now so rapidly propagating itself in Germany, but chiefly in Prussia, under the colour of orthodoxy, is really destitute of any religious or theological character whatever. It is simply a political movement, taking an ecclesiastical colouring. Its animating principle is the principle of absolute authority. This principle or sentiment is just now undoubtedly gaining a hold on the European mind. Power rests less than ever on bayonets; it is becoming respectable. It is raising itself into a right. Might is not merely submitted to, it is recognized. Absolutism is emerging from a fact into an opinion. In the same proportion all reliance on the results of thought, all the elasticity of the individual will, is failing. The rights of conscience, and the necessity for freedom of expression, are less and less keenly felt. The independent and manly sentiments in human nature are, for the time, giving way to the equally natural impulses to timidity—to crouch, to fawn, to flatter. This doctrine of Power, and the corresponding sentiments of submission, are the doctrine and sentiments which are really active and popular. Their alliance with 'Orthodoxy' is purely accidental. That is to say, a political conservative party seizes, for political purposes, on the creed which lay nearest to its hand. Any creed would answer equally well; for in putting forward the doctrines of the Confession of Augsburg, this party does not do so because those doctrines are true, but because they are the doctrines of 'the Church.' The old Confession is no longer now the expression of a subjective conviction, but one objectively imposed to overrule conviction. It came in the sixteenth century from the conscience, and is now used against the conscience. It was in its origin a positive thought, it is now a negation of thought. The present 'Orthodoxy' came into the world as a protest against orthodoxy; for, as Milton says, 'A man may be a heretic in the truth. If he believe things only because his pastor says so, or the Assembly so determines, without knowing other reason, though his belief be true, yet the very truth he holds becomes his heresy[1].' This modern Orthodoxy is no legitimate attempt to bring into currency a true theological system in the place of false systems. It

[1] [*Areopagitica.* Works, p. 113 (Bohn's edition).]

is a denial of Theology as a science altogether; a usurpation of force, to crush thought and supersede conviction.

The thorough determination with which this Neo-Lutheranism sets itself against all that is internal and subjective, and so against the very source of real religion, is seen in nothing more strikingly than in its language towards Pietism. So far is the new Orthodoxy from allowing the services of the old Pietist, or 'evangelical' party, in reviving religious sentiment, that it delights in disowning and denouncing it.

Now Pietism, whatever its defects, was undoubtedly the protest of the religious consciousness against the arid Rationalism of the eighteenth century. And in the genial warmth of Pietism was fostered the might of Schleiermacher. As Luther sprang out of the Mysticism of the thirteenth century, so did Schleiermacher out of the Pietism of the eighteenth. But the new Orthodoxy declares against Pietism, with its subjective and separatist impulses, its disposition to place practical piety above doctrinal adhesion. 'Spener,' says Kliefoth[1], 'was an exotic growth in the Lutheran Church. The Pietists and Rationalists, enemies to each other, were yet, like Herod and Pilate, ready to conspire against the Church.' Pure doctrine is everything, the first and dearest treasure of the Church. The inward and individual principle of Pietism is but another manifestation of Rationalism. In this subjective religiousness the abstract, external, divine dogma proposes itself as the one 'truth.' There is no difference between fundamental and indifferent dogmas. 'All is fundamental in the true system,' says Stahl, 'and let him who would swerve a tittle from the law be anathema.' No less emphatically do they repudiate the Theology of the school of Schleiermacher. It is Ideology; a theology of rhetoric, not of facts; a Utopian pursuit of 'the Church of the future.' On the other hand, the Lutheran Church is

[1] *Kirchliche Zeitschrift, ap.* Schwarz, p. 336.

no ideal Church. It exists. It is the historical Church of Germany; the Church that has been transmitted to us from the Reformation. It has defined rights, recognized by the Constitution of the empire, and, through that recognition, guaranteed by the public and international law of Europe. This lawyer-like tone is characteristic of the writers of the Orthodox party. Theology is not the expression of the spiritual consciousness, but a concatenation of formulae imposed upon the understanding. The Church is not a free association for purposes of edification, but an institution under solemnly ratified articles. No one can belong to it who cannot exhibit the old title-deeds of the Confession.

Such an ecclesiastical tendency is not likely to produce much in the province of Theology. The party has other purposes—secular interests occupy it, and theological thought is an alien and artificial effort. Their 'system' is not intended to supply material for the speculative activity, or an object for religious contemplation. It is a mere calculus, from which formal consequences only can be deduced. It has neither mind nor heart in itself, though it may be dexterously employed by the understanding to silence others. Their only theologian worth naming is Hengstenberg. His attempts have been chiefly confined to the Old Testament. His arbitrary and lawless interpretation, and outpourings of rabbinical lore, mixed with scholastic allegorizing, impose on the ignorant, but have been received with amusement and ridicule by scholars. The truth is, that what attention has been bestowed on these absurd displays of learning gone mad, has been attracted, not by any merits of the books themselves, but by the position their author occupies at Berlin. This position he has gained by means of his powerful organ, the celebrated *Evangelische Kirchen-Zeitung.* His history, as given by Schwarz (p. 91, fol.) is as follows.

Hengstenberg first appeared as 'Privat-docent' in

Theology in the University of Berlin in 1824. Just at that time, the party which is now grown into the great Orthodox party was beginning to show itself in the form of a semi-pietistic party. It was favoured, and indeed was in some measure created, by the late King. Hengstenberg attached himself to it. Royal favour, and the zealous backing of a thriving party, supplied the want of professional qualifications, and he was successively appointed extraordinary (1826) and ordinary (1827) Professor of Theology in the University, alongside of Schleiermacher and Neander. In 1827 he founded the *Evangelische Kirchen-Zeitung*. Under his clever management this journal rapidly became a power. With an instinctive knowledge of his field of operation, the court and society of Berlin, he brought into play every engine by which a newspaper can work upon the peculiar class of passions and jealousies which gather round our most sacred beliefs. A ramified system of espionage was established by correspondents on 'Church affairs' throughout the provinces. Students were encouraged to delate their Professors. Hinted suspicion alternated with loud denunciation and demands for expulsion from the Church. Growing bolder by success, it flew at higher game. At first the Rationalists were denounced in the mass. They were classed with demagogues as disturbers of settled order, while the Orthodox were shown to be firm supporters of 'the throne.' Then men like De Wette, Bretschneider, and Ammon, were signalled by name as unbelievers. And at last Schleiermacher himself became the great mark for these poisoned arrows. It was not, however, till after Schleiermacher's death that this terrorism reached its acme. The publication of Strauss's *Life of Jesus* (1835) brought the theological panic to a crisis, and created an irritable state of public feeling, which was the very atmosphere for such a journal to thrive in. A sort of Papal tribunal was erected in Berlin, before which everything alike was brought up to be sentenced. For the talent of the paper at no time consisted in its writing. It scarcely pretended to criticize; it only abused. Satire, sarcasm, irony, the finer weapons of even unfair criticism, were unknown to it. It did but denounce and damn decisively, and that was all that its applauding public wanted. The events of 1848-49, and the transference of public interest to another order of ideas, gradually weakened its power over opinion. Though the journal still exists, it has greatly given way before younger and more zealous rivals. Already indeed, within the bosom of Neo-Lutheranism itself, has risen up a young party, who appear likely to draw off into themselves all the sap and juices of the parent stock.

This 'Hyper-Lutheranism,' as Dr. Schwarz calls it, is rather a development, than a rival, of Neo-Lutheranism. The New Lutheran Orthodoxy has nothing but the name in common with the Lutheranism of the sixteenth century. Its whole principle, indeed, is that of the externality of the Christian Institute, against which Protestantism was an insurrection. It is, at bottom, the conservative Catholicism of the sixteenth century, though without the formal confession of Catholicism. The Young Lutheran or 'Church' party have advanced a step further in the same direction. Not that they adopt, or incline to adopt, the ceremonial or mythological developments of the Catholic Church. But those rites and those doctrines which have made most noise in the Romanist controversy, are those which are the least of the essence of Romanism. The Virgin and the Saints, Reliques, Images, Purgatory, and Masses,—these bywords with the vulgar and the unthinking, are powerless decorations, or natural development. The one essential principle of the Catholic system is the control of the individual conscience by an authority or law placed without it, and exercised over it by men assuming to act in the name of Heaven. Towards this principle Young Lutherdom has made, and is still making, open and avowed approaches. This German 'Puseyism' is represented by such names as Kliefoth, Vilmar, Kahnis, Delitzsch, Petri. This party not only repudiate all approximation to the 'Mediation-Theology' as heretical, but affect to look on Hengstenberg and his friends as already superannuated. They belonged to a period of transition. 'Hengstenberg,' says Kahnis, 'was useful in making the first breach in the fortress of unbelief.' He has done his work; the new era of 'Faithfulness' requires other strength. The ultra-Lutheran party have accordingly seized on the ideas of the Visible Church and the Sacraments, and are endeavouring, with perseverance and success, to bring them into vogue. It costs them, indeed, some little trouble to state these conceptions in harmony with the genuine Lutheran doctrine of 'Justification by Faith.' Still, in the inconsistent and clumsy Realism of Luther's teaching on the subject of the Sacraments, there is something which serves the purpose, and gives plausibility to this anti-Protestant view. But it is in their doctrine of the 'Ministerial Office' that this effort to escape under false colours betrays itself most palpably. Lutheranism laid down in the most distinct way the doctrine of the universal Priesthood of all believers, in contradiction to the doctrine of the Mass. The office of preacher or minister in the congregation is, in the Lutheran Church, always described as a 'means of grace.' It is so most strictly in conformity with the principle of Protestantism. For in preaching, the 'grace' is not conveyed by any material or physical medium; it is conveyed direct to the understanding through the intelligent vehicle of language. The process of communication is thoroughly human and rational. Divine 'grace' is here seen as an entirely moral influence, penetrating the human subject, but in subordination to the laws of that subject. Hence it follows, that faith in the hearer, that is to say, a moral receptivity of the subject, is an indispensable condition of the operation of the word spoken. This is the proper Lutheran doctrine. But such a doctrine is quite counter to the views of the new ultra-Lutherans. The difficulty they are in would not be felt in this country, where, at least south of the Tweed, no sensible educated person thinks of a sermon more than as an instruction in religion, a reminder of duty, or an aid to thought. But it is otherwise through a great part of Germany. However lax the attendance at church may be, the principle of the 'Preaching,' as a means of grace, has still a practical recognition. A party, therefore, affecting to be pre-eminently Lutheran and Orthodox, cannot, like English High-churchmen, run down sermons in order to exalt the Sacraments or the Prayers. They are obliged, therefore, to cast about for an indirect mode of evading the purely 'rational' doctrine of old Lutheranism. Kliefoth, e. g. lays down, that the preacher is a merely instrumental medium, like the material elements in Baptism or the Lord's Supper—a non-rational vehicle of the gracious infiltration. This instance is not cited for the sake of its absurdity—the absurdity of exalting preaching into a sacrament in order to depreciate it—but to show the spirit of this hyper-Lutheranism, and the shifts to which its 'Theology' has recourse, in order to maintain itself under the false mask under which it is necessary to its success to fight. For exposure of its essentially Catholic character is the obvious reply with which this illegitimate Lutheranism is met. But this line of opposition makes little impression upon it, and has apparently no power to check it. 'Kirchenthum,' so it designates itself, rides triumphantly on in Prussia, and openly boasts that the future is its own. If its theology is not patronized at court, it is at least not discouraged. Government and its adherents profess and support the New Lutheranism, but are willing to allow this advanced guard to essay at its own risks and perils the conquest of public opinion. If it fails, it can be disavowed; if it succeeds, it will draw the State Church along with it. The hierarchical Lutherans have, therefore, hitherto been cautious not to break with their old partizans, in the expectation that they should in time carry them with them. They have had recourse to the expedient of declaring the points on which they have innovated on Neo-Lutheran views, 'open questions.' Thus they have avoided the breach which took place in England some years ago between the Tractarian and the old High-Church party, and which proved so damaging to the former. Also, they have warily shielded themselves from the storms of popular Protestant indignation, by letting alone that mimicry of Romish ceremonial, and those accessories of minor fancies or beliefs, which, though really harmless, yet constitute the vulgar conception of 'Popery.' There is no jealousy lurking in the popular mind of the catholicizing Lutherans as likely to go over to Rome, either in a body or individually. They will not solve the situation by the weak device of going to the mountain; they will bring the mountain to Mahomet. A system identical in principle with that of Catholicism is to be established at Berlin, for the use and oppression of Prussia. Religion is to sanction and consecrate the bureaucratic absolutism of North Germany. Instead of a mere State Church supported by power, the deeper theology of Young Lutheranism will base the 'Throne' upon a religious doctrine contrived expressly in the interests of 'Order.'

The result to which our comparison of theological tendencies has come may be thus briefly summed up. Of the three categories in which we have arranged the present tendencies, that of the Middle party counts by far the largest number of adherents, including many and various shades of opinion within itself, as well as three-fourths of the sensible and well-educated among the clergy. But it is not strictly a school of Theology. It is determined by other than religious or critical considerations. It depends for its material on other than independent sources of thought. It ebbs and flows not by its own laws, but in sympathy with the tides of other seas. All doctrines may be found in it, but they are not native, but only naturalized citizens. It contains net results, and no productive powers. Such a denomination will always exist. When it is comprehensive, numerous, and respectable, it furnishes the best possible foundation for a national Church. It is unfavourable to religious zeal, and not generative of speculative development. But it is patient, tolerant, liberal, not repressive, though itself stationary. It will encourage learning, and the literature of Theology, though the earnestness of religious thought will probably seem to it disturbing and revolutionary. Were the Governments of North Germany even ordinarily prudent and clear-sighted, they would see that in the Moderate party, and on the basis of Mediation-Theology, might be reared the structure of a durable, comprehensive, safe church polity. These little governments however are, it seems, not a field in which even common-sense statesmanship can be acquired. Absolutism has definitively allied itself with the Orthodox party. In Hesse, the Naples of the North, Vilmar, at once dishonest and fanatical, has forced on, at the point of the bayonet, a hierarchical revolution, and set an example that other States are ambitious to follow. Prussia has enlisted Orthodoxy in its service, and smiles on the efforts of conservative divines to extemporize mushroom theories of the 'Church' which are to turn to the profit of irresponsible power. Of the prospects of this party, Schwarz says :—

If we are not mistaken, the zeal of the ultra-Lutheran party promises it wide diffusion and great power. And we are far from wishing that this natural progress should be checked. We heartily wish this 'churchmanship' a development such as itself could desire. For we hope that in and through that development will be thrown outwards all those unhealthy humours which are at present lurking in the constitution of our Reformed Church—the seeds of radical and dangerous disorder. Such a purge of Catholic leanings and sympathies is indeed sorely needed, for they have of late years risen to a formidable head. It is no mere question of theological crotchets. We have a deep moral need of Protestant ideas on the nature of the Church, on the value of authority, on the essence of the Sacraments, on the relation of a Confession to the inward conviction. All these questions demand to be answered afresh out of the depths of Protestant consciousness. Nor can we feel much sympathy for the Mediation-Theology, and the coalition of opinion so highly commended by its friends. It is highly improbable that victory will remain with that party. In the basis of their Theology there is a want of clearness and truth. The 'consensus' which they put forward as their scheme is not a harmony of existing belief or actual consciousness. The wide gulf that separates old Lutheranism from modern opinions is but artificially covered over. They themselves are not orthodox in the old and proper sense; and this not only on the points at issue between the Lutheran and Reformed Confessions, but in the generic and essential doctrines of Protestantism. On the other hand, they are unmistakably inoculated with the speculative temper of modern times, yet they follow where it leads only with a half-mind, with a timorous conscience, and stammering utterance. They have constructed a piecemeal Theology, dovetailed of affirmation and denial right and left; a system of half-truths, harmonies, caveats, and exceptions; a thing to which no one can give himself with hearty assent. It is undeniable that the divines of this colour—Nitzsch, J. Müller, Dorner—are in acquirements, insight, and refinement, far before their often coarse opponents. But their fine-spun and elaborate Theology wants one thing—simplicity. It has none of the penetrating power of creative genius, the sway of an idea capable of animating an organic whole. The rude and shapeless blocks of Orthodoxy with which the ground of controversy is strewn, look both respectable and enduring by the side of the porcelain ware of this Theology of reflection. We cannot question herein the justice of history, which has ever denied the eclectic a separate niche in her temple, and has obliged the theologian who has spent a life in accommodations and concessions to submit to be tried by the standard of strict Orthodoxy[1].

The two sections of Theology, then, which seem

[1] Page 429.

at present in possession of the field, have, it appears, no root in themselves, and can wield no permanent power over opinion. The Orthodox Theology is intrinsically the weakest, but externally the most powerfully backed. It is a mere ecclesiastical flag, hoisted to give a colour of legitimacy to the war against conscience. It may reign, but will not persuade ; and its fortunes are linked, for good and for evil, to those of the conservative and aristocratic party in Europe. The Mediation-Theology exercises a respectable sway over opinion, but is essentially shifting, indeterminate, and relative. Whether or not circumstances may occur which would rekindle a real and honest speculative Theology, it is idle to discuss. Should, however, some renovating impulse be communicated to thought from without, it is impossible that the experience of the past should be wasted. Real ground has been gained. Intelligent men understand each other better ; good sense and earnestness have more and more weight. Meanwhile, the solid acquisition to theological science has been won by the small and uninfluential circle of scholars who have devoted their conscientious industry to the critical and historical matters which have become so intimately bound up with the Christian religion. While all the speculative attempts confess more or less of defect and exhaustion, this school alone has established results. Its power has lain also in its possessing a definite aim, and a limited material. Criticism does not, like speculation, set out on a voyage of discovery, or undertake the construction of a religion *a priori*. Its problem is comparatively narrow, and even this is not its own selection. What is the character and value of the Christian records ? All of us were asking this question, either aloud, or in the silence of our own hearts, and receiving merely accidental and most unsatisfactory answers. Criticism attempts to answer this question, on distinctly stated principles of inquiry—principles not arbitrarily laid down, but the same by which all

other written records whatsoever must be tested.   When
it has once answered this question, its work is done.   We
are not to look for infinite discoveries in this direction.
The point can be settled;   and the time is ripe for a
settlement.   While speculation is in abeyance, this, the
preliminary of all theological speculation, can be arranged.
And once settled, historical criticism has discharged its
mission, the Renaissance movement is complete, and
philology may lay down her arms, with the satisfaction of
having removed at least one of the great stumblingblocks
in the way of the truth-loving and serious religious inquirer.

XVII.

LEARNING IN THE CHURCH OF ENGLAND[1].

(*National Review*, 1863.)

THE 'Ecclesiastical Reaction,' or 'Church Movement' within the Established Church, has attained a spread and momentum which raise it to the rank of one of the new social phenomena of our age. Yet it obtains little or no recognition from the superior and philosophical part of the press. It meets us everywhere—in society, in public meetings, in books, and finally on the bench—as a diffused but invisible influence. Yet we hardly ever see any serious attempts to estimate its import, or analyze its true character. Mr. Mill has, indeed, once or twice surveyed with the calm temper of a politician the ecclesiastical history of this country, but his glance has rather been retrospective than towards the present.

The reason for this neglect has probably been, that the significance of the reaction has been hitherto veiled under the guise of a theological squabble. As the practical statesman dreads before all things religious faction, so the philosophic politician throws theological controversy aside as irrelevant. It is too much a ruled point with him to take no notice of it. He leaves church parties to the clergy, and treats the clerical arena with contempt in proportion to the fuss and excitement which the party papers on either side maintain over it. He regards

[1] *Report of the Church Congress held at Oxford*, 1862.

doctrinal dispute as the normal condition of the religious world; a *mêlée* noisy and dusty, but having no bearing on the moral and spiritual welfare of England.

If this be an oversight, as we think it is, it is one which the few remarks now to be made do not pretend to make good. It were, indeed, much to be wished that impartial minds, superior to either 'church' or anti-church prejudices, should give more attention than they hitherto have done to the actual tendencies of religious opinion. We propose at present to touch upon one single feature of the church revival. The phrase 'decline of learning,' by which that feature is indicated, very imperfectly expresses its character.

It may be readily granted that doctrinal controversy, even where best conducted, has little more than a technical interest, and should be left in the hands of theologians. The 'church movement' of which we speak is, however, something more than a mere oscillation of the doctrinal pendulum from the doctrines and practices of the Puritan towards those of the Anglican school. It may be true that the leaders of the parties in the struggle view and represent it as being this. It may be that its professed object is to repeat or reproduce a state of things which has existed before in our church. But nothing in history ever recurs. The mental horizon of the seventeenth century has been broken up once for all, and no human art avails to replace it where it was. The tendency of parties is not to be measured by what they say of themselves. Deeper than opinions lies the sentiment which predetermines opinion. What it is important for us to know with respect to our own age or any age is, not its peculiar opinions, but the complex elements of that moral feeling and character in which, as in their congenial soil, opinions grow.

All theological controversy is distasteful to thinking minds, even when it is illuminated by intellectual power

and enforced by copious learning. When these human-
izing adjuncts are absent, and when nothing remains but
the pure passion of enforcing your own opinion,—the
temper of the ignorant,—the aversion of such minds
becomes complete. The High-Church movement appears
to be entering this phase. But this very fact, if it be one,
deserves most careful consideration from all those to whom
it is of importance to watch the signs of the times. The
time has arrived, long ago foreseen[1], when the church
cause 'would, as years went on, make less apparent
but more real progress.' If it be true that the feelings
and sympathies which make up this movement are yearly
spreading over a wider area, drawing yearly larger
numbers of both clergy and laity within their influence ;
and at the same time that learning, knowledge, liberal
cultivation, and intellectual grasp are becoming more and
more alienated from the movement; that whatever
amount of these gifts the English Church may contain
is taking another direction ; that the party, as it acquires
strength, is becoming more of a party, and making
common cause with all the social elements which are
against intelligence,—this is surely a feature of our
social life which cannot long be matter of indifference
to any of us.

Were this phenomenon nothing besides, it would be
at least an abandonment by the High Church of its
principal vantage-ground, a renunciation of its own peculiar
tradition.

Mr. Fitzjames Stephen recently called the Church of
England 'the most learned church in Christendom[2].'
Without by any means adopting this compliment in its
literal extent, we may yet say that learning, from Queen
Elizabeth's day onwards, has always been a conspicuous
mark of the church. The estimation it has commanded
has been sometimes more, sometimes less, in amount ;

---

[1] *Christian Remembrancer*, January, 1860.　　[2] *Defence of Williams*, p. 85.

but these ups and downs of opinion or policy do not
interfere with the general truth of the assertion, that in
the Established Church there has prevailed all along a
general respect for learning and learned men ; that a fair
proportion of our higher literature has been the work of
clergymen ; that the Episcopalian clergy as a body have
contrasted very favourably in respect of mental cultivation
and refinement with the Nonconformist clergy, and
especially with the Presbyterian ministers of Scotland.   It
may be that the highest type of learning has not been the
type exhibited by the Church of England ; but that
learning has stood its ground at all in this country, has
been owing wholly to the tradition of the church and
its habits of education.   The limits too of studies allowable for the clergy have been stretched quite widely
enough, and far more widely than in any other communion.
It has not by any means been held requisite that a
clergyman should confine himself to strictly theological
studies.   Classical philology the clergy have vindicated
as their proper domain.   During its whole career in this
country it has been in their hands.   Philosophy is not
the forte of our countrymen ; but such as English philosophy is, the church has had its fair share of it.   One of
the founders of political science was a clergyman, and
the present Archbishop of Dublin its first professor in
our universities.   In devoting time and talent to natural
science in various branches, Watson, Kirby, Peacock,
Buckland, Henslow, Sedgwick, Whewell, have not been
held to derogate from the sacred obligations of the
Christian ministry.   It is not to our purpose to assign
to our church its proper rank in competition with foreign
churches.   It may be that our learning has been at
best defective in grasp and independent thought.   The
works of our divines have been too occasional.   Even
those of which we have most reason to be proud are
tainted with a tone of advocacy, and want symmetry

and repose. In historical criticism we have been too timid and conservative, and have accordingly been left behind by the freer development of the Lutheran bodies· However this may be, it concerns the quality of our learning, and not the esteem it has obtained among us. We are only concerned now to insist upon the fact, that the tradition of the church has for nearly three centuries been on the side of a ' learned clergy.'

Further than this, it is by the High-Church section of the church that the tradition of education and secular learning has been emphatically cherished. It is not an accidental taste in them. It originated with them ; or rather both they and it grew up in the political position forced upon the church during the latter half of the reign of Elizabeth. Anglicanism is not, as is often repeated by ill-informed assailants, an artificial creation of Laud and the courtier-bishops of Charles I, but the legitimate and necessary form which the church intelligence of England took, as soon as it had time to repose from the turbulence and volcanic upheaving of the religious revolution. Thus it is that Anglicanism has always been the religion of the educated classes exclusively. It has never at any period been national and popular, because it implies more historical information and a wider political horizon than can be possessed by the peasant or the artisan. The masses require either an intuitional religion, such as is provided by the grosser forms of Dissent in Great Britain, or a ceremonial of drill and parade, such as the Latin and Greek churches offer to their subject populations. The apathetic attitude of the labouring class towards the Church is no nineteenth-century paralysis. It has been thus from the beginning, and its cause lies in the complex nature of the political problem of which the Anglican Establishment was the solution. The most recent historian of the Church is aware of this when he says :—

To the strong conservative element in the English Reformation we owe the sad but undeniable fact, that the uneducated classes have never heartily embraced and lovingly cherished the mild and temperate spirituality of the Established Church. They unlearnt the extravagance of the Roman superstition only to throw themselves readily into the arms of the scarcely less unreasonable Puritans ; and under one name or another, in varying forms but similar spirit, there has existed from the days of the Reformers to our own a popular antagonistic feeling to the church of the Reformation [1].

In defending against the sectaries the necessity of a 'learned clergy,' the Caroline divines were defending, not an outwork and accessory, but the very key of their position. By the Act of Uniformity, though zeal and piety were brutally expelled, yet learning, almost without an exception,—Baxter, though a voluminous writer, has no pretensions to learning,—remained within the pale of the Establishment. The Restoration divines handed on the torch of knowledge to the eighteenth century ; and when the Evangelical school arose, it was the high or orthodox party which again vindicated the prerogative of secular learning in the Church. Finally, in the present century, and within recent memory, the existing church revival owed its origin in no small degree to the professed contempt of all learned inquiry, which was a principle with the Evangelical school. Evangelism, in its origin, was a reaction against the High-Church 'evidences'; the insurrection of the heart and conscience of man against an arid orthodoxy. It insisted on a 'vital Christianity,' as against the Christianity of books. Its instinct was from the first against intelligence. No text found more favour with it than ' Not many wise, not many learned. ' It did its work : it retained in the Church, or attracted to it, thousands whom the learned 'demonstrations of the Being and Attributes,' etc. could never have reached. But it soon lost its vitality, and fell a prey to a dogmatism as

[1] Perry, *History of the Church of England*, vol. I. p. 15.
National Review, 1863.]

rigid, and far less rational than that of the High Church. It had forgotten its spirituality, and had replaced it by a new orthodoxy of its own. In 1833 Evangelism was already effete. The helpless imbecility of Evangelical writing and preaching; their obvious want of power to solve, or even to apprehend, the questions of which they are nevertheless perpetually talking; their incapacity to explain the Scripture, while assuming the exclusive right to it; their conceit of being able to arrive at conclusions without premises; in a word, their intellectual weakness, —contributed very greatly to the fall of the Evangelical school before a better-informed generation of men. Certainly there were other causes besides its ineptitude which concurred in producing the catastrophe. And the High-Church leaders had other recommendations above their learning. But at the first rise of the Tractarian school above the horizon in 1833, and before its other features were obliterated in one desperate effort of assimilation to Ultramontanism, it was instinctively felt to be a revival of the spirit of learned research. Hugh Rose, Newman, R. H. Froude, and Keble, were first awakened by the study of primitive antiquity in its original remains. The new leaders were recognized by all the orthodox party as descendants in the direct line from 'our great divines.'

In proportion (wrote Dr. Pusey) as every class of society advances in secular knowledge or intellectual cultivation, in that degree do men need a balance of increased religious knowledge; nor can their new wants be supplied without an enlarged compass of knowledge on the part of their spiritual instructors. Christianity is the same at all times and in all countries, yet the same truths may be conveyed in different modes to the cultivated and to the ignorant. . . . It is of importance that the nation shall have confidence in their instructors. Truth depends for its reception often more on the character of him who enforces it than on its own. What in the first preachers of the Gospel the extraordinary gifts of the Spirit, and the mighty works following them, were to the confirmation of the faith, such must now be a well-grounded knowledge of its evidences, and a deep insight into its nature[1].

Names such as those of Bilson, Bull, Patrick, Cosin, Waterland, who had long been laid on the shelf as unenlightened men, were again in honour; and the bookselling trade began to ask long prices for folios which a few years before had been selling as waste-paper. The appeal was very soon extended from the Fathers of the Anglican to those of the Catholic Church. The criterion of truth was found in a wide 'Apparatus Criticus.' The complex historical position of the Established Church in its birth and early growth was set in a true light; the fallacy of 'Scripture only' was exploded; and even new ground was ventured on in the theory of 'development.' All this was in the spirit of learned research. To those who were without some tincture of classical reading, even the terms of the dispute were unintelligible. All that the mass of Englishmen understood in it was, that the ultimate test of religious truth was taken out of their hands, and placed where they could no longer follow it. The very earliest objection urged home against the new 'doctors' was, that in their system the road to truth seemed to be laid through learning, and by consequence the plain and unlettered man was excluded from salvation.

This was the aspect of the church revival in 1833 and the subsequent years. Thirty years (January 1863) have now elapsed,—the life of a generation. From a school of writers the movement has grown into an influential party. Evangelism, then effete, now merely cumbers the ground with its ruins. The ranks of the Evangelical clergy are being thinned yearly. Their social ascendency has departed from them. Their organs in the press fight with the desperate recklessness of men who know that the day is irretrievably lost. The Church of England is

---

[1] Pusey, *On Cathedral Institutions* (1833), p. 27.

National Review, 1863.]

Anglicanized. Not that every young clergyman goes to his cure imbued with the tenets of Archdeacon Denison. Far from it. The extreme Puseyites, if we may use the term, form an inner nucleus, inconsiderable in numbers, of the whole High-Church party. But Anglican feeling and sentiment is now the feeling and sentiment generally diffused over the face of the Established Church. Its spread is not confined to the clergy. The educated laity, especially in the highest circles, have largely imbibed the same tone. The impression tells every year more and more upon the middle classes, but is far from yet having pervaded *them*. Below them it has not begun to penetrate. It has not yet, in its downward spread, reached the limits of education. Whether it can ever pass those limits, whether the Church of England can ever become a church of the people, is a problem for the future. The masses are outside the present question, and count for nothing in it.

How the Church may be brought home to the classes which have never yet been at home within it; how it may extend its area, and reach the uneducated,—this is a momentous question, and one that calls for far other consideration than it appears to have had. Our present inquiry is a different one. We are not consulting as to what should be done, but inquiring what is already effected. We wish to ask what the movement has done for the educated class in aiding them to realize and apply the principles of the church to which they belong. Has a movement which originated in a deeper hold of moral and religious truth continued faithful to its origin, to purify, elevate, and enlarge the religious ideas of English churchmen? The Church rebelled against the narrow bigotry of the Evangelical school, and threw off its yoke; has it found a freer system? With the rise of the Anglican on the ruins of the Evangelical party, has the Church of England gained in solid learning, in enlargement of view, in liberality of sentiment? Has it made a step towards freedom from the bondage of the letter, towards assimilating the results of science and the rich elements of modern thought? Has Christian truth been brought by it out of the state of frozen dogma to which it had been relegated, and become an inspiring source of spiritual life?

The influence which has been infused by the movement, and its action upon the understanding of the educated, has penetrated much deeper than is often suspected, but in so insensible a way that it is not easy to bring it before those who do not recognize it. In attempting to estimate the influence of orthodoxy on the moral ideal of our contemporaries,—any attempt must be exceedingly imperfect,—it is natural to begin with the clergy. Bishops' chaplains complain of the inferior calibre of candidates for ordination. Yet even the prelates themselves of recent nomination are apt to be thought by the public, perhaps unjustly, to be rather estimable for good intentions than to be looked up to as leaders of thought. If this were so, we should hardly expect the standard by which examining chaplains try their candidates to be a very high one. We believe that this standard is much below what the bishops, or many among them, would gladly see it. But, even at this depressed standard, it is found impossible to supply the cures with curates. While the population of England and Wales has been steadily increasing,—more than cent. per cent. in the last fifty years,— the number of persons ordained, literates included, is not relatively but absolutely smaller. An ordination examination, it is to be remembered, is confined to the very rudiments of professional information, and has nothing of scientific theology about it. It tests ability hardly at all, and general attainments not at all. These are supposed to have been tested previously during the university career. A little inquiry, however, at our universities reveals the fact, that the Church is almost entirely recruited from the Passmen—this is a name for the students who do not study; that the pass examinations are at the minimum of requisition, if anything at all is to be required, and that even this minimum is surmounted with great difficulty, and after many failures, by a large portion of the future clergy.

This, it may be said, has been always the case. The very earliest complaint which made itself heard in the beginnings of our Church was for a more learned and able clergy. If there be any alteration in this respect, it is for the better. We must distinguish between talent and mental refinement. If the amount of native talent engaged in the clerical profession be less, its average mental refinement is equal, even superior, to that of the other professions. The symptoms here are not those of decline, but of metamorphosis. Some conservative tempers have been disposed to indulge the wish that there were a little more simplicity of living, a little less of the frippery of the drawing-room, and the conventionalities of society, among our clergy. Whatever may be to be said for this, we gladly miss in our clergy the lineaments of the generation who haunted the fair and the race, who drank with the squire overnight and administered justices' justice by his side in the magistrates' room in the morning. But we cannot but remember that the grossness of clerical manners has been refined only because general manners have refined. One form of easy conformity has been substituted for another. The parson of the 'Freeholder's' day has not given place for the reproduction of the saintly type of earlier times, whether of the variety of Herbert or of Baxter, of Ken or of Horneck. The model clergyman of our own day belongs to a type which appears now for the first time in the Church of England, though it is one of which the prototype is very familiar to us in the history of the Church of Rome. The revival of the idea of 'churchmanship' rather than of the Church,—a revival which is in fact the degradation of the idea of Christ's kingdom into that of a secular party,—is forming a bond of union and sympathy among the clergy such as no previous era of our history since the Reformation has afforded. The *esprit de corps* of 'the cloth,' which could be evoked in the last century against the Dissenters or Catholic Emancipation, bore a very faint resemblance to the organization which the freemasonry of churchmanship is creating. Besides that, in the last century an independence, not of thought, but of character, often saved the beneficed country rector from being carried away by those church agitations which have become so frequent in our own time. The division of the clergy, too, into two hostile camps neutralized their power of combining against any other element of the body-politic. And the very torpor of which the Church of the Georgian era is accused consists, in part, in the absence of those public demonstrations to which we are accustomed. The awakening of zeal and professional energy in the clergyman can only be regarded with satisfaction, provided it be accompanied by a corresponding awakening of the conscience, and the ambition of spiritual growth. Otherwise zeal and organization are but materials upon which an ecclesiastical agitator may work—a ἕξις ἄνευ νοῦ. Not that sound practical sense is not still found among the English clergy. Even in Convocation there has been enough of this element to balance hitherto the doctrinal *entêtement* of the Archdeacon of Taunton. But good sense is a much rarer quality than is often imagined, and at best has never been found, at the moment when wanted, able to stand against either enthusiasm or party spirit. The spiritual mind, which was the chief ingredient in the power exercised on society by the early leaders of the Evangelical revival, was a purely moral force, and the sympathy built upon it could not be directed against any social interest.

Energy, without development of either mind or character, appears to define the type of clergyman which the church revival tends to form. There is a weakness of individual character which relies upon the lead of the chiefs of the party, and a feebleness of intelligence which supplies the place of judgment by tenacious adhesion to dogma. In such natures there is no foundation for a full and living Christian faith, as there is no appetite for the more accessory parts of knowledge. The tradition of learning is in this barren field fast drying up. Already the phrase, 'a divine and a scholar,' long the highest eulogy of the clerical character, sounds old-fashioned in our ears. 'Active clergyman' is now our favourite form of approbation. The term is an appropriate one; for the merit commended consists, in no small degree, of bodily locomotion. The active clergyman is much about in his parish doing parochial 'work.' He builds new schools, and looks in upon the schoolmaster daily. He substitutes open seats for pews, of course, and works the fabric of the old church, inside and out, up to the mark of the established fashion of the day in decoration. This is often done at a great sacrifice of his own, perhaps slender, means, and still greater sacrifice of his time and means in begging from his personal friends. He attends public meetings far and wide; there is an 'opening,' or at least a 'reopening,' once a month in the diocese. The number of societies to which he belongs is large: he is on the committee of half of them, is secretary of one, and treasurer of another. He is not 'idle,' as he can truly boast; for indeed he has not spent an hour a day in solitary and studious retirement since he was ordained. He speaks with complacent superiority of the sloth and worldliness of the clergy in the last century. And justly so; for he is as different from the easy-going divine and scholar of the eighteenth century as he is from the Hookers and Herberts of the seventeenth. Amid our

luxurious refinements, and in our growth of churchmanship, we are fast losing even the lowest form of the
tradition of learning,—the form of respect for the well-
read gentleman, which has been as a feeble ray from the
distant sun of knowledge, never leaving the Church of
this country wholly dark.

It so happens, too, that the High-Church party has come
into possession of the stage at a moment when there was a
better prospect than there has been at any time since 1688
of the final reconcilement between Christianity and science,
between the Church and the philosophers. All the philosophy that is now influential is spiritual. Scepticism and
materialism are daily losing their hold on the English
mind. Perhaps an exception ought to be made of the
Positivist tendencies which profess to deny 'God and a
soul.' 'God,' to use Mr. Curteis's words[1], 'is daily inviting us to higher though more difficult views of his
revelation.' No existing Christian community was more
favourably situated for the work of fostering the Christian
tendencies of modern ideas than our own Church. The
Anglican school especially was invited by its best traditions
to undertake that work. We fear that we must say that,
so far as the church movement is influencing our Church,
it is carrying her further away than ever from any such
renewal of her strength. If at this critical juncture the
spirit of orthodoxy shall succeed in enveloping her body in
its deadly coils, the little mental life which still animates it
must be crushed out. The everlasting contest is still
waging between science and opinion, knowledge and
ignorance, intelligence and majorities; and it is but too
plain with which of these the ecclesiastical movement will
side. It had its beginning in the appeal of a learned
minority from the shallow dogmatism of the Puritan creed
to the broad field of Christian history and antiquities.
The minority has become a majority, and has outgrown its

[1] *The Guardian*, Nov. 26, 1862.

learning. It prefers force to reasoning. The tone of the High-Church triumph, as it swells louder and louder on the breeze, becomes more vulgar, more violent, more partisan. Not merely learning in any sense of the word, but knowledge, is deserting it, and with knowledge the power of being impartial. It has long ceased to want discussion for itself. Now it will not suffer others to discuss in its presence. The calm tone of historical inquiry is intolerable to it. Storm and rage and commination, the borrowed note of Machale or *L'Univers*, is becoming its style. Instead of the comprehensive wisdom of a church-system winning its way to regain the esteem and affection of a nation which it had all but lost, we have the factious triumph of a party clamouring for more rigorous tests, to expel whatever of attainments and intelligence still harbours within the shadow of the Church. The illusory promise of the early days of the revival has come to nought, and a noble opportunity is being wasted. The best traditions of Anglicanism—its moderation, its learned repose, its tolerant comprehension—are thrust aside, and in their place we meet the passionate temper of its worst days, the spirit of Laud and Sheldon, and of the vengeances of the Restoration. To traduce critical inquiry as scepticism or rationalism, to hound on the mob to hunt down the small handful of clergymen who have dared, however unskilfully, to put their hand to theology, is the absorbing passion of a party which once sat at the feet of Dr. Newman. And such are the means of terrorism at the command of the party, that they can wrest a denunciatory *mandement* from the episcopal bench, can intimidate an aged ecclesiastical judge, and poison the atmosphere of social life with scandalous aspersion. The literature of the party sinks lower with each increase of its strength. The *Christian Remembrancer*, the Anglican quarterly, though it never rose above the level of a party organ, and though it discussed questions of criticism from a party, and not from a scientific, point of view, yet did so with candour and moderation. It has paid the penalty, we fear, in a gradually declining circulation; and now, to take the intellectual gauge of the Bishop of Oxford's party, we must descend as low as the *Literary Churchman.* This is the publication from which the party derive their notions of foreign theological literature; especially it undertakes to keep them *au courant* of German theology. That literature is, we need not remind our readers, of the most complex character. There is not a shade of modern opinion which is not represented in it by erudition, by searching discussion, by profound thought. We may see in it, in free play and collision, all the elements which coexist in the Church of the present. Of all this the High-Church instructor is entirely unaware. It lumps it all as 'scepticism.' Every work of first-rate learning which has appeared in Germany for some years past has been consistently vilified by it, without the least glimpse of the author's purpose or meaning. The only exception made is in favour of feeble Roman-Catholic manuals, or the books of the clique of Romanizing Lutherans who haunt the court of Berlin. With this exception, the whole is passed off as 'shallow rationalism'; and such is the level of information among the party, that the conductors of the journal probably utter this in as good faith as their readers swallow it.

The same phenomenon reveals itself in the Church Congress held in Oxford in July last. There was animation, unanimity, vigour, arrayed on behalf of the most meagre poverty of conception, the most disappointing barrenness of moral purpose. The Congress exhibited the party in a most imposing light, and spread out in the broad light of day its growth in numbers, in consequence, in union, in the consciousness of power. But though the Congress was held in academical halls, the learning and talent of both Universities was conspicuously absent.

Not a single professor or tutor whose attainments have earned respect or influence took an active part in the proceedings, if we except Dr. Acland, who good-naturedly lent his name. The leaders in the debate were either ' Bishop of Oxford's men ' or professors whose chairs have been reached by other qualifications than those of knowledge of the subjects they have to teach. The debates were sham-fights ; for the real difficulties of the Church of England were tabooed, to begin with. The discussions were mock-discussions, which led to a pre-arranged conclusion. The impartial onlooker turns from the Oxford Congress as he might go away from a field-day where some Continental monarch had reviewed his troops. We all know what a parade-day at Potsdam is worth. A great deal of powder is burnt, cuirasses flash, and plumes nod magnificently ; the commander-in-chief and his high-born officers have had important work, by which nothing was done. The party exult over the Congress as a 'success.' They have reason ; for it at once showed their strength and cemented it. It demonstrated at the same time the difficulty of erecting theology into a party bond, without at the same time degrading it into a party watchword. ' Summa nequiquam pelle decorus.'

It is peculiarly unfortunate that Englishmen have ever since the Reformation been accustomed to this partisan style in theology. To take up with a set of opinions, and then to enforce them in a damnatory spirit upon all comers, is a mental process so unhealthy, that in all other topics we are indefatigable in guarding ourselves and others against it. In religion it is the only procedure we know and practise. Nothing but inveterate habit could reconcile us to this daily violation of the first principle of intellectual education. Is this to be so for ever ? Is there any prospect that the elementary laws of correct thought will ever be exemplified in religious thinking ? that theology will ever be raised in the Church of England even to the rank of any of the other branches of knowledge ? For we dare hardly go further than this, and ask, as we might do, Is it within hope that religious truth, instead of the degraded instrument of clerical animosities, shall be reinstated as the ' mater scientiarum,' embracing in one compact hierarchy of science all the natural and historical knowledge now open to us ?

We must first ascertain the cause of the disease before we can say if any means of mitigation are within our reach.

There is a very common explanation current, which finds in endowments the sufficient cause of this mental malady, the perpetuation of opinion without faith. To endow opinion, it is said, is to bring about and render inveterate a collision with science. The whole external history of science is a history of the resistance of academies and universities to the progress of knowledge. The first discoverers have always been the heretics, and often the martyrs of science.

Without disputing the truth of the historical experience appealed to, it must still be allowed that it goes a very little way towards the explanation of the fact. For the same circumstance is found where endowments are wanting. The religious idea among the English Dis-senters, with whom opinion has no legal guarantee, is even more debased than it is in the Church. Intellect and knowledge are quite as much estranged from orthodoxy among the French Catholics, where the ministers of religion are paid a miserable pittance out of the annual budget. The desiccated and unspiritual Christianity of the orthodox communions in the United States, under the voluntary system, is a caricature of our own condition. Orthodoxy, as a cause, is rapidly rallying adherents. It is developing, in the same proportions, its intrinsic antipathy to the life of the intellect and the health of the soul. A stiff and blighting dogmatic spirit is destroying our intellectual life, while the Church is displaying an unparalleled energy in building, endowing, subscribing, and every form of material outlay. As its moral vigour dries up, its material wealth expands. This is a phenomenon which, if any, has its sources in the inner heart of our time. This religious condition is not an isolated effect, but is referable to the same general causes which are operating in other parts of our national life. Ecclesiastical history is not a series apart, in which events occur according to the will of the clergy; it is but one part of our whole development. The following considerations may aid to place the subject under the point of view from which it may best be seen.

The whole body of that knowledge to which man can attain may be divided into two sorts: 1. There is the knowledge of God and of the Divine economy in the present government and the prospective destinies of man : this is theology, natural and revealed. 2. There is the knowledge of man and nature, which we acquire by experience and reflection : to this class we refer all the sciences, natural or moral, all political and historical wisdom,—all knowledge, in short, which does not come under the first head.

These two great domains of knowledge may be present to the collective intelligence of any generation in one of two modes. Theology and natural knowledge may be in harmony throughout all their parts from foundation to summit, distinct yet one, mutually explaining and supplementing each other. Inconsistency, incompatibility, conflict, these are not dreamt of; they have never occurred and can never occur. They cannot occur; for the accumulating experience of the human race is for ever rectifying its own errors, and acquiring a deeper insight into the principles of things. This ideal perfection of human intelligence we suppose not to be realizable in this present scene, where we see the real only ἐν αἰνίγματι, through the symbol of the phenomenal. We may perhaps please ourselves with fancying that we find an actual approach to this magnificent conception of the Temple of Truth in the Christian world, as it emerged from the turbulence of the Middle Ages. The contemporaries of Albert or Aquinas had at least no difficulty in being at once devout Christians and comprehensive philosophers. The Christian ideas of the second century were gloriously transfigured, expanded, developed, in harmony with the laws of reason and nature, as these were then understood. The exterior hierarchical harmony which reigned for a brief space throughout the church of the West was but a type of the inner beauty of the great intellectual edifice, of which the apex was theology.

Again : the realms of natural and divine knowledge may present themselves to a given generation dissociated, entangled, conflicting with each other. This in one of two ways. Either natural knowledge may be in abeyance, and the human soul may abandon itself exclusively to working out its spiritual experience. In this case, the spiritual life will be real, but it will be fantastic, visionary, irrational, fanatical. Such was the spiritual experience fostered by the eremitical and monastic efforts of the fifth century. Or, natural and historical knowledge may make a vigorous leap, while the religious conscience of man may be suspended. The intellectual horizon may be suddenly enlarged, while theology may be in the rigid custody of a priestly class, who may prohibit any others from meddling with it, while they themselves do not partake in the scientific progress going on around them.

This last case was that of the Catholic Church of the West at the time of the Reformation. The Church having once committed itself to the fatal principle, that what it once sanctions becomes irrevocable, there is no retreat for it from the accumulating arrears of blunders— errors of policy or principle, to which all long-lived societies, even the best managed, are liable. Consequently the Catholic Church has never been able to re-enter upon the common line of European progress. All the social ameliorations which European states have made for many centuries have been made outside the Church, and in spite of its most strenuous opposition. It has been the consistent foe of every attempt on the part of the wise and good to employ past experience for the correction of legislative error, or for softening the harsh pressure of political institutions. Since the sixteenth century its power has declined, its consistency has never yielded. The consequence is, that the sum-total of our intellectual and political gains has accumulated itself outside of the pale, if not of Christianity, yet of the historically legitimate and venerable fabric of the Western Church. The Church's position, with feeble pertinacity anathematizing in the name of religion all the triumphs of human reason and genius, has often provoked the sarcasm of the scorner and the satirist. It is beginning now to awaken other thoughts among us. We are now disposed to mourn over the invincible barrier which the attitude of the Church opposes to that reunion of the intelligence of the West to its religious traditions, which must be regarded as a preliminary condition to the final organization of society on a basis which shall preclude crises and revolutions. Instead of sneering at the impotence of the papal pretensions, we stand in dismay before the impregnable strength of the position in which human Unreason has entrenched itself.

The Reformation, so far as it was an intellectual movement, was an attempt to restore the equilibrium of science and religion, which had been disturbed by the gradual growth of human knowledge. The early discoverers in science, the philosophers of the sixteenth century, found themselves outside the Christian pale, not because science and philosophy are anti-Christian, but because the Church's conceptions of God's truth were unscientific. Protestantism, on its intellectual side, was a movement to set right this inadequacy. A monstrous antagonism had grown up between the conclusions of human reason and the decisions of the Church. The church doctors solved this by a dualistic theory of the real repugnance of the two faculties of natural reason and illuminated faith. The antithesis is imaginary. At least it does not exist between the two terms, but between false conceptions of their meaning. The knowledge we arrive at by the use of our natural faculties is God-given, and so also is our knowledge of the gracious work of Christ. Protestantism does not set up reason against faith, but proclaims the unity of all knowledge, human and divine. When the Reformation is described as the emancipation of reason from the shackles of church authority, the account is not untrue, but imperfect. It is not the authority of the *existing* Church which is thrown off in the Protestant system. It was the authoritative decisions of a past generation of churchmen which the existing Church claimed to examine. The Reformation vindicates the right of each generation of Christian men to form its own conception, according to its best knowledge, of the economy of God's dealings with man. Were this Christian liberty exercised, under the restraints which a right reason imposes upon its own exertion, collision between science and religion would be impossible.

It is with reluctance that we press considerations so obvious, though to the impatience of undisciplined readers they will seem too speculative and abstract. Let us hasten to apply them to the history of our own Church.

When England separated itself, in the sixteenth century, from Rome, we claimed, as a national church, the right to repudiate its jurisdiction, to remodel its discipline, and to rescind a portion of its doctrine. The right was both claimed and in fact exercised. Having been exercised, it was vindicated by argument. Such argument could but proceed upon principles admitted by the persons to whom the argument was addressed. We have nothing to say at present on the validity or invalidity of either these arguments, or the admitted premisses on which they proceeded. But it has been a capital circumstance in determining the character of Anglican theology, that the principle upon which the secession was originally defended was gradually abandoned, and that another and quite opposite principle was substituted for it. This is as much a historical fact as the Reformation itself. But it was not a change made by power, and engrossed in a public act, but one wrought out by public opinion. Its date may be fixed—so far as such insensible changes admit of chronology—in the latter half of Elizabeth's reign. In the first period of our Reformation our divines made common cause with the foreign reformers. They alleged the supremacy of Scripture. Scripture was posited as a principle. It was not proved, but approved itself to the individual or congregational conscience. Our divines knew of no church but the 'coetus fidelium,' the saints upon earth, whose illuminated conscience was the 'witness' of Holy Writ (Art. 20). As the Church was emphatically the present church, so the Scripture was not regarded as a historical relic, but as the living oracles of God. Such a system, regarded as the basis of a theology, seems to give free scope to conscience, piety, reason, and science, but none to history, criticism, or what we may call learning. It breaks with the past; has no other use for it but to sweep it away as rubbish. Such was the career on which our Reformed Church seemed originally embarked.

But the circumstances of Elizabeth's reign induced or compelled the apologists of the Church of England to abandon this position. Threatened, like all reforming movements, by the 'extreme left' of its own friends, to prevent itself from being forced further in the direction in which it had made more than one step, it chose to relinquish the grounds on which those steps had been justified. Pressed by the Puritans, it was unable to resist their inferences, while it allowed their premises. The only course was to reform the basis on which the church institution, such as it in fact was, was rested. This the Anglican divines of James's and Charles's reigns did by claiming for the English Church a legitimate descent from the primitive Church. They gave up to the Puritans the theory of Scripture and the Congregation, and recurred to the Roman theory of church tradition. They occupied against the intestine foe the very position which, as held by Rome, they so long besieged with small success.

The first visible effect of this principle working in the minds of English divines was one favourable to learning. Their appeal to Catholic antiquity, and the church system as understood in primitive times, gave them, in the judgment of scholars, a vast superiority when compared with the arbitrary textualism of the Puritan divines, and the wilful egotism of the Independents and later sectaries. Round the names of Pearson, Bull, Hammond, Stillingfleet, and the rest of the Caroline divines, gathers a faint lunar reflection of the noon-day glory which surrounds the majestic edifice of the Catholic theology of the Middle Ages. The Anglican scholars appeared to have reopened for Christendom the long-lost records of its early faith and discipline. In those forgotten documents they believed with sincerity they had found the archetypal lineaments, at least in outline, of the pure and apostolical Church of England as it existed in their own day. It is true their learning went only a little way. It was the learning of the lawyer who searches for precedents, not of the historian who resuscitates the whole spirit and form of a buried age. A thorough philological inquiry reveals at once the vast gulf between the religious ideas and usages of the second and the seventeenth centuries. An inquiry into the whole contents of ante-Nicene Christianity was beyond the reach of these divines. But to admit this in no way interferes with the fact of the elevated tone which was communicated, both to the Church and to its theology, by this direction being given to study. Of all social forms, religious society, more than any, demands of those who are called to guide or govern it a knowledge of its history. We never break with the past with impunity. The pretence of the Puritans to legislate for the Church from the Law of Moses and the Acts of the Apostles was simply the presumption of ignorance. The opening of patristic antiquity by the Anglican divines was, at the beginning of the seventeenth century, a signal enlargement of the intellectual horizon of the English Church, and the admission of a new stock of facts, the knowledge of which was indispensable to the discussion.

But this hopeful beginning led to little or no substantial results. Like fruit in a wet autumn, learning in our Church promised well at first, but has hung on the tree ever since still immature. It is shrivelled and puny, from want of the sun and the winds which play freely everywhere else, but not on it. 'Multi pertransibunt, et augebitur scientia;' this process has been going on ever since Bacon placed these words in the front of the *Advancement;* only from theology has it been shut out. The consequence is, that we are on the eve of a collision between knowledge and opinion; with every prospect, as far as we can see, that our Church will make the same choice which has been made by the Roman Catholic Church, and will ally itself irrevocably with the cause of ignorance.

We are not writing the history of English theology, and

must therefore be content with selecting from among a number of circumstances two points in which the intrinsic weakness of the High-Church school of divinity betrays itself. In the first place, it received its whole form from the exigencies of controversy, and that, controversy under the special circumstances of the sixteenth century. The Caroline divines never conceived the idea of historical investigation; they wanted to refute an adversary. They looked into primitive antiquity for just so much as served their purpose. In the skill and learning with which they achieved this purpose they have probably never been surpassed by any advocates. They took from Rome its principle of church tradition. But they fixed a limit of time below which it was not to be valid. That the decrees of the Nicaean Council were not to be subjected to criticism was agreed between Anglican and Catholic disputants. They took from Protestantism its principle of re-examination. But they fixed a chronological limit above which such re-examination might not ascend. That all the later accretions of Catholic orthodoxy might be re-examined by the light of Scripture and reason, was agreed between the Anglican and the Protestant. With this composite basis of operations the Anglican disputant was in a situation eminently favourable for argumentative attack. He could sally out and overwhelm the foe on either side, while he could shelter himself from reprisals under cover of a principle which was admitted valid by either antagonist. To demolish the chair of Peter, canonization of saints, monasticism, relics, pardons, and indulgences, he reinforced himself with Protestant criticism. To sustain episcopacy, or sacramental efficacy, against the Calvinist, he could array the whole of primitive consent at his back. The strength of this position lay wholly in the attitude of the assailants. A ground may be impregnable polemically, and may yet be no basis for a scientific system. The *argumentum ad hominem* is a telling resource in disputation, but is useless as a medium of proof. The Catholic hypothesis of a perpetual living organ of true doctrine affords a broad basis for a scientific or logical exhibition of church law, upon that hypothesis. The Protestant principle, which demands the rigid application of the rules of historical evidence to historical phenomena and the written records of them, opens the vista of a retrospective induction which shall present the Incarnation of Deity, with all its momentous consequences to the past and future of mankind, not as an isolated intervention, but as a part of the whole evolution of our race. Catholic theology is a compact, harmonious, imposing whole of legislative dogma, exactly parallel, both in the fact of its growth and in the theory of its origin, to the imperial civil law. Protestant theology appeals to the Bible, i. e. to the whole spiritual history of the human race ; a precious experience, but an experience only then intelligible when interpreted by all the other experiences attainable by each generation according to its means. Either of these modes of dealing with Christianity is intelligible, and satisfies that human mind to which all verbal exhibition of Christian faith must appeal. But it is impossible to combine them into one system of theology, though it is possible to argue for controversial purposes upon each principle alternately.

If the unsteady position of the church establishment between two extreme parties imparted a vacillating character to its theology, the principle which Anglican orthodoxy adopted from Rome has had a still further incapacitating effect upon our divines. The first foreign reformers, and our own with them, had acknowledged no rule of belief but Scripture, as interpreted by the existing congregation of believers. This view was incorporated into our Articles. But though it remained in the Articles, it early disappeared from the writings of the Anglican divines. The word 'church' began with them to stand for a past abstraction, no longer anywhere to be found upon earth.   But the whole system of the church, or whatever could be attributed to it, was now covered with the same infallibility which the Roman Catholics attributed to the decisions of theirs.   This idea of the sacred inviolability of all notions and usages once adopted by the ' church,' an idea fatal to all improvement in human affairs, is the heritage—a *damnosa·hereditas*—which the Anglican school of English divinity carries over with it from Rome.

The paralyzing effect of this notion of unalterable precedents is one that is felt more the further the world advances in its destined course.   Any institution which is tied up to such a system drags at each remove a lengthening chain.   Each year the living thought and ideas of educated Englishmen are passing more and more out of sympathy with the orthodoxy of the Anglican school. And yet, at the same time, that party in the Church is at this moment (1863) the most numerous, wealthy, and influential.   It engrosses all the zeal and activity, and is fast winning its way to ascendency in the State.   It is proud of its success, and confident of still further victories.   But the victories are not intellectual victories. It gains numbers, enlarges its area, stirs up sympathies. But there is a fatal weakness within.   It has no true grasp of Christian history.   The only clue to the past is not in its hands.   It has a set of borrowed dogmata, but no theology.   It feels that intelligence is against it. Having renounced the use of reason, it is compelled to go on to denounce reason.   The Church of England has a historical position beneath the venerable shadow of English traditions.   It has committed mistakes of policy, but its faults, after all, have not been—like the bloody deeds of the Roman Church in the sixteenth and seventeenth centuries—unpardonable crimes against humanity. It has in these latter days awoke to a new sense of strength.   Its first impulse is to stand upon its political position ; to ally itself with a party in the State ; to strengthen its connexion with property ; to plant its fabrics over the face of the land ; to get the primary schools into its hands ; in short, to carry the visible institution everywhere. If it be the case that our clergy have awoke from a literary or self-indulgent lethargy to a sense of practical duty, it is not altogether unnatural that this desire of usefulness should take, in the first instance, an outward and material direction. It is the universal order of human progress. We attend to our material necessities first, and we go on to satisfy our spiritual wants afterwards. Material church extension has not kept pace with the material progress of the English people. Let this, then, be remedied by all means. Let churches and schools be built. Let there be more curates, more bishops, more services, and more people to attend them. Let 'every church in England have its stalled chancel, duly filled with its surpliced choir; let every church have at least its weekly celebration at its altar duly surmounted with the emblem of salvation [1].'

All this should be done. But when it is done, to what end will it have been done ? Something would certainly have been gained for the well-being of the community, should the clergy succeed in visibly reuniting the masses with the Established Church, in giving them one link which could connect them, even externally, with the existing institutions of their country. The great social difficulty of our time is the gulf between the rich and the poor ; the clash of interest, unsoftened by any bond of union, between labour and the employers of labour. If the revived energy of the parochial system can do anything whatever to heal *this* schism, it ought to be warmly welcomed and promoted by all true Englishmen. Our fear is, that the spirit in which the church revival is being pushed by the Bishop of Oxford's party is doing little or nothing towards this much-to-be-desired end. We do

[1] *Christian Remembrancer.*

U 2

not perceive that that party ever attempts to grapple intellectually with the actual facts of our social life. They are very zealous; but their zeal is too exclusively a blind zeal for the recognition of the Church. They march forward like a Saracenic host, with the Koran or death as their watchword. They wish to conquer, but not to reform or renew the social life of the regions they invade. The anti-intellectual stamp of the party interferes with its real comprehension of the elements of our daily life. The High-Church clergyman carries with him into everything he does a fatal stereotype of theological opinion. Trained not to employ his reason in his theology, he never thinks of employing it in any other direction. Hence it is that remedial measures of social relief originate outside the clerical body, and often find in it their most uncompromising opponents. The High-Church clergy are, as individuals, generous beyond their means, sympathetic with affliction, unselfishly ready to bestow their time and their money upon doing good among the poor. But let any public question, involving those very interests, be brought before them in at all an abstract shape, and they are as little capable of giving it an impartial and cordial examination as an assemblage of Belgian or Spanish priests.

Under these circumstances, we cannot look so hopefully as we could wish to do upon the practical portion of the church revival. Unfortunately, however, its practical side is its bright side. Parochial activity is its best element. In its ideal of public worship, it has, if that is of any moment, both the spirit and the letter of the Book of Common Prayer on its side. Its choir-service is, compared with the practices it supersedes, an immense step in the right direction; that direction being not a recurrence to usages of the sixteenth century, as if those usages derived any value from their date, but the development of an ideal form appropriate to the substance of worship.

But beyond parochial organization, and the beauty of praise, a Christian ministry is charged with duties which transcend those in excellence as in difficulty. A Protestant church does not save souls independently of their moral condition. It is an instrument of instruction, of training, of guidance ; a home of holy example, a nurse of pious sentiment. The function of teaching is one of quite other importance in a Protestant, from that which it is in the Catholic, Church. In the Roman Church, the teaching office of the church is only one among many other subordinate functions of the body. In a Protestant Church, it is not by the efficacy of a sacrament, but by instruction, and discipline, and moral preparation, that the heart is made ready to be the recipient of the influences of the Holy Spirit. The church is not merely a temple of worship, but a school. When the organ is hushed, and the congregation silent, and the teacher ascends the pulpit, then the weak side of Anglicanism reveals itself. Still more out of the pulpit, in that wide arena of teaching where all the world are learners, is this weakness painfully apparent. The impotence of the pulpit, it may be said, is the fault of our congregations, whose ear expects a recurrence of phraseology to which they do not attend, but will not dispense with. But what shall we say of the written theology of the Anglican school ? The press is wide and free to all. Through the press a prodigious amount of moral instruction is being given daily; the whole sum of our ideas is being constantly fed, modified, altered, through its instrumentality. The influences thus kept at work upon the public mind are some better, some worse. Of the good influences, how small a fractional part can be traced to an Anglican origin ! According to the theory of the Anglican school, the Church claims the exclusive right to teach the nation; claims therefore the whole of this influence. If the voluntary teachers were to abandon the field to-morrow, and the press as well as the pulpit were the monopoly of the Anglican school, what has it got to teach? When we look at the power of the Anglican school to grapple with moral difficulties, to adjust the social machine, to aid the soul to rise above the weary cares of life, or the distracting tones of controversy, to aid it to contemplate the 'depth of divine wisdom and philosophy'—βάθος σοφίας καὶ γνώσεως Θεοῦ,—what impotence, combined with what pretension, do we find there! The theme is the most sublime to which the powers of the human mind can be dedicated; the treatment of it the most grovelling and pettifogging. Having nothing to say itself, its chief effort is to run down the attempts of others to handle the mighty theme. Little angry books, in which the bad temper is more conspicuous than the bad writing, dealing in denunciation of certain imagined 'enemies of the faith;' an enormous mendacity and disingenuousness, which is not ashamed to enlist in its cause all the prejudices of the ignorant,—such is the staple of High-Church literature, the utterances of the party who claim to be the exclusive teachers of truth. While the practical success of the school has been great, its literature has sunk to the level of that of the Evangelical school, upon whose ruins it had risen. Its arrogance and its incapacity are commensurate, while it breathes anything but the calm temper of a mind in possession, as these persons claim to be, of absolute truth. 'If dogmatism were the result of sincere religion,' Dr. Donaldson writes, 'its effect would be to make us pity our brethren who thought erroneously; we should endeavour to point out their errors, but should leave the consequences in the hand of God. The dogmatism which now prevails refuses to enter upon any argument; it denounces a difference of opinion as *ipso facto* wrong; and proceeds by all available means to inflict personal injury on those whom it is unable to convert [1].'

[1] *Christian Orthodoxy*, p. 417.

The fact is, that all the intellectual capacity which exists in the Church of England has moved away in another direction. The Church is not now, more than in past times, destitute of learning, scholarship, mental cultivation, powers of thought. But what it retains of these gifts are not found attached to the Bishop of Oxford's party. The surd and irrational complexion of that party is due to the circumstance that all its best minds went from it, some in the Ultramontane direction, others in the Latitudinarian, leaving it only a residuum of practical men—the working clergy. All those various *nuances* vulgarly denominated 'broad' are in fact nothing more than an offshoot of Anglicanism ; they constitute the intelligence of Anglicanism. To have attempted in any degree to apprehend religious truth, to appropriate it as a living knowledge, to seek its meaning, to give it access to the understanding, to penetrate below words to that which they would convey,—this effort transports the mind which makes it immediately beyond the pale of the Anglican party, though the person may in other respects retain unbroken the ties which attach him to that party. Accordingly, a manifesto, which evidently proceeds from one who has a right to speak in the name of his party, claims these scholars and divines as substantially friends and allies.

The definition of a Broad Churchman, as such, is merely the negative one, that he does not choose to be called either High or Low. There are persons using the name who consider 'church' merely as an expletive, and in whose eyes 'broad' is synonymous with indistinct and undefined,—Christians unattached, in short, who have not openly left the Establishment. But it is most unjust to impute this character to Broad Churchmen as a class; for we are convinced that, under that vocable are included many men really zealous for the church cause, and for the *bene esse* of the actual Prayer-book Church, but to whom the name and idea of party in connexion with religious affairs is peculiarly offensive, and who accordingly take refuge in an appellation which they consider has come into existence as a protest against the High- and the Low-Church parties. To such as these we gladly bid God speed; and from their co-operation, whatever be its degree, more or less hearty, more or less complete, we anticipate great good for the cause, which might perhaps have continued unattainable, had they not found a name under which they could work for that cause, without identifying themselves with that party in which, from however unfounded suspicions, they were unwilling to enlist[1].

This does not at all overstate the sympathy and hearty attachment which the scholars and divines in question entertain towards the institutions of the Anglican Church, as these have come down to us. The majority of these clergymen would, we are persuaded, repudiate the epithet 'broad' by which they are designated, and claim to be simply 'Anglican.' They, and not the Cuddesdon party, are, to our thinking, the genuine representatives, *mutatis mutandis*, of the best traditions of the Church of England. But with party aims they never can be in sympathy, because the law of their thoughts is Christian truth, and they know that truth never can be promoted by party. They have learnt from Church history that, from the moment a doctrine is made a party watch-word, it has lost its religious significance, and becomes a mere cloak for sinister interests or fanatical malignity. Many indeed of those who most deplore the crusade against knowledge into which the Cuddesdon party is drifting, may not be unwilling to keep on good terms with that party at present. Every clergyman is compelled, on pain of professional ruin, to maintain a fair repute as 'orthodox.' His orthodoxy is his point of honour, and, like a woman, to be suspected is to be lost. If he would not debar himself all opportunities of future usefulness, a clerical writer must not allow the imputation of heterodoxy to be fastened on him. At the present moment the Church is under the terrorism of the faction, who are not slow to avail themselves of this powerful weapon to destroy their

---

[1] *Christian Remembrancer*, January 1860.

adversaries. When *incivisme* is a capital crime, and education is sufficient evidence of *incivisme*, every one is naturally anxious to prove that he can neither read nor write. We cannot but excuse the eager timidity with which almost all clergymen, especially those who had become theological *suspects*, hasten to whitewash themselves by denouncing the Essayists, and leaving them to their fate. We willingly allow all clergymen to take refuge from the storm under the denomination of Anglican. Let them by all means keep themselves beyond the reach of the 'judicial constructions' of an ecclesiastical court. But when the tempest of unreason and theological suspicion shall be allayed, and men are at leisure to reconsider their ground, it will be impossible for any man who possesses any share of philological or theological acquirement to countenance the party of ignorance in tendencies so injurious to the highest interests of the English Church.

Could we hope that the handful of scholars and divines who still represent the tradition of learning in our Church—they are but a handful out of 17,000 clergy— would be allowed to pursue their researches in peace and freedom, and to transmit the torch of learning to another generation, we might hope that the spirit which has recently been kindled in the Church might be productive of a new and noble result. The English Church, in the exercise of her measured freedom, might be the instrument of carrying on the work of the Reformation, and restoring the destroyed harmony between the Christian tradition and human science. At least the attempt, however little successful, would have a beneficial influence. As long as there is room within the Church of England for free learning and a philosophy having its roots in science, so long will that healthy intelligence be maintained, which is an indispensable element of the life of all teaching bodies. But we cannot be blind to the fact, that a spirit is slowly but surely gaining strength within the Church, a spirit which is incompatible with any exercise of the intelligence, and which, if it succeed in gaining the upper hand, must end in expelling all intellect from her bosom. The 'Conservative reaction' may be, as the Liberal press is ever endeavouring to show, a mere temporary movement, the oscillation of the pendulum of parliamentary politics, a reaction against over-liberalism, a reaction which is in antagonism to the general progress of society, and which will be ultimately absorbed by that progress. This may be so. But looking only at the condition of religion among us, we cannot but think that, far down in the deep waters of society, below the surface which party combinations agitate, causes are at work more fatal to freedom of opinion in religion than any crisis through which we have passed since the Reformation. These causes and influences are new to English society, and operate, not in antagonism to the general movement, but—and this it is which makes them formidable—are entirely of it, and are strong by its strength.

These causes are to be found in the general levelling tendency exerted by the advancing tide of civilization. In its superficial aspect, this tendency shows itself in that spectre of the Tory party which they call 'democracy.' Its deeper forces are found in the increasing influence exercised over Government by a certain dead level of 'public opinion.' Our national Church has happily escaped political revolution for nearly two centuries; but it has not been exempt from the silent revolution which is leavening society. The tyranny of opinion has been making steady advances in Western Europe; nowhere more rapidly than in England. At one time it was worth the Church's while to ally itself with the State, i.e. with the Government. But it is now understood that Government has a master, and it is found to be better policy to contract the alliance directly with that master. This master is the public opinion of the majority. He who has a good understanding with this can afford to quarrel with power, even though it be the power of a Napoleon. Whatever other merit the opinion of the majority may have, it is, in the present condition of our population, an unenlightened opinion. It must be founded on passion rather than on reason; on prejudice, not on knowledge; it will prefer the interests of its class to those of the whole, and its own immediate to its remote interest. The numbers of the wise who think are little capable of increase at any time; but the numbers of the public who are influenced by opinion become yearly greater. Knowledge has less and less influence on affairs, and opinion more and more. This is not only the case in secular politics, but in religion also. Theology has absolutely no weight in this country, where there is not even any faculty of canonists. But religious opinion operates over a larger area than any other opinion whatever.

The only home of theology, and the learning which must minister to it, in this country, were the cathedrals and the universities. Within the last thirty years the cathedral endowments have been broken in pieces, and scattered in dust over the English parishes. This wanton havoc has been committed, not by confiscating statesmen, but by the hands of the bishops, and the consent of the Church herself, which has come to believe that more churches and more services were what were wanted, and that if she got them, she would do well enough without learning. The English cathedral, as it now stands, re-formed in the spirit of the age, reformed by the Church herself as she now understands her mission, has been transferred from the learned class to the working clergy. A modern Bishop is a mere vicar-general, having a peculiar department of official business to transact. Up to the moment of his consecration he was a working clergy-man. If any crisis of opinion arises, he is sure to reflect the prejudices of the majority. Of the Deaneries only three or four have been left with an independence. Even those are threatened by the same public opinion which desires to utilize them by converting them into endow-ments for more bishops. The Canonries have come to be considered as mere means of rewarding some de-serving parish priest, and appendages to his income. The Universities have long been diverted from the pursuit of the higher branches of study to the purposes of elementary education. In 1854 the opportunity of re-storing the balance by the endowment of chairs was lost. After much flourish of trumpets, nothing worth speaking of was done in this way; while the compulsory theological degree was abolished, and a large portion of college revenues was converted into exhibitions for young students. The election of heads of colleges being left in the hands of the fellows, experience has shown that the man of business and social habits will be preferred by them to the man of culture and learning; while at Oxford the only two unappropriated canonries in the cathedral remaining to the Crown were recklessly sacri-ficed to the same furor for practical purposes. All this was done in compliance with public opinion, in the face of which it was found impossible to proceed with the creation of a professoriate. The public could not see the use of higher knowledge. In Oxford, too, the annual income is more and more voted away for non-academical objects by the Bishop of Oxford's party, which has now acquired a large numerical preponderance in the aca-demical convocation.

The same animus which has levelled the whole Church, including the episcopate, into a parochial machine, when it turns to theology, will tolerate nothing above the level of sermons. Not only must the clerical writer not rise above the pulpit level, nothing must come from his pen beyond the phrases which are expected in the pulpit. Anything which travels beyond these conventionalisms shocks the expectation which knew what ought to have come next. The Church party speak of all that a clerical writer utters as 'teaching.' Teaching is become their cant term. As if there were no such thing as discussion, or learned research; no unexplored fields in historical criticism; as if the relation of the theological writer to his reader was that of spiritual guide, and the public sat at his feet to receive dogma. It is an evil incident to the pulpit, as too often employed, that it spreads a loose and superficial conception of Christianity. Designed properly for Christian exhortation, it has become in our day chiefly a vehicle for a popular and attenuated theological opinion. But the evil is magnified a thousand-fold when the corrective which learned discussion out of the pulpit might furnish is withdrawn. What would be the condition of any other of those branches of knowledge which bear on social life, if all attempts to handle them had to be made with the halter round the neck? What sort of notions would prevail among us on political economy or jurisprudence, e. g. if Mr. Mill or Mr. Austin were required to put nothing on paper which could offend the prejudices of the common run of Englishmen? The matters which the divine would seek to treat, were it open to him to do so, are so high and intricate, that their intrinsic difficulty might alone deter him, without having error made criminal and punishable.

Even this might be borne, were it an honest desire to take security against error in treating topics so momentous. It is not error which is offensive to the world of religious party. It is the philosophical spirit which is so obnoxious to them. We know the hatred of practical statesmen for the 'ideologists.' It is ideology in religion which irritates beyond control the susceptibilities of the vulgar.

Philosophizing in other matters does not touch them.   It is an idle waste of time, which they can despise, but will not quarrel for.   But revealed religion, that is their affair. They understand it thoroughly.   There is nothing in it with which they have not been long familiar.   To have anyone endeavour to go behind these familiar phrases, to bring to light some part of their deep significance, to sound the unfathomable 'mystery of godliness,'—this is an insult to the popular religion which the modern religionist will not bear.   The suspicion that he has been all his life feeding on words is a very painful one.   To be told that just where his phrases leave off, there that which is indeed spiritual religion begins ; that the symbols of ideas are not those ideas ; that an effort of heart and mind and soul is requisite for the apprehension of spiritual truth ;—all this is extremely galling.   A man need not be a Pharisee to resent it.   But the mass of orthodox English is not merely well satisfied with its own notions, but with itself for entertaining them.   It can better bear to be contradicted than to be treated as of no account.   It can tolerate dissent, or even unbelief, but not ideology.   A philosophical Christianity which admits, but leaves below it, the popular formulae, trenches upon the egotism as well as the prejudices of the community.   Our church public is, perhaps we ought rather to say was, strongly opposed to Romanism ; yet it would hear with patience the Romanist arguments, and defend its own notions against them with temper.   But when, some twenty-five years ago, a rich genius within the Church of England, revolting against the popular theology, endeavoured to escape its arid barrenness by glossing it with patristic and catholic interpretations, the irritation of the religious public knew no bounds.   It was not the Romanism, but the 'treason within the Church' that excited the clamour.   Those who are old enough to remember 1840 will remember that 'mystical,' not 'popish,' was the public epithet of dislike for Dr. Newman's mode of treating Christian truth at that period. Its doctrine of 'reserve in communicating religious truth' was that which first embroiled nascent Tractarianism with the religious world. Just so in the recent ferment on occasion of *Essays and Reviews.* It was not the crudities, blunders, and hasty opinions that volume contains which has stirred all the indignation, but the transcendental treatment of religion from within. Newman's constant effort was to 'realize' the doctrines of the Church ; it was his favourite word at one time. Jowett is ever idealizing the language of Scripture. To the common understanding both alike are felt to be not only passing beyond its ken, but to be taking truth away with them into some region into which it cannot follow.

For, over and above the wound inflicted upon the vanity of the semi-instructed by these supercilious pretensions of an aristocracy of illuminated minds, we must remember that such persons are *bonâ fide* unable to see truths and relations of truths which are nevertheless matters of habitual intuition to those whose minds are further opened. The instincts of a democratic majority not only lead it to hate culture which it believes to be real, they compel it to disbelieve the existence of such culture. The public claims to be arbiter in religious controversy, because, like James I, it believes itself qualified to be so. The mass of religionists feel towards mysticism in religion as the artisan does towards political economy. He has an idea that it is his interests treated of in a pedantic jargon, for the purpose of being made unintelligible to him. The evil against which we have to strive is partly a denial of the utility of theology, but partly also the negation of its possibility. That the Gospel is for the poor, the simple, and the unlettered, is construed to mean, that there are no ideal elements in religion but what are accessible to them. Because the uninstructed can use the Bible for devotional reading, it is denied that the instructed can see in it a historical record of past events. In all ages the multitude of the semi-educated have resented these transcendental pretensions, whether of the philosopher or the saint. It is the old standing schism of the ψυχικός and the πνευματικός,—the man of the letter and the man of the idea. It is not the wholly unlettered who at first come into collision with these claims, but those who have gone through some educational routine without ever having had their minds awakened. Large numbers even of those who read and write books are in this predicament. To this large and increasing class abstract truth has as good as no existence ; but they have acquired a sort of vested interest in the language they have been accustomed to repeat about it. With respect to religious truth we are almost all in this condition. We have all got the Christian terminology by rote long before we quit childhood ; and we are most of us already immersed in practical life before we have capacity to follow the terms into their meaning. Affliction and the trials of life do something for many of us towards opening the mind to moral and spiritual ideas ; but many even these never touch. And at best how imperfect is the qualification thus given for passing judgment on the whole range of religious ideas, involving often special knowledge, critical and interpretative! Yet this is what our religious public assumes the right to do, and without any misgivings as to its own competence. How great is the contrast with the humility of true learning! 'I found,' said Porson, 'that I should require fifty years' reading to make myself thoroughly acquainted with divinity, to satisfy my mind on all points ; and therefore I gave it up. There are fellows who go into the pulpit assuming everything and knowing nothing ; but I would not do so.'

With this popular opinion to work upon, it is not difficult from time to time to bring an overwhelming amount of public reprobation to bear upon any original mind that dares to treat religion as anything beyond a superficial string of inefficacious commonplaces. It is a necessary consequence of the advance of education that every subject becomes vulgarized and superficialized. Superficial knowledge is a very different thing from incomplete knowledge. The knowledge which an occupied man has of any extra-professional subject must be imperfect. But be it ever so partial, if he be aware of its imperfection, that portion which he does not possess will be of some value to him. But of superficial knowledge it is the characteristic, that it believes itself exhaustive,—that is, it is negative of all beyond itself. A majority so educated will not require in its church ministers a body of teachers; for what has it to learn? There is too much truth in Dr. Donaldson's picture of the moral level of the lower middle class among ourselves, though we might wish it more charitably expressed.

The man of business is prone to acquiesce in the consciousness of his own respectability. This is the idol of his heart. He imitates the expensiveness rather than the refinements of the class above him. If he lays down the law in politics or religion, he is the unconscious mouthpiece of some short-sighted utilitarian or canting bigot, whom it is respectable to follow. He cares for little beyond the uncontradicted maintenance of the sentiments he has adopted from his newspaper or his preacher, his personal and domestic comfort, and the decencies of his outward appearance. Abundant meals, good clothes, and a well-furnished parlour, are the extent of his wishes. He measures things without his circle by the ideas which suffice for his narrow world. Hence he is too often the tool of bigotry, the echo of stereotyped opinions, the victim of class prejudices, the blind or obstinate advocate of measures which have no connexion with his own or his country's interests. He has no wish that his sons should be more cultivated and enlightened than himself. I regard the middle class as practically the great stumbling-block in the way of a general diffusion of higher cultivation in this country; for though they have really no opinions of their own, it is impossible to induce them to listen to any argument which runs counter to their inveterate preconceptions [1].

[1] *Classical Scholarship*, p. 88.

The increasing influence which minds of this stamp exercise in controlling the religious teaching of the clergy is a circumstance of very grave import. Hitherto the tendency of the congregation to legislate doctrinally has been kept in check by the presence, in the Church, of superior attainments and more comprehensive knowledge. The Church has (it is true, too faintly) maintained a protest against the grossness of popular conceptions, and opposed a higher standard of knowledge to the assumption of popular ignorance. But the continued degradation of the intellectual level of the clerical body on the one hand, together with the continued spread of the area of religious opinions on the other, is gradually doing away with this safeguard. The small band of men of mental acquirement in the Church is coming to occupy a more and more isolated position within it. Their knowledge appears alien, almost outcast, amid the recognized conventionalities of the popular theology. In another generation there will, in all probability, be no room for such within the Establishment. They are already struggling hopelessly against a majority,—a majority such as described by Mr. Mill,—a majority which is supreme, and therefore 'has no longer need of the arms of reason. It can make its mere will prevail. Those who cannot be resisted are usually far too well satisfied with their own opinions to be willing to change them, or to listen without impatience to anyone who tells them that they are in the wrong [1].'

If this result should be attained, if the High-Church movement should succeed in stifling the voice of conscience and reason, and the Church of England should be beaten down to the dead level of democratic orthodoxy, what would be the result to the Church, and through it to the nation?

We are not left to mere speculation to answer this question. History furnishes us with a parallel case. The

---

[1] *Representative Government*, p. 174.

Church of Rome had at the Reformation the same option
which the Church of England now has. It had to choose
between conforming its doctrine and discipline to the
accumulated knowledge of the time, or of breaking for
ever with the intellectual progress of Europe. We know
which side it took. Was its choice a right or a wrong one?
a wise or an unwise? The history of the three centuries
which have elapsed since that choice was made, is not
more than enough to enable us to answer this inquiry.
Looking to the spiritual duties which a church is called to
perform, it was the wrong choice. It threw up for ever
the office of teacher, renounced the dangerous and troublesome duty of raising man above himself, of guiding and
shaping the intelligence of Christendom. The Church
ceased at the Reformation to do that which it had done
ever since the first promulgation of Christianity. The
education of mankind was from that time forward handed
over to the impersonal and irresponsible moralists of the
press. That education went on, but outside the Church,
under its ban. On the other hand, looking to the temporal
and selfish interests of the Church as a corporation, it was
the wise choice. It was the wise instinct of the Italian
statesmen that led them to choose ignorance and the
masses as the solid foundation for the edifice of their
ecclesiastical power. An aristocracy of intellect is a very
precarious institution. Power always finds its way back
to the majority in the long run. The press may be
troublesome at times; but the majority can always tie it
up when they please to do so.

The church movement in the Church of England is
arriving at power at the moment of a similar crisis. It has
to choose between the knowledge of the few and the
ignorance of the masses. Will it rise to the high calling
of combating prejudice, resisting popular delusions, vindicating learning, maintaining the standing protest against
superficial religionism, restoring the superior education as

a preparation for the ministry, asserting its rightful place as the instructor of the nation? The party guided by the Bishop of Oxford will not be so unwise in its generation. To an arduous and responsible struggle it will prefer an easy and certain party-triumph. The loss of caste which the Church will suffer by an overt breach with the intelligence of the country will be far more than made up to it by its becoming more at home with the majority, whose opinion controls the Government. 'With a uniform £50 suffrage,' says Mr. Isaac Taylor, 'the Church would be politically omnipotent. With universal suffrage and electoral districts the power would be vastly greater than it is. The line is now drawn at that precise point which is most inimical to her interests. For it is with the class of the £10 householders that Dissent has struck its roots[1].' If the party now uppermost in the Church choose to act with a single eye to her interests, irrespective of her duties, they seem to be on the eve of strengthening her political position by a sacrifice of her moral and religious usefulness, to an extent which has not been achieved since the Restoration.

[1] *Liturgy and the Dissenters*, p. 7.

National Review, 1863.]

XVIII

PHILANTHROPIC SOCIETIES IN THE REIGN OF QUEEN ANNE.

———•——

(*Fraser's Magazine*, 1860.)

AT what date in our history did our religious and philanthropic societies originate? It is probable that most people asked this question would say that bene-volent associations are a very recent invention among us; that they were called into being somewhere about the beginning of the century by the labours of Clarkson, Wilberforce, and the other Abolitionists. Howard, who died in 1790, is called the Philanthropist, because he was the first of the order.

It is true that the last sixty or seventy years have been *the* era of philanthropic association; but it is not true that unions for benevolent purposes did not exist at an earlier period. Any one who has seen a Report of the 'Society for the Propagation of the Gospel,' will remember the date on its cover, 1701. Few, however, know that the era which this 'venerable' society can claim as that of its birth, was also a time fruitful of schemes of charitable co-operation. Mr. Secretan deserves our thanks for bringing forward some of these early attempts in a chapter of his *Life and Times of the pious Robert Nelson.* This chapter he entitles 'Nelson's ways and methods of doing good.' It offers some interesting details gathered from various sources.

Benevolent effort is a result of men's feelings, not of

their knowledge.   Its vigour varies accordingly as the feelings that prompt it are intense or languid.   As an individual has his vicissitudes of feeling—to-day all fire and warmth, to-morrow chill and torpid—so has a nation. The history of religious and moral sentiment is therefore a history of 'revivals.'   Piety, being a human sentiment, cannot be a constant quantity.   It is like a wood-fire, always passing into extremes.   One while we see it blazing, roaring, crackling ; catching hold of everything that comes near it, ' a good servant, but a bad master ;' then it sinks and sinks, till it seems all but out ; gives neither light nor heat, but just retains life enough to enable it to be resuscitated when the time comes.   That the ebb and flow of pious feeling can be converted into a steady and continuous stream by any machinery we can contrive, is probably out of the question.   Church establishments and voluntary societies are, however, a great safety-valve for these intermittent forces ; and are, it should seem, the natural channel they seek for themselves. Such a period of revival coincided with the Revolution of 1688.   Though of brief duration, it produced much valuable effect while it lasted.   It deserves more attention than it has received.   Church historians are usually so intent upon their theological battles, as to have little time left for the history of religion.   Battles, in ecclesiastical as in secular history, have engrossed a most disproportionate space.

The secular triumph of the Established Church at the Restoration, 1660, had like to have been more fatal to it than its persecution by the Roundheads had been.   It had been made a tool of by the Cavalier party for their own purposes.   When those purposes were answered, the Church was repaid by restitution of its temporalities, but it did not recover its moral hold upon the people. The Act of Uniformity ushered in a period of shameless moral depravity and political corruption.   It is vain to deny the fact that the interior decay of religion accompanied the exterior victory of the Church, though it is doubtless true that they were not related as cause and effect. The English nature was too sound at core to take heartily to the license and sensuality which reigned in the Court and the town, and a reaction was preparing beneath. Historians trace the Revolution of 1688 to political causes. They are no doubt right. But it is also certain that a vigorous moral reaction within accompanied that exterior dynastic revolution. This moral renovation is too humble to have attracted the attention it deserves. Mr. Secretan, who details some of the facts, does not attempt to put it in its true relation to public events. Indeed, it is the most difficult of the historian's tasks to describe phases of sentiment and opinion. Yet on these phases depends, in no small measure, the course of political affairs. In the present instance, the reaction of religious sentiment of which we speak, embodied itself in various societies, and so acquires a shape and entity which make it more possible to hold it up to view.

1. *The Religious Societies.* This brief 'revival' of piety and zeal which accompanied the Revolution of 1688, we seize in shape first in the capital, the scene on which the profligacies of the Court and the hypocrisies of the Popish plot had been enacted. There was no press in those days to disseminate these things through the kingdom. Only those who saw them done knew the rights of them. Only they, therefore, could feel the disgust which simple and honest souls must have felt when they came to know the rights of them. All the accounts refer the beginnings of the 'religious societies of young men' to somewhere about the year 1678, and to the congregations who attended the preaching of Dr. Horneck at the Savoy Chapel, and of Mr. Smithies at St. Michael's, Cornhill. It is necessary to remark that these societies had, in their origin, no political or ecclesiastical character whatever.

They were simply associations for mutual edification. They arose out of the natural desire for spiritual intercourse, the exchange of religious experience, and mutual encouragement in the practices of piety. The members were young men, of the middle station of life, in the cities of London and Westminster. 'The greater part of them were such as had enjoyed a sober education, and had not shared in the scandalous and heightened enormities of these latter days.' The little pamphlet from which the account of these societies is taken, was written by Dr. Josiah Woodward, minister of Poplar. Dr. Woodward was a clergyman of more zeal than judgment, as appears from another book of his, called *Fair Warnings* (1707), full of apocryphal stories of apparitions and divine interpositions. But nothing of this sort appears in his *Account of the Rise and Progress of the Religious Societies in the City of London, etc.*, beyond the earnestness with which he pleads their cause. For as soon as their existence came to be generally known, they became, not unnaturally, an object of suspicion. The idea of religious brotherhood is too little familiar in this country not to ensure that any such association would be credited with ulterior objects. These 'religious societies,' however, overlived the first period of jealousy. They had the approbation not only of Nelson and the Non-jurors, but of Tillotson, Compton, and many of the other bishops. They conducted themselves, too, with great prudence. During the dangerous time of the reign of James II, they changed the name of 'society' for that of 'club'; and instead of meeting at a friend's house, they adjourned to a tavern, where they could have a private room for their meetings. In other respects the Catholic zeal which then raged at Court only stimulated their devotion. The sight of the daily celebration of mass in the Chapel Royal induced them to set up daily prayers at 8 p.m. at St. Clement Danes, where 'they never wanted,' we are told, 'a full and affectionate congregation.' They made a collection at their weekly meetings for the relief of the poor, for charity schools, for the support of daily prayers and lectures in various churches, and for sending out missionaries to the plantations. In about twenty years from their first foundation they had increased to the number of forty-two distinct societies in London. Similar associations were formed at Oxford, at Cambridge, Dublin, Drogheda, and other large towns. Clergymen going from London to the charge of rural parishes instituted similar usages; borrowing or adapting to their purposes the rules of the London societies, with the most beneficial results, in the revival of at least the externals of religion and the decencies of public worship.

Dr. Woodward's *Account* is very imperfect. We should have liked to have known whether these societies were strictly of home origin, or whether they were propagated from a foreign source. Their resemblance to some of the lay confraternities established by St. Vincent de Paul is obvious. But from the share which Dr. Horneck had in their erection, it is more likely that they were copied from some Lutheran original. We find Jablonski, the King of Prussia's chaplain, translating Dr. Woodward's *Account* into German; and Dr. Francke, the Pietist professor at Halle, writes letters of sympathy and encouragement to the London Societies. Such associations are from their nature temporary, partaking of the ephemeral and convulsive character of all revivals. If their machinery is maintained after their spirit is gone, it is more than probable that it is employed for simply mischievous ends. Such was, it seems, the case with these societies. They began as 'religious' associations, degenerated into mere 'Church' societies, and deservedly perished in the ruin of Jacobitism. One of their last annual meetings was at Bow Church in 1738, where they listened to a sermon from Dr. Berriman, warning the members against being led astray by the irregularities of White-field.

2. *Societies for the Reformation of Manners.* The 'Religious Societies' have been placed first, as not only earlier in point of time, but as the root out of which the later really grew. The 'Societies for the Reformation of Manners' have sometimes been confounded with the 'Religious Societies,' but they were distinct bodies, and had different objects. The 'Religious Societies' had, in their origin, no other purpose than the promotion of individual piety among their members. The 'Societies for the Reformation of Manners' first bring us upon the questionable ground of union for philanthropic purposes. Their object was the enforcement of the existing laws against vice and profaneness. The excesses of outrageous impiety to which the High Church triumph had indirectly led called forth attempts to suppress them by the arm of law. A new Act of Parliament was obtained against cursing or swearing; another against impious books. Royal proclamations were issued, Parliament addressed the Crown, grand juries presented, and the gentlemen and magistrates united—Churchman and Dissenter alike—to put in force the laws against swearing, drunkenness, and the profanation of Sunday. A second society consisted of about sixty tradesmen and others, who made it their business to suppress the debauchery of the streets. Tenison recommended the societies to his suffragans in a pastoral letter. Affiliated branches were formed at Hull, Nottingham, Bristol, and other provincial towns. Blank warrants were sent down from town to the local associations. A compilation, containing an abstract of the penal laws for the guidance of their proceedings, was circulated. A Report of the London Society in 1736 states that in the forty-two years of its existence it had prosecuted 100,650 persons, in London only, for debauchery and profaneness. Seventy or eighty warrants were sometimes executed in a

week upon common swearers in the metropolis, 'so that our constables of late have found it difficult to take up a swearer in divers of our streets.' Sunday markets were suppressed. Bakers were not allowed to appear in the streets with their baskets, or barbers with their pot, basin, or periwig-box ; a strict watch was kept on public-houses, and no 'tippling' allowed in them on the Lord's day. Some thousands of 'lewd persons' were imprisoned, fined, or whipped ; and the 'Tower-end of the town purged from that pestilential generation of night-walkers.'

These societies seem to have come to an end about 1740. They did not die, however, till their inefficacy had been demonstrated by facts in the most complete way. All historians agree that the corruption of manners, as far as its external signs were concerned, was never greater in our country than about the middle of George II's reign, when these societies had been zealously prosecuting, and the magistrates fining and whipping, for half a century. De Foe alone, in this, as in so many other things before his age, seized their weak point when he suggested to the higher classes to try the effect of a little good example in reforming their inferiors.

3. *Society for Promoting Christian Knowledge.* Philanthropical aims took a better form, and one which has maintained its existence down to our days, in the wellknown Society for Promoting Christian Knowledge. This society has never yet had its historian ; and Mr. Secretan's notices, though short, will be read with interest. It was first established in 1698, by a few friends of Dr. Thomas Bray. This is its first resolution :—

Whereas the growth of vice and immorality is greatly owing to gross ignorance of the principles of the Christian religion, we, whose names are underwritten, do agree to meet together as often as we can conveniently, to consult, under the conduct of the Divine providence and assistance, how we may be able by due and lawful methods to promote Christian knowledge.

The first meeting was on the 8th March, 1699, when Lord Guildford, Sir Humphrey Mackworth, Justice Hook, Doctor Bray, and Colonel Colchester were the members present.   The two main objects to which the Society addressed itself were the establishment of charity-schools and the circulation of religious books.   Among their earliest publications were Nelson's *Festivals and Fasts,* and other shorter tracts by him; Dr. Woodward's *Tracts against Drunkenness and Swearing;* Ostervald's *Abridgment of the Bible;* Lewis's *Church Catechism Explained;* Bradford *On Regeneration;* Melmoth's *Great Importance of a Religious Life; Life of James Bonnell;* Scougal's *Life of God in the Soul of Man;*—all works which still retain their place in the list of the Society for Promoting Christian Knowledge.   Suitable books of devotion were dispersed among the patients in the hospitals.   Eight hundred *Kind Cautions against Swearing* were distributed in town among the hackney coachmen ; thirty thousand *Soldier's Monitor* sent to the army in the Low Countries.   A plan for the reformation of seamen was taken into consideration ; and Admiral Benbow and Sir George Rooke undertook to have similar tracts dispersed through the fleet.   The society, in its first two years, designed to embrace missionary effort in foreign countries and the colonies. But it was found, after that short experience, that this was too wide a field of exertion.   And accordingly—

4. *Society for the Propagation of the Gospel in Foreign Parts.* A separate society was organized in 1701 for these purposes.   The *name* was of older date.   Cromwell, in 1649, had erected a corporation under the name of 'The President and Society for the Propagation of the Gospel in New England.' The same corporation, or another under the same name, was promoted by Clarendon after the Restoration.   From this probably the name of the new society, which received its charter of incorporation June 16th, 1701, was adopted.   The charter

recited the insufficient maintenance, or total absence, of ministers of the Church in the plantations, colonies, and factories beyond the seas, so that the population 'do want the administration of God's word and sacraments, and seem to be abandoned to atheism and infidelity;' while 'divers Romish priests and Jesuits are the more encouraged to draw them over to Popish superstition and idolatry.' The new corporation is charged with 'the receiving, managing, and dispensing of charity given for the maintenance of an orthodox clergy, and for making such other provision as may be necessary for the propagation of the Gospel in those parts.' Besides the leading members of the Society for Promoting Christian Knowledge already mentioned, the following were active members of the 'Society for the Propagation of the Gospel':—Tenison, Bray, Beveridge, Mapletoft, Gastrell, Marshall, White Kennett, John Evelyn, Sir Richard Blackmore, etc. Robert Nelson, being a non-juror, is not named in the charter, but was elected a member in the following November, in company with Burnet and nine other of the bishops.

5. *The Charity Schools.* When public feeling is once excited in the direction of benevolent schemes, they tend to multiply, as commercial schemes do in times of speculative excitement. Instead of standing in each other's way, they tend to call fresh associations into being. The good that wants doing is practically infinite as soon as we conceive the ambition of doing it. The education of the children of the poor was one of the obvious fields of exertion. The idea of the State either providing the means or enforcing the acquisition of education was not yet started. It was a benefit which the rich now came forward to bestow as charity upon the poor. As our grammar-schools date from Edward VI, so our Bluecoat and Greycoat schools date from Queen Anne. The Jesuits, in the reign of James II, opened a gratuitous

school in the Savoy. This was the first charity school in London. To counteract their influence Tenison opened a Protestant school in St. Martin's parish, and some other zealous churchmen set up the Bluecoat School in St. Margaret's, Westminster. We must not ascribe this movement wholly to church rivalry. Tenison saw doubtless not only the influence that might be gained, but the good that might be done. This, too, was the great era of school foundation or improvement in the north of Germany. The celebrated Francke foundations at Halle, in Saxony, had been begun by August Hermann Francke in 1694, and his labours soon became widely known in this country. By 1701 there had been called into being in London and its suburbs forty schools, in which above one thousand children received gratuitous education, clothing, and facilities for being apprenticed. By 1712 the number of such schools had increased to one hundred and seventeen, with five thousand children. This was at a time when the population little exceeded five hundred thousand.

The standard of instruction was not ambitious. The boys were taught reading, writing, and the grounds of arithmetic to fit them for service. The girls were only taught to read, to knit, to sew, and mark, to make and mend their clothes. 'Some worthy persons are contriving expedients to teach our children *things* as well as *words*, and to render learning more useful to humane life, which has been greatly wanting [1]'. The adults were not forgotten: masters and mistresses were recommended to appoint some evening in the week to teach such grown people to read as have been neglected in their youth. Particular mention is made of the clergyman of Kepsall in Bedfordshire (Mr. Salmon), who 'has with great success prevailed upon the youth of his parish to go to school to learn to read and write, and their catechism, in the close of the winter evenings; and on the servants of the

[1] Woodward, *Account of the Religious Societies*, p. 95.

said parish to come to him once a week for instruction.' Thus the 'night-school' is not a modern invention. In many churches of the metropolis sermons were preached monthly or quarterly for the maintenance of the schools. General interest was still further maintained by catechizing the children at church; by quarterly school examinations at nine or ten places in town at five in the evening, open to the public; and by an annual assemblage of the school children at St. Sepulchre's Church, the original of the present anniversary meeting in St. Paul's.

The example of London was imitated throughout the country. At Shoreham the experiment of King's Somborne was anticipated—that, viz., of making the school self-supporting by the joint education of children of different grades. 'Persons of ability gave more than the schooling of their own children, that the master might have such an income as might enable him to teach the children of the poor gratis.' At Salisbury the whole expense of one school was borne by the Bishop (Burnet), 'who frequently visits and catechizes the children, and sets them portions of Scripture to get by heart, which he sees performed himself.' At the then fashionable resort of Tunbridge Wells, a school of seventy children was maintained by the contributions of the visitors. At Cambridge many of the colleges gave their communion money. In the minutes of the Society for Promoting Christian Knowledge, May 12th, 1708, we find that

Mr. Nelson communicated a letter he received from some unknown hands at Oxford, acquainting him that several gentlemen of the University, observing the streets filled with idle children, notwithstanding the city and University have set out two very considerable charity schools to which the said gentlemen have been subscribers, they have resolved to erect another, towards which they have subscribed between £50 and £60, and opened a school for about ninety children, most of 'em girls; upon which they desire Mr. Nelson's advice how to apply their fund to the best advantage, and likewise to furnish 'em with rules for the better government of the schools.

All these schools were distinctly Church of England schools. The master was not only to be a member of the Church, but 'one that frequents the holy communion, and who is approved by the minister of the parish before he is presented to be licensed by the ordinary.' His first business was to instruct the children in the Church Catechism, 'and shall afterwards more largely inform them of their duty by the help of the *Whole Duty of Man*.' He was to bring the children to church twice every Lord's day and holiday. In some cases he had to attend divine service with his scholars every day.

6. *The Designs of Dr. Bray.* Dr. Thomas Bray, Rector of St. Botolph's Without, Aldgate, and afterwards Commissary of Maryland, was one of the foremost persons concerned in setting up the Society for the Propagation of the Gospel. But the title of 'Associates of Dr. Bray' was specially given to a society founded by him for the erection of parochial libraries. He printed an 'Address to Persons of Quality and Estate.' He solicits their charitable consideration of this project; stating that there were then in England above two thousand parishes where the annual incomes of the ministers did not exceed £30. He proposes to establish parochial libraries, to be attached to such parishes, for the use of the minister for the time being. The libraries to consist of a 'competent number of the best comments on the Holy Scriptures, and the most approved treatises of practical divinity, and such books as may enable them to administer wholesome and sound doctrine to their flock, either by way of catechizing or preaching.' His exertions were so successful that before his death, in 1730, he had established sixty-seven parochial libraries for the use of the minister of the place, and eighty-three lending catechetical libraries in central localities, for loan among the neighbouring clergy. He had purchased nearly three thousand books in folio, and above four thousand in quarto and octavo.

The preservation of these libraries was secured by an act of Parliament, which he obtained in 1709. The trustees survive to the present day under the title of 'The Associates of Dr. Bray.' They possess an income of £450 a year, derived, partly from a sum of money invested in the funds, partly from an estate in Pennsylvania; but their aid is no longer given to the formation of libraries, nearly the whole of their revenue being spent on colonial schools. Surely libraries are no less required by the poorer clergy now than then. Perhaps the fate that has overtaken those which were established has been the reason of this diversion of the funds from their proper destination. What has become of these libraries, of the three thousand folios, and the four thousand quartos and octavos?

Mr. Edwards[1] has traced the existence of one or two, but no more, and these one or two seem dying a lingering death. Thrust into a chest in the vestry, torn up for waste paper, rotted by damp, the books appear to have perished by all the known forms of death. Even at Maidstone, which obtained, on the easy terms of raising £50, Dr. Bray's own valuable collection of the Fathers, 'the losses appear to have been serious.'

7. *The Commission for building new Churches.* The zeal displayed so far had been confined to private individuals, and directed to works of piety and religion. In 1710, the Tory and High Church House of Commons took the initiative in a more strictly ecclesiastical work, and voted £350,000 for church building in London and its suburbs. It appeared by the report of the committee that a population of 240,000 were unprovided with church room. The sum voted was intended to build fifty new churches, reckoning 4750 souls to each parish, and to provide a parsonage-house and burial ground for each church. The amount was voted unanimously, and was to be

[1] *Memoirs of Libraries*, vol. I.

raised by a tax of 3*s.* a ton upon all coals brought into the port of London. This method of providing the funds appears to have been a suggestion of Dr. Hickes, who, as early as 1705, had recommended that the Coal Act of Charles II, which was then expiring, should be continued for the purpose. Hickes had asked for one hundred churches; Parliament granted fifty, and voted £7000 a-piece for that number. The supineness of a Royal Commission and the extravagance of the architects, however, had not been allowed for. The £350,000 was got through before a fourth part of the fifty churches had been completed. Of some twelve which were built with the money, a Parliamentary Committee reported, Nov. 19th, 1718, that St. John's, Westminster, cost £29,277; Deptford, £19,367; Limehouse, £19,679; Spitalfields, £19,418; Ratcliffe Highway, £18,557; St. Mary-le-strand, £16,341. The first two, the committee complained, were erected by Mr. Archer, the architect, and one of the Commissioners, without any estimate.

After this gigantic specimen of jobbery, no more money was to be got from Parliament. The revived zeal in which these schemes had originated died out with that generation. Philanthropic project slumbered for nearly a century, with a few solitary exceptions, such as Bishop Berkeley, whose romantic enterprises in the middle of the church history of the eighteenth century look sadly out of place. In the last half century our societies have multiplied to such a degree that they have become a public nuisance. They crush, instead of promoting, individual charity, and tame our sympathy between man and man. Our social evils are come to that pass that it may be truly said, 'Nec vitia nostra, *nec remedia*, pati possumus.'

XIX.

LIFE OF MONTAIGNE[1].

———◆———

(*Quarterly Review*, April, 1858.)

MONTAIGNE supplies the French with what Shakespeare does ourselves—a perpetual topic. The *Essais* have a breadth and depth which criticism is not yet weary of measuring and re-measuring. And, notwithstanding all the excellent things that have been said on those unique effusions, doubtless there remains more still that can be said. There are some books which partake of the inexhaustible multiformity of our moral nature, and the *Essais* is one of such books. 'On y trouve tout ce qu'on a jamais pensé,' as one of Montaigne's admirers says.

But besides the book of essays, the author's life offers a fund for the regular investment of floating public curiosity. In this department the material for speculation is constantly on the increase. 'Montaignologie' is become a science by itself. Documentary research has yielded the French antiquaries year by year a residuum of 'new fact.' Each small bit of ore passes in its turn through the smelting-pot of public discussion, till the portion of precious metal it contains is extracted from it. When the grains have accumulated to a heap, comes a new 'étude,' which digests and arranges all the facts new and old into a consistent whole. One of these is now before us, and

[1] 1. *La Vie Publique de Michel Montaigne.* Par ALPHONSE GRÜN. Paris, 1855.
2. *Nouveaux Documents Inédits ou peu connus sur Montaigne.* Recueillis et publiés par le Dr. J. F. PAYEN. Paris, 1850.

gives occasion to our present notice. We shall confine
our remarks to Montaigne's life. We are not going to re-
dissect the *Essais.*

We have likened Montaignesque to Shakespearean
criticism, as two perennial streams supplied each by its
glacier on the far off mountain-top. The writings of the
two men stand in marked contrast as sources for their
biography. From Shakespeare's plays nothing can be
gathered about Shakespeare. The great charm of Montaigne's Essays is their egotism. They are a transcript of
his mind. 'Ce ne sont mes gestes que j'escris ; c'est moy,
c'est mon essence.'   When Henri III told him that he
'liked his book,' then, replied Montaigne, 'Your majesty
must needs like me. My book is myself.' But it is the
man—his habits and opinions, his tastes and likings that
we find there, not his history. The biographers, therefore,
have endeavoured to discover elsewhere the body belonging to this soul. They have ransacked libraries and
archives to resuscitate something of a frame-work of bone
and muscle to all this sentiment. They have had some
success. Indeed they have had as much success as could
be expected, considering that it was known beforehand
that all that could possibly be discovered lay within fixed
limits. They have ascertained dates, distinguished the
members of his family, and altogether given a local
colouring and verification of the course of his private life.
They have not turned the literary lounger into a careworn
statesman, or a fighting captain of the forces of the League.
In this as in many other cases, all the efforts of inquiry
have but repeated the lineaments of the traditional and
received biography. Such labour, however, is not thrown
away. We are not to propose a paradox, or a revolution
in opinion, as the only results worth arriving at. If we
can deepen the lines, or freshen the colours, cover a scar
made by time, or remove a little gathered dust, we do our
part towards maintaining the Gallery of Worthies. It is

only when the original portrait is discovered not to have been a likeness, that we should paint it over again.

The great feature of Montaigne's life, as impressed on his *Essais*, was, that it was a country life. Early in 1571, at the age of thirty-seven, he withdrew to his estates in Perigord —'with full purpose, as much as lay in me, not to trouble myself with any business, but to pass in repose so much of life as remaineth to me[1].' My design is, he repeats in the Third Book written after 1580, 'de passer doulcement, non laborieusement, ce que me reste de vie[2].' It was solitude at first. He declined society, and occupied himself with his family, his books, the care of his property. This lasted some little time, but his temper was sociable, and he found he could not support solitude. 'Je suis tout au dehors, et en évidence; nay à la société, et à l'amitié[3]'. And he disliked the cares of the *ménage.* He sought distraction, therefore, in the company of his neighbours, in travelling, and in writing. He wished retirement, not solitude. What he would shun was the pressure of business, not crowds. Repeated tours—one to Italy—a journey or two to Paris about the publication of his *Essais*, and his mayoralty at Bordeaux, in 1582, forced on him against his wishes, are the principal events of his life after his retirement. Such at least was the received biography. Nor had any of the disinterred facts disturbed the repose of the picture. His diary of his tour in 1580, written in Italian, was found at Montaigne 180 years after his death, and was published in 1774. Now De Thou had said in the 104th book of his history, that Montaigne was at Venice when he received the news of his election to the mayoralty. This journal enables us to correct De Thou. It was at the baths of Lucca, on the 7th of September, in the morning. The letter was dated Bordeaux, August 2, and had followed him into Tuscany,

[1] I. 8.   [2] III. 9.   [3] *Ibid.*

by way of Rome. Such *incrementa* reassure, instead of invalidating, history.

An attempt, however, is now made to wrest from us the Montaigne of our youth, the 'Gentilhomme Perigourdin;' to tear him from the frame in which he was set in our memory and our affections, from the 'librairie' and 'chambre d'études au troisième étage' of the old 'manoir' of Montaigne, and to make of him—good heavens!—to make of him a man of business, a man about court. M. Grün's volume is entitled *La Vie Publique de Michel Montaigne*. The titles of its several chapters are :—Ch. 2. 'De la Conduite publique de M.' Ch. 3. 'M. Magistrat.' Ch. 4. 'Relations de M. avec la Cour.' Ch. 5. 'M. Chevalier de l'ordre de S. Michel.' Ch. 6. 'M. Gentilhomme ordinaire de la chambre du Roi.' Ch. 9. 'M. Négociateur Politique.' Ch. 10. 'M. Militaire.' Ch. 11. 'M. aux Etats de Blois.'

Such a metamorphosis of our prose Horace, the man of whom 'la liberté et l'oysiveté sont les maîtresses qualités[1]' into a hardworking man of office, dressed in the imperial livery trimmed with red tape, is one of those harlequin tricks which paradoxical biographers try upon us from time to time. We have been lately told that Tiberius has been slandered by Tacitus; that the world was never better off than under Caracalla; and that Henry VIII was the victim of domestic infelicities. On examining M. Grün's volume we find there is no more evidence for the Imperialist transformation of Montaigne than there is in the other three instances. There is in M. Grün's mode of arranging his facts, indeed, a certain degree of art, but it is the skill of the special pleader. It is the argumentation of the Palais de Justice, not of the Court of History. The highest praise is due to French archaeologists for their zeal of research, but they cannot, apparently, apply their discoveries. Such a piece of historical reconstruction as this *Vie Publique de Mon-*

[1] III. 9.

taigne, in which hypothesis and imagination are the principal architects, would not stand a chance of a hearing in Germany. We shall add, however, that this attempt to disguise Montaigne has not passed unchallenged in France. With all the authority of his own name, and of the body to which he belongs, M. Villemain has in the gentlest language pointed out that the critic's evidence will not bear all the weight of his conclusions. To no one could this task fall with so much propriety as to Villemain. His own earliest step into publicity was an *éloge* of Montaigne. It was in 1812 that he carried off, though the youngest of the competitors, the prize proposed by the Académie Française on this subject. It is proof of the national feeling for Montaigne that the first of French living critics, after having made the whole circuit of his country's literature, returns after half a century to the object of his youthful devotion.

It is not our intention to controvert M. Grün's conclusions. It is unnecessary even to examine his reasoning. It is not merely that his evidence is inadequate, but his case is bad to begin with. His intention is worse than his argumentation. An able legist, government *employé,* and ex-chief-editor of the *Moniteur,* he brings into literature the habits and prepossessions of his position. The Academy, and the established reputations, look coldly on the administration from which they are systematically excluded. It is not from republican principle, from antipathy to despotism that they do so—it is from the repugnance which the lettered and cultivated man feels for the official man who is not so. Times are changed since the statesmen in France were the writers—when to be a journalist conferred *portefeuilles.* Statistics is your only reading now. Point and epigram, and sparkling style—how childish to be governed by such instruments. Let us have men of business, and have done with *mots.* All the great men—Sully, Richelieu—have been able adminis-

trators. And the great writers too? 'To be sure,' is the
answer, 'and in proof there is Montaigne. You think
he was a rustic recluse, who forswore the court for his old
Gascon château, but you are entirely mistaken.' This
baseless theory is not worth refuting. The real value of
M. Grün's *Vie de Montaigne* is as a painstaking collection
of the facts at present known. It includes all the new
discoveries, except those that have come to light since
its publication—and though it is only six months old,
there is already a considerable harvest.

It would we conceive be more than individual error,
it would be a fundamental misconception of the character
of French literature, to lose sight of the following general
distinction. The literature of the *Siècle* is the literature
of a court circle. It is fashionably dressed, it is modish,
Parisian. It comes not from the study, but from the
world. From a world, however, of etiquette, of polished
intrigue, a world with all its license, yet circumscribed
by conventional morals. Thought and judgment are there,
but they are conformed to a certain superficial standard
of good society. In a word, it is the literature of the
salons of Paris and Versailles. In contrast with this,
the few great pieces of literature of the previous age, from
Rabelais down to Pascal, were the offspring of the cloister,
the château, or the wayside. They are the *Vox clamantis
in deserto.* Their superior force and originality derive
directly from the rude independence of character, which
was generated by that free and unformal life. In Montaigne especially, it is the force of individual character,
coming out on us in every page of his book, that charms.
He stands in awe of no Café Procope, has heard of no
rules of writing, he is not composing. He has the hardy
and fearless spirit of a man who has no one to please but
himself. ' J'ay une âme libre et tout sienne, accoustumée
à se conduire à sa mode[1].' He complains somewhere

[1] II. 17.

that his times had not produced any great men. Greatness, to be manifested to the world, depends on the
conjunction of natural endowment with opportunity, and
must needs be rare. But we may surely say that the
average stamp of the men of that day was great. Compared with the feminine uniformity of the shaved and
tailor-made man of later court-dress days, how grand are
the bearded seigneurs of the sixteenth century! Intrepid,
not lawless ; disciplined in the school of action and suffering ; and conscious of all the restraints that limit human
will, these men had made their acquaintance with law
in its grandest form, not in that degenerate artificial shape
in which the victim of good society alone knows it.

Montaigne was born in 1533 and died in 1592. His
father's name was Pierre Eyquem. M. Gence, the writer
of the life in the *Biographie Universelle*, says that the
family was originally from England. That a French
biographer should be willing to make over one of the
greatest of his countrymen to England might surprise us.
It may well do so in this instance, as the self-denial is
wholly uncalled for. We cannot in honesty accept the
offer. ' Eyquem,' or rather ' Eyckem,' according to the old
spelling, is a compound of the common termination ' ham '
or ' heim,' and the name of that tree, which in the English
vocalization is ' oak.' The German ' eiche,' or the Flemish
' ecke,' come much nearer to the form in ' Eyquem.'
Accordingly, some of the biographers have thought of
looking to Flanders for the original stock of the family.
It is still an open question in ' Montaignologie,' and M.
Grün produces no evidence for his positive assertion that
the name is ' essentially of Gascon origin.' In the course
of the sixteenth century the personal was superseded by
the territorial appellation. This was derived from a
domain which they possessed five leagues from Bergerac,
in the department of the Dordogne. The château is
situated on a height—' une montagne '—' jonchée sur une

tertre,' he says : in this tower Montaigne was born, lived, and died. The possession of this domain was an acquisition, it should appear, which the Eyquem had only recently made ; their nobility, therefore, was of very modern date. Joseph Scaliger said in an off-hand way that the father of Montaigne 'était vendeur de harenc[1].' M. Grün, with the bitterness habitual to French writers when they have to speak of Scaliger, repels this as a false and malevolent insinuation. The main fact implied, however, that the ancestors of Montaigne were 'marchand,' and, therefore, 'bourgeois,' is indisputable. We must not omit, as he has recorded it himself, that he was an eleven months' child. As he was a third son of a family, now noble and not rich, his father, an excellent person, took particular pains about his education. He was put out to nurse at a poor village on the estate. Here he was kept all his infancy, with the view both of accustoming his taste to rude diet, and of inducing him to form attachments amongst the poor. His sympathy with peasant life he preserved to the last. 'The poor fellows,' thus he writes in a season of more than usual suffering in the country, 'those poor fellows whom we see all about, their heads bowed over their tasks, who never heard of Aristotle, or Cato, from them nature obtains heroic efforts of patient endurance, which may shame us who have studied in the schools. That man who is digging my garden, he has this morning buried a son, or a father perhaps. They never take to their beds but to die.'

The most curious experiment made in his education was that of teaching him Latin before French. A German preceptor who could speak no French was found for him. None of the rest of the household, mother, maid, or man, were allowed to speak anything but Latin to him.

It is not to be imagined how great an advantage this proved to the whole family. My father and mother by this means learned Latin

[1] *Scaligerana Secunda*, p. 457.

Quarterly Review, 1858.]

enough to understand it perfectly well, as did also those of the servants who were most with me. In short we Latined it at such a rate that it overflowed to all the neighbouring villages, where there yet remain, that have established themselves by custom, several Latin appellations of artizans and their tools. Thus I was above six years of age before I understood either French or Perigordin any more than Arabic, and without art, book, grammar, or precept, whipping or the expense of a tear, had by that time learned to speak as pure Latin as my master himself[1].

The same attention was extended to all the minutiae of his training. To save him from the shock of sudden awakening, some musical instrument was played by his bedside in the morning. Our readers will recollect the same usage in the early education of Bishop Horne, as described by his biographer Jones of Nayland.

When he quitted this careful paternal roof, it was to go to the college of Guienne at Bordeaux. At this school, quite recently established, some of the best scholars then to be found in France were masters. But as he left it at the age of thirteen, he could not have profited much by the higher scholarship which Muretus and George Buchanan were capable of communicating. As the sword belonged by birth to the eldest son, Michel, as the third, had to choose between the church and the robe. He chose, or rather his father chose for him, the latter. At thirteen he must have been incapable of choice, and he always looked to his excellent parent with a mixture of respect and affection, which disposed him to acquiesce in his least wishes. What school of jurisprudence he attended is not known. M. Grün makes it Toulouse, for he naturally wishes 'Montaigne Magistrat' to have been a pupil of the celebrated Cujas. It may have been so. There is not a particle of evidence to show that it was. The solitary text is Montaigne's own declaration: 'while a child, I was plunged up to the ears in law, and it succeeded.'

[1] I. 25.

As soon as he was qualified, his father provided him with a place in the Court of Aids of Périgueux. The law was entered there, as the army is with us now, by purchase. We cannot stay to debate with the antiquaries the knotty point whether Montaigne's father resigned in his son's favour, or purchased him the place of some other counsellor. In 1557 the Court of Aids of Périgueux was consolidated with the Parlement of Bordeaux. And thus, at the early age of twenty-four, Montaigne was seated on the bench of a Supreme Court of Justice without either of the troublesome ceremonies of purchase or examination.

Honourable it was for a younger son; but when by the death of his father and both his brothers, Michel became himself the Seigneur de Montaigne, the long robe no longer befitted him. By these events he became a 'gentleman,' and carried arms, as the phrase was. Ill-natured people said in after days that Montaigne was ashamed of having been counsellor cleric, and did not like to allude to that period of his life. M. Grün is able to repel peremptorily this imputation. It proceeded indeed from later days, when Parlements were fallen, and the magistracy, especially the provincial magistrature, was looked down upon by the courtier. The sneers of Balzac and the Port-Royalists are in the spirit of their own time, and are quite miscalculated for the age of L'Hospital, Pasquier, and De Thou. All Montaigne's friends, relations, and connexions—his father, uncle, brother-in-law—were parliament men. He himself married Françoise de la Chassaigne, daughter of one of the Bordelais counsellors and descendant of a parliamentary family. His most cherished friend La Boétie had been his colleague in the magistracy; and all the friendships he retained through life had been cemented during his own parliamentary career. So much, however, is true, that Montaigne did not relish his judicial functions. This distaste had two causes: dislike of law, and dislike of the religious fanaticism which animated the magistracy of Bordeaux.

He was never really a lawyer. The plunge up to his ears had succeeded in qualifying him for a charge, but had not given him the professional dye. The biographers have exaggerated this distaste into disgust. They make Montaigne into a law reformer; they ascribe to him an enlightened jurist's view of the contradictions of the customary law, and predilection for the luminous simplicity of the civil. This, again, is to read the sixteenth century by the reflected light of '89. Montaigne imbibed the views and aims of the more enlightened jurists of his own time, but he did not project the Code Napoléon. The opinions he has left on record on this subject are very general, but they are those of a wise and humane moralist, not of a jurist. They show how much of a philosopher and how little of 'a magistrate' he was. He has first an abhorrence of litigation, not less for others than himself; he declares against the multiplication of enactments, the contradictory judgments, the glosses of the commentators; but all this is in the spirit of a man of taste; revolted at the bad Latin of the Digest, and wishing to be reading his Cicero. It is a declaration against the language of law altogether rather than against its abuse in chicane. He condemns torture, and the horrible mutilations which were practised on the bodies of the unhappy criminals. But in this he only echoed the opinion of all the moralists of all time, and had with him all the great and wise of his own day. Against him, however, were the churchmen and Rome. Those passages in his Essays in which he pleads that all beyond simple death is pure cruelty, presented one of the chief obstacles to their passing the censure; the other, we may mention, was his assigning a high rank among Latin poets to Theodore Beza. He eloquently denounces the practice of selling the places in the courts of justice; and, to complete the list, he ridicules entails, or, as he calls them, 'masculine substitutions.' Sir W. Hamilton wishes to trace this opinion of Montaigne to the tuition of Buchanan[1]. Buchanan having quitted the college at Bordeaux in 1542, his pupil was only nine years old—an age at which we may doubt if he under-stood what 'masculine substitution' was.

In truth we believe Montaigne, when he says of himself[2] that he knew there was such a science as juris-prudence, and that that was all he did know. His amusing pleading against the lawyers[3] is nothing more than one of the many popular diatribes on that traditional butt. If it proves anything, it proves that he was no lawyer; as his vituperation in the same Essay of the medical prac-titioners does, that he was no physician. He is, in fact, merely using the contradictions of judges and the uncer-tainties of medicine, to enforce his favourite topic of the feebleness of human judgment. It is as great a fallacy to class him with the enlightened publicists, who saw and laboured to remedy the monstrous evils of the French judicial system, as it would be to class him among the revolutionists of the practice of physic. The Montaigne adorers exaggerate their idol in every direction. He is great enough: he is a man of universal sympathies, but they want to make him a man of profound acquirement, which he was not—not even in his own profession. We suspect that his professional history was the common one where strong literary tastes are early imbibed. Buchanan *may* have had something to do with this—may have laid the groundwork of classic predilections which made steady application to law impossible. Montaigne followed it as a career; he got a place, discharged its duties; he never had a vocation for it, and gave it up as soon as he wanted it no longer.

[1] Note in Hamilton's excellent edition of *Dugald Stewart*, vol. I. p. 100.

[2] I. 24.   [3] III. 13.

The second cause of distaste for his Parliamentary functions, to which allusion has been already made, was the violence of religious faction which disturbed it. In no quarter of France had Protestantism made more progress than in Guienne and Gascony. Everywhere the Parlements showed themselves the strenuous supporters of the Church. None was more untiring in the zeal for persecution than that of Bordeaux. Their registers for some years are one series of edicts, each more cruel than the last, against the professors of the new opinions. Montaigne was attached throughout to the Catholic and Royalist party. In this adhesion he never wavered, and it belonged to his characteristic frankness never to conceal it. But he was of too moderate a temper to be carried away by the passionate fanaticism of his party; too good hearted not to execrate their cruelty; and too wise not to see that the violence of the Catholics only provoked the more obstinate resistance of the Huguenots. But wisdom and moderation are no titles to the respect of religious faction. We shall not wonder then that Montaigne, whose spirit of tolerance went far beyond even that of tolerant men in that age, was glad to terminate his connexion with a court of justice, which seemed to have totally forgotten the duty of judicial impartiality, and to have made itself the organ of an infuriated party.

All the zeal of the antiquaries has not been able to retrieve a history for the thirteen or more years during which Montaigne occupied his seat in the Parlement of Bordeaux. M. Grün goes through the principal trans- actions of the Court during that period—a useful *résumé* and a very proper part of a complete life, but too extensive for our purpose. The single sentence in De Thou's history, 'Olim in senatu Burdigalensi assessor dignissimus,' is nearly the whole that is known of thirteen years of Montaigne's life.

The second period extends from 1570 to 1582, aetat. 37-49, and is that portion of Montaigne's life to which he owes his immortality. This period is really marked by a long and absolute retirement in the château of Montaigne, by the composition of the *Essais*, and by two or three journeys to Paris, chiefly connected with their publication. It is concluded by a long tour into Germany, Switzerland, and Italy. M. Grün, who will not resign even this period from his 'public life,' interpolates into it two visits to Court, which are wholly imaginary; a campaign against Henri of Navarre, which is in the highest degree improbable; and, by way of mingling pleasure with business, he exhibits his hero at the fêtes and galas which marked the progress of Catherine de Medicis in the south, in the year 1578.

The hypothetical history here spoils the authentic. The legend misleads instead of assisting the imagination. This retirement in the château of Périgueux, the solitary meditation in the turret chamber, is the canonical fact. A biographer would do good service who could paint for us in its true colours this Gascon interior. Communicative, garrulous even, as Montaigne has been about himself, what he has told us has only given us a reason for desiring to know the things he has not told us. He has made us so much his friends that we require to know all his secrets. He has drawn for us himself, his library; it is on the third floor of one of the turrets of the château. There are four stories in the turret. The first floor is the chapel; above the chapel is a bed-room with suite, appropriated to his own use. The library is above the lodging-rooms. From its three bay windows it commanded a view of nearly the entire premises, including the garden, the front as well as the base court. In the distance, the elevation on which the château stood afforded a very extensive view over a flat country. The shape of the room was that of the tower, round—all but one straight side where the chair and table were placed. From this seat the eye could command all the books as they stood ranged in five tiers of shelving round the walls: the room was sixteen paces in diameter. Opening into the library was a smaller cabinet; this was more elegantly furnished; it was fitted with a fire-place, to which he might retire in the winter. The only want he regretted was a long gallery, or 'promenoir,' to agitate his thoughts in by walking up and down. He could not resolve on adding this: not the cost, but the fuss, of building, deterred him. In this tower he passed the greater part of his time. There was his throne; there his rule was absolute. That only corner he preserved from the invasion of wife, children, or acquaintance. Elsewhere he possessed but a divided authority; for this reason he rejoiced that the access to his retreat was difficult, and of itself defended him from intruders. Here he lived, not studied; he did not so much read books, he says, as turn them over—he did not so much meditate as allow his reverie to follow its own course. The retirement was so strict at first as to produce melancholy and engender fantastic chimeras in his imagination. It was to allay these that he first betook himself to note down his thoughts on paper. Such was the parentage of the *Essais.*

The library, however, the imagination heated by solitary musing, the melancholy grown of long seclusion, should have given birth to a very different progeny. We might have had a *Pilgrim's Progress,* or a *Castle of Otranto,* or a third part of *Huon de Bordeaulx,* but for one quality which Montaigne brought with him into his retreat. This is the thorough good sense, the tone of the man of the world, which pervades, without being paraded, every page of the book. It is not a mere rectitude of judgment about men and things, but a judgment which has been exercised and tempered by actual trials and collisions—'a learned spirit of human dealing.' But for this life-giving flavour, the *Essais* would not have been the book they are. They might still have shown the varied reading of the scholar or the amusing gossip of the egotist, but they would not have been the universal favourite of 'courts, camps, and country mansions.' It is this which, with all their whimsical paradox, and often commonplace moralizing, makes them still instructive.   In tracing this element, M. Grün's chapter, 'Montaigne in his relations with the court,' affords all the materials that are to be had.   We cannot adopt his theory, which turns Montaigne into a courtier, and cuts out of his Life that period of privacy, almost cynical, which we think necessary to the conception of the *Essais*.   But there is evidence enough to show, what the Essays themselves require, that Montaigne had seen much of court and courtiers before he wrote them.

The Kings of France in the middle ages were surrounded by the high officers attached to their person.   Their court was constituted by great functionaries.   The nobles of the provinces who had no employments never approached the King except when they fought by his side, or were summoned by his order.   The decay of the feudal manners, and the policy of Francis I, broke through this estrangement.   He loved to surround himself with a brilliant court. The gentlemen flocked to it.   They laid aside the rudeness of their manners, but they lost at the same time the independence of their character.   The rivalry in luxury and expense ruined them.   To maintain their fortunes they were obliged to seek office.   Places were created on purpose, and the once haughty nobles fought like hungry hounds for these grants at the hands of an absolute monarch who dispensed them.   This revolution was gradual.   It was only in progress in the sixteenth century. But Montaigne found established the usage for French gentlemen to present themselves to the Sovereign without being officially placed about his person.   On succeeding

to the family estates, Montaigne did like the rest. He
was even appointed 'gentleman in ordinary of the bedchamber,' an office which did not demand residence at
court, but was much sought after, and for which nobility
was an indispensable qualification. His complexion, he
tells us[1], was not averse to the movement of a
court. He went gladly into company; he liked city life,
especially Paris. Paris had possessed his affections from
his earliest youth[2]; but these social impulses were
combined with another impulse urging him to seclusion :—

The solitude I love and preach is no more than what serves to
retire my affections and to redeem my thoughts. I would circumscribe
not my steps, but my desires. I would shun not so much the throng
of men as the importunity of affairs. Local solitariness, to say truth,
doth rather extend and enlarge me outwardly. I give my mind more
readily to state matters, and to the world, when I am alone. At the
Louvre, and in the crowd, I am apt to slink into my own skin (*je me
contrains en ma peau*). Assemblies thrust me back within myself. I
never commune with my own spirit so fondly, freely, and so much
apart, as in the resorts of grand company and lordly ceremonial. I go
gaily into great assemblies, yet doth this coyness of judgment of which
I spoke attach me perforce to privacy. Yea, even in mine own
house I see people more than a good many, yet few such as I love to
converse or communicate withal. Herein I exercise an unusual
privilege of liberty. I cry a truce to the established courtesies so
distressing to all parties, of being with my guests, and conducting
them about; but each one employs himself as he pleases, and en-
tertaineth what his thoughts affect. If I please, I remain silent,
musing and reserved, without offence to my guests or friends[3].

This piece of self-portraiture is at once true to history
and to nature. We read in it the parentage of the *Essais,*
to which the agitation of courts and the stillness of the
recluse's cell each gave their portion. And we find in it—
and in none of his self-disclosures more so—we find in it
one of the secrets of genius. Nay, not only of great, but
of all sound minds this is true, that for their sustentation

[1] III. 3.   [2] III. 9.   [3] III. 3.

and due nurture they require the two elements, society and solitude. No healthy life is ever lived, in which either of these is wanting. And if we turn to books—to judge of mind by its most enduring products—we see the same experience repeated from age to age. There are books enough left us by those who, having never tried to live, have shut themselves within the circle of their own meditations. Wonderful in its variety and richness is the literature of mysticism and sentiment! What a wealth of thought and feeling drawn from the pure depths of human consciousness! Again, turn to the memoir-writers and court gossips. What keen observation of manners, what infinite webs of intrigue they unravel before us, what countless characters they have distinguished! But what are the books that instruct us, that speak to us as men, that raise us, but raise us not too high for our duties and our destiny? Between the frivolous and the divine lies the truly human. Wisdom that is from above, yet that can give us light in this world! Theory without facts is not science, and moralizing without experience is not wisdom. A pallid and dreary jargon is the metaphysic of the schools by the side of the tangible and experimented maxim which flowers out naturally from the intellect that has lived. But unless to this experience be added the maturing influences of meditation and self-knowledge, the result is equally one-sided. We get then that unspiritual and debasing physiology of human conduct, that so-called philosophy of courts, which leaves out of the computation of motive all that separates man from any other species of mammal. In no writer perhaps are these two elements that make up wisdom mingled in happier proportion than in Montaigne.

Little has been added by the diligence of the collectors to the glimpses of his retreat which the *Essais* themselves supply. We need not wonder that the château of Montaigne has been repeatedly visited by enthusiastic pilgrims; some of these, among whom may be included poor John Sterling, have described what they saw. But they seem to have carried with them more enthusiasm than powers of accurate observation; at least they were not able to copy correctly the sentences which Montaigne had inscribed on the cornices of his library. Some of them are characteristic: and Dr. Payen has done good service by reproducing them, as they are fast being obliterated. 'Quid superbis, Terra et Cinis? Vae qui sapientes estis in oculis vestris! Ne plus sapias quam necesse est, ne obstupescas.' The first six are Scripture texts. After them come the classical, of which we may give—'. . . nostra vagatur In tenebris, nec caeca potest mens cernere verum,' from Lucretius; παντὶ λόγῳ λόγος ἴσος ἀντίκειται, from Sextus Empiricus. Still more interest attaches to an inscription in the 'cabinet du travail'; this is in Latin, and also in a state of decay. It is to the following effect, when the gaps have been conjecturally supplied :—

In the year of Christ 1571, the 38th of his age, on his birthday, to wit the last day of February, Michel de Montaigne, long wearied of court slavery and public employments, has withdrawn himself into the bosom of the Sisters of Learning, where, in peace and freed from care, he will pass through what little may yet remain of a life of which the most part hath already passed away, if only fate permit. This narrow abode and loved ancestral retreat he hath consecrated to his liberty, repose, and tranquillity.

If these lines be genuine they are autobiographical, and decisive against M. Grün's theory; he naturally, therefore, wishes to think them the product of some later hand. But he does not offer one critical argument for the suspicion he throws on them. 'The sentiment they express is too puerile for Montaigne, and not in keeping with his habits.' To bring up a loose analogy of this sort against epigraphic evidence is simply childish in the eyes of those who know what historical criticism is; but in this instance it happens that the analogy itself is not good. The inscription does but repeat that passage in the *Essais* which we have already quoted: 'Je me retirai chez moi, délibéré autant que je pourrais ne me mesler d'autre chose que de passer en repos et à part le peu qui me ,reste de vie.' Even if then the inscription were put up by a successor, the sentiment in it is derived from Montaigne himself, who more than once in the *Essais* enters into this engagement with himself to consecrate the remainder of his days to studious repose. The insertion of his age, and the solemn mention of his birthday, which M. Grün thinks 'puerile,' appear to us exactly in Montaigne's character. Dr. Payen has justly remarked that he is fond of noting his age at different epochs of his composition; that his *Natural Theology* is dated the day of his father's death, to whom it is dedicated; and reminds us that Montaigne liked to use his father's cloak, not because it fitted him, but because 'il lui semblait s'envelopper de lui.' We must, however, express our surprise that the date of this inscription should still be left matter of argument. Surely the shape of the letters, the style and colouring, or other indications would serve to ascertain if the epigraph were or were not contemporary with Montaigne.

The mention of the five tiers of shelving has naturally suggested to our painstaking friends an inquiry after the books which once filled them. For though the shelves are there, and the mottoes on the rafters above them are dimly visible, the books are gone. Dr. Payen has here had wonderful success. He has traced or recovered upwards of thirty volumes which were in the possession of Montaigne, and contain his autograph, or other notes. The history of his twenty years' siege and final capture of Montaigne's *Caesar* forms of itself a little epic, which we read in the *Débats* not long since[1], and which is too glad to talk of Montaigne's *Caesar*, since the other Caesar is

---

[1] *Journal des Débats*, Mars, 1856.

interdicted ground. It tells how M. Parison, the distinguished bibliophile, who, with an income of £250 a year,
left behind him the astonishing collection of books which
has just been dispersed by public auction, picked up the
Caesar in one of the quais bookstalls; how he guarded it
five years—not *thirty-five*, as the *Débats* exaggerates—
without breathing the existence of the treasure—how, in
1837, Dr. Payen, the chief of the 'Montaignologues,' got
scent of its existence—how he laid siege to M. Parison's
citadel on the fourth floor of a house on the Quai des
Augustins, by a series of dedications, notes, allusions
sometimes flattering, sometimes caustic, till the final
triumph in 1838, when the stubborn possessor surrendered
at discretion, yielded up the *Caesar*, took to his bed, and
died. Had we space we would not so curtail this
bibliographical episode. The *Caesar*, after all, is not
devoid of interest even for our purpose. It is the Antwerp
edition (*ex Officinâ Plantinianâ*) of 1570. Montaigne had
noted on it, as he did in all the books he read, the time
occupied in reading it. He commenced reading the three
books *De Bello Civili* on February 25, and finished the
De Bello Gallico July 21st, in the year 1578. After the
Anno Domini he has added 44-45—figures which indicate
his age at the time of reading, his birthday being, as will
be remembered, February 28. The marginal notes, of
which there are upwards of 600, do not offer much of
quotable interest. But in the minute care with which it
was read, and the fact that it was read continuously
between February and July, we gain some light upon
Montaigne's method of using books. All his reading
was not of the desultory kind we might infer from
what he says of it in the Essays:—'Je feuillette à cette
heure un livre, à cette heure un aultre, sans ordre,
et sans dessein, à pièces descousues [1].' He could, we
see, at the time he was writing his *Essais*, begin a

[1] III. 3.

book, and return to it day after day till it was read through. In the last page he has written, in his small and fine hand, a short appreciation of the book and its author. This was his usual custom when he had finished a work. He adopted it, he says[1], to meet the extreme treachery of his memory. This was so great that it had happened to him more than once to take up a volume which he had carefully read a few years before as if it was a new book. On comparison of the appreciation of *Caesar*, which occupies thirty-six lines of close writing, with the thirty-fourth chapter of the second book of the *Essais*, we find that the essay is a greatly improved development of the annotation. Indeed, it is more than improved. The judgment passed on *Caesar* in the annotation is imperfect, and fails in doing justice to him. In the essay Montaigne rises to a far higher elevation, and indicates a much more matured point of view. Now, the *aperçu*, as we have seen, was written in 1578. The *Essais* were published in 1580. Thus we gather that it was not Montaigne's habit to dismiss a book from his thoughts when he had finished it and recorded sentence on it. It might continue to occupy his meditations and grow upon his thoughts. The casual and discontinuous turning over · of books, he tells of, was the external aid to a methodical and solid process of digestion.

The duties, whatever they were, of 'Gentleman in ordinary to the bedchamber' were the only ones which Montaigne ever discharged at court. Difficulties still uncleared surround this function. Its date is uncertain, and we know not how to reconcile it with Montaigne's own assertion that he had never received from any prince a 'double' either as wages or free-gift. Leaving these interesting *nœuds* to the discussion of the biographer that is to come, we have to speak of the great question of the secretaryship. For many years all the lives and *éloges* of

---

[1] II. 10.

Montaigne had repeated that he at one time filled the office of secretary to the Queen Dowager Catherine de Medicis. This would have changed the complexion of his life indeed, and would have of itself turned the scale decisively in favour of M. Grün's views. This mistake, for such it is, and nothing more, arose from the negligent, assumptive habits of the literary biographers. There is preserved a letter of instruction from the Queen addressed, so it is indorsed in the MS. copy in the Bibliothèque Impériale (collection *Dupuy*), 'Au roy Charles IX peu après sa majorité.' It is a piece of no little curiosity in itself. It belongs, indeed, to general history, and is as widely known as the farewell letter which another Medicis addressed to his young twelve-year-old cardinal (afterwards Leo X). But it concerns us at present, not by its contents, but by a postscript of three lines as follows :—' Monsieur my son, do not take it amiss that I have made Montaigne write out this letter ; I did it that you might read it better.—Catherine.'

This letter made its first appearance in print in Le Laboureur's additions to the *Memoirs of Castelnau*, in 1659. Which of Montaigne's biographers may claim the credit of having transported the 'new fact' into Montaigne's biography we have not ascertained. But before the beginning of the present century Montaigne's Secretariate to the Queen had become an accredited event. One of them, M. Jay, comments thus :—' Those who have studied the character and manners of Catherine de Medicis, and who have read with attention the reflections of Montaigne himself on the rights and duties of princes, will easily recognise that the *Avis* are the composition of Montaigne himself.' Thus history made itself as it went on through the hands of slipshod *littérateurs*. From copyist, Montaigne became author of Catherine's letter. But as soon as a discerning eye was directed to the evidence on which the 'Secretariate' rested, it was seen at a glance that the identification of the amanuensis of the *Avis* with the essayist was a pure conjecture. And the indefatigable labours of Dr. Payen have brought to light the existence of a François Montaigne, Secretary in Ordinary of the Chamber of the King and the Queen-Mother. M. Grün devotes fifteen pages to the correction of this error. It is a piece of historical reasoning which is a fair specimen of his book. The case is plausibly and forcibly put: but that is all. He creates at least as much error as he rectifies. He makes out Catherine's Montaigne to be Jacques de Montagne, 'avocat-général' at Montpellier in 1560. The forensic skill with which the evidence is marshalled covers a quantity of conjectural assumption which, much more than the concluding blunders, must entirely destroy M. Grün's credit as a historical critic.

The third and last period of Montaigne's life extends from aetat. 50–59. This includes a portion of his career which may with more justice be entitled his 'public life.'

He received the announcement of his nomination to the mayoralty of Bordeaux at the baths Della Villa, near Lucca; but, faithful to his resolution to have done with 'public life,' he declined the honour, and, after a second visit to Rome, returned slowly into France, with the intention of resuming the peaceful and studious leisure which his long wanderings had made doubly sweet to him. He found, however, that his friends condemned his inactivity, and that the citizens of Bordeaux were resolved not to let him off. Finally he consented—not, however, till the King (Henri III) had interposed his authority—and entered on the office in January, 1582. His administration was more than usually capable, and he received the rare honour of re-election for a second term of office. During his mayoralty, and after it, he was engaged, on more than one occasion, in transactions of public importance. The history of these, as it

has been laboriously pieced together out of the correspondence, acts, registers, and other remains of the time,
will be gone through with interest by the circumstantial
student. The general reader may perhaps be satisfied
with a summary remark upon them. All the negotiations
in which Montaigne was thus engaged exhibit his character
in a light consistent with what we know of him. We see
that he was trusted and recognized on all hands as a
gentleman of worth, honour, and experience; to whose
management and discretion men were glad to entrust
their interests in critical cases. In a time of general
suspicion, during protracted civil and religious warfare
which had proved a 'veritable school of treachery and
dissimulation,' the open, loyal, straightforward conduct of
Montaigne gained him the confidence of both parties.
But we do not see him engaged, or ambitious to be
engaged, in strictly state affairs, or the more momentous
crises of the difficult politics of that shifting scene. His
character, wanting in energy and ambition, did not supply
the defect of birth, which had not placed him among 'les
grands.' He was not qualified, and did not affect, to
lead. Any expectation that he should have taken a
prominent part in the transactions of his time arises in us
from our looking back to his life through the halo of his
after-fame. We think that so much worldly wisdom and
solid sense must have made itself felt on the theatre of
public affairs. It is sufficiently apparent, notwithstanding
M. Grün's violent efforts to drag him forward, that
Montaigne's indolent and meditative temperament kept
him remote from the turmoil of public life. That he was
in any degree forced into active duties is to be ascribed to
the same easy disposition. He allowed his friends to
impose labours which he would never have assumed.
' Je ne me mets point hors de moi.' ' Il se faut prêter
à autrui, et ne se donner qu'à soi même.' These are
his characteristic maxims. He is no Hamlet, however.

When action is thrust upon him, he is vigilant, steady, and efficient in its performance.

Nothing, in fact, can be less logical than to allow the splendid fame that has gathered round the *Essais* to react on our conceptions of their author's life. It would be a very vulgar inference that one who has left us a great book must have done great things. No one, indeed, would seriously argue thus, but such a feeling may insensibly influence the expectation we form. The title of the work before us, *La Vie Publique de Montaigne*, appears as if it were a response to this illusory anticipation. It can only lead to disappointment. As the life of a private country gentleman, loved by his friends, respected by his enemies, trusted by all, and of whom all regretted that he shunned employment, it corresponds perfectly to the careless wisdom and unaffected sagacity of his written page. To attempt to pass him off as a public man only leads a reader to the mortifying exclamation, 'Is this all?' Montaigne, stripped of the essayist, looks to us as he did to the courtiers of his own time. How, Brantôme will witness :—

In our time we have seen lawyers issue from the courts, throw aside the cap and gown, and take to wearing the sword. We have seen those, I say, get the collar of St. Michael without having served at all. Thus did the Sieur de Montaigne, who had far better have stuck to his pen and gone on scribbling essays, than changed it for a sword, which did not sit so well on him. Doubtless his kinsman, the Marquis de Trans, got him knighted by the King, in order to turn the order into ridicule, for the marquis was always a great mocker[1].

Such was Montaigne to the courtiers of his own day. The essayist has indeed had his revenge! The growth of his fame, however, has not been continuous. During his own lifetime, and for some time after his death, it was steadily on the increase. He himself saw five editions of his *Essais* through the press, and thirty-one editions have

[1] *Capitaines Illustres*, art. *Tavanne.*

been counted between 1580 and 1650. There were very soon two complete translations into English, and, through Shakspeare's use of Florio's version, the blood of Montaigne may be said to have flowed into the very veins of our literature. Pascal had studied him till he almost knew him by heart. But as the growth of the Siècle literature gave a new direction to thought and taste, the credit of Montaigne declined. It was not without difficulty that he was admitted among the authorities of the Dictionary of the Academy. Bossuet only names him once, and then he is 'un Montaigne.' Fénelon mentions him, but it is to reproach him with his Gascon words. And it is a significant fact that from 1669 to 1724 not a single edition of the *Essais* was called for. Later times have made abundant atonement for this temporary neglect. Few other books of the sixteenth century could be named which issue from the press at the rate of one edition a year. The original editions sell at bibliomaniac prices. The *Caesar*, with his autograph, for which M. Parison gave 18 sous, was knocked down to the Duc d'Aumale at 1550 francs. Of late years especially, an amount of industry has been expended in elucidating his life and writings such as is only devoted to the great classics of a language. We believe that all his fellow-labourers will agree in assigning to Dr. Payen precedence in their joint efforts. His name, like that of Mademoiselle de Gournay, must ever be associated with that of Montaigne. But investigation is still in progress. It is far from complete. It has not arrived at that stage, nor have its results been yet sufficiently sifted to allow such a biography of Montaigne to be written as will last, and we must regard M. Grün's volume as a temporary and only partial substitute.

XX.

POPE AND HIS EDITORS[1].

(*British Quarterly Review*, 1872.)

THE time which has elapsed since this edition of Pope was first announced, more than twenty years, is long, but perhaps not unreasonably long. It might only be due to the fact that an editor had formed a high estimate of the duties he had undertaken, and intended something beyond meeting the immediate demands of the market.

There are doubtless many able literary men about town, who would not ask twenty months to turn out an edition of Pope's poems which should be useful and afford a good deal of help to the reader. But an editor who takes twenty years for his work is probably aware of the difficulties over which his rapid rival is content to glide, and has found by experience that the information required is not to be found merely by looking for it in libraries. To one who should set about the work of editing in a thorough spirit, the notes of previous editors, and bio-graphical dictionaries, those great resources of the pro-fessional editor, are no authorities. He must found himself upon contemporary documents only, and there is no recipe for turning up at the moment the illustration required. Nothing but patient plodding through the whole contemporary literature will do. And even this

[1] *The Works of Alexander Pope.* New Edition, including several hundred unpublished Letters, and other new Materials, collected in part by the late Right Honourable John Wilson Croker. With Introductions and Notes by the Rev. WHITWELL ELWIN. (London: John Murray.)

often leaves you in the lurch. Nothing baffles the annotator more than an attempt to elucidate any particular obscurity by a search through books. The fact sought for refuses to be found when wanted. At another time it reveals itself in some unexpected quarter. Sometimes the sense of a dark passage flashes upon the unprompted mind in a moment. And the co-operation of others is necessary: as Johnson says, 'A commentary must arise from the fortuitous discoveries of many men in devious walks of literature.'

Time, then, is the indispensable condition of a commentary which is to enable a modern reader to understand Pope as his contemporaries understood him. Pope's writing has so much the modern air that we are apt to forget that his poetry is now a century and a half old. It is further removed from us than Shakespeare was from Dryden; yet Dryden writes in 1672 that the language had been so changed since Shakespeare wrote, that anyone reading his plays and comparing them with what had been written since the Restoration would see the change almost in every line. The 130 years from Pope to our time has not seen anything like the change experienced by Dryden. The impoverishment of the language—though a few of Pope's words have been lost—has been arrested by the periodical press. But the change in ideas is very great, quite as great as the change noticed by Dryden. Pope, indeed, is not to be read as the exponent of the higher range of religious and philosophical ideas. Where he attempted them, as in the *Essay on Man*, he found himself out of his depth. But he is in a peculiar degree the mirror of the social passions and sentiments, the modes and tone of his day. To comprehend how much this is so, we have only to suppose the ten volumes of Pope's works annihilated. What a chasm would be created by the act of destruction! But in what? Not a single discovery, or truth, or thought, or idea, or character, or image, which

counts among the treasured possessions of human intelligence, would be thereby lost.   But in the history
of English literature and life what a gap would be
occasioned! There is no one other book in the language,
the loss of which would obliterate so much personal
anecdote, so much scandal, if you will, but also so much
true and firm drawing of character and personal relations,
such felicitous touches of manners and contemporary tone.
Indeed, for the particular moment of our history to which
Pope's best pieces belong—the third decade of the
eighteenth century—we have no contemporary authority,
except the *Memoirs of Lord Hervey*. Lord Hervey was
a person whom the world never appreciates, and does not
like.   To the English reading public, a courtier and
a hater of the clergy is always unacceptable.   This anti-
ecclesiastical eighteenth century tone is not forgiven either
in Gibbon or in Adam Smith, and to its presence in Lord
Hervey's *Memoirs* we must ascribe the fact that they are
so little relished.   They are, even in the mutilated state in
which we have them, one of the best productions in our
language of a kind of writing in which the French are so
rich, and we so poor.   No parallel is intended between
Pope's *Satires* and Lord Hervey's *Memoirs* on any other
point but the one of flashing a vivid light upon their
surroundings during a period little otherwise illuminated.
The two books have no other resemblance, and may be
obviously contrasted.   Lord Hervey paints the Court
from St. James's; Pope, at Twickenham, vents the spleen
of the opposition.   Lord Hervey relates matter of fact
in simple prose; Pope deals in distant allusions and veiled
sneers.   However, such as they are, the two together, Pope
and Lord Hervey, mortal foes as they were, are the two
most important witnesses of the period in question.   But
they require to be supplemented or illustrated from the
vast mass of fugitive literature, literature utterly worthless
except so far as it furnishes such illustration, from pam-

phlets, from the dreary pages of Bolingbroke's disquisitions, or the voluminous correspondences, the Marchmont, the Atterbury, the Suffolk papers, where an occasional gleam of fact is our only reward for toiling through reams upon reams of words signifying nothing.

This is the dreary labour which an editor of Pope imposes upon himself. And when he has done his best, when he has collected all his references and illustrations, he meets a new disappointment. This is the impossibility of presenting to a reader the result of his researches in the same fulness with which he possesses it himself. The acquaintance which he has himself acquired with the personages and affairs of the period cannot be transferred to paper. To him the characters live, and act, and move —the whole drama is full of life. Let him set about explaining in a note who is meant in this line, what event is alluded to in the next, and he will feel that he has only accumulated a dry list of unmeaning names, an index, a register of dates. He has dulled and dimmed the allusions in his author without elucidating them.

If this be so, it may be asked, why annotate English poets at all? If an editor cannot possibly succeed in conveying his own knowledge to a reader, he had better abstain from attempting it, and confine himself to giving a text unencumbered by information, which it seems is useless for the purpose for which it is affixed.

It is not, however, the case that an editor's explanation of names and allusions is useless. It is inadequate, but it is better than nothing. All that a commentator can say, in the compass of a note, of the life and history of the character brought up by the poet, cannot place his reader in the full enjoyment and appreciation of the poet's wit or point. In the case of a writer like Pope, where the allusions are penetrating and well aimed, this complete gust can only be attained by an intimate familiarity with the character and tone of his age, which only length of time and much reading can confer. But as this can only be reached slowly, an editor must provide a grammar or key. And as such complete knowledge can ever be the lot of but few, an editor must have an eye to that large class of readers who are neither wholly ignorant nor fully informed, and who are content in a hurried passage through life to take a snatch at the salient aspects of literature without having leisure to dwell specially or devotedly upon any one. An editor must regard his own notes, and readers must employ them, not as a compendium of all the accessible information, but as a key to its acquisition. They can only direct into collateral reading, they cannot supersede it. In the case of such a work as Pope's *Satires*, a reader's enjoyment will be exactly in proportion to his knowledge of the contemporary history.

There is indeed a doctrine about poetry current which leads its votaries to look with scorn upon all such matter of fact, which looks upon a poem as a work of art having its perfection in itself, and in no relation to real persons and events. According to this theory, poetry is ideal; it is produced by the writer's imagination, and is enjoyed by the reader through an aesthetic perception without any medium of knowledge. As soon as you copy reality, you are writing history, biography, description, and all that is below the province of art. Art is pure creation.

This theory is always extant, potentially even when not acknowledged. But it was towards the latter end of the last century, or the beginning of the present, that it began to dominate poetical criticism in this country. Sometimes Wordsworth's *Prefaces*, sometimes Coleridge's conversation, is credited as its source. But both Coleridge and Wordsworth derived it, whether consciously or unconsciously, from Kant—not perhaps from the study of Kant's own writings, but from that impulse and bent which Kant's *Kritik der Urtheilskraft* gave to aesthetic criticism in Europe. The ascendency of this doctrine, which made imagination the test of poetry, had an immediate influence upon the estimation in which Pope was held by his countrymen. The poetical dynasty which went by his name was dethroned. For nearly a century this school had occupied the field without a rival. Those who were quite aware of Pope's faults, and who, like Johnson, were ready to make the most of his negligences and irregularities, had never questioned the correctness of the principles, or the truth of the aims, which he and the whole tribe of poets professed. But all this was now at an end. Tried by the new test, the whole of English poetry from the Restoration down to Mason and Hayley was pronounced a mistake. It was declared to be mere versification ; the name of poetry was denied it. It wanted a soul. It wanted nature. It did not touch the heart. It had no trumpet call. Its rhythm was 'sing-song.' The very term 'taste' became a byword. Inspiration was everything, and as in other fanaticisms, he was thought most inspired who was most outrageously absurd. To find what they could admire, this generation recurred to the sixteenth century. The greatest extravagances of Shakespeare were held up as profound exemplifications of an inner law; even the fustian of the old dramatists was found to be genuine poetry after all. In the Pope controversy, which arose out of some remarks of Campbell in the first edition of his *Specimens of the British Poets*, 1819, the question was generally decided against Pope. It was unfortunate that Pope's chief defender, Byron, did not exemplify his doctrines in his own practice. Byron, who desired to please the public, took care to mix a good deal of tall talk in the most popular of his poems, *Childe Harold*.

The result of this revulsion in public taste upon the estimate of the eighteenth century poetry, was that Dryden was allowed to have vigour; and in consideration of this vigour, which was called indifferently 'imagination,' he was placed in a class above Pope. Pope was allowed the merit of a placer of words, an elegant rhymist, but declared to be 'no poet.' If any exception was made it was in favour of the *Rape of the Lock*, in which the imaginative critics discerned traces of the quality they required, and *Eloise to Abelard*, in which they said there was 'true passion.' This was the criticism of the romantic school, which read Keats and Shelley, and delighted in trampling under foot the eighteenth century.

We do not propose here to open this controversy, or to attempt to come to a decision as to what shall or shall not be called 'poetry.' This is an inquiry of the higher philosophical criticism, very interesting in itself, but not necessary as a preliminary to ascertaining the duties of an editor of an English poet. Instead of using the debatable term poetry, it will be safe to substitute the wider term literature. And then we go on to say that the primary value of all literature is not beauty, but truth. That which makes the written productions of a past age worth preserving and studying is their power of giving us a knowledge of that age, of reflecting and representing it, of making us understand its thoughts, works, and ways. Writers are great, and books are profitable, in proportion to their gift of doing this. Truth of representation is not truth of fact merely ; it must be truth of character and life. A work of fiction may easily be more valuable than a history. Smollett's *Roderick Random* is better worth preserving than the same author's continuation of Hume. As the ages go on, and the progeny of the teeming press accumulates far beyond the reading power even of men of complete leisure, a natural process of selection leaves more and more to die, and the few best books come to stand more prominently forward. The best books of each age are those which contain most information about the time. And that information is the best—not which chronicles most facts, but that which results from the keenest observation; not the statement of the man who has seen most, but of him who has seen most truly. Yet, as few books are entirely worthless, as nearly every one who writes has seen something truly, and may have mentioned it, this surplus literature, which no longer deserves to be perpetuated for its own sake, will remain in holes and corners to supply illustration and aid in the reading of the selected 'classics.'

This is the duty which is discharged by the professional commentator. An edition of an English classic is often regarded by the reader or purchaser as an aggravation of an already existing grievance. The original grievance is that the editor, out of his professional zeal, has raked together every line that his author has ever put on paper —bad as well as good—his failures as well as his successes. That is already an error, this ranking the sweepings of an author's study among his works. Then, as if this was not enough, comes the editor, and loads this mass of rubbish with more rubbish of his own, in the form of notes, till it becomes a serious labour to pick the grains of gold which there may be, out of the heaps of sand in which they have been elaborately buried. Editing thus wears the appearance too often of multiplying books, and of making what was already too long, longer.

But a good commentary upon an English classic is the reverse of this. So far from ministering to the overgrowth of literature, a good edition is really a process of abridgment and condensation. A commentary should be a collection of texts and passages from contemporary writers—a florilegium which should preserve their most pertinent and significant sayings. The ephemeral publications of each age should be passed through a sieve, by which what few grains of information they may contain

should be separated. These will find an appropriate
centre round which they will cluster, in the text of the
leading authors of their own age, and by adhering to
which they will be preserved. This is pretty nearly the
condition in which the destructive agencies of time,
weather, and fire, have transmitted the Greek and Latin
classics to our day. We have the texts of many (not all)
of the leading classics preserved, in part or in whole.
Around these texts the diligence of the commentators has
arranged all the scattered fragmentary matter that can be
discovered as illustration. What blind chance has done
in the case of the papyrus and parchment of the ancient
classics, must take place with the paper and print of our
vernacular literature by deliberate selection. It is not
only its want of merit, but its very mass that will be fatal
to the average productions of the printing-press. Indeed,
even to the works of the great masters themselves, the
time must come, if it has not already come, when the
same principle will have to be applied. It will no longer
be desirable or possible to read, or to transmit, the whole
works of even the principal writers. The maxim that the
half is more than the whole, will enforce itself in this case.
Of the dramatists—nay, even of Shakespeare, of Bacon, of
Dryden, of Swift, of Johnson, and of all our voluminous
writers—select works, not selections, will be all that we
shall reprint. It will be better for their fame, and for
their readers, that their inferior productions should pass
out of sight, and be remembered no more against them.

To no writer is this more applicable than to Pope. Mr.
Elwin truly says: ' Like most great authors, he published
not a little which is mediocre, but he is to be estimated by
the qualities in which he soared above the level, and not
by the lower range of mind he possessed in common
with inferior men[1].' One of Pope's chief titles to the
distinction he enjoys being polish and finish, where

[1] Elwin, II. 233.

he does not take pains he immediately becomes flat and insipid.   Where he is not speaking of his contemporaries, he has nothing to say that is particularly instructive. This creates a difficulty in making the selection among Pope's writings, and deciding what should be kept, and what may without loss be suffered to fall into oblivion. Taking the test of value proposed before, viz. fulness of representation of contemporary life and feeling, his *Satires and Epistles* are his most valuable production. Indeed, it is no paradox to say that these Imitations of Horace are the most original of his writings.   From this point of view the *Essay on Man* is the least valuable.   Its point of view is indistinct.   A good representation of the thoughts of that age on the great questions of natural theology would be always worth preserving.   But Pope's is far from being such a representation.   As is now well understood, it is like Lucretius's view of atomism, a blurred and marred picture.   But when we pass from the thoughts to the words, there are in the *Essay on Man* not only single lines and couplets, but whole paragraphs, so finely conceived, and expressed with such force and felicity, that it is impossible to part with them.   English literature, wordy, clumsy, and careless, cannot afford to spare a poem full of lines of such condensed energy and exquisite finish, as are thickly strewn up and down the four epistles of the *Essay on Man*.   The *Essay on Criticism* presents the same kind of difficulty as the *Essay on Man*.   Looking at its contents, its value to us is little or none.   De Quincey said of it—' It is the feeblest and least interesting of Pope's writings, being substantially a mere versification, like a metrical multiplication-table, of commonplaces the most mouldy with which criticism has baited its rat-traps.   The maxims have no order or logical dependency, and are generally so vague as to mean nothing.'   This censure may be overdone, with De Quincey's usual vehemence of language.   But it is true that the *Essay on Criticism* is

made up from books, and not from the poet's original
observation. It is not representative of its time. Yet we
can hardly make up our minds to lose it. Can we part
with a piece that contains epigrams that have lodged
themselves as household words in the language, such
as—

> A little learning is a dangerous thing,
> Drink deep, or taste not the Pierian spring.
>
> True wit is nature to advantage dress'd,
> What oft was thought, but ne'er so well express'd.
>
> True ease in writing comes from art, not chance,
> As those move easiest, who have learn'd to dance.
>
> Men must be taught, as if you taught them not,
> And things unknown proposed as things forgot?

And there are many more such couplets, or single lines.
It is true that this merit of putting a happy point upon
a commonplace is an inferior kind of merit. Yet we may
range through many sheets of Chalmers's *Poets* without
finding even this excellence. English literature must
become far richer than it is in witty *mots* or remem-
berable lines before we can afford to throw away the
Essay on Criticism.

Select Works of Pope would then contain only:—

> The Satires and Epistles, with the Prologue and
>   Epilogues;
> The Moral Essays;
> Essay on Man;
> Essay on Criticism;
> The Dunciad;
> The Rape of the Lock.

This selection will probably form the *Pope's Works* of
future generations. If posterity preserves and continues
to read all these, it will have as much as it will care to
have of Pope. It will lose nothing in what is left behind.
Especially is Pope's correspondence of the smallest possible interest. If the value of literature consists in its

reflection of the age, letters ought to be one of the most effective media. And they often are so. Voltaire is nowhere greater than in his correspondence; and without the letters of Horace Walpole, what should we know of 'society' in the middle of the last century? But Pope seems to have contrived his correspondence as if on purpose to make it uninteresting. He composed his letters to his friends with a view to publication. The affectations of Horace Walpole sit so gracefully upon him, and are so much a part of the man, that they lend a lustre and reality to the pictures he is drawing. Pope's affectation is artificiality; it is scheme, deception, mystery. He is labouring to act a part, and this so clumsily, that he is at once seen through. This tissue of petty imposture which forms the bulk of Pope's letters is not redeemed by any merits of expression. A *dictum* of Lord Byron is often quoted, to the effect that Pope and Dryden were as great masters of prose as of verse. Of Pope, this is certainly not true. His peculiar power of condensation is confined entirely to the couplet. Even in verse he is often beaten by the double requirements of metre and clearness. But in a prose sentence he is rarely successful. He probably often has spent as much pains in elaborating, and as much diligence in retouching his letters as his poetry. But the result was, from the nature of the case, different in each. The couplet is, in its nature, an artificial thing, and is indefinitely improvable by chiselling. The letter must flow freely from the feeling of the moment, or else it becomes untrue to its character. There are, no doubt, occasional passages, and even whole letters, which ought to be excepted from any summary condemnation. Pope's reply to Atterbury, of date Nov. 20, 1717, is manly, sincere, and not ungraceful. Atterbury writes to him on the death of his father, and suggests with great delicacy that now he has an opportunity of reconsidering the question of conformity to the Church of England.

Pope declines the suggestion with a firmness and simplicity which are too seldom found in his letters. Of these, in general, it may be said that they are pervaded by an unpleasant insincerity, and that the want of straightforwardness in the sentiment finds its mirror in the entanglement of the expression.

This being the general character of Pope's letters, it is no longer desirable to rank them with the poet's *works.* Information certainly they do supply, but thinly distributed through the mass. All that is important in their contents may be left to be used up by the biographer and the commentator. To these the letters will be always indispensable. It may be ingratitude, but in the interest of the general reader we can hardly feel glad that the researches of Mr. Elwin—the most industrious editor whom Pope has yet had—have enabled him to add so largely to the published mass. The last edition published in the lifetime of Pope contained 354 letters. These were increased by Warburton to 384; by Warton to 502; by Bowles to 644; and by Roscoe to 708; exactly double the number published by Pope himself. The present edition will contain more new letters than were collected by all these editors combined. In fact, it will form the largest section of the edition, for it is to fill five volumes, while the poetry will be comprised in four. And it is not only in bulk that it will be considerable—it receives prominence from the attention Mr. Elwin has bestowed upon it, and the laborious dissertation he has prefixed, unravelling all the mystery of Pope's intrigues to get his letters published, which has never before been so clearly elucidated.

But before any examination of the work which Mr. Elwin has done upon Pope, and the spirit in which he has approached it, we may shortly survey what had been effected by previous editors.

Pope was not one of those writers who care not what becomes of their books as soon as they have answered

a temporary purpose of profit or renown. He had spent
too much labour on polishing his lines to be indifferent to
their fate. His life had been, from first to last, an author's
life. He had lived to write, and after production had
ceased, up to the very time of his death, he was unceasingly occupied in revision. So solicitous was he to
preserve his lines as he left them, that he provided for
their integrity by his will. He left the property of his
printed works to Warburton, with the proviso that they
should be 'published without future alterations.' Johnson
calculated the value of this bequest at £4,000. What Pope
did was, in effect, to bind Warburton under a penalty of
£4,000 to print his poems as the author left them. There
is strong evidence, both direct and circumstantial, that
the injunction in the will was carried out to the letter.
Warburton had, at Pope's request, made some alterations
in the *Dunciad* and the Preface to the Homer. These
were adopted by the poet in his lifetime. For the few
alterations made in the text after Pope's death, Warburton
states that he had the sanction of a corrected copy
delivered to him by Pope. Warburton, who had upon
his hands his edition of *Shakespeare*, his *Lincoln's Inn
Sermons*, and a host of adversaries whom he was engaged
in mowing down, required seven years to bring out his
edition of Pope's works. It appeared in 1751. As far as
the text of the poems is concerned, Warburton's edition
must be considered a standard from which there can be no
departure. Errors of the press apart, and they are not
numerous, we conceive that every editor is bound to
adhere to this text with critical exactness. Mr. Elwin
has taken the liberty in his edition to do what reviewers
call 'modernize the spelling.' We cannot but regret this
licence. We claim to have the text of every English
classic, to a letter, as it came from the pen of the author.
To tamper with the letters of which the author's words
are composed, is not more allowable than to correct his

language. He who steals a penny would steal a pound. Mr. Elwin has not gone the length of modernizing Pope's language. But we see from his annotations that he is occasionally dissatisfied with it, and would prefer to have, instead of the words actually used by Pope, the modern equivalent, such as a reporter would put into the mouth of a Parliamentary speaker. Were the point of correct spelling of no consequence in itself, it would become of importance as a test of editorial accuracy and fidelity. But it is in itself a thing which ought to be rigidly exacted. For every classic is not only a mirror of the thought of its age, but a monument of its language. Even Mr. Elwin himself would not propose to re-write all the English poets in the spelling of the nineteenth century. There was a time when we were content with an Elizabethan Chaucer; but editors now are all agreed to go back to the contemporary MSS. The editors of the new Clarendon Press Wiclif have been most scrupulous in adhering to the original orthography, and have even reproduced the thorn letter, and the old form of g. Whatever reasons could be given for conforming the spelling of a poet of George II's time to our standard, would hold good of the time of Edward III. Nay, there would be more reason for printing Chaucer and Wiclif as we now print; for the text of these writers must be taken from MSS. which are very diverse in their orthography; while the text of Pope has, in the edition of 1751, a rigid standard, any departure from which is an arbitrary act of an editor.

In Warburton's edition, the notes and commentary occupy a very undue share of the page. But this is their least demerit. Warburton thrusts his author into the shade to occupy the foreground himself with pretentious matter, in which is to be found neither wit, nor learning, nor information, nor illustration. The character of Warburton's commentaries on Pope was decided by the circumstance in which they originated. When he first wrote on the subject, Warburton did not contemplate *Notes* on Pope, still less an edition. What he did was to write a series of letters in a literary periodical of the day, called *The Works of the Learned*, which letters were a polemical retort to two pamphlets in which Crousaz had attacked the *Essay on Man*. This was in 1738; and it was not till 1742 that these letters were collected into a volume, and it was not till the following year, 1743, that Pope resolved upon publishing an edition of the *Essay*, in which these letters were cut up into lengths and printed as notes on the same page with the poem. Pope's gratitude for the controversial service rendered him, led to a friendship with Warburton; and this friendship led to Warburton being left by Pope, who died in the following year, 1744, his literary executor. Pope's will gave Warburton the copyright of 'such of my works as he hath written, or shall write commentaries or notes upon.' Thus Warburton was in the position of being compelled to comment whether he had anything to say or not, in order to preserve his rights. When these circumstances are considered, we shall see that we are not to look in Warburton's notes for the explanation of allusions or elucidation of difficulties. Nor, indeed, was there any call for explanation of that character, on the part of the poet's contemporaries, to whom his allusions were generally intelligible enough. It is not till a later generation that these difficulties become formidable. Warburton regarded himself not as an interpreter, but as a champion. He had to fight the poet's foes, theological and literary. It is, therefore, scarcely fair to complain of him for not having accomplished what he never undertook. Even Mr. Elwin's somewhat violent language does not exaggerate the bad taste and irrelevance of Warburton's notes on Pope. We must agree that he 'fabricated hollow paradoxes'; that he 'tortured language into undesigned

meanings'; that 'his lifeless and verbose conceits provoke
by their falsity, and fatigue by their ponderousness'; and
that 'he has left no worse specimen of his perverse propen-
sity than the spurious fancies and idle refinements he has
here fathered upon Pope.' If this is all true, surely the
inference to be drawn is that which De Quincey drew
long ago, in reviewing Roscoe in 1825, that Warburton's
commentary ought to be discarded from the editions of
Pope. It must seem curiously inconsistent with his own
invective that Mr. Elwin has preserved the whole of the
'bulky excrescence' in his edition, though he had already
placed on the same page with Pope's verses a no less
bulky annotation of his own. None but antiquarian
students of the history of literature can have any call to
read Warburton's commentary. And such students will
require to have it, not in the abridged form in which it
appeared in Warburton's edition of Pope, 1751, and in
which Mr. Elwin has reprinted it, but in the original
shape of 1742, with a dedication, a preface, and many
other amusing *naïvetés* and self-complacencies, which were
afterwards omitted. Mr. Elwin's edition is thus burdened
with sixty octavo pages of close print, which do not serve
in the least to elucidate Pope, but which illustrate only
the personality of Warburton. And yet, as illustrative of
Warburton, it is not the genuine document, which he who
wants to read Warburton requires to have. If Pope is to
be edited as a classic poet, the vulgar pamphlet in which
one of his poems is dragged through the mire of the
theological polemic of the day has no place in *Pope's
Works*. If an edition of the *Works* is to be a repertory of
the original pieces written for or against Pope, there was
no reason for not giving Warburton's pamphlet in its
genuine form.

The truth is, that the title of *Commentary*, and the
sanction given it by the poet himself, have had such an
imposing effect upon the minds of all editors, that they

have shrunk from separating what Pope had joined together. But as soon as it is recognized that the notes in question are not in our sense a commentary, but a polemical defence of the supposed theological doctrines of a piece which we read as a classical poem, and not as a system of doctrine, it will be felt at once that when Warburton's notes had answered their temporary purpose they were done with. When we read Pope, what we want is, not to have it proved to us that he was right or that he was wrong in any of his abstract propositions, we want simply to understand what it is that he has said. We no more think of vindicating or of refuting his reasoning than we do of vindicating or refuting the philosophy of Lucretius. As Mr. Elwin has committed the error of spending his editorial strength in refuting his author's text in his foot-notes, we must assume that it was in a spirit of fairness that he decided on reprinting Warburton's vindication at the end of the volume, in order that the other side might have a hearing. Both attack and defence appear to us to be equally out of place.

Thus it was to an accident—to the accident, viz. of finding himself enveloped in the flames of the theological controversy of the day—that Pope owed the singular distinction of seeing his poetical works published with the honours of a regular commentary in his lifetime. He perpetuated the distinction by compelling his literary executor to write commentaries on the whole of his poetry, under a heavy pecuniary penalty. But for the accident that made it necessary to his safety to retain an orthodox fighting-man near his person, it is possible that an annotated edition of Pope might have been waited for as long as one of Gray, or Young, or Thomson, or Addison. The *Spectator*, the *Seasons*, the *Night Thoughts* were all highly popular, and were reprinted again and again without any attempt to edit or illustrate them. Warburton's commentary was, as we have seen, not an annotated edition in our sense, but a bullying apology addressed to a particular purpose. But it became the occasion or the provocative of the first regular attempt at illustration and elucidation.

Warton's notes on Pope were undoubtedly called forth by Warburton's commentary. The personal altercation and literary feuds in which Pope and Warburton delighted were repugnant to Warton's temper. He would not engage in controversy. Without naming or directly alluding to Warburton, he published, five years after the appearance of Warburton's edition, a volume of notes on Pope, which were calculated to counteract the bad taste of the *Commentary*, by presenting a better model of editing and juster principles of criticism. He did not meditate an edition, indeed he could not seek to invade the copyright of the poems, but called his work an *Essay on the Genius and Writings of Pope*. After Warburton's death, and after the expiration of the copyright, Warton undertook and published a complete edition of Pope, and used up the materials of his *Essay* in the notes to it. This was in 1797. He now did not scruple to refer to the Bishop of Gloucester's commentary, and in terms of deserved, but still dignified censure. His delay in following up the first volume of his *Essay* with a second, and the long period of forty years which elapsed between his first volume and his edition, have led to its being asserted that he abstained, from fear of Warburton. This assertion is not supported by Dr. Johnson, who, when asked the reason of Warton's delay in bringing out the second volume of his *Essay*, said, he supposed 'it was because he could not persuade the world to be of his opinion about Pope.' But Warton may, very likely, have been afraid of Warburton. If he was, such fear would have been no imputation on his courage and honour. He may, nay, he must, have feared Warburton, not as cowed by his superiority, but as a just and reasonable-minded man fears the contact of the irrepressible slanderer. He feared dirt, not confutation. It was impossible to suppress Warburton, and Warton was too refined a scholar to fight him with his own weapons of scurrility and abuse. When a man is incurably wrong-headed, the only resource is to avoid him. If it seems unhandsome in Warton to have spoken his opinion of the Bishop after his death, having preserved silence for so many years, it should be remembered that what might have been presumptuous in him at thirty-five, when he was only beginning to be known, was no longer so at seventy-five, when he had a long and honourable career of a life devoted to learning behind him. Joseph Warton was not one of those original men of genius who rouse our curiosity and leave their mark on their age. Johnson, with far less learning, and Gray, who left only a few hundred lines of fragmentary poetry, will count as more remarkable men than Warton. But if, from want of force of character, Warton does not hold a first place among his contemporaries, he will always claim the regard of students of our literature, both for what he was himself, and for the new direction which he impressed on poetical criticism in this country.

Joseph Warton, born 1722, died 1800, spent the whole of a long life in the pursuit of letters, and in the society of literary men. Neither academical endowments nor Ministerial patronage came near him, and he was compelled for a maintenance to continue the drudgery of teaching to the verge of the grave. In those political days, Church patronage was an appanage of the great Parliamentary families ; and while deaneries and canonries were lavished in return for political support, the most eminent literary scholar of the day owed what small Church preferment he ever got to private patrons. Thirty-eight years master at Winchester, his Virgil, and his Horace, and his Latin metres, must have become more than familiar to him. This sound foundation served to carry a much more extensive reading of the classics than was demanded by the requirements of his class. He was not indeed a scholar after the type of Porson or Dobree; he was a literary scholar. He read the classics as literature, and he could marshal alongside of his Greek and Latin classics a still wider variety of modern reading. Equipped with this information, and able to expatiate freely over this wide field, he brought to the business of criticism a just poetical taste, which, without being susceptible, was not insensible to any kind of beauty. His principal attraction lay towards literary history, and he was one of the many who have meditated, and have not executed, a history of the classical revival. His criticism and his conversation leant towards the side of anecdote or quotation, rather than that of abstract principle. Yet it was not unguided by principle. To him we must ascribe the chief share of that revolution in the tone of poetical criticism which took place in England about the middle of the eighteenth century, and which is generally known as the reaction against what is called the School of Pope, but which we should prefer to call the classical school. In 1746, only two years after the death of Pope, when Warton was only twenty-four, he announced the principle of his criticism in an apologetic preface to a book of poems.

'The public,' he says, 'has been so much accustomed of late to didactic poetry alone, and essays on moral subjects, that any work, where the imagination is much indulged, will perhaps not be relished or regarded. The author, therefore, of these pieces, is in some pain lest certain austere critics should think them too fanciful or descriptive. But as he is convinced that the fashion of moralizing in verse has been carried too far, and as he looks upon invention and imagination to be the chief faculties of a poet, so he will be happy if the following odes may be looked upon as an attempt to bring back poetry into its right channel.'

These simple words are a declaration of war against the reigning school. To this cause Warton remained ever faithful, though he was able to promote it more effectually by his criticism than by his example. His own poetical powers had not force enough to lead the way to a new form of writing. A few pieces linger in the collections, but they do not rise above the level of elegant academical exercises. 'Dr. Warton,' says Campbell, 'so far realized his own idea of inspiration as to burthen his verse with few observations on life which oppress the mind by their solidity.' This was in allusion to Warton's having laid it down, 'that the most solid observations on life, expressed with the utmost brevity and elegance, are morality, not poetry.' This principle he gradually expanded and applied in his notes on Pope. It must not be inferred, however, that his attitude in his edition of Pope is a hostile attitude. He is quite alive to Pope's merits, and never fails to draw attention to the surprises and felicities of expression which occur so frequently in everything Pope wrote. Such a taste as Warton's could not be insensible to the classical keeping and finish in which Pope would treat the most uninteresting matter.

But the sympathy of the commentator with his author extended in the case of Warton and Pope beyond mere style and language. It is true that Warton's theory of poetry condemned 'observations on life,' or didactic moralizing, as unfit material for the poet's art, and demanded imagery, figures, and what he vaguely called 'the romantic.' Warton insisted upon description from Nature, but it is plain, from his own attempts, that though his remoter sympathies were open to rural and out-door life, his nearest and quickest interest lay in the world of society and books. He feels for painter's nature, for cheerful scenes and pretty effects, but he has not the real eye of an observer. He is the student who has sallied out from his library and pleases himself, by contrast, with the song of the birds and the gambols of the lambs. His taste for rustic imagery was not affected, it was real, but it did not go very deep, and it was overpowered by the

literary interest. For this class of mind, Milton and Pope
will, of all our poets, always have the strongest attraction.
They are the most classical. They invite the annotator;
every line is pregnant with allusion which stimulates
the memory of the scholar. Warton's taste was thus
of wide compass. He had room in his affections for the
naturalness of the Elizabethan writers, and for the
artificial epigram of the French school. Long before
Coleridge, Wordsworth, and Southey, he called for
admiration for our early poetry.   Drummond of Hawthorn-
den is 'that charming but neglected poet'; Drayton's
Nymphidia is 'not so much attended to as it deserves.'
He was aware that Milton's *Lycidas* 'is superior to all
pastoral poems in our language,' and that ' Dryden
must rank as a poet for his music-ode, and not for his
Religio Laici.' His appreciative power stops nowhere,
but ranges from Pascal and Racine to Hearne's
Chronicles, to *Clarissa* and *Tom Jones.*

With this rare combination of just principles of criticism
to guide him, poetical sensibility, classical correctness,
a wide range of literature, ancient and modern, and a fair
acquaintance with the personal history of the previous
generation of our writers, Joseph Warton was well
equipped to be the editor of *Pope.* Though the proposal
came from the booksellers, it was no uncongenial task that
was imposed upon him. Unfortunately, he was turned
seventy when he undertook it. His advanced age, but
even more, the want of a clear conception of what a
commentator's duties are, did not allow him to produce
a book which can be called a good edition of a classic.
His notes are garrulous and irrelevant, and many a
difficulty is left untouched. He has indulged to the full
the two editorial privileges—silence where explanation
is needed, diffuseness where it is superfluous. But if he
has not left a model edition of Pope, it cannot be denied
that he has produced a most amusing book. Regarded as

ana, Warton's *Pope* is one of the most entertaining and instructive in the language. However irrelevant, he is always fresh and buoyant. His egotism is genial without being obtrusive, and his book-quotations are relieved by personal anecdotes, the reminiscences of an old man, who had moved all his life in the best informed company of the capital. He had conversed with Lord Bathurst, who had known three generations of poets and politicians ; he had lived many years on terms of intimacy with Adam Smith ; he mixed with the circle of the Literary Club. Young, Collins, Pitt (the translator of Virgil), Steevens, Dr. Campbell, Sir Joshua Reynolds, Mr. Berenger, and Lord Lyttelton, are quoted by name for some anecdote or other. The Duchess of Portland had described to him the scene when the character of Atossa was read to old Sarah, Duchess of Marlborough. From the report of Hoadly he had heard how the same Sarah had sworn in his presence at Dr. Mead, and was going to tear off his wig. He had heard Lord Huntingdon talk of his friend Fontenelle, and he knew Mr. Hans Stanley, who had read Lord Hervey's *Memoirs,* then in manuscript. Warton's notes on Pope must always be resorted to by those who wish to become acquainted with his period. Printed by themselves, without the poems, and without the notes of Pope and Warburton, with which they are intermixed, they would make an independent and entertaining volume. But as an annotated edition of Pope, it would not be difficult to surpass Warton's book.

Yet strange to say, though Warton's *Pope* was published in 1797, and though it has been superseded in the market, it has never yet been improved upon. Twice, indeed, the attempt has been made, but without success. Bowles re-edited Pope in 1806, but he succeeded only in introducing into the subject the Coleridge and Wordsworth criticism, a criticism which knew nothing of the eighteenth century, and treated the artificial or 'periwig' school with

indiscriminate contempt.   Bowles had himself the feeling
of a true poet, and no ordinary eye for natural phenomena.
One of his criticisms, however, which has been cited as
evidence of his gifts as a naturalist, does not prove much.
It is on a line of Marvel's, well known since Bowles
singled it out,

> And through the hazels thick espy
> The hatching throstle's shining eye.

On this Bowles says 'the last circumstance is new, highly
poetical, and could only have been described by one
who was a real lover of Nature, and a witness of her
beauties in her most solitary retirement.' Familiarity with
the 'hatching throstle's shining eye,' only proves that
Bowles and Marvel had both been schoolboys, and
addicted to birds-nesting.   But keen sympathy with Nature
constitutes a positive disqualification for being a commentator on Pope, as it only quickens the sense of one
of the deficiencies of Pope's school.   Bowles was without
an ear for the versification, and without knowledge of the
history of the eighteenth century, and contributed nothing
to the elucidation of the confessed obscurities of Pope's
allusions.

Of the disgraceful bookseller's job called *Roscoe's Pope*,
nothing need be said.   The booksellers could not have
pitched upon a worse editor.   For Roscoe, though well
versed in the Italian writers of the *renaissance*, knew
nothing of the eighteenth century.   He was not a classical
scholar.   And though his English style is easy and
elegant, and his *Life of Pope* very pleasant reading, his
command of the facts is so slight, that Roscoe's memoir of
the poet is entirely superseded by Mr. Carruthers' more
correct, though less elegant biography. 'Roscoe has
shown,' says Mr. Adolphus Ward, in the *Globe* edition of
Pope's poems, 'that Bufo was not meant for Lord Halifax.'
Without wishing to be disrespectful to Mr. Ward, we
must say that Roscoe has not shown it, and his attempt to

disprove a reference which is as certain as any anonymous allusion in Pope can be, is only one among many instances which might be given of how little versed Roscoe was in the period he had to illustrate. Of this edition, which is justly called by Mr. Croker 'the worst,' the public have absorbed two large issues, under the name of the standard trade edition.

We have now enumerated the leading editions of Pope, but we must not omit mention of one who, though not editor, was an illustrator, and of whom Mr. Elwin says that, though the least known and appreciated, he has done the most for his author. This was Gilbert Wakefield, a personage in the latter half of the eighteenth century, who, though obnoxious to bishops for his opinions, and to scholars for his dabbling with textual emendation, hit upon the one right track for an editor of Pope. For Pope, as Sir W. Hamilton said, 'was a curious reader.' 'He collected,' says Warton, 'gold from many a dunghill.' Pope had no thought, no mind, no ideas, but he had the art of rhymed language in a degree in which no English poet before or since has possessed it. And this he had acquired by unremitting labour from the nursery. He was very industrious, and had read a vast number of books, yet he was very ignorant,—ignorant, that is, of everything but the one thing which he laboured with all his might to acquire, the art of happy expression. He read books to find ready-made images, and to feel for the best collocations of words. His memory was a magazine of epithets and synonymes, and pretty turns of language. Wherever he found anything to his purpose, he booked it for use, and some time or other, often more than once, it made its appearance in his verse. This mosaic of phrase, this 'emblema vermiculatum,' as the old Roman poet called it, was just the workmanship which tempts a professional reader to take it to pieces to see how it was made, and to trace back the gems of thought to their former owners. Gilbert Wakefield was not particularly well fitted for this time-devouring occupation. His mind was too restless and flighty, and not sufficiently ' confined within the pale of words,' and he was at the same time labouring for a subsistence. Still he did a great deal in this way, and collected an abundant harvest of parallel passages. Mr. Elwin says of them, that many of the parallelisms are too slight to be applicable, as they are the common phrases which are the property of every Englishman. Besides collecting passages, Wakefield proposed to explain, and by aid of Dr. Bennett, Bishop of Cloyne, did succeed in explaining, many historical or personal allusions. By confining his notes to these two objects, Wakefield has the merit of having at least pointed out the right road to an editor. He only pointed it out, for he never proceeded beyond vol. I. of his edition. Warton's edition, which was going on simultaneously, had the support of the booksellers. Wakefield, whose opinions in Eldonian days exposed him not only to obloquy, but to persecution, was obliged to print at his own expense, and he perhaps found the patient labour of editing too much for his desultory habits.

Such as we have described being the state of Pope's works in the standard edition of Roscoe, it is no wonder that a new edition became a desideratum. The task was undertaken by Mr. J. Wilson Croker, who was engaged for many years in collecting materials. Mr. Croker had some qualifications for the office. He was conversant beyond almost any man of his day with the personal anecdotage of the period. He had edited the *Suffolk Correspondence*, the *Hervey Letters*, and above all *Lord Hervey's Memoirs*, then for the first time printed. He had edited Boswell's *Life of Johnson*, with notes, which, though leaving much to be desired, do not deserve Macaulay's description as ' worthless.' He was not averse to raking for materials in the sinks and sewers of literature, though the thin disguise of rebuke that he pretends gives an unpleasant impression of character. He had much sagacity in discerning what it was probable people would do or say. But Mr. Croker had also many disqualifications. He was not a scholar. His acquaintance with Latin was probably slender, but be that as it may, he had not even the average reading of the scholar. He was an Irishman, and had the inaccurate mind of his countrymen. It was not only that he was liable to mistakes, such, e. g. as confounding the two brothers Warton—who is not liable ?—but he had not an accurate habit of literary language. He had no sense of poetry, and no cultivated taste. He knew little or nothing of the history of our language or literature, and did not even know that there was anything to be known. As Secretary to the Admiralty, he had shared the odium of mal-administration or jobbery, which attached to that department. He had augmented it by his violent Tory politics, especially by a tone of virulence which pervaded his conversation, and his articles in the Tory journal. It is to be regretted that Macaulay should have forgotten the dignity and decencies of criticism in his attack upon him (in his review of Madame D'Arblay's *Diary*), yet it is not perhaps going too far to say that Mr. Croker's mind had the stamp which is generally called 'low.'

If any one now could do so, Mr. Croker perhaps could have cleared up the doubtful allusions to persons in Pope's *Satires*. Beyond this we could not have expected anything from his editing. We congratulated ourselves when, after Mr. Croker's death in 1857, it was announced that his papers had been placed by the publishers in the hands of Mr. Elwin. Mr. Elwin announced his determination to adhere to the plan of editing sketched by Mr. Croker. Of the plan we know only what Mr. Elwin tells us in his introduction :—

The faults of plan and execution in the editions of Warburton,

Warton, Bowles and Roscoe, stand out in strong relief, and Mr. Croker resolved, as far as possible, to correct the mistakes, retrench the superfluities, and supply the omissions.   Warton and Bowles dismissed a large proportion of the barren, oppressive commentaries of Warburton.   Roscoe put back the whole of the bulky excrescence. Most of it had been adopted by Pope, and to relieve the text, without excluding interpretations sanctioned by the poet, Mr. Croker determined to print the pedantic lumber in appendixes.   The notes of the other editors rested on their intrinsic merits, and he intended to sift out the surplusage, and only retain what was pertinent.   To curtail is easy.   The difficulty was to clear up the many obscurities which remained, and Mr. Croker was anxious to furnish his share of explanation, though he was convinced that numerous contemporary allusions would always baffle curiosity.   His chief attention was directed to the *Satires*, and he continued for many years to pursue his investigations, and accumulate materials.   His busy life was succeeded by failing health, and he died before he had prepared his notes for the press.   The results of his research have luckily all been preserved, for his habit was to write them out in full at the time. He was an acute and eager inquirer into political, personal, and social history, and no man could have been more competent to bring to the surface the undercurrent of forgotten circumstances [1].—

Mr. Elwin's antecedents pointed him out as a fit person, nay, as much fitter than Mr. Croker himself, to become the editor of Pope. He possesses all the qualifications in which Mr. Croker was conspicuously deficient. To a scholar's training and literary habits of mind, Mr. Elwin adds not only a poetical taste, but a special study of the history of English poetry. Years ago he announced a book on the subject: and though no part of this has yet appeared, articles understood to be from his pen have shown with what pains and thoroughness he would investigate the personal history, and what a sound judgment he would bring to bear upon the works, of the poets. During the period—too brief—for which the *Quarterly Review* enjoyed his superintendence, it became for a short time an organ of literary criticism, and rose

[1] *Elwin's Pope.* Introduction, xxv.

above the level of party strife. Everything, therefore, concurred to raise our anticipations, and we looked for an edition of Pope which Mr. Croker's persevering investigation and Mr. Elwin's classical taste should combine to make the final edition.

Two volumes of the poetry and two volumes of the correspondence are now before the public. It is but an instalment, but it is enough to leave no doubt as to the character of the whole work. We are not to have from Mr. Elwin a classical edition of a classic poet. We have, instead, in the Introduction, a bitter pamphlet in the style of one of Mr. Croker's 'slashing' articles, and in the notes to the two volumes of poetry a running fire of theological polemic on the level of a leading article in the *Morning Advertiser*. What has driven Mr. Elwin upon this quicksand it is vain even to guess. It is the more extraordinary, as he is quite alive to the irrelevancy of Warburton's commentary. He has relegated this 'bulky excrescence' to an appendix, and would probably have dismissed it altogether, had it not been for Mr. Croker's determination to retain it. But he has supplied its place at the foot of the text with a no less bulky and no less irrelevant excrescence of his own. It is true that the two commentaries look two different ways. Warburton's commentary was a far-fetched paradoxical defence of the orthodoxy of the *Essay*. Elwin's is a commonplace and insipid, though violent tirade against the heterodoxy of the poet's *Essay*. Warburton wrote a stilted and hyperbolical panegyric; Elwin offers a counterblast in flat abuse. They take different sides, but the irrelevancy of the modern commentary seems to us to be as flagrant as that of the older.

Nothing, indeed, can well be a greater offence against taste than panegyrical comment. To be ordered, as we are by Warburton, to admire in every page beauty and sublimity, and to take note of a constant superiority to

Horace, inevitably disgusts. The iteration of such determined advocacy defeats its purpose. But if a surfeit of
eulogy nauseates, what are we to say of professional
detraction? Is it possible to read the text of a poet
with comfort—nay, to any purpose at all—when we
have a running fire of depreciation kept up at the foot
of the page—a critic ready to give an unfavourable
turn to every doubtful expression, to sneer at the poet
when he tries to mount, to throw cold water on him when
he tries to be witty, and generally to damp and dull the
effect of everything he tries to say? The question raised
by this edition is not one as to Pope's moral or literary
character, but one as to the duties of an editor, and
what is the shape in which it is desirable that we should
have our classical writers. Even if everything which
Mr. Elwin's industry has enabled him to suggest to Pope's
disadvantage were strictly true, we should say that
three-fourths of it is out of place here. Much of it
properly belongs to the biographer, not to the annotator,
and would form the proper materials of a critical article.
But in an *edition*, the text is the primary consideration ;
notes are only admissible when they are actually required,
and they are only required when something occurs which
is not in itself fully intelligible. This is a general rule
imperative upon all editors. To this must be added, in
the case of Pope, whose system of borrowing makes it
necessary, a selection of imitated or parallel passages.
In making this selection, mere parallelism is not the point
of interest ; what is wanted is that the passage which was
before the mind of the poet when he was writing his
own lines should be produced. In the case of Pope it is
possible to do this, as we have said, to a great extent.
Here is ample work for an editor—enough, indeed, to
deter any but men of great leisure and resolute industry
from the task of editing. He need not desire to extend
his sphere of labour by undertaking the duties of critic

and biographer at the same time. A short biography, for
the sake of dates, which are always necessary in the
reading of a poem, and select criticism in the shape of
introductions, are traditionally held proper appendages
of the works of the poets.

Mr. Elwin has constructed his edition upon a different
plan. In the two volumes of poetry the text is quite
subordinate to the annotator's accompaniment, not only in
quantity but in importance. Pope is not illustrated, he is
crushed under a pile of opprobrium. We are made to
feel from beginning to end that the object had in view in
editing Pope was to induce us to desist from reading him.
Pope is a liar, a cheat, and a scoundrel, and his so-called
poetry is ungrammatical, ill-rhymed, unmeaning trash.
And these are not the slap-dash *dicta* of a young journalist,
trying to make a reputation for himself by pulling down
somebody else's, they are the deliberate convictions of a
sober and judicious critic, who has spent years in investigating the case and arriving at this conclusion. We
cannot recall a parallel case in the annals of editing
where a man of learning, whose time and information are
valuable, has imposed upon himself the ungrateful task of
labouring so long upon what he thinks so unworthy of his
pains. If Pope's works be what Mr. Elwin evidently
thinks they are, of what value are Mr. Elwin's labours
upon them? The upshot of his book seems to be a
demonstration that it ought never to have been written.
If Mr. Elwin is taken at his word, and should bring the
public to be of his mind as to Pope, the sale of Mr.
Murray's edition would be summarily stopped.

It is not the intention of this notice to undertake a
defence of Pope's conduct, or to examine his literary
merits. We wish to be confined to the narrower question
of what are the functions and duties of an editor. From
much of Mr. Elwin's harsh summing-up we find it impossible to dissent. At the most we might venture to

suggest that there are extenuating circumstances. There
are merits and even virtues which might have had a
passing mention, if only to give relief to a picture of
meanness and deception which is depressing from its
monotonous depravity. We are by no means for a policy
of concealment, and in a Life of Pope we would have
everything told; but Mr. Elwin does not preface the
Poetry by a biography of the summary kind, which it has
been said would be useful to a reader of the poems.
There is not even a chronological table of events, or order
of publication, which might be a substitute for a Life.
Instead of this the first volume of the *Poetry* leads off with
nearly 150 pages of an investigation into the circumstances
attending the publication of the successive volumes of
Pope's correspondence. In this examination Mr. Elwin
has exhibited a patience and sagacity which place him in
the highest rank of literary inquirers. He has unravelled
with a merciless hand the web of artifice and petty intrigue
which it pleased Pope to weave round each of his publications of his letters. It is true that the late Mr. Dilke led
the way, and pointed out the track of investigation in his
papers in the *Athenaeum*, but Mr. Elwin has gone through
for himself the painful task of verifying Mr. Dilke's conclusions. Not once, but again and again—that is on each
occasion of publishing a volume—did Pope *finesse*, and
scheme, and pretend, and equivocate, and lie. Mr. Elwin
has not only waded through all the evidence of this silly
trickery himself, but he has marshalled it at full length for
the benefit of the reader, and prefixed it as a suitable
introduction to the first volume of the *Poetry*. The story
is well told, and the evidence, though minute and circumstantial, clearly arranged. In an original biography such
a digression would have found a proper place; in an
annotated edition of the works it is surely an encumbrance.
We want results when we sit down to read Pope himself,
and not investigation. But for prefixing an original inves-

tigation into the publication of Pope's *Correspondence* to the first volume of his *Poems*, we can discover no reasonable motive. The arrangement has, however, one undesigned consequence; the damning evidence of Pope's treachery and duplicity which is arrayed in the Introduction disposes the reader of the Notes which follow, to receive the fire of carping remark and perpetual suggestion of mean intention which is kept up from the editorial half of the page.

It is impossible that any partisan of Pope should offer any defence which can obliterate Mr. Elwin's partisan impeachment. We repeat that we question, not its truth, but its relevancy. But, after all, what does the story of the letters amount to? All this trickery and cunning which Pope thought proper to surround his publications with, had what mighty object? The gratification of the little fellow's small vanity, that he might see his letters in print in his lifetime, and yet that it might not be known that he had published them himself! That was all he took by it. And though big words may be applied to the conduct of the hoax—words which, if seriously pressed, cannot be denied to be literally true— most people will think that the pettifogging nature of the whole transaction makes it hardly worth while to fall upon it with the whole weight of moral rebuke. It is true a lie is a lie, be it great or small, and a trickster is odious. It is not quite comfortable to think that Scott, to preserve the anonymity of the Waverley novels, was obliged categorically to deny that he had written them. A satirist, of all men, should have his own hands clean. When we take in hand the *Novum Organum*, it is not wholly out of place to remember that Bacon took a bribe. So much we should expect an editor of that treatise to remind us of. But we should hardly wish to have him detail, in his introduction to it, the history of Bacon's corruption, his black behaviour to Essex, the

murder of Raleigh, the torture of Peacham. Though, no
doubt, if it were designed in the notes to lower our
estimate of the lofty aspirations of the *Advancement of
Learning,* no introduction could be more calculated to do
so than a narrative of Bacon's political career. It is just
and necessary that these facts of any great writer's life
should be recollected. When Pope is inclined to spread
his plumes and hint at his own virtues, let it be remembered that he cheated his friends Swift and Lord
Oxford out of the originals of his own letters. But a
single sentence would say on the subject all that an
editor need say. Pope had had a Catholic education,
and wanted rectitude and openness. He was not only
an invalid, but a *malade imaginaire.* Deception was a
second nature. 'He cannot drink a cup of tea without a
stratagem,' said Lady Mary. 'Il fait de la diplomatie
à propos de carottes et de navets,' said Lady Bolingbroke.

The charge of duplicity and trickery which Mr. Elwin
has established against Pope, even to supererogation, is
unhappily, true. Another, even more serious, with which
he has taken great pains, rests entirely upon a false
hypothesis. We are obliged to dismiss this in a very few
words. Mr. Elwin has adopted an opinion that Pope was
engaged in a conspiracy with Bolingbroke for the writing
down of the Christian religion, and the substitution of
Bolingbroke's irreligious metaphysics in its place. Pope's
contribution to the scheme was the *Essay on Man.* On
this thesis Mr. Elwin descants for about seventy pages
of small print, coupling with it a refutation, from Mr.
Elwin's point of view, of these metaphysics. Really, the
relation of the *Essay on Man* to Bolingbroke, to metaphysics, and to the deistical movement, is a thing so clear
and well ascertained, that any clearing up of the confusion
which our editor has superinduced upon the subject,
involves a repetition of what has been said so often that it

has become trite. We may be excused for being very brief under each of these three heads.

1. For obligations to Bolingbroke, Mr. Elwin produces the well-known story of Lord Bathurst. Lord Bathurst, who died at a great age in 1777, was in the habit of ascribing a principal share in the *Essay on Man* to Lord Bolingbroke. The reporters are not agreed upon the terms he used, Warton saying only that he had seen the whole scheme of the *Essay* in manuscript in Lord Bolingbroke's handwriting; while Hugh Blair goes beyond this, giving the words, as that the *Essay* was 'originally composed by Lord Bolingbroke in prose.' When this statement was repeated to Dr. Johnson, he immediately put his finger upon its weak point: 'Depend upon it, sir, this is too strongly stated. Pope may have had from Bolingbroke the philosophic stamina of his *Essay*. . . . But the thing is not true in the latitude that Blair seems to imagine; we are sure that the poetical imagery which makes a great part of the poem was Pope's own. It is amazing, sir, what deviations there are from precise truth in the account which is given of everything.' Johnson had read Spence's *Anecdotes* (then in manuscript), but he did not recollect, when he said this, that Pope himself, so far from concealing his obligations to Bolingbroke, distinctly stated to Spence, that he 'had received seven or eight sheets from Lord Bolingbroke in relation to it.' And if the conjecture be right, that these very sheets seen by Lord Bathurst were the *Fragments or Minutes of Essays* printed in Lord Bolingbroke's works, we have the means of judging for ourselves what was exactly the amount of Lord Bolingbroke's written contribution to the *Essay on Man*. But whatever may be the truth as to the identity of these *Fragments*, the moral doctrines, such as they are, of the *Essay*, sufficiently declare their own origin. They are doctrines having no peculiarity about them by which they can be

stamped as Bolingbroke's ; they are to be found in the books of the time, and were commonly current in the conversation of reading and thinking men. So familiar did they seem to Johnson, that, instead of finding a special paternity for them, he sneers at them as 'the talk of our mother and our nurse.'

2. So much on the *dictum* that the substance of the *Essay* was supplied to Pope by Bolingbroke. Of the relation of the poem to philosophy little need be said. Mr. Elwin spends many pages of careful writing in a furious denunciation of the *Essay* as shallow metaphysics, a tissue of incoherence and inconsistency. This, again, is a charge which no one can attempt to deny, and which, we may add, no one need have attempted to prove. It is understood by every one who reads the *Essay.* But we would ask, why is the *Essay on Man* still read, when many a volume of the same age, of the same shallow metaphysics, is forgotten ? It is much to be lamented that Pope attempted philosophy. He was very ignorant; ignorant of everything except the art of versification. Of philosophy he knew nothing beyond the name. In 1739, he told Warburton he had never read a line of Leibnitz, nor knew there was such a term as 'pre-established harmony,' till he saw it in Crousaz's review of himself. It were to be wished that he had always kept to what he calls 'ethical epistles, in the Horatian way,' and had never written either a *Dunciad* or an *Essay on Man.* In the selection of his subject, he was determined against the bent of his own genius by the direction in which the curiosity of his reading public happened to be running. His ambition as a poet led him beyond his powers. Unless he was to be content to be the poet of social life, and to be read only by 'the town,' he must apply himself to the larger argument which was then absorbing the attention of all serious minds. He had no interest in the subject. Though a great reader, 'he only skimmed

literature to pick up sentiments that could be versified, and to learn attractive forms of composition.' He quarried his stone anywhere. But what he was engaged in building was a beautifully contrived and adorned piece of verse, not a philosophical system. The want of reflection his works discover 'was the fault of an intellect unconscious of its weakness. To him the disjointed bits of philosophy presented no gaps. He had no conception of philosophical thought, no glimmer of the combination of philosophical ideas into an integral design.' These are Mr. Elwin's words, and we unhesitatingly subscribe to their truth. But surely they are incompatible with Mr. Elwin's own theory, that Pope was engaged in a conspiracy with Bolingbroke to propagate Bolingbroke's system of 'irreligious metaphysics.'

3. Lastly, Mr. Elwin affirms that Pope had renounced Christianity and professed Deism. The evidence for this, he says, comes to us from various independent sources. Chesterfield said so, and Mrs. Mallett told General Grimouard so. Lord Stanhope thinks the passage a spurious interpolation in Chesterfield's character of Pope; but be this as it may, we have better evidence as to Pope's religious sentiments than either Chesterfield's statement or what Mrs. Mallett told General Grimouard. It would probably have been in vain to have alleged to Mr. Croker, whose sensitiveness to religious truth is apparent from his notes to Lord Hervey's *Memoirs*, that Pope was a Catholic, that he persisted in adhering to his church in spite of every temptation to leave it, and that he not only received absolution, but that the priest who discharged the last office came out from the dying man penetrated to the last degree with the state of mind in which he found his penitent—resigned, and wrapt up in the love of God and man. It could so easily be replied that this was only a crowning act of hypocrisy, not uncommon with deists. We are sorry to find even Mr. Elwin sneering at Pope's

adherence to Catholicism, as not proceeding from conscientious motives, but from the wish to spare his mother's
feelings.   We are content to refer any reader, less pre-
judiced than our antipathetic editor, to Pope's reply to
Atterbury, above cited, one of the few straightforward and
genuine letters to be found in Pope's correspondence.
But we decline to contest the point of Pope's private
religious sentiments *apropos* of the *Essay on Man*, because
it is irrelevant; and secondly, because no one can handle
the Georgian phase of thought who sets out with assuming, as Mr. Elwin does, that there was a hard line between
those who renounced Christianity and those who did not.
The only question we raise here is, Was the *Essay on
Man* written to abet deism?   The answer to this question
is very simple.   It was not.   As it stands it does not, as we
have seen, promulgate any system of belief.   Mr. Elwin
tells us that Pope 'understood little beyond the separate
thoughts, and was insensible to the want of coherence,
consistency, and purpose.'   Crousaz says he knew persons
who were persuaded that Pope had tacked together a
number of fragments he had composed at various times,
before he had the idea of an *Essay*, which was a contrivance to work up his collection of odds and ends.   But
the question touches not only what was actually effected
by the poem, but what was intended to be effected.   It is
as certain, in our belief, as anything about human intentions can be, that Pope had no notion of writing against
revealed religion.   But for the dust and confusion in
which the present editor has enveloped the subject, we
should never have thought it possible that this theory
would have been again propounded.   Mr. Elwin has
revived the buried calumnies of Crousaz, and supported
them by a tissue of argument woven from a knowledge of
the partly-printed remains which Crousaz could not
possess.   The *Essay* is not a system at all.   But it is
certainly not a system of deism, because that term

connotes along with natural religion a negation of the truth or reality of the Christian revelation. But rational theism stands on its own basis; nay, it is only then rationally expounded when its evidence is set forth independent of the republication of it in Christianity, as it is set forth in the first part of Butler's *Analogy.* This much Pope did understand, and he left out, accordingly, by the judicious advice of Berkeley, an invocation which he had prepared to the Saviour. But though confining its scope scrupulously within the limits of natural religion, the *Essay* is not a treatise which even professes to be co-extensive with the whole of natural religion, through all its doctrines. It is named an *Essay on Man.* But the title imperfectly describes its contents. It is less a treatise on man than on the moral order of the world, of which man is a part. It is not a theistic system, but a Theodicée. It is only by a circuitous ingenuity of circumstantial reasoning that the preposterous thesis can be maintained, that the poem is a shaft levelled by Bolingbroke against Christianity. There is not in the whole poem a single line of such import, or the least savour of an *animus* against revelation. If it is against anything, it is against a kind of Manichean reasoning, such as was strongly pushed, even current at the time, founded on the prevalence of evil in the world. We must regret that Pope was not more competent to deal with his subject; but that he meant to be on the side of natural religion is sufficiently evident from his eagerness to be defended by Warburton. When Warburton first read the *Essay* in the country, he expressed great dissatisfaction at its doctrines. But when he came to know the author personally, he saw that the intention had been good, however lame the performance. Pope, who had never contemplated metaphysical heterodoxy, and had meant nothing but embroidery, was quite willing to have principles which he had imperfectly comprehended explained by a commentary which was even less intelligible, but which said, what was true, that he had meant orthodoxy.

To what Mr. Elwin has said of Warburton's commentary, we can make no objection. But he has sadly laid himself open to a *tu quoque* retort, by reproducing against Pope the same strained interpretation, the same imputation of meaning never meant, and the same inconclusive prosing on moral problems, which he objects to in Warburton. But Mr. Elwin's special interpretations in detail are not the grounds of his general assertion that the poem contains Bolingbroke's infidelity, but the general theory of the infidelity is the justification for forcing upon the passage the worse sense. It reminds us of Bentley's proceeding with the text of Milton. Bentley first created a fictitious editor, who had corrected the poem for the blind author. Having set up this imaginary personage, he could attribute to his forgery every word or line which he wished to correct. Mr. Elwin sets up the hypothesis of an antichristian conspiracy, and deduces from it the meaning of particular passages. Without the blinding influence of an *a priori* hypothesis, it would be impossible that so judicious and clear-headed a critic could have allowed himself to wrest the sense in the way he does, not once, but again and again.

To take an instance. Pope had said in an exquisite passage, which has fixed itself in the memory of every classical scholar—

> Scarfs, garters, gold, amuse his riper stage,
> And beads and prayer-books are the toys of age.

The drift of the whole paragraph, as of the corresponding passage in Horace, is, we should have thought, obvious enough. It puts in a striking light the emptiness of human pursuit, by putting it on a par with the eagerness of children in their play. The 'beads and prayer-books' point to the folly of devoteeism, a phenomenon common in Pope's time, though more common in France than in England, among women of fashion, when grown too old for pleasure. Will it be believed that Mr. Elwin extorts from this line an intention of an infidel to degrade and ridicule religious aspirations? Had Mr. Elwin pointed to parallel but more severe passages in the religious Boileau, or said that the comparison was so common in satire as to be even trite, though never so well expressed, the note would have been in place.

Pope, in dwelling, as nearly all moralists have done, on the trifling amount of human acquisitions in science, lets fall the following tolerably harmless couplet—

> Then, see how little the remaining sum,
> Which served the past and must the times to come.

Upon this Pope is seriously taken to task by Mr. Elwin, for depreciating physical science. He observes that 'there was one scientific region, which was destined to unlimited extension, and of which it was not correct to say that a little sum must serve the future, as it had served the past.' The spirit of contradiction can hardly be carried further than this. Yet it can be. For not satisfied with refuting what Pope has said, Mr. Elwin, on more than one occasion, refutes what Pope did not say, because he might have said it. Pope had expunged a couplet in the later edition. Mr. Elwin quotes the suppressed lines in the note, and then enjoys the satisfaction of refuting them. But indeed the passion for refutation extends beyond Pope. Mr. Elwin confutes Statius for ascribing the attitude of reluctance—'indignata'—to the heifer conducted by Mithras. On another occasion Pope is scolded for condemning as absurd something which was not absurd. In the first draft of the Pastorals, Pope had placed 'wolves' in his forest, but left them out in the revision, because 'of the absurdity of introducing wolves into England.' He is told he is wrong in his reason for the omission. For wolves were not extinct in the reign of Edward I, and the golden age, the time of the Pastorals, must have been previous to that date.

To recur to a more serious charge—

> If the great end be human happiness,
> Then nature deviates, and can man do less? &c.

Mr. Elwin's remarks on this very forcible passage imply that he takes the words, 'can man do less,' as an invitation to man not to do less than deviate from the moral order.   But surely it is plain that their meaning is that we are not to be surprised if man does the same.   If this is to 'justify the ways of wicked men,' as Mr. Elwin says, then any form of predestinarianism is an equal justification.   We should, indeed, be glad to have from Mr. Elwin's pen, on any other occasion than an edition of Pope, a refutation of the proposition that the Lord 'hath created all things for himself, even the wicked for the day of evil.'   Pending this refutation, we may be satisfied with the fact that the religious predestinarian, as well as the philosophical necessitarian, have always maintained that their systems are reconcilable with moral responsibility. Mr. Elwin must have recollected this fact, which lies on the surface of the history of morals, if his eagerness to find fault with Pope had not suspended the faculty of memory.

With such a model before him as Gilbert Wakefield's notes, it seems strange that Mr. Elwin should have committed the error of burying his author under a pile of monotonous railing and contumely.   Our criticism has still much to learn even from the French.   Whether we praise or whether we blame, we must do it grossly. Even where Mr. Elwin is right, a just taste must be offended by the savageness of his expressions.   But, right or wrong, he must be insulting his foe, and his foe is the text he is editing.   Pope's dunces are now at last avenged for the malignant atrocity with which they were treated in *The Dunciad.* The personal passions of Pope's age are revived in Mr. Elwin's notes, but the victim now is Pope himself. Such is the heat of the onset that Pope cannot apply a word or a metaphor without contradiction or insult. E. g. Pope speaks of the insect world as—

> The green myriads in the peopled grass.

Upon this he is insultingly told that 'a very little observation would have told him that "green" is not the prevailing hue' of insects. Pope's ignorance of natural objects was very great; yet even he did not mean to assert that all insects were 'green.' If Mr. Elwin had not been already in a rage, he must have recollected that poetry is not prose, and that nothing is commoner in classical poetry than transference of epithet. In Propertius Mr. Elwin himself, no doubt, admires the line—
'Et modo formosis incumbens nescius undis;' and does not object to Horace saying, 'Flebis in solo levis angiportu;' nor would he be prepared to deny to Gray his 'odorous shade,' his 'sickly dews,' and his 'poetic mountain.' After his remark that most insects are not green, we are rather surprised that Mr. Elwin allows—

> No craving void left aching in the breast,

to pass without rebuke. Surely Pope ought to have been told upon this occasion that a 'void' cannot 'ache.'

Though Pope deals largely in innuendo, it is innuendo of the palpable kind. He is afraid of having his hits missed, and seldom slides into one of those imperceptible suggestions which make the refined humour of Fielding or Miss Austen. Perhaps he was right in trusting little to the reader's sagacity. One such stroke of humour, however, he has put into the mouth of 'the Wife of Bath.'

> In all these *trials* I have borne a part.

Her *trials* were of the nature of Henry VIII's 'matrimonial infelicities.' Mr. Elwin seriously takes Pope to task because it was not her own matrimonial woes, which had been slight enough, which she was about to set forth, but the miseries of those whom it was her boast to have worried into obedience to her will.

It is not the least evil of the theological polemic which Mr. Elwin carries on, that besides being out of place itself, it displaces the legitimate illustrations which a reader of Pope demands. We have much of theology of a dubious character, and we have no attempt to track Pope's sources. Mr. Elwin, in two volumes, has hardly added a dozen references to those which Warton and Wakefield had collected. A scholar like Mr. Elwin might have been expected to bring more classical reading to bear. Perhaps he might say that Pope did not read the Greek poets in the original. Even if this were the case, there still remain the Latin poets, of whom, old and new, Pope was a diligent reader.

But to all the minutiae of illustration and criticism, Mr. Elwin's attitude is one of an indifference somewhat contemptuous. We have alluded to his disregard of the contemporary orthography in the text. And his rough and ready mode of passing by difficulties does not leave a curious reader in a satisfied state of mind. When Pope talks of Zoroaster as a conjuror, we don't want to have Pope refuted out of Smith's Dictionary, but we should like to know the parentage of that false rendering of the term *magian,* and how far it was current in Pope's time. On the line, 'Favour'd man by touch ethereal slain,' Pope writes in a note: 'Several of the ancients, and many of the orientals since, esteemed those who were struck by lightning as sacred persons, and the particular favourites of heaven.' It has puzzled scholars to divine where Pope got the notion that death by lightning was a mark of heaven's favour, seeing that the uniform tenor of classical tradition is to regard it as an effect of divine vengeance. Mr. Elwin makes no difficulty. 'Superstitions,' he says, 'often clash. Plutarch mentions that persons struck with lightning were held in honour.' The difficulty consists, not in finding 'clashing superstitions,' but that Pope should have found an authority for a statement so direct and categorical, which we cannot find. We will undertake to say he did not find it in Plutarch. It is hazardous to deny that any passage is to be found in a Greek author, whose works run to some dozen volumes, yet we will venture to challenge Mr. Elwin to produce any words of Plutarch, to the effect he mentions. The words which Mr. Elwin ascribes to Plutarch are, indeed, to be found in a Greek writer of a later date than Plutarch. But, besides the improbability of Pope having read Artemidorus's *Oneirocriticon*, even in Rigaltius's Latin version, the words there found would not authorize Pope's direct assertion that the thunderstruck were thought to be heaven's favourites. Mr. Elwin's memory may have confused the words of Artemidorus with a passage in Plutarch [1], which, however, affirms the received belief, and not Pope's fancy. 'In many parts of the world,' says the speaker in Plutarch, 'the bodies of those killed by lightning are surrounded by a fence, and left, where they lay, unburied'; burial not being thought allowable for the enemy of heaven.

This kind of research consumes a great deal of time. But Mr. Elwin has shown, at least that, as an editor, he will spare no pains. All that we venture to ask for is, that instead of spending his time in abusing his author, he would try the more useful, though more difficult, plan of explaining and illustrating him.

[1] *Conviv. Serm.*, IV. 2. p. 665. [III, part 2, p. 721 (Wyttenbach), Plutarch says further that the bodies were untouched by decay. Perhaps this notion gave rise to the error.]

XXI.

HISTORY OF CIVILIZATION IN ENGLAND[1].

———•———

[*Westminster Review*, 1857.]

THIS volume is certainly the most important work of
the season ; and it is perhaps the most comprehensive
contribution to philosophical history that has ever been
attempted in the English language. It is full of thought
and original observation ; but it is no speculative creation
of a brilliant theorist. It is learned in the only true sense
of the word. A mere glance at the matter accumulated in
the notes will show the labour and reading which it has
cost to quarry the materials. These are as judiciously
selected as they have been widely sought, and make the
volume, besides its proper merits, a most instructive
repertory of facts. The style of the text is clear, and
always easily followed. It is too diffuse, and a little
cumbrous ; but it is never tedious.

This first volume carries us no further than the end of
the first part of the General Introduction. It is an exposition of general principles, a survey of preliminary
matters, and an investigation in outline of the nature of
civilization in France. This is to be followed up in
a second volume with a similar summary of the civilizations of Germany, America, Scotland, and Spain, each of
which presents a different type of intellectual development.

[1] *History of Civilization in England.* By HENRY THOMAS BUCKLE. Volume I.
London : J. W. Parker. 1857.

Westminster Review, 1857.]

Then the causes of this diversity will be generalized, and thus we shall obtain certain principles, as fundamental laws of European thought. Having arrived at these in possibly a third volume, we may then enter upon the work itself, which is to apply these fundamental laws to the history of our own country, and to 'work out by their aid the epochs through which we have successively passed, fix the basis of our present civilization, and indicate the path of our future progress.' The reader, seeing in prospect the abundant supply of intellectual food which is thus being prepared for him, may be disposed—such is the ingratitude of mankind—to feel less regret than he ought at the announcement, that the author has abandoned his original intention of writing the history of *general* civilization. He was induced to limit himself to the narrower field, and to be content with the history of a single country, not only by the vast proportions of the subject, but by the state in which he found the materials he had occasion to use. The general historian, of course, must look to the special historians for the first collection of the facts which his master-hand is to elaborate. But the work of history-writing has been mostly performed by inferior men, who have not known what was worth recording and what was not. The important facts have been neglected, the unimportant ones preserved. Hence the philosophic historian finds nothing ready to his hand. He must be the mason as well as the architect; and make his own bricks as well as lay them. The drudgery of compiling the facts on which his generalizations have to be based is so vast, that the most protracted industry will not suffice to enable any one to comprehend adequately even a couple of centuries of the human annals. He selects the History of England in preference to that of any other country, not because it is his own, but because its progress has been the most normal. The English development has been least disturbed by foreign agency. The importance

of a national history in this view depends, not upon the
splendour of the exploits it has to show, but upon the
degree to which its events are due to causes springing out
of itself. In England we have been less affected than
other nations by the two main sources of interference, viz.
the authority of government and the influence of foreigners.
We have borrowed from the French manners, dress,
cookery; we have not borrowed in any of those things
by which the destinies of. nations are permanently altered.
On the other hand, the French have copied many of our
political institutions; are treading in our steps, at a
humble distance, in our financial and commercial experience; and the most important event in French history,
the Revolution of '89, was mainly instigated by men who
had learned their philosophy and principles in England.
If France cannot claim to be the representative country,
still less can Germany. In Germany we see an unhealthy
tripartite division : (1) the Governments ; (2) the Intellectual
Class; (3) the People. The governments exclusive,
narrow-minded, inquisitorial, meddlesome; the small intellectual class, possessing a compass of knowledge, and
a breadth of thought, which make it lead the speculative
intellect of the world; the people more superstitious,
more really unfit for political power, than the inhabitants
of England. This divergence of interests between classes
is due to the fact, that the intellectual stimulus of Germany
was a stimulus administered from without. They received
their impulse from their contact with French intellect
imported wholesale by the great Frederick. Hence the
highest intellects in Germany have so far outstripped the
progress of the mass of their fellow-countrymen, that they
have absolutely no influence upon them. Their great
authors write a dialect of philosophical slang, which is
unintelligible to their own lower classes ; and they address
themselves, in fact, not to their country, but to each other.
The United States will not serve as the illustrative

country; its history has been too short, its physical condition so extraordinary, and its institutions so largely adaptations from Europe. In America, too, cultivation exists in a very different state of diffusion from that which we notice in Germany. In Germany, the speculative classes and the practical classes are entirely disunited. In America, they are altogether fused. In Germany, speculation has shot far ahead of practice; in America, theoretical science of any kind receives little attention. The stock of American knowledge is small, but it is the common property of the whole nation; the stock of German knowledge is immense, but it is in very few hands. Thus Germany is unfitted for our purpose by a serious failure in the diffusion of knowledge; America by a deficiency in its amount.

These are the considerations that have determined the author to write the history of his own country, in preference to that of any other.

But though England be taken as the country whose development has been most regular and normal, there are important intellectual peculiarities which cannot be found sufficiently exemplified in English civilization. These, therefore, will be most conveniently studied in the history of some one or other foreign country, and then applied analogously to England. The author will therefore track the phenomenon of the accumulation of knowledge in Germany; that of its diffusion in America. Of government interference he will select France as the type; Spain will afford an example of the influence of superstition. He considers the deductive habit of mind to be an intellectual peculiarity of such great social importance as to require to be ranked among the leading influences. And as the prevailing character of English science is empirical, he selects Scotland, with its strikingly inquisitive and innovating literature in broad contrast with the vulgar bigotry of its middle and lower classes, as the model in which to study the effects of the deductive spirit. These partial inquiries are to form so many separate historical studies, introductory to the history of England.

The choice made, of the history of England, is one to which no objection will be taken, whatever we may think of the reasons assigned for it. The reasons sustain a character of symmetry and exterior completeness, rather than of solid force. Has England had this normal, or nearly normal, development rather than France? Our insular position has excluded foreign influence. Good. But the same insulation has cut us off from the general march of Europe—from the steady and uniform, as well as from the disturbing, forces. Our institutions, customs, national ideas, are, in many respects, highly eccentric and exceptional. The Englishman's manners are typical of his country. See our worthy countryman when he is travelling on the Continent. How strange, and awkward, and unconformable he is! What foreigners call our ' pride,' is only the result of ignorance and *gaucherie*. We have not been to the great school of the world, and learnt there how to behave. We feel this, and try to carry it off by swell and swagger. No one would select the English milord's manner as an average specimen of that of the European gentleman. We should have as little thought of finding in our British institutions—institutions so heterogeneous, discordant, and self-contradictory, as to have nothing in common but the fact of co-existence on English soil—an approach to a condition of normal and inherent development. In one department of progress the English development has indeed been complete, regular, and from within. In commerce and manufactures, England may be said to have conducted, on behalf of the world, but at her own risks and perils, the one great commercial experiment that has yet been made. Our practice has been so extended and diversified, that from it

alone, with but little reference to that of the other
trading nations of antiquity, or of modern times, the
laws of economics have been inferred, and a new science
constructed on a solid and indisputable basis. In the
science of politics, English history offers a memorable and
instructive, but almost unique, case for analysis. But
the economical phenomena of England are of a permanent
and universal type. The conditions and laws of exchange
may be understood and proved, from our commercial
history alone ; and in our present practice alone can they
be seen fully and freely exemplified. As, then, Mr.
Buckle proposes Germany as the case in which he
will study what he calls the laws of the accumulation
of knowledge, or Spanish history, as that in which
he will trace the effects of the reign of superstition,
so he might fairly have held up Great Britain as the
most perfect example of industrial and commercial
phenomena. But our vast industrial system, while,
taken by itself, it yields to science its best and simplest
data, becomes itself a disturbing momentum to the
functions of that body politic of which it forms a part. In
other words, the rapid and abnormal growth of our
manufacturing interests within the last hundred years
has revolutionized the social aspect of our country,
has distanced precedent, created an entirely new class
of experiences, and complicated our social fabric with
new and unknown agencies to an extent hitherto without
parallel. If what is sought is a fair average specimen
of European progress, everything appears to us to point
to France as the country in whose fortunes it is to
be found. The one marking exceptional element in
French progress has been the retarding force of the
central government. But against this must be set the
following considerations :—First, France has only shared
this in common with the other great continental nations.
Secondly, notwithstanding some appearances to the

contrary, it has suffered from this Conservative spirit very much less than any other continental people, and scarcely more than ourselves. For that retrogressive influence which in France flows from centralized power through an organized system of *bureaux*, is exerted in England quite as effectually through the unwholesome intellectual tone of the clerical and governing classes. Lastly, the drag which has throughout and unceasingly acted on *our* momentum, has at several epochs been entirely thrown off in France. Our efforts at freedom have been regular: theirs have been convulsionary. We have had steady reform: they, periodic revolution. The sum total of the national sentiment for progress, if not of its solid institutions, may be taken as nearly equal. We are not sure that the amount of illiberality pervading public opinion in England is not more powerful for evil, than the amount of repression exerted over public opinion in France. To all this may be added, that the French have really borrowed from others as little as any people. We are surprised to find Mr. Buckle say that the French have adopted our political institutions (p. 215). He also adopts in its full extent the popular view of the influence of English thought on the French mind, as preparing the explosion of '89. This view, repeated by Villemain, and a hundred writers, has a certain superficial truth. But, in spite of the array of witnesses with which (pp. 657-667) Mr. Buckle overwhelms and intimidates us, we venture to think that the *Anglomanie* of Voltaire's youth was an exterior symptom—at best, a sympathy, and not a discipleship. Questions of priority should not be discussed in the spirit of Arago's *éloges*. To the philosopher it can be of no consequence whether his own country led or followed on any particular occasion—took the first, or only the second, step in some great progressive movement. But in tracing the transmission of ideas, it is of the utmost importance to observe the distinction between the act of origination and the function of disseminating and popularizing. Now, if we take the philosophical and religious literature of England for the earlier half of the eighteenth century, we shall find upon it the stamp of a second-hand and derivative character. The writings of the English Deists—Shaftesbury, Chubb, Toland, and Woolston—have that sort of originality which proceeds from ignorance of what has been thought or written. The speculative impulse came from the Continent: from two or three leading minds—from Descartes, Spinosa, and Bayle. In England it obtained notoriety, publicity, and diffusion. But when we recollect the wide circulation of the periodicals edited by Le Clerc, in the French language, not to cite any other instances, we shall see that a sceptical spirit, such as that which broke out in Huet's celebrated *Traité de la Foiblesse*, was, before the death of Louis XIV, already naturalized in France. When the French travellers found their way to England, and Frenchmen began to read English books, they recognised with pleasure a tone and spirit with which their own was already in unison. The only difference was, that what was contraband with them was legitimate with us. What they saw in us with such admiration and surprise was, not the novelty of our ideas, but our power of expressing them. 'Que j'aime la hardiesse Anglaise! que j'aime les gens qui disent ce qu'ils pensent!' is Voltaire's expressive exclamation.

But, though obliged to dissent from Mr. Buckle's reasons for his selection of English History as his theme, we may express the highest satisfaction at the selection itself. Besides the natural and obvious wish to secure so much power and so much industry for the service of our own neglected history, there is another consideration, which deserves to be stated. A man who can deal with history at all, can deal best with that of his own country.

A foreigner has to consume labour and time in arriving slowly at a comprehension of minor characteristics, which to the native had been familiar from childhood. The disadvantage hereby incurred is not to be measured by the trivial blunders which he might make. When we write in a foreign language, it is not the slight solecisms in expression which weaken our style—not the few false notes, but a general want of power over the instrument on which we play. In this very circumstance lies, to speculative minds, the peculiar attraction of the history of other countries. Knowing their affairs only, or chiefly, from books, the understanding is not baffled by the complexity and contradictoriness of the phenomena. We can turn the history of a foreign people into doctrine, and reduce it to general theorems, with a rapidity and undoubtingness which fail us when we attempt our own. Baron Bülow, on his return to Prussia, said, in reply to some one who asked him what opinion he had formed of the English during his long sojourn among them—'At the end of my first three weeks I was quite ready to write a book on England; at the end of three months, I found that the task would be more difficult; now that I have been there three years, I feel that it is impossible.' A mind like Mr. Buckle's, facile to the seductions of complete and systematized views, was likely to have yielded to the attractions of foreign history, as more pliant to receive the yoke of his 'laws' than our own. We rejoice to have so ingenious and forcible a theorist self-condemned to frame his inductions in a field where it is in our power to keep him within bounds by confronting him with facts.

We proceed to present a summary of the method which the author proposes to apply to the History of England.

A person undertaking to describe the past transactions of men, must necessarily hold one of three possible views as to the cause or origin of those actions :—

Westminster Review, 1857.]

(1) Human actions, unlike material changes, obey no fixed laws, but are the result of a peculiar force in man called free-will. This freedom, itself the cause of all actions, is caused by none, but is an ultimate fact, admitting of no further reference. (2) Every event is linked to its antecedent by an inevitable connexion, absolutely pre-ordained from the beginning by the Will of the Supreme Being. (3) The actions of men have the same uniformity of connexion which physical events have, and no other; and the law, or laws, of these uniformities can be inductively ascertained in the same way as the laws of the material world.

The two former hypotheses the author sets aside, and adopts the last. The two first hypotheses are unproved. Though the third is still only an hypothesis, it is rendered highly probable by the general analogy of all knowledge, and the constant tendency of discovery to reduce to order classes of facts, once thought irregular and unpredictable. As all the antecedents of human action are either in the mind, or out of it, all the changes of which history is full must be the fruit of a double action—an action of External Nature upon the Mind, and an action of the Mind upon External Phenomena. These are the materials from which alone a philosophical history can be constructed.

On this distinction we may build the first grand division of History. All the civilizations on record will fall into one of two classes. (1) Those where the external world has influenced man more than man has influenced it. (2) Those where the reverse has been the case, and man has subdued nature. This division will nearly coincide with that obvious division which geography suggests, into (1) Civilizations external to Europe; (2) European Civilization.

In studying the first division, or the Civilizations out of Europe, we must, then, begin with a consideration of the physical agents by which the human race is most powerfully influenced. These are, chiefly—climate, food, soil, and a fourth influence, to which the name of the general aspect of nature may be given. Mr. Buckle has not overlooked *race*, but has deliberately excluded it. This arbitrary exclusion of so important an influence on the formation of character is an instance, in the outset, of that determination to purchase symmetry at the cost of completeness, which we notice throughout the Introduction. When we can leave out what we don't like, we can demonstrate most things.

Climate, Food, and Soil, are agencies which operate in connexion, and must therefore be considered together. The first result of these three combined agents is the accumulation of wealth: the soil regulating the returns made to any given amount of labour; the climate determining the regularity and constancy of the labour itself. The second result is the distribution of wealth; and this is chiefly affected by the remaining agent, or the food of the people. In warm and moist climates it is more plentiful, more cheap, and goes further than in temperate climates. Hence population is stimulated, and consequently wages are low. Low wages mean an unequal distribution of wealth, and unequal distribution of wealth means an unequal division of political power, i.e. an oppression of the mass of the population by a small and superior class.

We have but to turn to Hindostan, and there we shall see a perfect illustration, verifying in the most minute particulars the conclusion at which we have thus arrived *a priori*. In India, where the most general food of the people has been from the earliest period, rice— the most nutritive of the cerealia, containing a very large proportion of oxidizable food, and which yields to the labourer an average return of at least sixty-fold,—we find the upper classes enormously rich, the lower classes universally poor. An immense majority of the people, broken by incessant labour and oppression, pinched by the most galling poverty, have always remained in a state of physical debasement, crouching in abject submission beneath their masters. And this state of things we find in the oldest records—records 2000 or even 3000 years old, taking Elphinstone's date for *The Institutes of Manu.* Without going through the collateral confirmation which the author draws from the history of Egypt, from that of Central America, Mexico, Peru, and Brazil, we may accept the following general summary. In such countries—

Slavery, abject, eternal slavery, was the natural state of the great body of the people; it was the state to which they were doomed by physical laws impossible to resist. The energy of those laws is so invincible, that, wherever they have come into play, they have kept the productive classes in perpetual subjection. There is no instance on record of any tropical country in which wealth having been extensively accumulated, the people have escaped their fate; no instance in which the heat of the climate has not caused an abundance of food, and the abundance of food caused an unequal distribution, first of wealth, and then of political and social power. Among nations subjected to these conditions the people have counted for nothing; they have had no voice in the management of the state, no control over the wealth their own industry created. Their only business has been to labour; their only duty to obey. Thus there have been generated among them those habits of tame and servile submission by which, as we know from history, they have always been characterised. For it is an undoubted fact, that their annals furnish no instance of their having turned upon their rulers, no war of classes, no popular insurrections, not even one great popular conspiracy. In those rich and fertile countries there have been many changes, but all of them have been from above, not from below. The democratic element has been altogether wanting. There have been in abundance wars of kings, and wars of dynasties. There have been revolutions in the government, revolutions in the palace, revolutions on the throne; but no revolutions among the people, no mitigation of that hard lot which nature, rather than man, assigned to them. (p. 73.)

From the effects of Food, Climate, and Soil, we pass to

consider that other class of influences, to which the author gives the name of *The Aspects of Nature.* We find that in all the civilizations exterior to Europe, the mind of man has been powerfully affected by those sublime and terrible phenomena which tropical or juxta-tropical regions present. Both the fixed and permanent phenomena—such as the scale of mountains, rivers, forests, deserts,—and the occasional—such as earthquakes, tornados, hurricanes, pestilences,—make the external world much more formidable than it is within the temperate zone. Man is awed and crushed in the presence of the forces of nature ; the imagination is stimulated, and, as a consequence, the understanding is discouraged. Instead of investigating the natural causes of these overwhelming phenomena, the people who live among them and suffer from them are ever ready to imagine supernatural causes for them. The phenomenon presenting itself in the shape of a threatening danger, the ready impulse of the man is to endeavour to pacify by worship his gigantic foe. The destructive agencies become deities : where the ignorance is extreme, the tiger, the serpent, or the bear is worshipped ; where the ignorance is less, the earthquake or the plague is regarded as a manifestation of the divine displeasure. A spirit of reverence prevails among the people ; a mythological theory of nature is constructed, fenced round by prejudice, and becomes a new obstacle in the way of the inquisitive action of the understanding. Here again we find in the literature of India the fullest illustration of our deductively ascertained laws. In the first place we have the preponderance in it of verse over prose. The Sanscrit can show metres more numerous and more complicated than have ever been possessed by any European languages. In the contents again of that literature, we may almost say that reason is set at defiance, and that imagination, luxuriant even to disease, runs riot. An exaggerated preference for antiquity not only tramples upon the present, but has rendered all history of the past impossible. Indian history is fiction. All nations have been ready to imagine a golden age, a time when man was innocent, fed without labour, was ten feet high, and still young at the age of 100. But the ideas of European nations on this primeval state are tame and rational when compared with those which pervade Hindu literature :—

On this, as on every subject, the imagination of the Hindus distanced all competition. Thus, among an immense number of similar facts, we find it recorded that in ancient times the duration of the life of common men was 80,000 years, and that holy men lived to be upwards of 100,000. Some died a little sooner, others a little later ; but in the most flourishing period of antiquity, if we take all classes together, 100,000 years was the average. Of one king, whose name was Gudhishther, it is casually mentioned that he reigned 27,000 years ; while another, called Alarka, reigned 66,000. They were cut off in their prime, since there are several instances of the early poets living to be about half a million. But the most remarkable case is that of a very shining character in Indian history, who united in his single person the functions of a king and a saint. This eminent man lived in a pure and virtuous age, and his days were indeed long in the land, since, when he was made king he was 2,000,000 years old ; he then reigned 4,300,000 years ; having done which he resigned his empire, and lingered on for 100,000 years more. (p. 123.)

We may illustrate this effect of external nature in intimidating the will and subjugating the understanding by contrasting Hindostan with Greece. In Greece the aspects of nature are small and feeble. Of narrow limits, easier access, temperate climate, its highest mountains nowhere attaining the limits of perpetual snow, without one navigable river,—nature in Greece offers neither danger nor mystery. Here man asserted his supremacy. The Greek gods were human. In Greece we for the first time meet with hero-worship. Here the understanding gradually awoke to a sense of its own power, and the imagination was proportionably confined within limits. In this balance of the faculties consists the grand preeminence of Greek literature and art, the inquiring and sceptical powers of the intellect being freely developed, without destroying the reverential and poetic instinct of the imagination.

So much on the civilizations exterior to Europe, or those in which the destinies of man are mainly governed by agents external to himself. We have now to follow the author into Europe, where we find a civilization whose momentum is due to the skill and energy of man. The laws of this moving force must therefore be sought in the laws of the human mind, which, when ascertained, will be the basis of the history of Europe. Now mental laws are either moral or intellectual. But the progress of society has been determined exclusively by its intellectual acquisitions; intellectual truth being in its very essence traditive and progressive, while good feelings and good deeds die with the individual. The degree of civilization attained by any country depends on the amount, the direction, and the diffusion of the knowledge it possesses. The actions of individuals are greatly affected by feeling and passion; but these being antagonistic to the passions and feelings of other individuals, are balanced by them. The effect therefore of passion, good or bad, of vice as well as virtue, is, in the great average of human affairs, nowhere to be seen; and the totality of human actions is ultimately governed by the totality of human knowledge The business therefore of the philosophical historian will be nothing more or less than that of tracing the progress of knowledge; not indeed the whole of knowledge, but so much of it as is causative of human conduct. Before entering on the wide field of such a history, wide even for a single country, there are three topics of vast importance, which it is necessary to dispose of. For, in the general opinion, the prime movers of human affairs are, not knowledge properly so called, but Government, Religion, and Literature.

Westminster Review, 1857.]

1. The belief that Government is one of the principal influences by which the course of affairs is impelled or guided is so widely spread, that we may almost say that all our histories have been written on this assumption. This fallacy, for it is nothing more, is one we should have thought Mr. Buckle would have expatiated in refuting. But he only brings forward some of the more obvious illustrations of the principle, that the government of any country whatsoever always follows, never leads. The measures adopted by rulers are the results of social progress, not the cause. The only difference between governments absolute or constitutional lies in the greater or less remoteness which the ideas on which they rest bear to the ideas prevalent in the country. In constitutional states, as the government must always give effect to the opinions of the majority, and as the majority, even in the freest countries, will always be behind the place reached by the enlightened minority, legislative measures will be a little in arrear of the best knowledge of the day. In despotic countries, the measures of administration may be inspired either by the most retrograde, or by the most advanced party in the state, without reference to the numerical strength of such party; but, in either case, it is inspiration, not origination. Looking at the history of Europe in particular, it is so far from being true that its civilization is due to its rulers, that they have, in every country, been its most steady and persistent opponents. In England, a history of English legislation would be a history of the efforts of our governing classes to prevent progress. Every European government may be said to have legislated against commerce. It has been said by Blanqui, that if it had not been for smuggling, trade must have perished under the Prohibitive System. To the mischievous effects of government interference with commerce must be added, the equally mischievous

consequences of a protective policy applied to opinion. Every government thinks it a part of its duty to legalize certain religious and political opinions, and to prohibit others. Such interference not only destroys the healthy balance of opinion, and prevents the natural ascendency of truth, but necessarily generates a vast amount of hypocrisy, insincerity, and even perjury.

2. Another very common opinion is, that Religion is a main cause of social improvement. In every manual of history we take up we find it assumed that Christianity has been the great civilizer of modern Europe. This opinion is as unfounded as the other. The religious opinions which prevail at any period are among the symptoms by which the period is marked. Where a reaction changes its religion, it is in consequence of some previous advance in intelligence. No people will ever discover that their religion is bad until their reason tells them so ; but if their knowledge is stationary, the discovery will never be made. The Teutonic hordes adopted Christianity as a consequence of their having first imbibed something of the civilization of the Empire. Herein we see the cause of the almost entire failure of modern missionaries among the heathen. Men of excellent intentions, but of little knowledge, have expected to bring over savage tribes to Christianity by simply communicating to them, in their own language, the Christian doctrines or history. They have even persuaded barbarous communities to make a profession of the Christian faith. But if we confront the sanguine reports of the missionaries with the evidence of general travellers, we find that such profession is only nominal, and that what these ignorant tribes have really adopted is nothing more than the externals.

In the same way, if we trace the history of Christianity from its first introduction into the West, we shall find that it has even varied, from time to time, with the amount of enlightenment possessed by the age. Instead of Christianity enlightening and purifying the barbarous invaders of the Empire, and raising them to its level, they degraded it to theirs. The superstition of Europe, instead of being diminished, was only turned into a fresh channel. For centuries after Christianity had become the religion of Europe it failed to bear its natural fruit. Persons, indeed, observing that at the present time nearly all the more civilized countries are Protestant, and the more uncivilized are Catholic, have, not unnaturally, inferred that this enlightenment is due to Protestantism. They thus overlook the fact that, until the enlightenment had begun, Protestantism was not required. The Reformation was the result of the intellectual advance made in the fifteenth century.

3. The supposed influence of Literature on progress may be shortly disposed of. Literature is simply the form in which the existing opinions of a country are registered. It is palpably a product and measure of the intellectual attainment of a people, not its source. The utility of the most finished literature depends upon the power a people may possess of appropriating its contents. The monks were all along in possession of the literature of Greece and Rome ; but they could not use it. It was pitched at too high a level for them, and they preferred the *Legenda Aurea*. Nay, at all times there are minds which derive no benefit from the most laborious study of the best books. Whole systems of education, that of our schools and colleges, for example, propose for their end the knowledge of books—thus making the end subservient to the means. It is because this is done, that we often find what are called highly educated men, the progress of whose knowledge has been only retarded by the activity of their education,—men whose erudition ministers to their ignorance, and of whom it may be said that the more they have learned the less they know. For

every literature contains something that is true and much that is false, and the effect it produces will depend upon the judgment by which the true is discriminated from the false.

These are the general ideas upon the foundation of which the author proposes to write the History of England. The exposition of principles occupies the first two hundred and sixty-four pages of his first volume; the remainder is taken up with the application of the principles to the course of events in France, and to English History in the way of summary, introductory to the extensive history which is to follow. It has been our wish, in the preceding pages, to lay before the reader, in as condensed a form as possible, the author's leading views. It may now be expected that some attempt should be made to appreciate the value of this new historical method, which announces itself with no little pomp and pretension, and claims to regenerate History.

All philosophic minds have long been feeling the inadequacy of our historical methods. It is the one weak point in the Palace of Truth. In every other science, though there are facts which we cannot combine, laws which still baffle our powers to grasp, and whole regions as yet unexplored, there is none in which we are dissatisfied or doubtful of the methods of investigation we employ. We may not have gone very far in some subjects, as, e. g. Biology, or Electricity; but so far as we have gone, we feel sure of our ground. Very different is the profound distrust we feel of our historical knowledge. Here all is chaos; and the intellectual anarchy is made more apparent by the enormous accumulation of details which modern research has achieved. It is true, there are good histories, and there are bad; the interval between Guizot and Alison is wide; but the silly and the sagacious, the driveller and the philosopher, seem equally helpless when they tread that shifting quicksand called History. The difference between them disappears, or dwindles to that of literary qualification. We read a Grote or a Michelet with the same intellectual gratification which we derive from a superior novel. Our reflective faculty is excited by sympathy with the penetration, the lofty aim, and the generalizing dexterity of the historian to whose guidance we, for the time, have resigned ourselves. We dwell upon his figures, we enjoy the variety and the distinctness of the characters which his tale evolves; but we are not the less conscious that they are beings of his own creation, and that the next enchanter who arises will attach the same names, and ascribe the same fortunes, to a quite different set of spiritual creations. Even those who have no doubt themselves, whose minds are so constituted that they embrace with confidence one of the competing views of European events, are yet disturbed and irritated by the presence of a vast mass of hostile opinion, and look around imploringly for the aid of some scientific method to which appeal may be made, and which shall coerce the dissidents, and silence controversy, as effectually as it is silenced by the onward progress of discovery and physical science.

If scepticism thus undermines narrative history as a source of instruction, the more ambitious philosophic history is set aside with unlimited disdain. In narrative history we recognise a certain approximation to reality, as in a Claude or a Poussin we see that there is a foundation in nature. Thus it comes to pass, that no philosophy is at a greater discredit than the Philosophy of History, while none is more universally and imperatively demanded. The attempts at a general Philosophy of History which have been made, from Montesquieu downwards, are singularly lamentable failures. They contain, as does even the superficial *Esprit des Lois*, valuable detached suggestions; but as attempts to ascertain the general laws of political changes, they are

repudiated by common consent as arbitrary and unsub-
stantial hypotheses.

There is, indeed, one theory of human affairs which,
though no longer received by the more advanced thinkers,
yet exercises over the minds, even of the educated, a very
extensive though occult influence, and which is the
avowed theory of classes whose intellectual development
is limited. This is the theory of General and Special
Providence. The most elaborate and successful statement of this theory is that in the well-known *Universal
History* of Bossuet. Taking for his pattern the historical
books of the Old Testament, in which the fortunes of the
Jewish nation are displayed to us as regulated by their
fidelity to, or rebellion against, the one true God, who
had adopted them as His peculiar people, Bossuet extended the idea to the subsequent history of Christian
Europe. What the Hebrew people are for the whole
period B.C., viz. the point on which the affairs of the
universe are made to turn, that for the period A.D. is the
history of the Orthodox Catholic Church. This is the
consistent and ingenious form in which the doctrine
is embodied by the Roman Catholic Bishop. But in order
to include the history of Protestant countries, the same
doctrine of Providential Government receives, in the
popular apprehension of it, a much wider application.
Not only are the more remarkable casualties and epochal
crises of affairs ascribed to the interposition of the Deity,
but the whole of the ordinary sequence of events is
supposed to be overruled by His controlling Will, in a
way in which the nexus of cause and effect in the physical world is not. The adjustment of the special and the
general interference of Providence varies with each
theorist; nor are speculative difficulties which embarrass
the theory deliberately attempted to be cleared up in any
book which has attained general acceptance. A general
sense of the difficulties of the scheme serves to keep it in

the background. A disinclination to relinquish it altogether maintains it a secret existence. It influences many
more minds than is often suspected, and those, too, much
higher up in the scale of intellect. Yet, as no one, except
the utterly uninstructed, now feels any temptation to refer
physical phenomena to supernatural agency, or rather,
as that agency is now seen to be placed only at the commencement of the whole series, and not at each point
along the line, we might wonder why it is that the hypothesis of supernatural influence has not also been expelled
from history. The answer undoubtedly is, that there
exists no other hypothesis of equal generality. It is a
great mistake to suppose, as is often done, that mere
scepticism has ever overthrown the dominion of any
generally received belief. Improbabilities and difficulties
weaken the influence of an idea ; they oppress, but do not
destroy it. One hypothesis can only be displaced by
another which recommends itself more to the reason and
religious instincts. Revolutions in thought are occasioned
by the conquests of new ideas. And in a healthy state of
the social intellect, no old notion will be supplanted by a
new one, unless the new theory be closer to the facts, be
the result of more correct observation, and based upon
wider experience, than the old theory which it supplants.
All reflecting and religious men have long felt that the
hypothesis of Interferences is not the key to the source of
human events. Even the most unphilosophical minds are
struck with the contradictory applications made of the
One Cause ; the opposite results which can be elicited
from the same premiss. While in the hands of Bossuet,
the theory of a Divine superintendence of the favoured
people, and the Orthodox Church, was saved by its very
exclusiveness and consistency ; but when it was found
that the same theory was equally capable of interpretation,
in their own exclusive favour, by a dozen different Protestant Churches, it fell to pieces by its own universality.

It was merged in the general notions of the subordination
of the Human to the Divine, of man's dependence on God,
and was seen to be a truth so universally applicable, as to
be incapable of serving as the special solution of the
enigma of history.   Were this arbitrary introduction of
Providence into history nothing more than useless for its
professed purpose, it would not need to be discussed.
But it is not innocuous.   The belief that it is, in a
peculiar way, the *religious* view, and that it is treason to
the Almighty to question it, presents a powerful obstacle
in the way of truer and more improving conceptions of the
moral world.   This is not a question of mere theory.   It
is not even a question between the true and the false only,
or one which interests only science and men of letters.   It
is an eminently practical speculation.   It concerns the
method to be pursued in the study of a subject in which
every man has an equal interest.   The material which
makes up history is the same material from which our
every-day experience must be drawn.   Without the illumi-
nation to be drawn from a knowledge of the past, the
soundest common-sense is helpless.   Unless he can
rightly use the lessons of experience, man must remain
always a child ; and a partial or ill-interpreted experience
is worse than none.   That which we seek from history,
and which history can afford us, is a real enlightenment
of the practical judgment ; a wisdom which can embrace
in one comprehensive view the whole of the past history
of mankind, and read aright the lessons it conveys ;
which, keeping ever in view the future, and instructed by
the experience of the past, shall be able with perfect
calmness to rise above and to estimate the present, discern
clearly its wants—what can and what cannot be done with
it.   Such wisdom, based upon knowledge and disciplined
by social morality, shall in its large conclusions be applicable to all the demands of life [1].

[1] See Congreve, *Gibraltar*, p. 45.

It is not, then, as a question of literature, but as the first
condition of practical wisdom, that the interpretation of
history presses itself upon the attention; and a theory
which excludes events from the operation of fixed laws
cannot but be detrimental to the best interests of mankind.
A fatalist, whether Christian or Mohammedan, can learn
no lesson from the past. So far as such men do learn, it
is by being untrue to their own doctrine. Predestination
can teach but one lesson—resignation; Arbitrary Interference can inculcate but one sentiment—the folly of human
wisdom. But if we conceive that the liabilities and
obligations of our position can best be fulfilled by ascertaining what that position is, and how it has been created,
it is of the first consequence to us to know whether human
events have, or have not, their own laws, which can be
inductively established. It is impossible here to exhibit
the evidence in favour of Regularity. Mr. Buckle rightly
assumes, and does not attempt to prove the principle. No
work on any single science ought to engage in the proof
of the possibility of Science. That is a question of logic—
and a very difficult one too, though not more so as applied
to events, than to physical phenomena. The early history
of Physics shows that the 'possibility of speculative truth'
was a truth not established in general belief by the logical
reasonings employed in its defence, but by the gradual
growth of numerous bodies of undeniable truths. As the
special sciences attained importance and solidity, the
position of the Sceptics, 'That nothing can be known,'
slowly lost its influence. Plato might defeat the position
by the most brilliant logic—it still lived on, but has died a
natural death, time and experience having refuted it.
Similarly in history: we shall not find it easy to establish
a priori the abstract doctrine that social changes have the
same character of uniformity that physical changes have.
But let us once obtain a body of undeniable generalizations of social facts, as universally admitted as are our

established truths of natural knowledge, and we shall hear no more of the sceptical theory of arbitrary interpositions. For the present, the philosophical historian must be content to lie under the imputation of employing an hypothesis as the basis of his reasonings. Let him not shrink from admitting most freely that it is an hypothesis. The 'Uniformity of Nature' was equally so in the beginning of Physics. Even now that it has become an article of faith among scientific men, it is neither demonstrated nor demonstrable. It is guaranteed by its success, and can point to its achievements as its legitimation. We cannot prove that the social series is analogous to the material series. Let us not pretend to prove it; let us not even say that it is provable. Let it be honestly and openly an assumption. We shall do no good at present by trying to place it on a higher pedestal.

This preliminary settled,—it being agreed that history shall be a science, we are ready to begin to proceed to our facts. And the first inquiry is, Where? What are we to observe? In this 'incoherent compilation of facts' called History—in the treasured archives of the human race, what documents are we to select for examination? Here we are met by a distinction of the first importance, and which is the corner-stone of historical science. It is the distinction between society and the individuals of which society is composed. In dealing with the individual human being, everything is uncertainty; it is only of man in the aggregate that results can be calculated with accuracy. Quetelet enunciates the theorem thus: 'The greater the number of individuals, the more completely does the will of individuals disappear, and allow the series of general facts which depend upon the causes by which society exists and is preserved to predominate.' The consequences which immediately follow from this general law are then,—

    1. All observation of units of society, or record of the

actions of individuals, is useless for the purposes of the scientific historian.

2. The value of any observation depends upon the extent of the area from which it is drawn. Hence, all our statistical generalizations are at present wholly empirical ; that is, the highest of them can only be taken as a fact of the particular society from which it is collected, and not as a law of society as such.

Of this last consequence, as it is common to all sciences of observation, as opposed to those of experiment, nothing further will be said. It is only brought forward for the purpose of correcting a not uncommon tendency to take statistical results as already attained uniformities. So small and insignificant, compared with the whole social area, has been the area from which our statistics have been drawn, that we are not justified in regarding any result yet obtained as more than approximative.

Our corollary No. 1 has a more immediate application to Mr. Buckle's labours. The inference that the actions of individuals afford no materials for science, disqualifies at one stroke all the records of past events which have hitherto been preserved. We cannot found on them anything more than conjectural inference as to the state of society. A social history can only be composed upon statistical *data*. And as these *data*—even if they were real generalizations, which they are not,—extend only to a very small number of social phenomena, it will follow that a history of society, in the present state of knowledge, is an impossibility. If this be so, what are we to think of Mr. Buckle's 850 pages ? From what materials are they drawn ? On what *data* are they founded? Will it be believed, that after laying down, in the outset, that individual experiments can effect nothing, and that certain consequences can only be tracked by comprehensive observation of society in the aggregate ; that after pouring unmeasured contempt on previous historians for neglect-

422 XXI. HISTORY OF CIVILIZATION IN ENGLAND.

ing this principle, and on the metaphysicians for their narrow method of studying the human mind in single specimens, and that after insisting that we must apply to the history of man those methods of investigation which have been found successful in other branches of knowledge, Mr. Buckle employs the remainder of his volume in exemplifying the very method of writing history which he had condemned? We have in several chapters (chap. viii.—xiv.) a summary of the progress of society in France; a masterly sketch, of which it is not too much to say, that in breadth and comprehensiveness of view, no English writer on French History has yet equalled it. If the details are not new—and they could not be,—the whole effect is new. If the principles are not original, they are brought to bear on the facts with a precision which lightens up every corner of the subject, and endows with a general purpose traits which have hitherto served to illustrate only a solitary character. But all this is effected without the slightest reference to the principles of historical science avowed in the opening. In the beginning of the volume, we have the author true to the principles of Positive Science. In his own practice, we find him sailing triumphantly down the broad stream of a deductive process. The revolutionary theory, with which he starts in life, is silently exchanged for a conformity with established practice. Instead of general averages, we have the opinions of eminent individuals. Instead of the fatality of social law, we have the force exerted on national life by the single will of a Louis XIV. The reader finds, indeed, his account in this forgetfulness of his own principles by the author. We find his history practical, entertaining, instructive, in a degree beyond that of most writers who have gone over the same ground; but by his own definition of History, it is excluded from any claim to that title. It bears the same relation to the science of History, which a narrative of the commercial fortunes of the great house of Hope, or the successes and reverses of the family of Rothschild, would bear to the science of Political Economy.

On the whole, it appears as if Mr. Buckle was not quite free from a confusion which prevails over minds far inferior to his, between the Science of Society, and History, as it is, and must be written. That fixed laws of social changes exist, we believe. That we possess a collection of observations sufficient to establish those laws, is very doubtful. That those laws have not, as yet, been established, is certain. But the history of any particular state, or system of states, such as that of Western Europe, is not that Social Science. European progress must, of course, have conformed to the general laws of progress; and till we know those general laws, we cannot properly do what Mr. Buckle claims to have done—'reconstruct the history of the eighteenth century according to the order of its social and intellectual development' (p. 699). Our order must necessarily be empirical; but an empirically deduced series may be highly instructive. This cannot be better stated than in Mr. Buckle's own words, when speaking of another subject :—

The desire to grasp at truth by speculative, and, as it were, foregone conclusions, often led the way to great discoveries; but when it is universally followed, there is imminent danger lest the observation of mere empirical uniformities should be neglected, and lest thinking men should grow impatient at these small and proximate generalizations, which, according to the inductive scheme, must invariably precede the larger and higher ones. Whenever this impatience actually occurs, there is produced serious mischief: for these lower generalizations form a neutral ground, which speculative minds and practical minds possess in common, and on which they meet.— (p. 225.)

This is true of all science, but it is more particularly true of History and Economy. Here, more than in any other field, do we feel that theory exists for the sake of the facts, and not facts for the sake of the theory. In these practical sciences we are less liable to that science-worship which infests the more theoretical, in which the more abstract and general the expression the better. The economists and statisticians have not yet learnt this fanaticism. The history of Europe, however ill it may fare in other respects, is not sacrificed to symbolical notation: it labours under the opposite defect of being abandoned to the opinions of the chance-comer—of having no basis of principle whatever. If this is to be remedied, it must be by a treatment sensible, practical, and individual, such as Mr. Buckle has himself given a specimen of in the latter portion of his volume; not by attempting to apply the highest abstractions of Social Science, if we possess any such. Let us move a little more slowly, that we may make an end the sooner. The nebular hypothesis is a brilliant generalization, but it would have done no service to astronomy had Kepler begun with it.

The wide difference between Social Science and History, and the degree in which the one is confounded with the other in Mr. Buckle, will appear further, on examining a little more closely his fundamental principle, that 'The totality of human actions is governed by the totality of human knowledge.'

The first consideration which shakes the claim of this proposition to be a 'Law,' is the necessity for limiting its application to Europe; for, as we have seen, in tropical civilizations, external nature takes the place of knowledge, as the 'governing' principle. We are to suppose, then, that the accident of geographical position subjects society to one or other of two distinct and mutually exclusive 'laws.' In other words, in the proposition, 'The totality of human actions is governed by the totality of human knowledge,' we have no law of society as such, but an empirical generalization from the course of affairs in

a particular region. Such a generalization may be, and
is, highly instructive, and of fertile application ; but it is
deposed from the pretensions it assumed to be a scientific
'law' from which deductive inferences could be confidently drawn. Its application has no tendency whatever
to assimilate History to the Inductive Sciences. We see
at once a difference in kind between the facts called
historical, and the facts which can combine into one
inductive science. A physical law is a universal and
constant property. The mechanical properties of fluids
are so. This so-called 'law' of Progress is a collection of
observed places, like the eastward course of the Gulf-
stream, which can be laid down in charts.

Passing this, and taking Mr. Buckle's 'law' at this
reduced value, let us inquire into its validity as a generalized fact of European history. We will no longer ask, Is
it the true law? but, Is it a correct description of
European movement to say that the totality of human
actions in Europe, since the rise of the existing state-
systems, has been governed by the totality of knowledge
possessed by the nations composing that system ? It is
not possible to exaggerate the importance of obtaining
a correct decision on this question. Even in the reduced
form in which we have now taken the proposition, could
we establish that knowledge is not only progressive in its
own nature, but that it is the one force which has controlled social and political changes for a thousand years,
what a presumption this would raise as to the continuance
of such a force through coming centuries! Though we
might be forbidden by the aspect of great stationary
societies, such as those of China or Hindustan, from
extending our hopes for the human race to all time,
and to all aggregations of it, yet what hopes and prospects
it would open to ourselves!—not the mere vanity of
'Science grown to more,' the barren creed of most scientific men, the miserly accumulation of heaps of glittering

truths, but the true triumph of Mind. Such a hope would amount to a faith—a political faith, which would exert upon our public action the same elevating effect which religious faith does on the private conduct. It would remove anxiety, and lighten what is dark; it would disperse that gloom which is the ordinary consequence of the thoughtful study of history and politics, and which events that the present generation has witnessed have tended in no small degree to aggravate. It would restore elasticity and confidence to our motions; it would endow the will of public men with that purpose in which they are so sadly deficient; it would dignify the debasing drudgery of parliamentary and official life; and inspire the party of Progress with that far-sighted confidence in their cause which itself would accelerate their victory.

Such being the value of this view of history, could it be established as true, the philosophic mind will be all the more on its guard against the temptation to adopt it for its utility, and without a rigorous inquiry into its grounds. We shall not attempt, in our narrow limits, to argue against Mr. Buckle's position. But it may be useful, as assisting the judgment of some readers, briefly to indicate the competing theory of historical action which Mr. Buckle's view excludes. We may, then, very securely reject, as Mr. Buckle does, the common notions of the influence of moral principle on the progress of civilization. The great truths which compose our systems of morality were among the earliest ideas acquired by mankind, and have undergone the least alteration. More than this, their restraining operation was perhaps more direct and universal in the simpler stages of society than now, when, in the complexities of men's relations, and the technicalities of business, the application of the simple moral rule is become embarrassed. The distance through which the electric current is transmitted weakens its force. Thus much may be granted to Mr. Buckle. But because moral sentiments (as they are called), or rules of moral conduct, are influences not subject to an appreciable variation, it by no means follows that the passions and desires may also be thrown out of the account. The passions of men play a most important—indeed, far the largest—part in the history of nations, as of individuals. Nor are their effects transient; 'the passions and feelings of one part of society being balanced,' as Mr. Buckle argues, 'by those of the other part' (p. 208). Passion, it is true, can do nothing itself, but allied with power, and animating it, it becomes the most formidable, and not the least permanent, of the agencies that disturb or control the doctrines of society. Force, indeed, or the muscular power of the animal, combined and armed, is an element of history which the author contemptuously overlooks. We suppose—for he does not himself vouchsafe an explanation—that he would say that force is nothing, unless guided by knowledge; that it is the mere servant of thought, the mechanism by which an idea imposes itself on numbers ; and that 'even bayonets think.' True : power is a machine, but it is one of which the moving force is passion, much oftener than knowledge. This is the agent with whose effects and consequences history has to occupy itself. This is the force which moves the world, small and great, from the intrigue that turns out a minister, to the revolution that changes the face of a continent : passion, creating and animating power, degrading knowledge to be the skilled artificer that forges chains for its subjects. Power, once constituted, has a tendency to perpetuate itself : it is at the discretion of power how much, or how little, intellectual progress its subjects shall be permitted to make. For though knowledge be itself a power, yet as it grows up and finds passion already seated on the throne, it cannot raise its head, except so far as the monarch in possession licenses it. Power, however, though excessively jealous, is not clear-sighted.   It has always entertained suspicions of knowledge, and has usually set its face against it, and kept it under.   But it has not done so in all countries with the same thoroughgoing consistency which it has in some, and which it always could show.   Hence, in these countries, as in England, the classes in possession of knowledge were able to wrest a considerable share of power from the classes in possession of the landed property, i. e. capitalized power.   And as knowledge, the moment it is at all free, has an irresistible tendency to increase, it has, in England, made those encroachments on property, and shows that disposition to encroach more and more on the prerogatives of property, which theorists mistake for a uniform law of progress, and ascribe to the inherent vitality and expansiveness of knowledge. The history of Europe teaches quite another lesson.   In it we see written, in characters of blood, the weakness of intellect when separate from force and passion—its utter powerlessness when against them.   Talk of progress! look at Italy in the fifteenth century, and Italy now. What is the moral of Italian history?   The collapse of knowledge in the presence of power and passion.   Talk of progress! look at France: after the gigantic effort of '89 (an effort, too, brought about by passion, this time enlisted on the side of knowledge)—after the slower and steadier labour of forty years, 1815–1851, the bayonets marched in again, and installed the ignorance of the rural population supreme in her capital.   In our own country, though we are justly proud of a historical progress which has gone on uninterruptedly since the sixteenth century, yet we are not to blind ourselves to the fact that it contains elements of ignorance and fanaticism, on which education has yet exercised no dissolving force.   When we think of our aristocracy in possession of half the property, and the whole of the government of the country—of the servility and timidity

of our middle classes—of their scripture-worship, sabba-
tarianism, and intolerance—we see that a persecution of
knowledge is possible at any moment. There has never
been a time in the history of Europe when the ignorant
classes, whether they stand at the top or the bottom of
the social scale, have not vastly outnumbered the instructed. If ever they have let knowledge grow in peace,
it has been because they are little alarmed at it—are not
aware of its hostility to their tenure of power. Let them
but become aware of this, and they can at any moment
seize a club, and dash its vaunted fabric to the ground.

Such is the rival theory, or ordinary view of European
history, in place of which Mr. Buckle substitutes his
irresistible advance of knowledge. It may be as well to
obviate the reply which he might possibly make to what
has been now advanced. He might say, that he does not
write the History of England, but of Civilization in
England; of progressive, not of stationary society;—
that, while he has selected for his subject the fact of
progress, we have dwelt on the obstacles to progress;—
that he does not ignore the fact of resistance to progress,
nay, has specially treated of it, under the name of 'The
Protective Spirit;'—but that all that is not progress only
falls within his plans, so far as it has acted as a retarding
force.

In answer, let the objection taken in our foregoing
paragraphs be stated thus :—

No writer is obliged to include the whole of any subject :
he is at perfect liberty to select any part of it. Mr. Buckle
can, as others have done before him, trace the progress of
European mind, or of English mind. No one could
object that such a history did not contain Napoleon's
campaigns, or recite the events of the American War.
But, as 'Progressive Knowledge' is brought before us in
this volume, it is not as a single thread running through
the whole web of history, but as the whole of history.

The 'totality of human actions,' nothing less, is explained by it; it is not a part, it is the whole. Now it is not questioned that intellectual progress is a fact; that its course can be traced; that it is an element of national history—perhaps the most attractive element. But what is of vital consequence to us to know is, whether intellectual advance is an inevitable necessity. Will society be re-generated by its intellect in spite of its passions? The condition of every society yet known to us has been, a small minority of educated persons in a combination, either of conflict or harmony, with an overwhelming unen-lightened mass. The enlightened minority who are in possession of the knowledge, have, more or less, leavened the whole. Where this practice of leavening has pro-ceeded, unchecked, for any considerable time, an appear-ance is presented which may easily be mistaken for an intrinsic power in knowledge to conquer every other motive of action. But is it more than an appearance? What security have we that the sleeping volcano of passion will not flame forth with irresistible violence? That the ocean of imagination, and false opinion, will not break in, submerge a continent, and sweep away every trace of the Palace of Truth?

> To shame the boast so often made,
> That we are wiser than our sires.

The vitality of knowledge consists in its advance. Let power arm the protective spirit sufficiently, and it can prohibit advance. We cannot suppress liberty to save civilization. The condition of true knowledge is freedom of speech and opinion. But who is to guarantee the freedom of the press? Let beneficent power, by strength of arm, maintain its freedom, and it will teach and enlighten ; but knowledge cannot maintain its ground for an hour against force. Let selfish power step in, and in its own interest close the printing-presses, and where is know-ledge? Shut up in the bosoms of a few silent worshippers, it dies a lingering death beneath the frown of power. It passes through all the stages of decay. Taste becomes pedantry, science becomes magic, Virgil is turned into an enchanter, and civilization has become the prolific mother of the thousand forms of barbarism.

Aspice convexo nutantem pondere mundum !

INDEX OF NAMES.

Hervey, Lord, *Memoirs,* ii. 352, 373, 387.
Hesiod, i. 185, 369, 394.
Hesse, ii. 259.
Heubner, H. L., ii. 249.
Heyne, C. G., i. 171, 265, 344 *sqq.*, 376, 378 *sq.*, 383, 387 *sqq.*, 394; ii. 172.
Hickes, George, ii. 109, 322.
Hieronymite brotherhood, the, i. 243.
Hilgenfeld, A., ii. 236.
Hoadly, Bp. B., ii. 68 *sq.*, 112, 128, 373.
Hobbes, Thomas, i. 221, 333, 484; ii. 78.
Hochstraten, Jacob, i. 58 *sq.*
Hoffmann, von, i. 362.
Hohenstauffen, the, i. 34.
Holbein, Hans, i. 45.
Holywell (Flintshire), i. 331.
Homer, i. 88, 138, 164, 198, 200, 209, 244, 268, 274, 337, 346, 349, 352, 369 *sq.*, 372, 377 *sqq.*, 399; ii. 170, 173, 363.
Hooke, [Sergeant] J., ii. 316.
Hooke, Nathaniel, i. 2.
Hooker, Richard, ii. 12, 20, 275.
Horace, i. 87, 258, 263, 279, 410; ii. 146, 326, 369, 380, 390, 393.
Horne, Bp. G., ii. 331.
Horneck, A., ii. 273, 311, 313.
Hort, F. J. A., ii. 84.
Hostager, i. 230.
Hôtel Rambouillet, the, i. 262.
Hotman, i. 106, 230.
Hough, Dr. J., i. 322, 324, 328.
Houtteville, Abbé, i. 275.
Howard, J., ii. 309.
Huber's *English Universities,* i. 448.
Huen, Isle of, i. 249.
Hüpeden, Sophia, i. 354.
Huet, P. D., i. 138, 157, 198, 244–305 ; ii. 403.
Hughes, Thomas, i. 306.
Huguenots, i. 223, 227, 233 *sqq.* ; ii. 180, 198, 335.
Hull, i. 51 ; ii. 314.

Humanist party in Germany, i. 57, 78.
Humboldt, W. von, i. 365, 383, 385 *sq.*, 398 *sq.*, 404 *sqq.*
Hume, David, i. 2, 252, 298 *sqq.* ; ii. 46, 51, 54, 110, 356.
Huntingdon, Selina, Countess of, ii. 70.
Huntingdon, Lord, ii. 373.
Huon de Bordeaulx, ii. 337.
Hurd, Bp. R., i. 264; ii. 119, 121, 123, 128, 131 *sqq.*, 145 *sqq.*
Huss, John, ii. 108.
Hutten, Ulrich von, i. 54.

I.

Ilfeld, i. 342, 350 *sqq.*
Ilgen, i. 372.
Illustrium Virorum Epistolae ad Io. Reuchlinum, i. 60.
Independent Whig, The, ii. 102, 105 *sq.*
Indian Civil Service Commission, i. 457, 489.
Innocent XII, Pope, i. 284.
Irenaeus, St., i. 146; ii. 233.
Irnerius, i. 441.
Ironside, Gilbert, i. 329 *sq.*, 332, 334.
Isabella, Empress (sister of Henry III), i. 33, 49.
Ivry, Battle of, i. 174, 179, 237.

J.

Jablonski, D. E., ii. 313.
Jackson, Cyril, i. 453.
Jackson, J., ii. 162.
Jacobs, F., i. 371.
Jacobson, Dr. W., i. 483.
James I, King of England, i. 46, 146, 149, 250, 331, 449 ; ii. 286, 303.
James II, i. 313, 320 *sqq.* ; ii. 312, 317.
Jane, Joseph, ii. 150.
Jansenists, i. 295.
Jarnac, Battle of, i. 225.
Jay, M., ii. 345.
Jeannin, i. 176.
Jeffreys, Lord Chancellor, i. 322.
Jena, i. 386, 401 *sqq.*
Jena Literary Gazette, i. 370, 375, 387.

Jenkins, R., ii. 77.
Jenson, i. 86.
Jerome, St., i. 164 *sqq.*
Jersey, i. 29.
Jests, ephemeral character of, i. 54.
Jesuit-Latin, i. 291.
Jesuits, the, i. 187 *sqq.* ; 295, 426.
Jewel's *Apology,* ii. 111.
Jews, admission of the, to Parliament, ii. 45.
John, King of England, i. 40.
Johnson, Dr. S., i. 152, 244; ii. 49, 65, 67 *sq.*, 122, 124, 139, 143 *sqq.*, 158 *sqq.*, 162, 351, 355, 358, 363, 368 *sq.*, 376, 385 *sq.*
Jones, W., ii. 331.
Jortin, J., ii. 131 *sqq.*, 159, 162, 169 *sq.*, 172, 175.
Josephus, i. 379.
Journal des Débats, i. 392.
Jovius, Paulus, i. 54.
Jowett, B., ii. 303.
Juvenal, i. 279; ii. 87.

K.

Kahnis' *German Protestantism,* ii. 210, 216, 256.
Kant, i. 474; ii. 45, 219, 354.
Keats, John, ii. 356.
Keble, J., ii. 269.
Ken, Bp. T., ii. 273.
Kennett, Bp. White, ii. 317.
Kent, arms of the county, i. 39.
Kepler, i. 276; ii. 424.
Kepsall, ii. 318.
Kilvert, Francis, ii. 120.
King, Dr. W., ii. 141.
King's Somborne, ii. 319.
Kingsley, Charles, i. 306 *sq.*
Kirby, W., ii. 266.
Kippis, Dr. A., ii. 158.
Kliefoth, Th., ii. 252, 256 *sq.*
Knapton, Paul, ii. 151.
Knox, J., i. 333.
Kocher, D., ii. 135.
Köchly, i. 381.
Königsberg, i. 51.
Körte, W., i. 338, 375, 381, 389, 391, 394, 402, 412.

* [See *A Chapter in English Church History*: being the Minutes of the S.P.C.K., 1698-1704. Edited by the Rev. Edmund McClure, M.A. (London: S.P.C.K., 1888).]

THE END.

ERRATA.

Vol. I. p. 256, l. 31, *read* Bouillaud
,, p. 436, foot, *read* 1855
Vol. II. p. 95, l. 15, *read Analogy*
,, p. 193, l. 21, *read extraordinaire*
,, p. 412, l. 36, *read* ever

Ingram Content Group UK Ltd.
Milton Keynes UK
UKHW020230270423
420850UK00005B/80

9 781010 225881